> "Nolo's home page is worth bookmarking."
> —WALL STREET JOURNAL

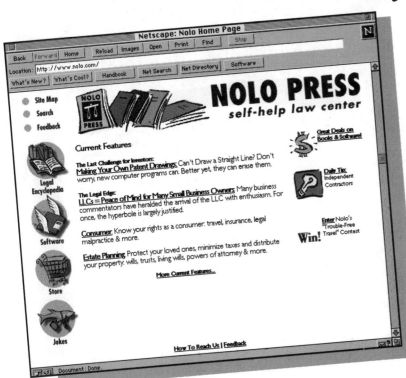

LEGAL INFORMATION ONLINE

www.nolo.com

24 hours a day

AT THE NOLO PRESS SELF-HELP LAW CENTER ON THE WEB, YOU'LL FIND

- Nolo's comprehensive **Legal Encyclopedia**, with links to other online resources
- **Downloadable demos of Nolo software and sample chapters of many Nolo books**
- An online law store with a secure online ordering system
- Our ever-popular lawyer jokes
- Discounts and other good deals, our hilarious Shark Talk game

THE NOLO NEWS

Stay on top of important legal changes with Nolo's quarterly magazine, *The Nolo News*. Start your free one-year subscription by filling out and mailing the response card in the back of this book. With each issue, you'll get legal news about topics that affect you every day, reviews of legal books by other publishers, the latest Nolo catalog, scintillating advice from Auntie Nolo and a fresh batch of our famous lawyer jokes.

SECOND EDITION

COPYRIGHT
YOUR
SOFTWARE

by Attorney Stephen Fishman

Nolo Press  Berkeley

Your Responsibility When Using a Self-Help Law Book

We've done our best to give you useful and accurate information in this book. But laws and procedures change frequently and are subject to differing interpretations. If you want legal advice backed by a guarantee, see a lawyer. If you use this book, it's your responsibility to make sure that the facts and general advice contained in it are applicable to your situation.

Keeping Up To Date

To keep its books up to date, Nolo Press issues new printings and new editions periodically. New printings reflect minor legal changes and technical corrections. New editions contain major legal changes, major text additions or major reorganizations. To find out if a later printing or edition of any Nolo book is available, call Nolo Press at 510-549-1976 or check the catalog in the *Nolo News*, our quarterly publication. You can also contact us on the Internet at www.nolo.com.

To stay current, follow the "Update" service in the *Nolo News*. You can get a free one-year subscription by sending us the registration card in the back of the book. In another effort to help you use Nolo's latest materials, we offer a 25% discount off the purchase of the new edition of your Nolo book if you turn in the cover of an earlier edition. (See the "Special Upgrade Offer" in the back of this book.) This book was last revised in **September 1998**.

Second Edition	SEPTEMBER 1998
Editor	STEPHEN ELIAS
Illustrations	MARI STEIN
Book Design	TERRI HEARSH
Cover Design	LINDA WANCZYK
Production	SARAH TOLL
Index	NANCY MULVANY
Proofreading	SHERYL ROSE
Printing	CUSTOM PRINTING COMPANY

Fishman, Stephen.
    Copyright your software / by Stephen Fishman. -- 2nd ed.
        p.   cm.
    Includes index.
    ISBN 0-87337-494-0
       1. Copyright--Computer Programs–United States--Popular works.
  I. Title.
    KF3024.C6F57 1998
    346.7304'82—dc21   98-8533
                                           CIP

For information on bulk purchases or corporate premium sales, please contact the Special Sales Department. For academic sales or textbook adoptions, ask for Academic Sales. Call 800-955-4775 or write to Nolo Press, Inc., 950 Parker Street, Berkeley, CA 94710.

Acknowledgments

Many thanks to:

Jake Warner for giving me the opportunity to write this book.

Steve Elias, whose ideas and superb editing made this a much better book.

Linda Wanczyk for her imaginative front cover design.

Terri Hearsh for her outstanding book design.

Sheryl Rose for her thorough proofreading.

Mari Stein for her illustrations.

Table of Contents

Copyright Registration: The Basics

 The Registration Process

 After You've Mailed In Your Registration

 Scope of Copyright Protection for Software

Transferring Software Copyright Ownership and Use Rights

Software Copyright Infringement: What It Is, What to Do About It, How to Avoid It

International Software Copyright Protection

15 Other Legal Protections for Software

16 Help Beyond This Book

Appendix I

Sample Forms

Appendix II

Blank Forms

- Form TX
- Form PA
- Form VA
- Request for Special Handling
- Form _____ /CON (Continuation Sheet for Application Forms)
- Form CA
- Search Request Form
- Document Cover Sheet

Index

How to Use This Book

This book is about copyright protection for computer software. It is for the entire universe of people who deal with software, including programmers, software developers, software publishers, companies and individuals who hire software developers to create software on their behalf, and people who work for software developers and publishers.

⚠ You May Not Need This Book

If you have already purchased the second edition of *Software Development: A Legal Guide*, by Stephen Fishman (Nolo Press), you don't need to buy this book. *Software Development* covers much the same information on software copyrights as this book.

A. How This Book Is Organized

Chapters 2–6 consist of a short overview of copyright law as it applies to software (Chapter 2), "how-to" guides on copyright notices (Chapter 3) and registering with the Copyright Office (Chapters 4–6).

Chapters 7–16 serve as your software copyright resource; they discuss the most important aspects of software copyright law in detail. If you are unable to find the answers to your questions in these chapters, the final chapter (Chapter 16, *Help Beyond This Book*) tells you how to do further research on your own and, if necessary, find a copyright attorney.

Citations to Copyright Law

As you read through this book, you'll come across references—called citations—to court cases and statutes on copyright law. See Chapter 16, *Help Beyond This Book*, Section A, for a discussion on how to interpret the citations and use them for additional research.

B. Which Chapters You Should Read

Not everyone will want to read the whole book. Which parts you do want to read will of course depend on why you bought the book.

Most of you bought the book for one of these three reasons:

- You want to know how to satisfy the procedural requirements to obtain maximum copyright protection for your software.
- You have a specific question or problem concerning copyright protection for software.
- You want a general education about copyright protection for software.

Assuming you fall into one of these three categories, here is how you can make best use of this book.

1. Readers Who Want to Know How to Satisfy the Procedural Requirements for Maximum Software Copyright Protection

If you just want to know how to place a valid copyright notice on your software (that's the © followed by a date and name you usually see on published works) read Chapter 3, *Copyright Notice*. Placing a valid copyright notice on your work will make it easier to enforce your copyright.

If you want to register your software with the Copyright Office, refer to Chapter 5, *The Registration Process*, for a step-by-step explanation. You'll find all the registration forms you need in the tear-out Appendix at the end of the book. By registering your software shortly after it is published (no later than three months), you will be sure to significantly increase your copyright protection.

2. Readers Who Have a Specific Copyright Question

If you have a specific question or problem, start with the Table of Contents at the front of the book. For example, suppose you want to know who owns software created by an employee. By scanning the Table of Contents you would discover that Chapter 11, *Initial Copyright Ownership*, is probably the place to start. And by examining the section headings under Chapter 11, you would find that Section A, Independent Authorship by an Individual, is the place to start reading.

If you didn't find what you were looking for in the Table of Contents, you could use the index at the back of the book and search under such terms as "copyright ownership" and "employees."

3. People Who Want to Learn All About Copyrighting Software

If you simply want to learn more about copyright protection for software, read Chapter 2, *Copyright Basics,* and Chapter 15, *Other Legal Protections for Software.* Then read as much of the material in chapters 5–12 as you wish. You can skip Chapters 3–6, since these chapters are intended for people who want to take specific steps to obtain maximum copyright protection for their software.

C. What This Book Is Not About

This book only covers copyright protection for computer software. This means it is not about any of the following:

- software contracts such as software publishing agreements, custom software development agreements, employment contracts, multimedia license agreements, trade secret agreements and independent contractor agreements. See *Software Development: A Legal Guide,* by Stephen Fishman (Nolo Press) for a detailed discussion of all these types of agreements and sample forms.

- copyright protection for written works like books, magazines, letters and so forth. See *The Copyright Handbook: How to Protect and Use Written Works*, by Stephen Fishman (Nolo Press) if you want to know about this.

- patent protection for computer software. Refer to Chapter 15, *Other Legal Protections for Software*, for a brief overview of patent law, to *Software Development: A Legal Guide,* by Stephen Fishman (Nolo Press) for a more detailed discussion of this topic, and to *Patent It Yourself,* by David Pressman (Nolo Press) for detailed guidance on how to draft and file patent applications (Patent It Yourself is also available as a computer program).

- protecting titles, logos or slogans. These items may be protected under federal and state trademark laws, which have nothing to do with copyright. For a brief overview of trademark law, refer to Chapter 15, *Other Legal Protections for Software*. For a detailed discussion of trademark law, refer to *Trademark: How to Name a Business & Product* by Kate McGrath and Stephen Elias (Nolo Press).

- protecting ideas. Copyright only protects how ideas are expressed—not the ideas themselves. Ideas can be protected as trade secrets, which involves committing anyone who learns of the ideas to secrecy and maintaining security procedures to prevent the ideas from leaking out. For a brief overview of trade secret law, see Chapter 15, *Other Legal Protections for Soft-* *ware*. For a more detailed discussion of trade secret protection for software, see *Software Development: A Legal Guide*, by Stephen Fishman (Nolo Press). ■

Copyright Basics

This chapter is an introduction to some basic copyright concepts and vocabulary. This chapter is designed to pave the way for more detailed discussions in later chapters. We therefore urge you not to use this material to reach a final conclusion about any particular issue. Only after reading one or more of the later chapters will you be in a position to make a judgment about a particular question or course of action.

A. Why Have a Copyright Law?

The Founding Fathers recognized that everyone would benefit if creative people were encouraged to create new intellectual and artistic works. When the United States Constitution was written in 1787, the framers took care to include a Copyright Clause (Article I, Section 8) stating that "The Congress shall have Power... To promote the Progress of Science and useful Arts, by securing for limited times to Authors ... the exclusive Right to their ... writings."

The primary purpose of copyright, then, is not to enrich authors; rather, it is to promote the progress of science and the useful arts—that is, human knowledge. To pursue this goal, copyright encourages authors in their creative efforts by giving them a minimonopoly over their works—termed a copyright. But this monopoly is limited when it appears to con-

flict with the overriding public interest in encouraging creation of new intellectual and artistic works generally.

Although the Constitution only mentions copyright protection for "writings," over the past 200 years the scope of the copyright laws has been expanded to cover all forms of creative expression, including computer software.

B. What Is a Copyright?

A copyright is a legal device that provides the creator of a work of authorship the right to control how the work is used. The Copyright Act of 1976 (17 U.S.C. 101 et seq.)—the federal law providing for copyright protection—grants creators (called "authors") a bundle of intangible, exclusive rights over their work. These rights include the:

- *reproduction right*—the right to make copies of a protected work
- *distribution right*—the right to initially sell, rent, lease or lend copies to the public (but this right is limited by the "first sale" doctrine which permits the owner of a particular copy of a work to sell, lend or otherwise dispose of the copy without the copyright owner's permission—for example, libraries may lend the books they purchase without getting permission)
- *right to create adaptations* (or "derivative works")—the right to prepare new works based on a protected work
- *public display right*—the right to show a copy of a work at a public place or transmit it to the public, and
- *public performance right*—the right to perform a protected work in public.

An author's copyright rights may be exercised only by the author or by a person or entity to whom the author has transferred all or part of her rights. (See Chapter 12, *Transferring Software Copyright Ownership and Use Rights*). If someone wrongfully uses the material covered by the copyright, the copyright owner can sue and obtain compensation for any losses suffered as well as an injunction (court order) requiring the copyright infringer to stop the infringing activity.

In this sense, a copyright is a type of intangible property—it belongs to its owner and the courts can be asked to intervene if anyone uses it without permission. And, like other forms of property, a copyright may be sold by its owner, or otherwise exploited for her economic benefit.

C. What Can Be Protected by Copyright?

Copyright protects all kinds of original works of authorship. This includes, but is not limited to:

- literary works—this comprises any work "expressed in words, numbers, or other verbal or numerical symbols or indicia" (17 U.S.C. 101), including novels, plays, screenplays, nonfiction prose, newspapers and magazines, manuals, catalogs, text advertisements and compilations such as some business directories.
- motion pictures, videos and other audiovisual works—this includes movies, documentaries, training films and videos, television shows, television ads, and interactive multimedia works.
- photographs, graphic works and sculpture—this includes maps, posters, paintings, drawings, graphic art, display ads, cartoon strips, statues and works of fine art.
- music—this includes all types of songs, instrumental works and advertising jingles.
- sound recordings—this includes recordings of music, sounds or words.
- pantomimes and choreographic works—this includes ballets, modern dance, and mime works.
- architectural works—this includes building designs, whether in the form of architectural drawings or blueprints, or the design of actual buildings.

1. Copyright Protection for Computer Software

The Copyright Act specifically classifies computer programs as "literary works" and affords them full copyright protection. But just what do we mean by computer programs? The Copyright Act defines computer programs as "sets of statements or instructions to be used directly or indirectly in a computer to bring about a certain result." (17 U.S.C. 101.) But all experts agree that many aspects of software—in addition to computer programs—are protected by copyright. Copyright not only protects all forms of computer code, but may extend to:

- program design documents—that is, schematic or other representations such as flowcharts or detailed specifications that describe a program's structure, sequence and organization,
- supporting materials such as users' manuals, software documentation and instructions,
- at least to some extent, the way a program itself is structured, sequenced and organized, and
- at least to some extent, a program's user interface. That is, the way it presents itself to and interacts with the user; this is often called "look and feel," and may include the design of computer screen displays as well as how the user actually operates the program.

As we discuss in detail in Chapter 7, *Scope of Copyright Protection for Software*, any of these additional elements of software (particularly the user interface and program structure and organization) may in fact receive little or even no copyright protection because of various copyright doctrines. In any event, what all this means is that the owner of the copyright in software as we define it here (including computer code, documentation, and, to some extent, user interface and structure, sequence and organization) has the five exclusive rights outlined in Section B above.

> **EXAMPLE:** AcmeSoft, a small software developer, has its employees create a software package called AcmeMap—Website mapping software that allows a Webmaster to see a graphical description of all the pages in a Website. The package consists of the AcmeMap program itself and an extensive manual. AcmeSoft is the sole copyright owner of every element of the AcmeMap package that is protected by copyright. This may include the program's source code and object code; the structure, sequence

and organization of the program modules, routines and subroutines; the user interface; and the program's online and written documentation.

As the owner of the copyright in AcmeMap, AcmeSoft has the exclusive right to copy it, to distribute it to the public, to create derivative works based upon it (new or enhanced versions, for example), and to perform and display it in public—for example, over the Internet. Subject to some exceptions discussed below, no one else can exercise AcmeSoft's copyright rights without its permission. If they do, AcmeSoft is entitled to sue them in federal court for copyright infringement to make them stop the infringing activity and to obtain damages.

Can Computer Languages Be Copyrighted?

No court has ruled on whether high-level computer languages like C++ or Java can themselves be protected by copyright. However, the Copyright Office apparently believes they cannot be protected since it refuses to register a work consisting solely of a computer language. The Copyright Office's view is supported by decades-old copyright cases involving telegraphic codes and stenographic systems. The courts in these cases held that the component elements of shorthand systems and telegraphic codes—that is, the individual coined words or symbols that form the vocabulary of the system—are not protected by copyright. But a particular arrangement of such symbols is protected if it meets the originality, fixation and minimal creativity requirements discussed for copyright protection. (*Hartfield v. Peterson*, 91 F.2d 998 (2d Cir. 1937).) It seems likely, therefore, that anyone is free to write any program in any computer language. Although the language itself is not protected, a particular program written in that language is, just as the English language itself is not protected, but a poem written in English is.

---

2. Screen Displays Protectible as Audiovisual Works

The copyright law defines audiovisual works as "works that consist of a series of related images" intended to be shown through the use of a machine or device. (17 U.S.C. 112.) Computer screen displays may constitute an audiovisual work that is separate and distinct from the "literary work" comprising the actual computer code. For example, several early software copyright cases held that the computer screen displays contained in video games such as *Pac-Man* were protectible as audiovisual works. In more recent years, audiovisual copyrights have been claimed, with varying degrees of success, in the "look and feel" of computer programs such as *Lotus 1-2-3* and in the Apple Macintosh graphical user interface. (See Chapter 7, *Scope of Copyright Protection for Software,* for detailed discussion.)

3. Software Distributed Online

Today, much software is distributed online over the Internet, commercial online services such as America Online and CompuServe and BBS's. Software distributed online is entitled to exactly the same copyright protection as software that is sold by mail order or in stores. That is, it is illegal to download or otherwise use the software without the copyright owner's consent. Of course, due to the ease of copying works in the online environment, huge amounts of software are illegally copied from and to the online world every day.

D. Copyright Ownership and Transfer of Ownership

The exclusive rights outlined in Section B above initially belong to a work's author. However, for copyright purposes, the author of a work is not necessarily the person(s) who created it; it can be that person's employer—a corporation, for example. There are four ways a person or business may become an author:

- An individual may independently author the work.
- An employer (whether a person or business entity such as a corporation or partnership) may pay an employee to author the work, in which case the employer is an author under the work made for hire rule. (See Chapter 11, Section B.)
- A person or business entity may specially commission an independent contractor to author the work under a written work made for hire contract, in which case the commissioning party becomes the author.
- Two or more individuals or entities may collaborate to become joint authors.

(See Chapter 11, *Initial Copyright Ownership,* for detailed discussion of initial copyright ownership and the work for hire rule.)

The initial copyright owner of a work is free to transfer some or all of his, her or its copyright rights to other people or businesses, who will then be entitled to exercise the rights transferred. (See Chapter 12, *Transferring Software Copyright Ownership and Use Rights,* a for detailed discussion.) For example, a software copyright owner may license its software to end users.

The majority of software is created by employees or independent contractors who transfer their copyright rights to the hiring firms. As a result, most software is owned by businesses, not by the people who actually created it.

E. Scope of Copyright Protection

Copyright protects only the new material a creative person produces. Since the main goal of copyright is to encourage creation of new intellectual and artistic works, it follows that copyright protection does not extend to material copied from others.

There is also no reason to protect works whose creation is a purely mechanical or clerical act. Protecting certain databases such as phone book white pages or certain blank forms would not help develop the arts and sciences. An author must employ a minimal amount of creativity in producing the work. This does not mean that to be protectible a work has to be a work of genius or a great advance in the field, but a minimal amount of thought or judgment must have been involved in its creation. (See Chapter 7, *Scope of Copyright Protection for Software,* for a detailed discussion of the scope of copyright protection for software.)

A work need not be entirely new to be protectible. Copyright protects new material an author adds to a previously existing work. For example, copyright protects "derivative works." A derivative work is a work that is created by adapting or transforming previously existing material into a new work of authorship. Examples in the software field include updated versions of existing programs and the translation of a program to operate on a different platform. A computer game based upon a movie or television show is another example of a derivative work. (See Chapter 8, *Derivative Works and Use of Preexisting Material,* for detailed discussion.)

Copyright can also protect compilations. These are works in which preexisting materials are selected, coordinated and arranged so that a new work of authorship is created—for example, electronic databases. (See Chapter 9, *Computer Databases,* for a detailed discussion.)

F. Limitations on Copyright Protection

We've seen that the purpose of copyright is to encourage intellectual creation. Paradoxically, giving authors too much copyright protection could inhibit rather than enhance creative growth. To avoid this, some important limitations on copyright protection can be found in the federal copyright laws and the federal court cases that interpret them.

The most important limitation is that copyright protects only the particular form that a program, book, manual, record, screen, script, etc., takes. It doesn't protect the ideas or concepts contained within it. Ideas, methods, systems, concepts, discoveries, algorithms and facts are not copyrightable. (See Chapter 7, *Scope of Copyright Protection for Software* for a detailed discussion.)

Copyright protection also is limited by the fair use doctrine. To foster the advancement of the arts and sciences, there must be a free flow of information and ideas. If no one could make any use at all of a protected work without the copyright owner's permission—which could be withheld or given only upon payment of a permission fee—the free flow of ideas would be greatly impeded. To avoid this, Congress created a special fair use exception to copyright owners' rights. Under this exception, as a general rule, you are free to copy from a protected work for purposes such as research and editorial comment so long as the value of the copyrighted work is not diminished. (See Chapter 13, *Software Copyright Infringement: What It Is, What to Do About It, How to Avoid It,* for discussion of how the fair use rule can apply to software developers.)

1. Material in the Public Domain

An intellectual creation that is not legally protected is said to be in the public domain. Public domain material belongs to the world, and anyone is free to use it in any way she wishes. For copyright purposes, a creative work enters the public domain when the term of the copyright expires (see Section G below). This means that the work can be used without obtaining permission from the copyright owner. We discuss the public domain in the context of copyright law in detail in Chapter 7, *Scope of Copyright Protection for Software.*

However, even if a work—or some aspect of the work—is not protected by copyright, it still may not be in the public domain in the sense that you are definitely free to use it without having to get *anyone's* permission. This is because there are many different ways to legally protect software. Software may be protected not only by copyright—which is

the focus of this book—but by patent, trademark and trade secret laws as well. We discuss these laws in Chapter 15, *Other Legal Protections for Software.*

The fact that all or part of a software product may not be protected by copyright doesn't necessarily mean it isn't protected by one or more of these other laws. For example, we said above that the ideas, discoveries, methods, procedures, processes, systems, concepts, principles, algorithms and facts embodied in software (or any other work) are not protected by copyright. But all these things possibly could be protected by patents or trade secrecy.

If you're not sure whether an item you want to use is in the public domain, seek legal assistance or get permission to use it from its owner.

G. Copyright Duration

One of the advantages of copyright protection is that it lasts a very long time—far longer than the vast majority of software copyright owners will ever need. The copyright in a program or other protectible work created after 1977 by an individual creator lasts for the life of the creator plus an additional 50 years. If there is more than one creator, the life plus 50 term is measured from the year-date the last creator dies.

The copyright in works created by employees for their employers (probably the majority of software) lasts for 75 years from the date of publication, or 100 years from the date of creation, whichever occurs first. This term also applies to works created by:

- individuals under a work made for hire contract, and
- individuals who choose to remain anonymous or use a pseudonym (pen name) when they publish their work.

Copyright protection lasts so long that it is highly likely that any software you create will have long been obsolete by the time the copyright expires.

1. Pre-1978 Published Works

Software and other works published before 1978 have a different copyright term. Software published before 1978 but after 1964 has a 75-year term from the date of publication. Software published before 1964 had an initial 28-year copyright term and an additional 47-year renewal term if a renewal application was filed with the Copyright Office during the 28th year after publication. (See *The Copyright Handbook: How to Protect and Use Written Works,* by Stephen Fishman (Nolo Press) for a detailed discussion.)

H. Copyright Infringement

Copyright infringement occurs when a person other than the copyright owner exploits one or more of the copyright owner's exclusive rights without the owner's permission. Infringement of software usually involves the unauthorized exercise of a copyright owner's exclusive rights to reproduce and distribute the work or prepare derivative works based on it. In plain English, this means that someone incorporates your protected expression into their work without your permission. Here are some examples of infringement:

> **EXAMPLE 1:** Tush, Rose, a large accounting firm, buys one copy of *TaxEze*, a tax preparation software package, and makes 100 copies for its employees without the copyright owner's permission. The purchaser of a computer program may legally make only one copy of the program for archival purposes without the copyright owner's permission. (See Software Purchasers' Limited Right to Make Copies and Adaptations, below.) Thus, the making of the 100 unauthorized copies constitutes infringement on the copyright owner's exclusive right to reproduce and distribute *TaxEze.*

EXAMPLE 2: Without authorization, Larry creates a Mac version of a popular PC computer game and sells copies over the Internet. Larry has infringed on the game owner's right to create derivative works from its game—that is, the right to create new works based upon or derived from the PC game.

EXAMPLE 3: BigTech, Inc. creates a database program for medical records. In doing so, it obtains a copy of the source code for a preexisting, similar program owned by Medidata, Inc. from a former Medidata employee. BigTech copies hundreds of lines of code from Medidata's program. BigTech has infringed Medidata's exclusive right to reproduce (copy) the code in its program.

The Copyright Act doesn't prevent copyright infringement from occurring, just as the laws against auto theft do not prevent cars from being stolen. However, the Copyright Act does give copyright owners a legal remedy to use after an infringement has occurred—they may sue the infringer in federal court.

A copyright owner who wins an infringement suit can stop any further infringement, get infringing software destroyed, obtain damages from the infringer—often the amount of any profits obtained from the infringement—and recover other monetary losses. This means, in effect, that a copyright owner can make a copyright pirate restore the author to the same economic position she would have been in had the infringement never occurred. And, in some cases, the copyright owner may even be able to obtain monetary penalties that may far exceed her actual losses. (See Chapter 13, *Software Copyright Infringement: What It Is, What to Do About It, How to Avoid It* for a detailed discussion.)

Software Purchasers' Limited Right to Make Copies and Adaptations

Earlier we said that a software copyright owner has the exclusive right to reproduce his work and create adaptations (derivative works) from it. However, there is an important exception to this rule. A person who purchases a computer program has the right to copy or adapt the program if the copy or adaptation is either:

1. "an essential step in the utilization of the computer program in conjunction with a machine and that it is used in no other manner"—in other words, the purchaser has to adapt the program to get it to work on his computer; or
2. the copy or adaptation is for archival purposes only (a single back-up copy) and is made and kept only by the person who owns the legally purchased copy. (17 U.S.C. 117)

This limited right to make a back-up or archival copy is not really very generous. Since the copy is for back-up purposes only, it cannot be used on a second computer. This means, for example, that if you own a desktop computer and a laptop, and want to use your word processor on both, legally you must buy two copies. In an effort to make their customers happy, some large software publishers are now including provisions in their license agreements permitting their customers to use a program on two different computers. For example, Microsoft permits purchasers of *Microsoft Word* to use the program on both an office and home computer. (See Chapter 12, *Transferring Software Copyright Ownership and Use Rights* for a detailed discussion.)

I. Copyright Formalities

There are certain simple technical formalities that must be attended to in order to obtain maximum copyright protection.

1. Copyright Notice

Before 1989, all published works had to contain a copyright notice (the © symbol followed by the publication date and copyright owner's name) to be protected by copyright. This is no longer true. Use of copyright notices is now optional. Even so, it is always a good idea to include a copyright notice on all works distributed to the public so that potential infringers will be informed of the underlying claim to copyright ownership. Besides deterring potential infringers, inclusion of a copyright notice makes it impossible for an infringer to claim she didn't know the software was copyrighted; this may enable the copyright owner to obtain greater damages if a copyright infringement suit is brought. In addition, copyright protection is not available in some 20 foreign countries unless a work contains a copyright notice.

It has never been necessary to include a copyright notice on unpublished works. A work is published for copyright purposes when copies are sold, rented, lent, given away or otherwise distributed to the public on an unrestricted basis. Software that is distributed to the public without a signed license agreement is normally considered published. Software that is under development or licensed to a limited number of users under a signed license agreement is usually considered unpublished. However, since unpublished copies of your work may receive limited distribution—to beta testers for example—it is a good idea to include a notice on them as well. (See Chapter 3, *Copyright Notice*, for a detailed discussion of copyright notices for software.)

2. Registration

Copyright registration is a legal formality by which a copyright owner makes a public record in the U.S. Copyright Office in Washington, D.C. of some basic information about a copyrighted work, such as the title of the work, who wrote it and when, and who owns the copyright. When people speak of copyrighting a work, they usually mean registering it with the Copyright Office.

Contrary to what many people think, it is not necessary to register a work to create or establish a copyright in it. As mentioned above, copyright protection begins automatically the moment an original work of authorship is fixed in a tangible medium of expression. However, registration is required before a copyright owner may file a lawsuit to enforce her rights. In addition, timely registration in the U.S. Copyright Office—within three months of publication or before the infringement begins—makes a copyright a matter of public record and provides three very important advantages if it is ever necessary to go to court to enforce it. (See Chapter 4, *Copyright Registration: The Basics,* for a detailed discussion.)

J. Masks Used to Manufacture Computer Chips

Until 1985, a burning (and economically important) question was whether the intricate designs imposed on a computer chip in the form of masks were protectible as intellectual property—as an expression subject to the copyright laws or as a physical invention covered by the patent laws. Congress stepped in and passed the Semiconductor Chip Protection Act, a law that extends a type of copyright protection for a ten-year period to these designs (masks) and the three-dimensional templates (mask works) that are used to create them. To qualify for this protection, the mask or mask work must be truly original and independently created, and the owner of the mask or mask work must be:

- a U.S. national or resident on the date the work is registered with the U.S. Copyright Office or first commercially exploited anywhere in the world;
- a national or resident of a country that is a signatory to a mask work treaty;
- the owner of a mask or mask work that is commercially exploited in the U.S.; or
- an owner who is made subject to protection through presidential proclamation.

Because the creation of the mask works and masks used to manufacture integrated circuits involves a process costing many millions of dollars, we assume that the creators have ample access to lawyers who specialize in this area. Accordingly, we don't go further into this subject. If you want more information on protection of mask works and masks, short of visiting a lawyer, we suggest you call the Copyright Office at 202-707-3000 for more information. ■

3

Copyright Notice

This chapter is about copyright notice. The copyright notice is "c" in a circle—©—followed by a publication date and name, usually seen on published works. The purpose of such a notice is to inform the public that a work is copyrighted, when it was published, and who owns the copyright. A copyright notice is not required as a condition of obtaining or keeping a copyright. Nonetheless, it's a very good idea to include a notice anyway on all your software and other copyrightable works.

A. Why Use a Copyright Notice?

Contrary to what many people believe, a copyright notice is not required to establish or maintain a copyright in the United States or most foreign countries. Nor is a notice necessary to register a work with the Copyright Office. (However, as discussed in Section G below, a notice was required for software and other copyrightable works published in the U.S. before March 1, 1989.)

So if a notice is not mandatory, why bother to include one on your published software and other copyrightable works? There are several excellent reasons.

1. Notice Helps Makes Infringement Suits Economically Feasible

Authors and other copyright owners are able to enforce their copyright rights only because they can sue those who violate them. Unfortunately, copyright infringement litigation is expensive (copyright attorneys charge at least $150 an hour and often much more). As a result, copyright infringement lawsuits may be economically feasible only if the author can obtain substantial damages (money) from the infringer and use some of this money to pay the attorney.

The easiest way to get substantial damages is to prove that the infringement was *willful*—that is, that the infringer knew that he was breaking the law but did so anyway. Courts usually award far more damages where the infringement was willful than where the infringer didn't realize what he was doing was wrong. (See Chapter 13, *Software Copyright Infringement: What It Is, What to Do About It, How to Avoid It,* for a detailed discussion.)

Proving "willfulness" can be difficult if a published work lacks a valid copyright notice. The reason for this is what's known as the innocent infringement defense. If a person infringes upon a published work that does not contain a copyright notice, the infringer can claim in court that the infringement was innocent—that is, he or she didn't know the work was protected by copyright. If the judge or jury believes this, the infringer may still be liable for infringement, but the damages (monetary compensation) may be drastically reduced from what they otherwise would have been. On the other hand, if there is a valid copyright notice on the work, the infringer cannot claim innocence and will be treated as a willful infringer.

EXAMPLE 1: Art self-publishes a utility program for the Power Macintosh. He sells the program by mail order and over the Internet. He fails to place any copyright notice in the program itself or the floppy disks he sells to mail-order buyers. Suzy, a programmer employed by NastySoft, obtains a copy of the program, decompiles it and incorporates much of the code in a program she creates for NastySoft. Art finds out about the copying and sues Suzy and NastySoft for copyright infringement. Art doesn't know how much, or even whether, Suzy's copying harmed the sales of his program, so he is unable to prove that he suffered any actual damages (dollar losses). Nor can Art prove what profits, if any, NastySoft made from the illegal copying. For this reason, Art asks the judge to award him special statutory damages—damages up to $100,000 that can be awarded against a copyright infringer even if no actual damages are proved. (See Chapter 13, *Software Copyright Infringement: What It Is, What to Do About It, How to Avoid It*). However, Suzy, while admitting that she copied Art's work, claims that she thought the code was in the public domain because it lacked a copyright notice. The judge buys Suzy's story, and as a result awards Art only $1,000 in statutory damages. The judge tells Art that had his program contained a copyright notice he would have awarded substantially more statutory damages because Suzy's copying clearly would have been willful.

EXAMPLE 2: Assume instead that Art included a valid copyright notice in his program. He sues Suzy and NastySoft for copyright infringement. Since his program contained a valid notice, Suzy cannot claim that she did not realize the book was protected by copyright. As a result, the judge awards Art $20,000 in statutory damages.

Note that this rule applies only to *published* software. Theoretically, an alleged infringer of an unpublished work can raise the innocent infringement defense whether or not the work contains a notice.

However, it does not seem likely that an alleged infringer could convince a judge or jury that his infringement of an unpublished work was innocent if the work contained a copyright notice.

2. Copyright Notice May Deter Potential Infringers

Another important reason to place a copyright notice on all copies of your published software is that it may help deter copyright infringement. The notice lets users know that the work is protected by copyright and may not be copied without the owner's permission. Moreover, since copyright notices appear on the vast majority of published software and other copyrighted works, a user of software not containing a notice might mistakenly assume that it is not protected by copyright, and feel free to copy it or otherwise infringe upon your copyright.

3. Notice Informs the World Who the Copyright Owner Is

A copyright notice contains the name of the copyright owner(s) of the work. This information will help third parties—who might want to obtain permission to use or purchase the work—to identify and locate the owner.

4. Notice Protects Your Work In Countries Not Adhering to the Berne Convention

Finally, several foreign countries do not afford copyright protection to works unless they contain valid copyright notices. (See Chapter 14, *International Software Copyright Protection,* for a detailed discussion.) Providing a copyright notice on your work will enable your work to be protected in these countries.

B. When Should You Place a Copyright Notice on Software?

Many people are confused about exactly when to place a copyright notice on their software or other copyrighted works. Should you use a copyright notice from the day you write the first line of code, when you test the first module, or only when you first market your software to the public?

The best practice is to put a modified informal copyright notice on your work (described in Section C4 below) even before it is published, and put a formal copyright notice (described in Sections C1–3) on your work when it is published.

1. Copyright Notices for Published Software

A full-blown formal copyright notice of the type described in Section C below should be used for all *published* software and other published works. A work is published for copyright purposes when copies are sold, licensed, rented, lent, given away or otherwise distributed to the public. Selling copies to the public through retail outlets or by mail order, publishing code in a magazine, selling a program at a widely attended computer show, and allowing a number of educational institutions to use your program without restriction are all examples of publication.

However, publication occurs only when software is made available to the general public on an unrestricted basis. Distributing copies of software to a restricted group of users does not constitute publication. For example, sending copies to a few friends or beta testers would not constitute a publication. Similarly, a court held that software used by a company's salespeople solely for sales presentations for customers was not published. *(Gates Rubber, Inc. v. Bando American*, 798 F. Supp. 1499 (D. Colo. 1992).)

In addition, software licensed to a select group of end-users who sign license agreements imposing confidentiality requirements probably is not published for notice purposes. However, one court has held that software distributed to automobile and rec-

reational vehicle dealers throughout the country was published even though signed licenses were obtained. The court reasoned that all the auto dealers in the United States did not constitute a select group. *(D.C.I. Computer Systems, Inc. v. Pardini,* 1992 Copr.L.Dec. 27,005 (9th Cir. 1992).)

Finally, a publication does not occur for copyright notice purposes when software is made available only for use on a time-shared computer system or simply displayed on a computer terminal (for example, in an on-line library catalog). But even in these situations, it is wise to use a copyright notice.

Software Distributed Online

It is common to distribute software by uploading it to sites on the Internet, commercial online services such as America Online and CompuServe and computer bulletin boards. It's not entirely clear whether making a program available online constitutes publication. However, you should assume it does. Accordingly, all such programs should carry a proper copyright notice to achieve maximum copyright protection.

If you're not sure whether your software has been published for copyright notice purposes, the best course is to assume that it has been published and include a copyright notice.

2. Copyright Notices for Unpublished Software

Placing a copyright notice on unpublished software provides all the benefits discussed in Section A above except that technically it will not prevent an infringer from raising the innocent infringement defense discussed above. For these reasons, it is sensible to place a copyright notice on unpublished software before sending it to beta testers, potential publishers, product reviewers and other third parties.

C. Form of Notice

There are strict technical requirements as to what a copyright notice must contain if it is to serve its purpose of preventing an innocent infringer defense. A valid copyright notice contains three elements:

- the copyright symbol or the words "Copyright" or "Copr.,"
- if the software or other work is published, the year of publication, and
- the name of the copyright owner.

It is not required that these elements appear in any particular order in the notice, but most notices are written in the order set forth above. We'll discuss each element in turn.

Errors in Copyright Notice

If you discover an error in the copyright notice for your published software, it's wise to have it corrected when subsequent copies are produced. However, it is not necessary to recall any copies already distributed.

---

1. Copyright Symbol or the Words "Copyright" or "Copr."

In the United States either the © symbol or the words "Copyright" or "Copr." may be used. Or you can use the © symbol *and* the words Copyright or Copr. (This will help make it clear to even the dullest minds that your work is copyrighted.)

However, in those foreign countries that require that a copyright notice appear on a published work for it to be protected by copyright at all, you must use the © symbol (you can also use the words Copyright or Copr. if you wish). So if your work might be distributed outside the U.S., be sure to always use the © symbol.

Virtually all word processing programs come with alternate character sets which include the c in a circle. However, if, for some reason, your computer is unable to make a © symbol, the word Copyright or abbreviation Copr. should be used along with a c in parentheses—like this: (c). This will be a valid notice in the U.S., but there might be problems in some foreign countries. So if your work has particular international application, use a © symbol.

Sound Recordings

A different copyright symbol is used for sound recordings. A capital P in a circle ℗ is used instead of the © symbol.

---

2. Year of Publication

The copyright notice must also state the year the work was published. For initial versions of software, this is easy.

As discussed in the preceding section, a publication date should not be provided in a notice for unpublished software.

a. Software updates

Of course, many publicly distributed software programs are continually revised and updated. The copyright notice doesn't have to be changed if a update consists only of minor revisions.

However, if an update contains a substantial amount of new material, it is considered to be a separate work of authorship in its own right. The notice for such a derivative work should contain the date the new work was published. The notice need not contain the date or dates of the prior version or versions; however, it is common practice to include such dates in the copyright notice. One reason is to let the user know when the earlier versions were created. Another reason to do this is that it is not always easy to tell if a work qualifies as a derivative work under Copyright Office rules. (See Chapter 8,

Derivative Works and Use of Preexisting Material, for a detailed discussion.)

> **EXAMPLE:** AcmeSoft, Inc., published version 1.0 of a VRML authoring tool in 1999. The copyright notice read "Copyright © 1999 by AcmeSoft, Inc." The software was revised and republished as a new 2.0 version in 2000. If the 2.0 version qualifies as a new derivative work, the notice need only state "Copyright © 2000 by AcmeSoft, Inc." However, AcmeSoft is not sure whether the changes it made were substantial enough to make the 2.0 version a new derivative work. AcmeSoft decides to err on the side of caution and writes the notice like this: "Copyright © 1999, 2000 by AcmeSoft, Inc."
>
> If AcmeSoft revises the program again in 2001, it may write the copyright notice like this: "Copyright © 1999–2001 by AcmeSoft, Inc."

b. Form of date

The date is usually written in Arabic numerals—for instance, "2000." But you can also use:
- abbreviations of Arabic numerals—for instance, "'00";
- Roman numerals—for instance, "MM"; or
- spelled out words instead of numerals—for instance, "Two Thousand."

3. Copyright Owner's Name

The name of the copyright owner must also be included in the notice. Briefly, the owner is one of the following:
- the person or persons who created the work
- the legal owner of a work made for hire, or
- the person or entity (partnership or corporation) to whom *all* the author's exclusive copyright rights have been transferred.

a. Person or persons who created the work

Unless a work is made for hire (see below), the original creator(s) initially own all the copyright rights. Where all these rights are retained, the creator's name should appear in the copyright notice.

> **EXAMPLE:** Eli Yale creates a database program for churches. He distributes the program though religious bookstores and from his Website. Eli is the sole copyright owner of the program. The copyright notice should state: "Copyright © 2000 by Eli Yale."

If there are multiple creators, they should all be listed in the copyright notice. The names can appear in any order.

b. Works made for hire

A work made for hire is a work made by an employee as part of her job, or a work specially ordered or commissioned under a written work for hire contract. (See Chapter 11, *Initial Copyright Ownership.*) The creator's employer or other person for whom the work was prepared is considered the author of such a work for copyright purposes and that person's (or entity's) name should appear in the copyright notice as owner unless the copyright has been assigned to someone else. The creator-employee's name should not be included in the notice.

> **EXAMPLE:** A team of systems analysts, software designers and programmers employed by Datavue Publications, Inc. create a multimedia scripting and presentation software package. The software is a work made for hire created by Datavue's employees as part of their job. Datavue is considered the author, and thus the owner, and only Datavue's name should appear in the copyright notice: "Copyright © 2000 by Datavue Publications."

c. Transferees

If all of the copyright rights owned by a software author or authors (whether the author is the actual creator or the owner of a work made for hire) are transferred to another person or entity, that name should appear in the copyright notice on all copies produced and distributed after the transfer. However, any copies produced before the transfer occurred may be distributed without updating the notice.

EXAMPLE 1: Assume that Datavue Publications published its presentation package in the example above in 1999. In 2000 Datavue, a small closely held corporation, is purchased by Behemoth Software Inc. As part of the purchase, Behemoth acquires all the copyright rights in the presentation package. Behemoth can go ahead and distribute all unsold copies of the presentation software without updating the copyright notice they contain, even though the notice states that Datavue is the copyright owner. But if Behemoth produces and distributes any new copies, its name alone should appear in the copyright notice.

EXAMPLE 2: Cheapskate Software hired over a dozen freelance programmers to create a new program. All the programmers signed independent contractor agreements transferring all their copyright rights in their work to Cheapskate. Cheapskate's name alone should appear in the copyright notice.

What Name Goes on Notice Where Rights Are Transferred to Different People or Entities?

We explain in Chapter 12, *Transferring Software Copyright Ownership and Use Rights,* that a copyright is completely divisible—that is, the owner may transfer all or part of her exclusive copyright rights to whomever and however she wishes. For example, a copyright owner can transfer less than all of her rights and retain the others, or transfer some rights to one person or entity and all the others to other transferees.

Because copyrights are divisible, it can be confusing to determine just who the owner of copyright is for purposes of the copyright notice. The general rule is that unless the author—whether it is the actual creator or the owner of a work made for hire—transfers all her copyright rights to a single person or entity, the author's name should appear in the notice.

EXAMPLE: Dick and Jane create an educational computer game for young children. They sell to Moppet Publishing Co. the right to publish the game in North America. Dick and Jane sell the right to publish the game outside North America to Foreign Press, Inc. They sell TV, video and film rights based on the game to Repulsive Pictures. Dick and Jane's names alone should appear in the copyright notice in all published versions of the game. In contrast, had Dick and Jane sold all their rights to Moppet, its name should appear alone in the notice.

The one exception to this general rule is where a collective or derivative work is created from preexisting material (see Section D3, below).

d. Form of name

Usually, the owner's full legal name is used. However, it is permissible to use an abbreviation of the owner's name, a last name alone, a trade name, nickname, fictitious name, pseudonym, initials or some other designation as long as the copyright owner is *generally known* by the name or other words or letters used in the notice. For example, International Business Machines Corporation could use the abbreviation IBM. Remember, however, that the point of a notice is to notify, so don't be cryptic or cute.

If You Want to Remain Anonymous

The word "anonymous" should not be used in a copyright notice because an author is obviously not generally known by that name. Likewise, it is not advisable to use a pseudonym by which you are not generally known. You can avoid revealing your name in a copyright notice, and still ensure the notice's validity, by transferring all of your copyright rights to a publisher. This way, the publisher's name may appear in the notice. Another approach would be to form a corporation, transfer your entire copyright to it, and then use the corporation's name in the notice.

If the copyright owner is a corporation, it is not necessary to include the word "Inc." in the name, even if this is part of the corporation's full legal name. Nor is it necessary for the word "by" to precede the copyright owner's name, although it is commonly used—for example, a notice can be written as "Copyright © 2000 by AcmeSoft" or "Copyright © 2000 AcmeSoft."

4. Form of Notice for Unpublished Works

All the rules discussed above should be followed for notices on unpublished software with the exception that you can't include a publication date in the copyright notice. Instead, the notice should indicate the work's unpublished status. A copyright notice for an unpublished work should be in one of the following forms:

- *Copyright © AcmeSoft, Inc. (This work is unpublished.)*
- *Copyright © AcmeSoft, Inc. (Work in progress.)*

In addition, it's a good idea to include a trade secret notice on your unpublished work. (See Chapter 15, *Other Legal Protections for Software* for discussion of trade secrets.) Here's an example:

THIS IS AN UNPUBLISHED WORK CONTAINING [YOUR COMPANY NAME] CONFIDENTIAL AND PROPRIETARY INFORMATION. DISCLOSURE, USE OR REPRODUCTION WITHOUT AUTHORIZATION OF [YOUR COMPANY NAME] IS PROHIBITED.

D. Notice on Compilations and Derivative Works

Compilations and adaptations are formed all or in part from preexisting material. Nevertheless, it is usually not necessary that the copyright notice for this type of work refer to the preexisting material.

1. Compilations

A compilation may be a collective work—that is, a work that consists of separate and independent works assembled into a collective whole. A good example in the software realm is a computerized encyclopedia. Hard copy or digital versions of serial publications, such as periodicals, magazines and newspapers, are also collective work compilations. A compilation may also be a work in which preexisting materials—usually data of various types—are selected, coordinated and arranged so that a new work is created—for example, a catalog. (See Chapter 9, *Computer Databases*, for detailed discussion.)

Unless the person or entity who creates a compilation uses material in the public domain, he must either own the preexisting material used in the work or obtain the permission of those who do own it. If the creator of a compilation does not own the preexisting material, all he owns is the copyright in the compilation as a whole—that is, the copyright in the creative work involved in selecting, combining and assembling the material into a whole work. Nevertheless, a compilation need only contain one copyright notice in the name of that copyright owner. That notice will extend, for the purposes of defeating the innocent infringer rule, to the individual components of the compilation.

> **EXAMPLE:** Hardsell, Inc. compiles and publishes a CD-ROM containing the 100 best new Java applets. The copyright owners of each applet gave Hardsell permission to publish them on the CD-ROM, but still retain all their copyright rights. The CD-ROM need contain only one copyright notice in Hardsell's name: "Copyright © 2000 by Hardsell, Inc." Separate copyright notices need not be provided for the 100 Java programs.

Although an individual contribution to a compilation does not have to have its own copyright notice, a notice is permissible where the copyright in the contribution is owned by someone other than the owner of the compilation as a whole. This may help deter a potential infringer and make clear that the owner of the copyright in the compilation does not own that particular contribution. It will also make it clear to end users whom to contact for permission to use the particular contribution.

> **EXAMPLE:** The owner of a program included in Hardsell's CD-ROM above could include a copyright notice on the user's computer screen upon start-up of the program and/or continuously on-screen (for example, in a status line). A notice could also be provided in a written manual or other documentation accompanying the CD-ROM.

a. Publication date for compilations

The copyright notice for a compilation need only list the year the compilation itself is published, not the date or dates the preexisting material was published.

> **EXAMPLE:** The publication date for the notice on Hardsell's CD-ROM would be 2000, the year the CD-ROM was published.

b. Advertisements

The rule that a single notice for a compilation as a whole covers all the material in the work does not apply to advertisements. Advertisements in serial publications such as periodicals, magazines and newspapers must carry their own copyright notice. However, an advertisement inserted in a compilation on behalf of the copyright owner of the compilation need not contain its own notice—for example, an ad inserted in *PC Magazine* by its owners urging readers to subscribe would not need its own notice.

2. Derivative Works

A derivative work is a work that is created by recasting, transforming or adapting a previously existing work into a new work of authorship. Examples in the software world include revised versions of preexisting programs. "Porting" a program from one type of hardware to another—from a Mac to a PC, for example—is another type of derivative work.

Unless the preexisting material used by a derivative work is in the public domain or owned by the creator of the derivative work, the creator must obtain the copyright owner's permission to use it. (See Chapter 8, *Derivative Works and Use of Preexisting Material.*)

As with compilations, the copyright notice for a derivative work need only contain the name of the owner of the copyright of the derivative work itself, not the owner of the preexisting material upon which the derivative work was based.

EXAMPLE: Inumeracy Software published a mathematical equation-writing program for the Macintosh back in 1998. Oxymoron Software, Inc. obtains permission to create an updated and revised Windows version of the program. The Windows program is a derivative work based upon the preexisting Macintosh program. However, only Oxymoron's name need appear on the copyright notice for its program, since Oxymoron is the owner of the copyright in the derivative work.

a. Publication date

As with collective works, the publication date in the notice for a derivative work should be the year the derivative work was published, not the year or years the preexisting material was published.

3. Work Containing Previously Copyrighted Material

If your software is not a derivative work but nevertheless includes code or other material that was previously published by another copyright owner, you needn't include a separate copyright notice for the work unless this is required by the other copyright owner. Your single copyright notice protects the entire work as a whole. However, if the copyright owner of the earlier work you use wishes his copyright to be specifically noted, you would do it like this:

- © *Copyright 1999 Sid Simm*
- © *Copyright 1998 Mary Moron*

4. Works Containing United States Government Materials

The rule that a single general notice is sufficient for a compilation or derivative work does not always apply to publications incorporating United States government works. United States government publications are in the public domain—that is, they are not copyrighted and anyone can use them without asking the federal government's permission. However, if a work consists *preponderantly* of one or more works by the U.S. government, the copyright notice must affirmatively or negatively identify those portions of the work in which copyright is claimed—that is, that part of the work not consisting of U.S. government materials. This enables readers of such works to know which portions of the work are government materials in the public domain.

It's up to you to decide if your work consists preponderantly of U.S. government materials. Certainly, if more than half of your product consists of federal government materials, your notice should enable readers to determine which portions of the work are copyrighted and which are in the public domain.

EXAMPLE: Databest Inc. publishes a CD-ROM containing analyses of U.S. census data and including several appendices containing U.S. Census Bureau material. The CD-ROM is a collective work in which independently created contributions have been combined to form a collective whole. The appendices amount to over half the CD-ROM. The copyright notice for the work could state: "Copyright © 1999 by Databest Inc. No protection is claimed in works of the United States Government as set forth in Appendices 1, 2, 3, 4, 6."

Alternatively, the notice could affirmatively identify those portions of the work in which copyright is claimed—that is, those portions not containing government materials. In this event, the notice might look like this: "Copyright © 1999 by Databest Inc. Copyright claimed in Sections 1 through 10."

Failure to follow this rule will result in the copyright notice being found invalid. This means that an infringer of the material in which you claim a copyright would be allowed to raise the innocent infringement defense at trial. (See Section A above.)

E. Where to Place Copyright Notice

Although it's not strictly required by law, you should place your copyright notice in lots of different places to ensure that it serves its intended purposes—to be seen and give notice of your copyright to the world. Indeed, every component of a published software package should contain a copyright notice. This includes:

- the package or box the software comes in
- the manual and other written documentation
- the computer disks or other media containing the software, and
- the appropriate computer screens

1. Packaging

Most published software that is not distributed solely online is sold in some sort of box or other package. A copyright notice should appear somewhere on the box. It is often placed on the back of the box, but you can also place it on the front or sides. The notice will apply to your cover art and graphics as well as to the software and other materials inside the box or package.

2. Computer Diskettes, CD-ROMs

A copyright notice should also be printed on a label permanently affixed to the computer diskettes, CD-ROM disks or other magnetic media containing the software.

3. Computer Screens

According to Copyright Office regulations, providing a copyright notice on the box or disk containing published software is sufficient. But it shouldn't be sufficient for you. Remember, you want to make sure that users do really see your notice. It should appear somewhere on the computer screen when the software is used. This can be done in one or more of the following ways:

- by printing the notice in or near the title of the program or at the end of the program
- displaying the notice when the program is first activated (on the opening screen or in an about or credit box), or
- displaying the notice continuously while the program is being used (for example, in a status bar).

A good rule is to display it on the screen at the beginning and end of a program, as well as every time the program title is displayed. Also include a notice in any "read me" files.

⚠️ **Caution**
Certain programs have more than one mode or version when they are running or performing their task. For example, many complicated programs have a training mode, separate from the program itself. Each mode should have a correct copyright notice.

4. Software Documentation and Other Materials in Book or Pamphlet Form

Documentation includes everything that accompanies, explains, illustrates or otherwise complements your program. Many manuals, such as user manuals, programmer reference manuals, and training manuals, look more or less like books. Short manuals and program documentation often take the form of a pamphlet. The rules for placing your copyright notice are the same for both, as long as the pamphlet consists of at least two pages.

The copyright notice for a manual or other similar written work may be placed in any of the following locations:

- the title page
- the page immediately following the title page (this is the most commonly used location for books)
- either side of the front cover
- if there is no front cover, either side of the back leaf of the copies—that is, the hinged piece of paper at the end of a book or pamphlet consisting of at least two pages
- the first or last page of the main body of the work.

5. Single-Leaf Works

Single-leaf works consist of one page. For copyright purposes, it makes no difference whether printed material appears on one side of the sheet or both. As long as only one piece of paper is involved, the notice can be anywhere on the front or back of the page.

6. Magazines and Periodicals

If you publish a magazine, periodical, newsletter, journal or other serial publication, the copyright notice may be placed in any of the locations provided for manuals (above), or:

- as part of, or adjacent to, the masthead (the masthead typically contains such information as the periodical's title, information about the staff, frequency of issuance and subscription policies)
- on the same page as the masthead, but not as part of the masthead itself, provided that the notice is reproduced prominently and set apart from the other matter appearing on the page, or
- adjacent to a prominent heading appearing at or near the front of the issue containing the periodical's title and any combination of the volume and issue number and date of the issue.

7. Pictorial, Graphic and Sculptural Works

This category includes computer-generated art, charts, graphs, etc. Notice must be affixed directly or by label that is sewn, cemented or otherwise durably attached to two or three-dimensional copies. The notice must be attached to the front or back of copies, to any backing, mounting, base, matting, framing or any permanent housing. Again, the idea is to give notice, not bury it, so be sure your notice can be seen easily.

FIRST THE WORD COPYRIGHT OR THE © SYMBOL OR COPR. THEN THE DATE, THEN YOUR NAME, THEN ALL RIGHTS RESERVED.

F. Other Information Near Notice

Certain other information in addition to the copyright notice itself is commonly included on the same page as the notice.

1. Trade Secret Notices

Most software qualifies for trade secret protection as well as copyright protection. For this reason, it's a good idea to include a trade secret notice along with a copyright notice.

a. Unpublished programs

A confidentiality notice such as the following can be used for unpublished programs and other unpublished materials:

THIS IS AN UNPUBLISHED WORK CONTAINING [your or your company name] CONFIDENTIAL AND PROPRIETARY INFORMATION. DISCLOSURE, USE OR REPRODUCTION WITHOUT AUTHORIZATION OF [your or your company name] IS PROHIBITED.

b. Published programs

When you publish a program—for example, mass-market it in computer stores or over the Internet—include a combined confidentiality notice such as the following in the program itself and on any diskettes, manuals and other documentation:

THIS [choose one: program, document, material] IS CONFIDENTIAL AND PROPRIETARY TO [your company name] AND MAY NOT BE REPRODUCED, PUBLISHED OR DISCLOSED TO OTHERS WITHOUT COMPANY AUTHORIZATION.

2. All Rights Reserved

Until recent years, some Central and South American countries required that the words "All rights reserved" be used along with a copyright notice. This is no longer true. Nevertheless, out of force of habit, you sometimes see the words "All rights reserved" accompanying a copyright notice on published works. These words are unnecessary, but do no harm if they are used.

3. Warning Statements

Since many people do not really understand what a copyright notice means, many copyright owners include various types of warning or explanatory statements near the copyright notice. The purpose is to make clear to users that the work is copyrighted and may not be reproduced without the copyright owner's permission. It does not cost anything to place this type of statement near the copyright notice, and it may help deter copyright infringement. But remember, such statements do not take the place of a valid copyright notice as described earlier in this chapter.

a. Statements used in software

Here's a simple warning statement that could be used near a copyright notice contained in software itself—both on diskette labels and on the computer screen when the program is activated (for example, it could be placed inside an about or credit box or near the program's title):

This software is copyrighted. The software may not be copied, reproduced, translated or reduced to any electronic medium or machine-readable form without the prior written consent of [Name of Copyright Owner] *except that you may make one copy of the program disks solely for back-up purposes.*

b. Statements commonly used in manuals

Here is an example of the type of warning statements that are commonly used in software manuals:

This manual, and the software described in this manual, are copyrighted. No part of this manual or the described software may be copied, reproduced, translated or reduced to any electronic medium or machine-readable form without the prior written consent of [Name of Copyright Owner] *except that you may make one copy of the program disks solely for back-up purposes.*

Friendly Copyright Statements

A growing number of software publishers are departing from negative sounding statements like those above. Rather, they employ friendly language that is positive and inviting. The reasoning behind this is approach is that appealing to an end-user's sense of fair play will get better results than attempting to scare him. Here's an example of such language:

We have worked very hard to create a quality product and wish to realize the fair fruits of our labor. We therefore insist that you honor our copyright. However we want to encourage the use of our product in all possible circumstances and will work very hard to meet your needs if you will call and ask us for permission.

G. Copyright Notice Requirements for Pre-1989 Published Software

Prior to March 1, 1989, a copyright notice was absolutely essential for all published works. Failure to have one could result in loss of all copyright protection.

1. Works Published Before 1978

Until 1978, all works published in the United States had to contain a valid copyright notice to be protected by copyright. Failure to provide the notice resulted in automatic loss of the copyright in the work—that is, the work was injected into the public domain, meaning that anyone could copy or otherwise use it without the author's permission. There was nothing authors could do about this.

The only exception to this rule is where the copyright owner failed to provide notices on a *very few* copies by accident or mistake. In this event, the copyright owner may be allowed to enforce his

copyright rights against an infringer who had actual notice of the copyright. However, this exception has rarely been successfully invoked.

There's probably not much pre-1978 software that is still valuable today, so these rules don't have much meaning for the software industry.

2. Works Published Between 1978 and March 1, 1989

The pre-1978 notice requirement often had draconian results—authors lost their copyright protection just because they failed to comply with a mere technical formality. The harshness of this rule was moderated somewhat by the Copyright Act of 1976, which provided that a work without a valid notice that was published after January 1, 1978 did not enter the public domain if—within five years after the publication—the work was registered with the Copyright Office and a reasonable effort was made to add a valid notice to all copies of the work distributed after the omission was discovered.

EXAMPLE: Sam created a simple home accounting program back in 1987 and distributed it by mail order and at computer trade shows. The program was published for copyright purposes. However, Sam didn't know anything about copyright so he failed to register the program with the Copyright Office or include a copyright notice. In 1988, he found out about his error and decided to correct it in order to "rescue" his copyright. He registered the program with the Copyright Office and made a reasonable effort to add a notice to all copies of the program distributed after he found out about his error. By doing so, he saved his copyright in the program.

Unfortunately, by the time you're reading this book it is too late for any copyright owner to rescue her copyright by doing what Sam did in the example above. This is because such corrective efforts had to be made within 5 years after the work was published prior to March 1, 1989. Thus, a program published on February 28, 1989 without notice entered the public domain unless corrective action was taken by February 28, 1994. Works published before February 28, 1989 entered the public domain earlier.

It is now too late to save any of these pre-1989 unnoticed works. They have entered the public domain (at least for copyright purposes) where they will forever remain. The only exception is where the notice was inadvertently left off a relatively small number of copies distributed to the public. Omission of notice from 1% or fewer of published pre-1989 copies probably satisfies this criteria. Anything more, likely doesn't, although it's not entirely clear.

3. Works Published After March 1, 1989

The copyright notice requirement for published works ended altogether when the United States signed the Berne Convention, an international copyright treaty. The Berne Convention is discussed in detail in Chapter 14, *International Software Copyright Protection.* All you need to know about it now is that it required the U.S. to get rid of its notice requirement, which happened on March 1, 1989. Any work published after that date need not contain a copyright notice, even if it was originally published prior to that date. ■

CHAPTER

4

Copyright Registration: The Basics

This chapter is about the basics of copyright registration. You'll learn:

- what registration is
- when to register
- who may register
- how many times to register a particular work, and
- registration of new versions and other derivative works.

A. What Is Copyright Registration?

Copyright registration is a legal formality by which a copyright owner makes a public record in the U.S. Copyright Office in Washington, D.C. of some basic information about a copyrighted work, including:

- the title of the work
- who created the work and when, and
- who owns the copyright.

When people speak of copyrighting software or other works, they usually mean registering them with the Copyright Office.

To register, you fill out the appropriate pre-printed application form, pay a small application fee, and mail the application and fee to the Copyright Office along with one or two copies of all or part of the copyrighted work.

Contrary to what many people think, it is not necessary to register a work to create or establish a copyright in it. This is because an author's copyright comes into existence *automatically* the moment a work is fixed in tangible form. (See Chapter 2, *Copyright Basics.*) However, as discussed below, it is a good idea to register any work that may have commercial value.

B. Why Register?

If registration is not required, why bother? There are several excellent reasons.

1. Registration Is a Prerequisite to Filing an Infringement Suit

If you're an American citizen or legal resident and your software or other copyrighted work is first published in the United States (or simultaneously in the U.S. and another country), you may not file a copyright infringement suit in this country unless your work has been registered with the Copyright Office.

It's as simple as that. You legally own a copyright, whether you register or not, but you may not use the legal process to enforce your rights unless you've first followed the legal procedure for registration. This doesn't mean that infringers of unregistered copyrights can never be sued—you can register your copyright at any time and then sue.

You may be thinking, "Big deal, I'll register if and when someone infringes on my software and I need to file a lawsuit." If you adopt this strategy, you'll probably end up having to register in a hurry so you can file suit quickly. You'll have to pay an extra $500 for such expedited registration. (See discussion in Chapter 5, Section F.) Moreover, if there are problems completing and sending in the application or getting it approved by the Copyright Office, there could be a substantial delay before you can file your suit.

Works First Published Abroad

Copyright owners who are not U.S. citizens or legal residents and whose work is first published in foreign countries that are members of the Berne International Copyright Convention need not register to sue for infringement in the U.S. (See Chapter 14, *International Software Copyright Protection*, for a list of Berne countries.) But, if they do register, noncitizens and nonresidents will obtain the important benefits discussed below.

2. Registration Protects Your Copyright by Making It a Public Record

When you register your copyright, it becomes a matter of official public record. In practical terms, this means:

- you're the presumed owner of the copyright in the material deposited with the registration, and
- the information contained in your copyright registration form is presumed to be true.

These legal presumptions are applied if you become involved in a court dispute. Does this mean that if you register you automatically win a copyright infringement case? No. Registration only causes the court to make these presumptions in the absence of proof to the contrary. In other words, if another author claims original authorship in a work that's identical or similar to yours, everything you state on your registration form, including the date you created your work, will be taken by the court as true unless the other author proves differently. However, you will still have to prove the other elements—access to your work and substantial similarity—described in Chapter 13, *Software Copyright Infringement: What It Is, What to Do About It, How to Avoid It,* in order to prevail.

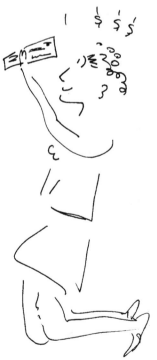

Potential Problems Arising From Copyright Registration

Let's assume we've convinced you that registration is wise. Before you register, you should know about a possible down side to making your work a public record by registering it with the U.S. Copyright Office: Your copyright application and at least some part of your work become available for public inspection when you register. Others will have the opportunity to examine your work. They can view everything you send to the Copyright Office, although they cannot normally make copies.

If making your material public in this way concerns you, make sure to read Chapter 5, Section D. There we address this concern in detail and suggest several practical ways to alleviate it. Those readers who plan to maintain the trade secret status of their work will also want to read Chapter 15, *Other Legal Protections for Software.*

We believe that, in most situations, the danger that copyright registration will disclose your work is usually more fanciful than real, assuming you take several routine self-protection steps described in Chapter 5, Section D.

3. Timely Registration Makes It Easier to Win Money in Court

The benefits discussed in Section 2 above are available whenever you register. However, if you register either before an infringement of your work begins or within three months of publishing the work, you'll become entitled to two additional benefits if you have to sue an infringer and prevail in the case:

- the court can order the other side to pay your attorney fees and court costs, and
- you may elect to have the court award statutory damages (special damages of up to $100,000 per

infringement) without your having to establish what damage you actually suffered.

Details on how to fulfill the time limit requirements for registering a work are discussed in detail in Section C, below.

From a real-life standpoint the potential to recover attorney fees can determine whether you can afford to sue. In many copyright infringement cases, attorney fees exceed the potential benefits of winning the lawsuit. However, if your case is a strong one, the infringer has the apparent ability to pay and attorney fees can be collected because you promptly registered, a lawyer may well take your case for little or no money down and hope to collect from your opponent.

The ability to collect statutory damages is also an important benefit. Proving a specific monetary loss can often be far more difficult than establishing that infringement occurred. With statutory damages, you don't need to prove the infringement caused you any monetary loss. If you've promptly registered your work, a judge may award from $250 to $100,000 in statutory damages, depending on the circumstances of the case. (Refer to Chapter 13, *Software Copyright Infringement: What It Is, What to Do About It, How to Avoid It* for more details about statutory damages.) Either way, the possibility of statutory damages is a real incentive to register early.

EXAMPLE: AcmeSoft publishes a diet maintenance program called *You Are What You Eat.* A former AcmeSoft programmer uses some of the code from AcmeSoft's program to help create a competing program published by ShadyWare. AcmeSoft easily proves in court that ShadyWare's program contains code copied from *You Are What You Eat.* But when it comes to damages, AcmeSoft cannot show any direct losses caused by the copyright infringement. Sales of *You Are What You Eat* remained about the same after the infringing program was published. For this reason, AcmeSoft elects to ask the judge to award it statutory damages. The judge decides to award $25,000, since she decides ShadyWare's copying was willful—that is, it knew the copying was wrong but did it anyway.

It may seem that all the benefits of prompt registration relate to litigation. You're also probably aware that the overwhelming majority of copyrights are never involved in a lawsuit. Why, then, should you go to the trouble of registering? The answer is that registration is a very inexpensive type of insurance. As with other forms of insurance, you buy protection against fairly unlikely occurrences, but occurrences that are so potentially devastating that you're willing to plan in advance to cushion their impact.

Timely registration may actually help keep you out of court because an infringer may be more willing to negotiate and settle your claim if he knows that you could recover substantial statutory damages in court. For example, ShadyWare in our example above might have elected to pay AcmeSoft a substantial sum to settle the case rather than facing a potentially hefty statutory damages award.

Since registration is very easy to accomplish, currently costs only $20 per work registered and provides significant benefits, we believe it to be one of the great insurance deals of all time.

Of course, no insurance, whether it consists of copyright registration or a more conventional variety, makes sense if what you're protecting has little or no value. Some published instruction materials, promotion copy and, occasionally, even a program—may have no realistic value to anyone but you. In this situation, placing a copyright notice on the material and not bothering to register may be a wise choice. You'll have to decide that question. However, we strongly believe that in most situations, if your work is valuable enough to publish, it's valuable enough to register.

C. When to Register

A work may be registered at any time. However, to receive the benefit of statutory damages and attorney fees in infringement suits, copyright owners must register their works within the time periods prescribed by the Copyright Act. The time periods differ for published and unpublished works.

1. When to Register Published Works

The copyright owner of a published work is entitled to statutory damages and attorney fees only if the work is registered:
- within *three months* of the date of the *first* publication, or
- *before* the date the copyright infringement began.

A work is published for copyright purposes when copies are made available to the public on an unrestricted basis. Obviously, a software product is published when it is made available to the public in stores or by mail order. It's not entirely clear whether software distributed online is considered published. But, to be on the safe side, you should assume that it is. (See Chapter 2, *Copyright Basics,* for a detailed discussion of what constitutes publication.)

EXAMPLE 1: SuperWare, a small software publisher, publishes a new database program on July 1 and registers it with the Copyright Office in mid-September. In December, SuperWare discovers that BadSoft obtained a source code copy of the program from a former SuperWare employee and copied substantial portions of it into a competing database program that was released in August. If SuperWare sues BadSoft for copyright infringement, it will be entitled to receive statutory damages and attorney fees, since the registration was completed within the three-month period.

EXAMPLE 2: Assume that SuperWare registered the database program in the above example on November 1, four months after it was published. Also assume that BadSoft didn't get its competing program out until December. Although the program was not registered within three months of publication, SuperWare will still be entitled to attorney fees and statutory damages if it sues BadSoft because the program was registered before the infringement occurred.

EXAMPLE 3: Assume instead that SuperWare's program was never registered. After discovering BadSoft's infringement in December, SuperWare registers the program with the Copyright Office and files suit against BadSoft. Super-Ware will not be entitled to receive statutory damages and attorney fees and costs. Reason: SuperWare's program was neither registered within three months of publication nor before BadSoft committed the infringement.

The above examples aside, in the real world it's important to get your work registered within the three-month postpublication period because many infringements begin shortly after publication.

2. When to Register Unpublished Works

If an unpublished program or other work is infringed upon, its author or other copyright owner is entitled to obtain statutory damages and attorney fees from the infringer only if the work was registered *before the infringement occurred.*

You cannot get around this requirement by publishing the work and then registering it within three months of the publication date. The three-month rule discussed in Section C1, just above, applies only if the infringement began *after first publication.*

D. Who May Register?

Any person or entity, such as a corporation or partnership, that owns all or part of the rights that make up a work's copyright may register that work, as can that owner's authorized agent (representative). This means registration may be accomplished by:
- the author or authors of a work
- anyone who has acquired one or more of an author's exclusive copyright rights, or
- the authorized agent of any of the above.

Ownership of copyrights is discussed in detail in Chapter 11, *Initial Copyright Ownership,* and Chapter 12, *Transferring Software Copyright Ownership and Use Rights.* The following discussion briefly describes ownership solely for registration purposes.

1. Registration by a Work's Author(s)

Unless a work is a work made for hire (see Section b, below) the copyright initially belongs to whoever created it.

a. Individually authored works

The copyright in a work created by a single individual is owned by that individual (unless it was a work made for hire as discussed below). An individually authored work can be registered by the author or his authorized agent—that is, someone he asks to register it for him).

> **EXAMPLE:** Shelby has written a computer game based on the history of the Civil War. Shelby can register the game himself, or it can be registered by his authorized agent on Shelby's behalf, for example, his business manager.

b. Works made for hire

A work created by an employee as part of her job is a work made for hire. For registration purposes, the author of a work made for hire is the creator's employer or other person for whom the work was prepared. The employer normally registers a work made for hire, not the employee-programmer.

> **EXAMPLE:** Bruno, Hilda, Eric, Hans, Gertrude and Heinrich are programmers employed by BigTech, Inc. Their latest project was creating an English-German translation program. The program is a work made for hire and should be registered by BigTech, their employer.

Certain types of works created by independent contractors—that is, nonemployees—can also be works made for hire. But this is so only if the contractor signs a work made for hire contract before the work is created and the work falls into one of the work made for hire categories enumerated in the Copyright Act. These categories include contributions to a collective work (a work created by more than one author), instructional texts, parts of an audiovisual work, translations and compilations.

> **EXAMPLE:** Heidi, a self-employed technical writer-translator, is hired by BigTech on a freelance basis to translate a computer manual into German. Before undertaking the work, she signs an agreement stating that her translation shall be a work made for hire owned by BigTech. The resulting manual is a work made for hire and should be registered by BigTech, the hiring party.

However, it is unclear whether software—computer code itself—falls within any of the work made for hire categories. For this reason, persons who hire independent contractors to work on software should never rely on the work made for hire rule. Instead, they should have the independent contractor assign all copyright rights to the hiring party. (See Chapter 11, *Initial Copyright Ownership*, for detailed discussion.) The hiring party can then register the software as a transferee as discussed in Section 2 below.

c. Joint works

If two or more persons jointly create a program or other protectible work with the intent that their respective contributions be combined into a single work, the work so created is called a joint work. A joint work is co-owned by its creators (unless it's a work made for hire), and can be registered by one, some or all of the authors or by their agent.

> **EXAMPLE:** Bob, Carol, Ted and Alice decide to create a stock market investment program. They agree that they will each own 25% of the copyright in the program. After it is written, the program may be registered by any combination of Bob, Carol, Ted and Alice, or their authorized agent.

(Again, for a detailed discussion of these categories, see Chapter 11, *Initial Copyright Ownership.*)

2. Registration by Publishers and Other Transferees

As discussed in Chapter 2, *Copyright Basics*, an author's copyright is really a bundle of separate exclusive rights. These exclusive rights include the right to reproduce, distribute and adapt a work. A copyright owner can sell or otherwise transfer all or part of his exclusive copyright rights. Indeed, this is usually how an author benefits economically from his work.

Persons or entities who obtain copyright rights from software authors (transferees) need to be concerned about the timing of the registration. If the work is not timely registered (accomplished before an infringement begins or within three months of publication), they will not be entitled to obtain statutory damages and attorney fees if they successfully sue someone who infringes on the copyright.

Fortunately, transferees do not have to rely on authors to register. Anyone who obtains any of an author's exclusive rights is entitled to register the author's work. For example, if the exclusive right to publish a popular computer game were divided geographically and licensed to distributors in 18 states, there would be at least 18 persons or entities that could register the work.

Although a number of people may be entitled to register a work, normally only one registration is allowed for each version of a published work. It makes absolutely no difference who gets the job done. The single registration protects every copyright owner. It behooves a transferee to register a work immediately if the author has not already done so.

As a practical matter, registration is almost always accomplished by a work's author or publisher. The publisher usually has a right to register either as an owner of all or some exclusive rights or as the author's authorized agent.

In the software publishing business, it is common practice for authors to sign over all copyright rights to their publishers by contract. When this occurs, the publisher usually registers the copyright on its own behalf as the owner of these rights. Remember, however, that except for work made for hire situations, the author always has the original power to register, and should do so unless a publisher is already in the picture who will accomplish this.

Who May Register Works Created by Independent Contractors

The copyright in a computer program created by an independent contractor generally is owned by the contractor, not the hiring party, unless the contractor transfers her ownership rights in the program to the hiring party. Absent such a transfer agreement, only the contractor would be entitled to register the program.

Other types of works created by independent contractors—for example, translations, contributions to collective works, audiovisual works, indexes—may be works made for hire if the contractor signs an agreement to that effect before the work is created. In these cases, the hiring party is deemed the author for registration (and all other) purposes and should register the work.

E. Registering All the Elements of a Single Software Package

Computer software is a multifaceted product that usually consists of several different works of authorship, including:

- computer code,
- documentation, and
- screen displays and other elements of the user interface.

Moreover, software is rarely one giant program, but is usually a system of modules, including screens, overlays, drivers, help files, config files and so forth. Many or even all of these modules and files may be able to stand on their own as independent works of authorship.

The question naturally arises: "Do I register each type of authorship separately or everything together at the same time?" Fortunately, the answer is that you usually register every element of a software package together on one application form for one fee, saving you both time and money.

A Copyright Office decision provides that "all copyrightable expression owned by the same claimant and embodied in a computer program, including computer screen displays, is considered a single work and should be registered on a single application form." (53 Fed.Reg. 21817 (June 10, 1988).)

In other words, you may register any number of *separate* works of authorship together on one application if:

- the copyright claimant is the same for all elements of the work for which copyright registration is sought, and
- all such elements are either unpublished or are published together as a single unit—that is, sold together in a single package.

1. Who Is the Copyright Claimant?

Because the copyright claimant must be the same, you'll need to know who this is. When a work is first created, it is owned by the original author—the creator or the original owner of a work made for hire. If the work is registered at this point, the author is the claimant.

However, as we discuss in detail in Chapter 12, *Transferring Software Copyright Ownership and Use Rights*, an author is free to transfer all or part of her exclusive copyright rights to others. These exclusive rights are the right to copy, distribute, display, perform or create derivative works from an original work. When an author transfers *all* her exclusive copyright rights in one bundle to a single person or entity (the transferee), the transferee becomes the copyright claimant for registration purposes. Such a transferee must have a written transfer document from the author—for example, a software publishing agreement transferring the original author's "entire right, title and interest" in the software.

Often an author transfers some of her copyright rights and retains others, or transfers some rights to one person or entity and others to another person or entity. This may occur where an author transfers fewer than all her exclusive rights to a publisher, or where a person or entity that acquired all the author's rights transfers some, but not all, of the rights to a third party. In this event, nobody will own all the copyright rights. If the work hasn't been registered already, any person or entity that owns one or more exclusive rights in the work may register. (See Section D2 for a detailed discussion.) The original author is listed as the claimant on the application, even if someone else is registering the work. In effect, this means that the author(s) will always be listed as the copyright claimant unless somebody else ends up owning all the exclusive copyright rights before registration occurs.

In the case of a work made for hire, the author is the creator's employer, or person or entity for whom the work was created. This means the copyright claimant is either (1) the employer or hiring party; or (2) the person or entity to whom the employer or hiring party has transferred all of its exclusive rights in the work.

Consider these examples:

EXAMPLE 1: FrancoSoft publishes a French language instruction software package called *Lingua Franca*. All the elements of the software package—code, documentation, screens—were created by FrancoSoft employees or independent contractors who assigned all their copyright rights in the work to FrancoSoft. FrancoSoft is considered the author of this work made for hire. As such, it initially owns all the copyright rights in every element of *Lingua Franca* and is the copyright claimant for registration purposes. Assuming all the elements are sold together, the entire package can be registered by FrancoSoft on a single application.

EXAMPLE 2: Assume instead that *Lingua Franca* is part of a series of instructional language programs and that the documentation and other written reference materials are sold separately by FrancoSoft. Because these materials are not a part of a single unit of publication, they cannot be registered with the program on the same application.

EXAMPLE 3: Assume instead that *Lingua Franca* was a joint venture between FrancoSoft and DataDoo, another software company. DataDoo employees wrote the extensive written instruction manual and FrancoSoft created the program itself. The parties' joint venture agreement provides that DataDoo owns all the copyright rights in the manual and FrancoSoft owns all the rights in all the other program elements. Two registrations will be required for this software package. DataDoo will have to register the manual and FrancoSoft will have to register the code and other program elements that it separately owns.

EXAMPLE 4: Assume instead that *Lingua Franca* was initially developed solely by DataDoo employees. FrancoSoft purchases all the copyrights in the program from DataDoo. Since the program has not been registered by DataDoo, FrancoSoft decides to register it. The entire software package can be registered on one application with FrancoSoft listed as the copyright claimant (owner of all the rights in the work).

EXAMPLE 5: Assume the same facts as in Example 4 above, except that FrancoSoft purchases from DataDoo only the exclusive right to distribute *Lingua Franca* on the Macintosh. FrancoSoft may still register the entire software package on one application (or DataDoo may do so, it makes no difference who does; see Section D2 above). DataDoo, the initial author of this work made for hire, would be listed as the claimant since no single person or entity now owns all the rights in *Lingua Franca*.

Copyright Tip

If you're still confused after reading all these examples, call the Copyright Office at 202-707-3000 during working hours and ask them whether one or more registrations are required for the work you wish to register.

2. Registering Computer Screen Displays

Computer screen displays—the way a program looks on the computer screen—form an important part of a program's user interface, and as such are a very valuable component of any software package. As we discuss in detail in Chapter 7, *Scope of Copyright Protection for Software*, whether and to what extent user interfaces are protected by copyright has been the subject of much litigation and is still an unsettled question.

As discussed earlier in this section, it normally is not necessary to separately register computer screens. A single registration of the entire program will extend to the screen displays. The only exception is where the copyright claimant in the underlying program is different from the claimant for the displays—that is, where the code and displays are owned by different parties. In this event, separate registrations by each claimant are required. (See Section 1, above, for a discussion of identifying copyright claimants.)

Indeed, the Copyright Office takes the position that screen displays *cannot* be registered separately from a program itself where the displays and program are owned by the same copyright claimant.

Nevertheless, because computer screen displays are so valuable, some software publishers have sought to separately register them. Doubtless the primary motivation for this was to make it clear to the world that the displays were protected by copyright and thereby deter potential copiers and make it easier to win an infringement case. One well-known software publisher, the video game maker Atari, sued the Copyright Office when it refused to register the displays for a video game called *Breakout* as a separate audiovisual work. The court held that the game displays were copyrightable and should be registered by the Copyright Office. *(Atari Games Corp. v. Oman*, 979 F.2d 242 (D.C. Cir. 1992).)

However, it really isn't worth the trouble to try to separately register screen displays. If you want to make it clear your displays have been registered, simply mention the displays in the nature of authorship space on your one basic registration application (see Chapter 5, Section C). Also, include photos or other identifying material for them with your deposit as discussed in Chapter 5, Section D5. This is not required, but will make it abundantly clear that your displays have been registered. Be aware, however, that this will probably delay approval of your application because the copyright examiner will have to examine your identifying material to determine whether your computer screens are copyrightable.

3. Registering Documentation

Where documentation—such as manuals, user guides and tutorials—is sold along with a program as a single unit, the documentation can and should be registered along with the program on a single application. The only exception to this rule would be the unusual situation where the copyright owner of the documentation is different from the copyright owner of the program.

Documentation published or distributed separately from the program it describes or supplements must be registered separately.

4. Registering Complex Computer Systems

Most modern sophisticated software packages consist of numerous subsystems or modules that can be considered independent works of authorship in their own right and that might be independently worth stealing. For example, a software package for designing Websites might, among other things, consist of an HTML editor, a Web graphics editing tool and a collection of Java applets.

Again, the Copyright Office's rule is that, if the various modules making up a computer system are all published for the first time in a single software package as an integrated unit, they should be registered together on one application form. The only exceptions are where:

- there are different copyright claimants for the various modules, or
- one or more of the modules have been previously published.

If any modules or subsystems of a program that is registered on one application are subsequently published or otherwise marketed independently, they can and should be separately registered.

5. Registering Online Works

You register on-line materials such as websites in much the same way any other material is registered. If the work consists primarily of text, use Form TX to register. If the work consists primarily of graphics, use Form VA. See Chapter 5 for a detailed discussion about how to fill out these forms.

When you register an online work, the registration extends only to the copyrightable content received by the Copyright Office in your deposit. These means that if the online work is subsequently revised or updated, the registration will not protect the new material. This means you'll have to separately register each new version of your online work and pay a new application fee.

However, there is also a group registration procedure for electronic databases that permits you to register all material in a database created within any three-month period. (See Chapter 9.)

6. When to Reregister a Work

Subject to the exceptions noted below, a software package constituting a single integrated unit of publication (that is, all elements of the package are sold together) need be and can be registered only once.

a. Reregistering published works

A second registration may be made if the prior registration was unauthorized or legally invalid—for instance, where registration was effected by someone other than the author, owner of exclusive rights or an authorized representative.

If the facts stated in the registration application change after the work has been registered—for instance, the work's title is changed—corrections should be made on an application for supplemental registration filed with the Copyright Office. (See Chapter 6, Section D.)

b. Unpublished works

A work originally registered as unpublished may be registered again after publication, even if the published and unpublished versions are identical. If they are identical, it is still a good idea to register the published version of a previously registered unpublished work. If you ever become involved in an infringement suit, it may be helpful to have the published version of the software on deposit with the Copyright Office—the deposit shows exactly what was published and the second registration establishes the date of publication, which may later aid you in proving that an infringer had access to your work. (See Chapter 13, *Software Copyright Infringement: What It Is, What to Do About It, How to Avoid It.*)

F. Registering New Versions and Other Derivative Works

A derivative work is a work based upon or recast from preexisting material. We discuss derivative works in detail in Chapter 8, *Derivative Works and Use of Preexisting Material.* To qualify for registration, the new material in a derivative work must be significant enough to constitute copyrightable authorship.

If you own the preexisting material and your alterations don't have independent value, there's no pressing reason to register. If, however, the derivative work involves a significant new and creative effort, as is often the case, registration is recommended.

> **EXAMPLE:** AcmeSoft first published a small business accounting program for the Macintosh back in 1995. The program, called *Bean Counter*, was not a success and AcmeSoft withdrew it from the market in 1997. In 1999, AcmeSoft creates a new accounting program called *AccountHelp* using a substantial amount of *Bean Counter* in addition to much valuable new code. *AccountHelp* should be registered as a derivative work.

1. Registering New Versions of a Work

Computer software is never really finished; it is constantly being updated and otherwise revised and modified. A new version of a preexisting program is one type of derivative work.

Once you've registered a version of a software program, all material contained in that version is covered, regardless of how many new versions are produced. New material contained in new versions, however, is not covered.

If the changes are minor, or merely correct routine errors, registration is probably not necessary—and will not be allowed. This is particularly true where the changes are sprinkled here and there and do not make sense standing alone.

If, on the other hand, your changes are significant (say you issue a new release of your work containing literally hundreds of changes, because the old one is out-of-date or simply not up to speed), then you'll want to register the new release as a new version of the original. Examples of software modifications that can and should be registered include situations where:

- substantial new program code is added to a previously published program to enable it to accomplish new functions,
- a previously published program is translated from one computer language to another,
- a previously published program is adapted to run on a different model or brand of computer (as long as the changes are not functionally predetermined— that is, the basic software that is being changed was specifically designed to accommodate such changes; see sidebar in Chapter 5, Section C).

Where modifications such as these are registered, the registration covers only the new material added to the preexisting software. Note carefully that under Copyright Office rules, registering a later version of the same software will not constitute registration of any earlier versions. Consider the following example:

EXAMPLE: MicroArt, Inc. creates a new computer graphics program called *Draw All*. MicroArt publishes versions 1.0 and 2.0 of the program without registering them with the Copyright Office. MicroArt then registers version 3.0. This registration covers only the copyrightable materials added to the program since the last published version of the work (version 2.0). Obviously, MicroArt needs to separately register versions 1.0 and 2.0 as well as 3.0.

2. Registering Software Under Development

You may, if you wish, register your unfinished software as it undergoes various stages of development. This may be useful if you're worried about others claiming you've copied from them. When you register your software, you deposit a copy of the work with the Copyright Office. (See Chapter 5, Section D.) The deposit can help you show that your software was independently created, not copied from others. ■

The Registration Process

n this chapter we discuss going through the copyright registration process. You'll learn how to fill out the registration forms and comply with the Copyright Office's deposit requirements.

A. Overview of Registration Process

To register your software with the Copyright Office, you'll need to take these four steps:

Step 1: Select the appropriate registration form (Section B).

Step 2: Fill out the registration form correctly (Section C).

Step 3: Decide how to satisfy the Copyright Office's deposit requirements (Section D).

Step 4: Place your application, deposit and appropriate fee in one package and send it to the Copyright Office (Section E).

Where to Get Help

If you have difficulty understanding any aspect of the registration process, you can get help by calling the Copyright Office at 202-707-3000 between 8:30 a.m. and 5:00 p.m. eastern time, Monday through Friday. An Information Specialist will be available to give you advice on selecting the proper form, filling it out and making the required deposit. Copyright Office Information Specialists are very knowledgeable and helpful; however, they are not allowed to give legal advice. If you have a particularly complex problem that calls for interpretation of the copyright laws, consult a copyright attorney. (See Chapter 16, *Help Beyond This Book.*)

B. Selecting the Appropriate Registration Form

The Copyright Office has developed several different preprinted registration forms used to register various types of works. But don't worry if you're not sure which form to use. The forms are virtually identical and the Copyright Office will accept your registration on either form.

1. Form TX

Software is usually registered on Form TX, the form used to register all types of writings and other literary works (software is classified as a literary work for registration purposes).

2. Form PA

Where pictorial or graphic authorship predominates, registration may be made on Form PA as an audiovisual work. If your registration consists primarily of display screens or other audiovisual elements, rather than computer code and documentation, you should use Form PA. An arcade game is a good example of a software work that would be registered on Form PA. Form PA is also normally used to register multimedia programs. (See Chapter 10, *Multimedia Programs*, for detailed discussion).

3. Short Forms TX and PA

The Copyright Office has created simplified versions of Forms TX and PA called Short Form TX and Short Form PA. These forms are only one page instead of two and are easier to complete than the regular Forms TX and PA. However, these forms may only be used if:

- there is only one author *and* copyright owner of the work
- the work was not made for hire—that is, was not created by employees or freelance programmers under a work for hire agreement (see Chapter 11), and
- the work is completely new—that is, does not contain a substantial amount of material that has been previously published or registered, or is in the public domain.

In addition, the short forms must be signed by the author personally—no one can sign on his or her behalf. This means, for example, that a software publisher may not sign the form on behalf of an author.

It's likely that relatively few computer programs will be eligible to be registered on the new short forms. Most software today is created by more than one person and is created by employees and freelancers. Such software does not qualify.

Short Forms TX and PA will most likely be used by hobbyists and others registering programs they've created themselves. Keep in mind, however, that the form may only be used for the first version of a work, not a revised or updated version.

4. Other Forms Not Used for Software

The Copyright Office has several other registration forms not used for software itself, but which may be used for software-related items. These include:

- **Form VA.** This form is used for pictorial, graphic and sculptural works, including photographs, maps, diagrams and technical diagrams. Form VA would be used, for example, to register a work consisting primarily of graphics-based flowcharts. Similarly, the owner of photos or other graphic elements licensed for use in a multimedia program would separately register them on Form VA. (See Chapter 10, *Multimedia Programs.*)
- **Form SR.** This is the correct form to register phonograph records, tapes, CDs and other recorded music or sounds. Form SR should be used to separately register the sounds contained in a software program or to register a software instructional tape. If sounds are owned by the same copyright claimant as the computer program itself, a single registration on Form TX will register the sounds.
- **Form SE series.** There are several different Form SEs, which are used to register all types of serial publications, including magazines, newspapers, newsletters, journals and the like. One of the SE forms would be used to register a computer magazine, journal or newsletter. They are also be used to register a magazine, newsletter or similar publication distributed online.

For a detailed discussion of how to register all types of writings (other than software) refer to *The Copyright Handbook: How to Protect and Use Written Works,* by Stephen Fishman (Nolo Press).

5. Where to Obtain the Forms

The tear-out Appendix at the end of this book contains copies of the application forms discussed here.

Electronic copies of the forms can also be downloaded from the Copyright Office's Internet site at http://lcweb.loc.gov/copyright. You must print the forms out and then complete them by hand or typewriter. The forms are in Adobe Acrobat PDF format. You must have the Adobe Acrobat Reader installed on your computer to view and print the forms.

You can obtain hardcopies of the forms by calling the Copyright Office. Call 202-707-9100 24 hours a day (you may have an easier time getting through at night). Leave your name, mailing address and identify the type of forms you need according to the class or title—for example, "Form TX." The Copyright Office will send up to ten copies of each form; specify how many you want.

The forms can also be obtained by writing to the Copyright Office at the following address:

Information and Publication Section LM-455
Copyright Office
Library of Congress
Washington, DC 20559

Copyright Tip

To save the U.S. taxpayer paper and printing costs, the Copyright Office encourages applicants to use photocopies of the blank application forms. The photocopies must be clear, on a good grade of white 8½-inch by 11-inch paper, and reproduced in two-sided copies with the top of the reverse side of the form at the same end as the top of the first side. Applications on forms not meeting these requirements will be returned by the Copyright Office.

C. How to Fill Out Forms TX and PA

Form TX and PA are virtually identical, except that Form TX has one additional space to be filled out. We'll give step-by-step instructions on how to fill out both forms. Each form consists of several numbered blank spaces calling for specific information.

Type your application form or use only *black* ink. When filling out the form, remember that it could end up being submitted in court to help prove your infringement case. If any part of it is inaccurate, your case could suffer—perhaps greatly. Moreover, a person who intentionally lies on a copyright registration application may be fined up to $2,500.

Space 1: Title Information

You must provide information about your work's title in Space 1.

Title of This Work

The Copyright Office uses the title for indexing and identifying your software. If your software has a title, fill in that wording. This should be the same title that appears on your deposit. (See Section D, below.) If your work is untitled, either state "untitled" or make a title up.

If the title includes a version number (such as, *AccountHelper, Version 1.0)* list it along with the title. Note carefully that under Copyright Office rules registering a later version of the same software will not constitute registration of any earlier versions. Consider the following example:

> **EXAMPLE:** Microstuff, Inc. creates a small business accounting program called *Account-Helper*. Microstuff publishes versions 1.0 and 2.0 of the program without registering them with the Copyright Office. Microstuff then registers version 3.0. This registration covers only the copyrightable materials added to the program since the last published version of the work (version 2.0). Obviously, Microstuff also needs to separately register versions 1.0 and 2.0 as well.

 Copyright Tip

Titles and other identifying phrases cannot be copyrighted. This means that registration will not prevent anyone from using the title to your work. You may, however, be able to protect titles under the trademark laws. (See Chapter 15, *Other Legal Protections for Software.*)

FORM TX
For a Literary Work
UNITED STATES COPYRIGHT OFFICE

REGISTRATION NUMBER

TX	TXU

EFFECTIVE DATE OF REGISTRATION

Month	Day	Year

DO NOT WRITE ABOVE THIS LINE. IF YOU NEED MORE SPACE, USE A SEPARATE CONTINUATION SHEET.

1

TITLE OF THIS WORK ▼

PREVIOUS OR ALTERNATIVE TITLES ▼

PUBLICATION AS A CONTRIBUTION If this work was published as a contribution to a periodical, serial, or collection, give information about the collective work in which the contribution appeared. **Title of Collective Work ▼**

If published in a periodical or serial give: **Volume ▼**   **Number ▼**   **Issue Date ▼**   **On Pages ▼**

2

a

NAME OF AUTHOR ▼

DATES OF BIRTH AND DEATH
Year Born ▼   Year Died ▼

Was this contribution to the work a "work made for hire"?
☐ Yes
☐ No

AUTHOR'S NATIONALITY OR DOMICILE
Name of Country
OR { Citizen of ▶_____
Domiciled in ▶_____

WAS THIS AUTHOR'S CONTRIBUTION TO THE WORK
Anonymous?   ☐ Yes ☐ No
Pseudonymous?   ☐ Yes ☐ No
If the answer to either of these questions is "Yes," see detailed instructions.

NATURE OF AUTHORSHIP Briefly describe nature of material created by this author in which copyright is claimed. ▼

NOTE

Under the law, the "author" of a "work made for hire" is generally the employer, not the employee (see instructions). For any part of this work that was "made for hire" check "Yes" in the space provided, give the employer (or other person for whom the work was prepared) as "Author" of that part, and leave the space for dates of birth and death blank.

b

NAME OF AUTHOR ▼

DATES OF BIRTH AND DEATH
Year Born ▼   Year Died ▼

Was this contribution to the work a "work made for hire"?
☐ Yes
☐ No

AUTHOR'S NATIONALITY OR DOMICILE
Name of Country
OR { Citizen of ▶_____
Domiciled in ▶_____

WAS THIS AUTHOR'S CONTRIBUTION TO THE WORK
Anonymous?   ☐ Yes ☐ No
Pseudonymous?   ☐ Yes ☐ No
If the answer to either of these questions is "Yes," see detailed instructions.

NATURE OF AUTHORSHIP Briefly describe nature of material created by this author in which copyright is claimed. ▼

c

NAME OF AUTHOR ▼

DATES OF BIRTH AND DEATH
Year Born ▼   Year Died ▼

Was this contribution to the work a "work made for hire"?
☐ Yes
☐ No

AUTHOR'S NATIONALITY OR DOMICILE
Name of Country
OR { Citizen of ▶_____
Domiciled in ▶_____

WAS THIS AUTHOR'S CONTRIBUTION TO THE WORK
Anonymous?   ☐ Yes ☐ No
Pseudonymous?   ☐ Yes ☐ No
If the answer to either of these questions is "Yes," see detailed instructions.

NATURE OF AUTHORSHIP Briefly describe nature of material created by this author in which copyright is claimed. ▼

3

a **YEAR IN WHICH CREATION OF THIS WORK WAS COMPLETED** This information must be given in all cases.
◀ Year

b **DATE AND NATION OF FIRST PUBLICATION OF THIS PARTICULAR WORK** Complete this information ONLY if this work has been published.
Month ▶_____ Day ▶_____ Year ▶_____
◀ Nation

4

See instructions before completing this space.

COPYRIGHT CLAIMANT(S) Name and address must be given even if the claimant is the same as the author given in space 2. ▼

TRANSFER If the claimant(s) named here in space 4 is (are) different from the author(s) named in space 2, give a brief statement of how the claimant(s) obtained ownership of the copyright. ▼

DO NOT WRITE HERE OFFICE USE ONLY

APPLICATION RECEIVED

ONE DEPOSIT RECEIVED

TWO DEPOSITS RECEIVED

FUNDS RECEIVED

MORE ON BACK ▶ • Complete all applicable spaces (numbers 5-11) on the reverse side of this page.
• See detailed instructions.   • Sign the form at line 10.

DO NOT WRITE HERE
Page 1 of _____ pages

Previous or Alternative Titles

Provide additional titles under which someone searching for the registration might be likely to look, if any. You don't need to include additional titles known only to you or a few others, such as working titles.

If you're registering a new version of software under a new title that contains substantial new material, you don't need to list the old title here.

Space 2: Author Information

Here you must provide information about the work's author or authors. Space 2 is divided into three identical subspaces: "a," "b," and "c." Subspaces b and c are filled out only if there is more than one author.

Name of Author

Following is a brief review of who the author is for registration purposes. If you need still more information, reread Chapter 4, Section D1. You'll also find detailed information in Chapter 11, *Initial Copyright Ownership,* and Chapter 12, *Transferring Software Copyright Ownership and Use Rights.*

- Works *not* made for hire: Unless the work was made for hire, the person or people who created the work are the authors. Give the full name—full first, middle and last name—of the first (or only) author. (For use of anonymous or pseudonymous names, see below.)
- Works made for hire: We briefly defined works made for hire in Chapter 4, Section D1b. If the work to be registered is a work made for hire, the author for registration purposes is the employer or other person or entity for whom the work was prepared. The full legal name of the employer or commissioning party must be provided as the "Name of Author" instead of the name of the person who actually created the work.

EXAMPLE 1: MicroWeird, Inc. publishes a jury trial simulation game called *Litigator.* The program was created by MicroWeird employees within the scope of their employment. MicroWeird Inc. should be listed in the "Name of Author" space.

EXAMPLE 2: Assume instead that MicroWeird purchased all the copyright rights in *Litigator* from its creator, a self-employed programmer named Jane Milsap. Jane Milsap should be listed as the program's author since it was not a work made for hire.

EXAMPLE 3: Assume instead that when Jane Milsap created *Litigator* she was employed by MicroGames, Inc. and that the game was originally a work made for hire owned by MicroGames. MicroWeird purchases all the rights in the game from Microgames. Who should be listed as the author? Microgames. The employer is the author of a work made for hire for copyright purposes. But a person or company that buys all the copyright rights in such a work for hire from the employer does not become the author (the new owner should just be listed as the copyright claimant in Space 4 below).

While not required, the name of the employee(s) who created a work made for hire may also be included if you want to make this part of the public record—for example: "MicroWeird Incorporated, employer for hire of Ken Grant, Jack Aubrey, Mona Wildman and Jane Kendall."

Copyright Tip

Don't guess about the full legal name of a corporation, partnership or other entity. Find out the organization's full legal name and use it. For example, do not state "ASC, Inc." when the full legal name is Acme Software Company, Incorporated. The full legal name may be found on the entity's organizing document, such as the articles of incorporation, partnership agreement or registration certificate filed with the appropriate state filing office (often called the Secretary of State).

Anonymous or Pseudonymous Authors

A work is anonymous if the author or authors are not identified on the published copies of the work. A work is pseudonymous if the author is identified under a fictitious name (pen name).

If the work is published as an anonymous work, you may:

- leave the Name of Author line blank (or state "N/A" for not applicable),
- state "anonymous" on the line, or
- reveal the author's identity.

If the work is pseudonymous, you may:

- leave the line blank
- give the pseudonym and identify it as such—for instance, "Nick Danger, pseudonym," or
- reveal the author's name, making it clear which is the real name and which is the pseudonym—for example, "Harold Lipshitz, whose pseudonym is Nick Danger."

Of course, if the author's identity is revealed on the application, it will be a simple matter for others to discover it because the application becomes a public document available for inspection at the Copyright Office.

Dates of Birth and Death

If the author is a human being, his or her year of birth may be provided here, but this is not required (the birth year is used for identification purposes). However, if the author has died, the year of death must be listed unless the author was anonymous or pseudonymous. This date will determine when the copyright expires (50 years after the author's death).

Leave this space blank if the author is a corporation, partnership or other organization. Corporations, partnerships and other business entities do not "die" for copyright purposes, even if they dissolve.

Was this contribution to the work a "work made for hire"?

Check the "Yes" box if the author is the owner of a work made for hire. Always check this box where the author is a corporation, partnership or other organization.

Author's Nationality or Domicile

This information must always be provided, even if the author is a business, is anonymous or used a pseudonym.

If the work is a work made for hire and the author is a corporation, partnership or other entity, state the country where the business has its principal office or headquarters. If this is anywhere in the U.S., simply state "U.S.A."

If the author is a person, his citizenship (nationality) and domicile could be different. An author's domicile generally is the country where she maintains her principal residence and where she intends to remain indefinitely. An author is a citizen of the country in which she was born or moved to and became a citizen of by complying with its naturalization requirements.

> **EXAMPLE:** Evelyn is a Canadian citizen, but she has permanent resident status and has lived year-round in Boston since 1997 and intends to remain there for the indefinite future. She is domiciled in the United States. She can state "Canada" in the citizenship blank or "U.S.A." in the domicile blank.

Was This Author's Contribution to the Work Anonymous or Pseudonymous

Check "Yes" box if the author is anonymous or used a pseudonym as described above. Check the "No" boxes if the author is identified by her correct name. Don't check either box if the work was made for hire.

Nature of Authorship

You must give a brief general description of the nature of the author's contribution to the work. Of all the boxes on the registration form, what you put in this box will determine whether your registration sails through without incident or whether you're in for a round of correspondence. The Copyright Office primarily relies on this box to determine whether your work is deserving of registration under the copyright laws.

The Copyright Office maintains a manual for use by its examiners containing specific words and phrases that are, and are not, acceptable to describe the nature of the authorship. The main idea underlying these guidelines is that some descriptions adequately describe a work as something subject to copyright protection while others don't. When we suggest you use some words and phrases and not others, we base our advice on these internal Copyright Office guidelines.

What you put on the Nature of Authorship line will vary most depending on whether this is:

- your first registration for an original work (discussed under "How to Describe Original Works," just below), or
- a registration for a new version of a previously published work or a derivative work (discussed below under "How to Describe New Versions and Other Derivative Works").

HOW TO DESCRIBE ORIGINAL WORKS

Most computer programs or code can be described using general descriptive terms like "entire text of computer program." The Copyright Office takes the view that this simple phrase registers every aspect of the program that is within the scope of copyright protection, including screen displays.

Other terms the Copyright Office will accept include:

- "program listing"
- "computer program code"
- "program text and screen displays"
- "program text"
- "computer software"
- "routine"
- "entire program"
- "entire program code"
- "software"
- "entire text"
- "subroutine"
- "entire work"
- "text of computer game"
- "module"
- "text of program"
- "program instructions"
- "wrote program."

If documentation is included with the program registration (which is only appropriate if all items are published as one unit—see Chapter 4, Section E) you should add

- "with users' manual," or
- "entire text of computer program with accompanying documentation."

Pick a term that accurately describes your work. If your deposit doesn't match the descriptive term you choose, you'll get a letter asking for clarification and your registration will accordingly be delayed.

Unacceptable Terms

Here is a listing of terms that will cause the Copyright Office to bounce your registration back for another try:

- "algorithm"
- "analysis"
- "cassette"
- "chip"
- "computer game"
- "disk"
- "encrypting"
- "eprom"
- "firmware"
- "format"
- "formatting"
- "functions"
- "language"
- "lay-out"
- "logic"
- "menu screen"
- "mnemonics"
- "printout"
- "programmer"
- "prom"
- "rom"
- "software methodology"
- "structure"
- "sequence"
- "organization"
- "system"
- "system design"
- "text of algorithm"

Should you mention computer display screens in the nature of authorship statement? As noted above, a simple statement in the nature of authorship space like "entire text of computer program" or "entire work" will cover any copyrightable computer screen displays included in the work. It is not necessary to separately mention the displays; however, it is permissible to do so. But if you do, there are two consequences:

- You will have to deposit identifying materials for the screen displays with your application (that is, photos, drawings or printouts clearly revealing the screens; see Section D5 below).
- The Copyright Office examiner will look at the identifying material to see if it is copyrightable (which will probably delay approval of your application).

If the examiner determines that the displays are not copyrightable, a letter to this effect will be sent to you and placed in the file for your application. The existence of such a letter could have a deleterious effect on any subsequent copyright infringement suit regarding the displays.

Clearly, then, you should never mention screen displays in the nature of authorship space if your displays are essentially not copyrightable. The Copyright Office has expressed the view that menu screens and similar functional interfaces consisting of words or brief phrases in a particular format generally are not registrable. (See the discussion of the copyrightability of the "look and feel" of computer screens in Chapter 7, *Scope of Copyright Protection for Software.*)

On the other hand, if you are certain that your computer screens are copyrightable and you are really want to protect the look and feel of your screen design, you may wish to indicate that screen displays are part of your authorship and deposit identifying material for the screens with your program code. Although this is not required, it will make it clear that both you and the Copyright Office thought your screens were copyrighted. This could deter a potential infringer and might help in any infringement litigation.

In this event, you should state "entire text of computer program and screen displays" in the Nature of Authorship space; or, if you are also registering documentation, state "entire text of computer program and screen displays with user documentation."

Another approach is to include identifying material for your screen displays but *not* to mention them in your nature of authorship statement. Instead, simply say "entire work," "computer program" or "all." When you do this, the copyright examiner will not examine the displays to see if they are copyrightable. The screens will ride along with the code without comment by the Copyright Office. This has the advantage of avoiding having approval of your application delayed. The disadvantage, however, is that you won't get a determination by the Copyright Office that your screens are copyrightable. But at least they will remain on record with the Copyright Office as part of your deposit.

HOW TO DESCRIBE NEW VERSIONS AND OTHER DERIVATIVE WORKS

If you're registering a new version or other derivative work (see Chapter 4, Section F for discussion of new versions, and Chapter 8 for detailed discussion of derivative works), you have more to consider in explaining your "Nature of Authorship" under Space 2.

To be eligible for separate registration, a work based on a prior work must involve enough changes in the prior work to be separately copyrightable. The Copyright Office uses the term *de minimis* to describe works (or changes in existing works) that aren't significant enough to warrant a separate copyright registration. This concept applies whether or not the whole work is registered as a derivative work or the changes are registered separately, as might be the case if whole new sections of code added to an existing program are able to stand on their own.

If the new material you wish to register consists of changes in or revisions to a prior program, you must use very precise language. Your registration should sail through if you describe the nature of the new material as:

- "editorial revisions"
- "revised revisions of [name of program]"
- "computer program"
- "text of program"
- "programming text"
- "program listing"
- "program instructions"
- "text of computer game"
- "module"
- "routine"
- "subroutine"
- "additional program text and extensively modified text"
- "wrote program."

EXAMPLE: MicroWeird Inc. issues a new release of its *Litigator* game program, which it originally registered as one package. MicroWeird adds three new programs and modifies four others substantially. In the Nature of Authorship box, it states "additional program text and extensively modified text." MicroWeird's registration is quickly approved.

Functionally Predetermined Changes Are Not Registrable

If you state "error corrections," "debugging," "patching," "features," or "enhancements" in the Nature of Authorship box you'll receive a letter from the Copyright Office requesting that you either submit a new application with a better statement of authorship, or abandon your registration by notifying them that the changes are too minor or "functionally predetermined" to warrant registration as an original work of authorship.

What does functionally predetermined mean? This is when the basic software that is being changed has been specifically designed to accommodate such changes. For example, many operating systems and applications software are deliberately made to easily accept preplanned changes (patches) that will permit them to compatibly operate with a number of different central processors (i.e., boards or chips). When such patches are made, they're considered functionally predetermined and ordinarily don't either alter the work or stand by themselves sufficiently to warrant a new registration.

TRANSLATION NOTE

Programs that are significantly adapted or translated to another computer language are usually considered to be a derivative work and registrable as such. In this situation, to correctly describe what is going on in the Nature of Authorship box, you need to include the name of the language into which the work has been translated. Thus "translation to C++" is deemed sufficient, while "translation" by itself is not. If, however, it appears to the Copyright Office that your translation really only enables the preexisting program to operate on a different machine without the need for a different language, your registration may or may not be approved as a new version, depending on the magnitude of the changes.

For example, if you simply change some of the initial commands to the computer and make a few minor format changes to enable an already registered program to run on different hardware, the Copyright Office will usually consider this to be *de minimis*, and thus not registrable. (This would also be an example of a functionally predefined modification described in the sidebar above.)

INFORMATION FOR ADDITIONAL AUTHORS

If there are two or three authors, go back now and fill in subspaces 2b and 2c for each of them using the above discussion as a guide. Space 2 only has enough subspaces for three authors. If the work you're registering has more than three authors, provide the required information for all the additional authors on a Copyright Office "Continuation Sheet" and clip (do not tape or staple) it to your application. A copy of a Continuation Sheet can be found in the tear-out Appendix at the end of this book. You can obtain additional copies from the Copyright Office.

Space 3: Relevant Dates
Year In Which Creation of This Work Was Completed.
Fill in the year in which the work you're registering first became fixed in its final form, disregarding minor changes. This year has nothing to do with publication, which may occur long after creation. Deciding what constitutes the year of creation may prove difficult if the work was created over a long period of time. Give the year in which the author(s) completed the particular version of the work for which registration is now being sought, even if other versions exist or further changes or additions are planned.

Date and Nation of First Publication of This Particular Work. Leave this blank if an unpublished work is being registered. Publication occurs for copyright purposes when a work is made widely available to the public. (See Chapter 2, *Copyright Basics.*) Give only one date, listing the month, day, year and country where publication first occurred. If you're not sure of the exact publication date, state your best guess and make clear it is approximate—for example, "November, 15, 200X (approx.)." If publication took place simultaneously in the United States and one or more foreign countries, you can just state "U.S.A." Make sure the publication date you list is for the version of the software being registered, not for some previous version.

If the software is being distributed online, it's up to you to decide whether it is published or not. The Copyright Office will not second-guess you on this.

The nation of publication for a work distributed online is either the nation from which the work is uploaded or the nation containing the server where the work is located. Use the name of a real country such as U.S.A. or Canada. Don't use nonspecific terms such as "global," "worldwide" or "Internet" in the nation of publication space.

Space 4: Information About Copyright Claimants

Copyright Claimant(s). Provide the name and address of each copyright claimant, which must be:

- the author or authors of the work (including the owner of a work made for hire, if applicable), or
- persons or organizations that have, on or before the date the application is filed, obtained in writing ownership of *all* the exclusive United States copyright rights that initially belonged to the author, or

- persons or organizations that the author or owner of all U.S. copyright rights has authorized by contract to act as the claimant for copyright registration (there is no legal requirement that such contract be in writing, but it's not a bad idea). (37 C.F.R. 202.3(a)(3) (1984))

See Chapter 4, Section E1 above for a detailed discussion of who qualifies as the copyright claimant.

A copyright claimant must be listed even for anonymous or pseudonymous works. You can provide the claimant's real name alone, the real name and the pseudonym, the pseudonym alone if the claimant is generally known by it or, if the claimant wishes to remain anonymous, the name of the claimant's authorized agent.

DEAR COPYRIGHT PERSON: I AM WRITING REGARDING COPYRIGHT REGISTRATION NO. 286 286 286 0...

Copyright Tip

When the name listed for the claimant is different from the name of the author given in space 2, but the two names identify one person, explain the relationship between the two names.

EXAMPLE: John Smith is the author of the work he is registering, but all of the copyright rights have been transferred to his corporation, Smith Software Publishing Company, Inc. of which Smith is the sole owner. Smith should not just state Smith Software Publishing Company, Inc. Rather, he needs to explain the relationship between himself and his company claimant—for example, "Smith Software Publishing Company, Inc., solely owned by John Smith."

Transfers

If the copyright claimant named just above is not the author or authors named in Space 2, give a brief general description of how ownership of the copyright was obtained. However, do not attach any transfer documents to the application. If there is not enough space to list all the claimants on Form TX, you can list additional claimants on the reverse side of Form/CON.

This statement must indicate that all the author's United States copyright rights have been transferred by a *written agreement* or by operation of law. Examples of acceptable transfer statements include: "By written contract," "Transfer of all rights by author," "By will," "By inheritance," "Assignment," "By gift agreement."

Unacceptable Transfer Statements

Examples of *unacceptable* statements include:

- words indicating that possibly less than all the author's United States copyright rights have been transferred to the claimant—for example: "By license," "By permission."

- statements suggesting that the person named as the claimant simply owns a copy of the work being registered, not the author's copyright rights—for example: "Author gave me this copy," "Author asked me to keep it for him."

- statements indicating that the named claimant has a special relationship to the author, but that do not show an actual transfer of ownership—for example: "Claimant is author's publisher" or "Author is president of claimant corporation."

See Chapter 12, *Transferring Software Copyright Ownership and Use Rights*, for a detailed discussion of copyright transfers.

Copyright Tip

Note that the transfers space is used only to inform the Copyright Office about transfers that occurred before registration. If a copyright is transferred after registration, there is no need to reregister (indeed, it is not permitted). However, although not required, it is a good idea to record (send) a copy of the postregistration transfer document to the Copyright Office. (See Chapter 12, *Transferring Software Copyright Ownership and Use Rights*, Section F.)

If the author or owner of all rights has authorized another person or organization to act as the claimant, this should be indicated by including language like the following: "Pursuant to the contractual right from [author *or* owner of all U.S. copyright rights] to claim legal title to the copyright in an application for copyright registration."

Space 5: Previous Registration

If none of the material in the work you're registering has been registered before, check the "No" box and skip ahead to Space 6.

If all or part of the work has been previously registered, check the "Yes" box. Then, you need to check one or more of the next three boxes to explain why a new registration is being sought:

- Check the first box if you are now registering a work you previously registered when it was unpublished.
- Check the second box if someone other than the author was listed as the copyright claimant in Space 4 in the prior registration, and the author is now registering the work in her own name. For example, where an anonymous or pseudonymous author previously listed an authorized agent in Space 4 and now wishes to re-register in her own name.
- Check the third box if the previously registered work has been changed, and you are registering the changed version or new edition to protect the additions or revisions.

Then provide the registration number and year of previous registration in the blanks indicated. The registration number can be found stamped on the certificate of registration. It is usually a multi-digit number preceded by the two-letter prefix of the application form used—for example: TX 012345. The Copyright Office places a small "u" following the prefix if the registered work is unpublished—for example: TXu 567890. If you made more than one prior registration for the work, you only need to give the latest registration number and year.

Space 6: Description of Derivative Works or Compilations

You'll usually need to complete Space 6 if your software is:

- a derivative work (a work based upon or derived from one or more preexisting works),
- a changed version of another work (this is really just one type of derivative work), or
- a compilation of preexisting works (a work created by selecting, arranging and coordinating preexisting materials into a new work of authorship).

(Derivative works are discussed in detail in Chapter 8, *Derivative Works and Use of Preexisting Material*. Compilations are discussed in Chapter 9, *Computer Databases*.)

You'll need to complete Space 6 only if the software or other work being registered contains a *substantial* amount of material (such as subroutines, modules or textual images) that was:

- previously published
- previously registered, or
- in the public domain.

Preexisting Material (6a): If your software is a derivative work and the preexisting material was substantial, you must generally describe the preexisting material here. You can simply state "previous version"; you need not provide any more detail. If the derivative work was based on a series of preexisting works, it is not necessary to list every one.

Don't fill out Space 6a if the software is a compilation.

Material Added to This Work (6b): Describe the new "protectible" material you are registering.

Typical examples of descriptions of new material for derivative works in Space 6b include "revised computer program," "editorial revisions," and "revisions and additional text of computer program." Often, you can simply repeat what you stated in the Nature of Authorship line in Space 2.

> **EXAMPLE:** AcmeSoft created and registered version 1.0 of a database program in 1998. AcmeSoft later thoroughly revises the software, adding many new features and redesigning the user interface. This new version 2.0 is published in 1999. AcmeSoft should state "revised computer program" in Space 6b when it registers version 2.0.

As we mentioned earlier, you shouldn't use words such as "enhancements," "error corrections," "patches," "features," or "debugging." This is because the Copyright Office tends to rule that these types of changes aren't significant enough to warrant another registration.

EXAMINED BY	FORM TX
CHECKED BY	
☐ CORRESPONDENCE Yes	FOR COPYRIGHT OFFICE USE ONLY

DO NOT WRITE ABOVE THIS LINE. IF YOU NEED MORE SPACE, USE A SEPARATE CONTINUATION SHEET.

PREVIOUS REGISTRATION Has registration for this work, or for an earlier version of this work, already been made in the Copyright Office?

☐ **Yes** ☐ **No** If your answer is "Yes," why is another registration being sought? (Check appropriate box) ▼

a. ☐ This is the first published edition of a work previously registered in unpublished form.

b. ☐ This is the first application submitted by this author as copyright claimant.

c. ☐ This is a changed version of the work, as shown by space 6 on this application.

If your answer is "Yes," give: **Previous Registration Number** ▼   **Year of Registration** ▼

5

DERIVATIVE WORK OR COMPILATION Complete both space 6a and 6b for a derivative work; complete only 6b for a compilation.

a. Preexisting Material Identify any preexisting work or works that this work is based on or incorporates. ▼

b. Material Added to This Work Give a brief, general statement of the material that has been added to this work and in which copyright is claimed. ▼

6

See instructions
before completing
this space.

—space deleted—

7

REPRODUCTION FOR USE OF BLIND OR PHYSICALLY HANDICAPPED INDIVIDUALS A signature on this form at space 10 and a check in one of the boxes here in space 8 constitutes a non-exclusive grant of permission to the Library of Congress to reproduce and distribute solely for the blind and physically handicapped and under the conditions and limitations prescribed by the regulations of the Copyright Office: (1) copies of the work identified in space 1 of this application in Braille (or similar tactile symbols); or (2) phonorecords embodying a fixation of a reading of that work; or (3) both.

a ☐ Copies and Phonorecords   **b** ☐ Copies Only   **c** ☐ Phonorecords Only

8

See instructions.

DEPOSIT ACCOUNT If the registration fee is to be charged to a Deposit Account established in the Copyright Office, give name and number of Account.

Name ▼   **Account Number** ▼

9

CORRESPONDENCE Give name and address to which correspondence about this application should be sent.   Name/Address/Apt/City/State/ZIP ▼

Be sure to
give your
daytime phone
◀ number

Area Code and Telephone Number ▶

CERTIFICATION* I, the undersigned, hereby certify that I am the

Check only one ▶
- ☐ author
- ☐ other copyright claimant
- ☐ owner of exclusive right(s)
- ☐ authorized agent of _____

of the work identified in this application and that the statements made by me in this application are correct to the best of my knowledge.

Name of author or other copyright claimant, or owner of exclusive right(s) ▲

10

Typed or printed name and date ▼ If this application gives a date of publication in space 3, do not sign and submit it before that date.

_____ Date ▶_____

☞   Handwritten signature (X) ▼

MAIL CERTIFICATE TO

Name ▼

Number/Street/Apt ▼

City/State/ZIP ▼

Certificate will be mailed in window envelope

YOU MUST:
• Complete all necessary spaces
• Sign your application in space 10

SEND ALL 3 ELEMENTS IN THE SAME PACKAGE:
1. Application form
2. Nonrefundable $20 filing fee in check or money order payable to *Register of Copyrights*
3. Deposit material

MAIL TO:
Register of Copyrights
Library of Congress
Washington, D.C. 20559-6000

11

*17 U.S.C. § 506(e): Any person who knowingly makes a false representation of a material fact in the application for copyright registration provided for by section 409, or in any written statement filed in connection with the application, shall be fined not more than $2,500.

May 1995—300,000   ☆U.S. COPYRIGHT OFFICE WWW FORM: 1995

If the work is a compilation, the statement should describe both the compilation itself and the material that has been compiled.

EXAMPLE: *Internet Magazine* compiles a number of previously published and public domain Java applets onto a disk. It should state in Space 6b: "Compilation of Java applets and text."

If your software is both a derivative work and compilation, you may state "Compilation and additional new material."

EXAMPLE: *Internet Magazine* in the example above not only compiles preexisting Java applets, but has its staff create a number of new applets as well. It could state in Space 6b: "Compilation and additional new material (programming and text)."

If the preexisting material in your work is not substantial or was not published, registered or in the public domain, put "N/A" in Space 6.

EXAMPLE 1: You would not need to complete Space 6 for a computer program entitled "X-103 Program, Version 3" incorporating material from two earlier developmental versions that were unpublished and unregistered.

EXAMPLE 2: You would not be required to complete Space 6 for a program containing a total of 5,000 lines of program text, only 50 of which were previously published.

There are two situations where you should provide an explanatory cover letter to the Copyright Office if you don't complete Space 6:
- the title of your work contains a version number other than 1 or 1.0, or
- the deposit for the software has a copyright notice containing multiple year dates.

In either case, the examiner will question (by letter or phone) whether the program is a revised or derivative version if Space 6 has not been completed.

If the software is not a derivative work and the version number or multiple year dates in the copyright notice on the deposit refer to internal revisions or the history of development of the program, put that information in a cover letter to the Copyright Office to help speed up processing.

EXAMPLE: PubSoft developed a desktop publishing program called *Practical Publisher* over a number of years. It produced several versions of the program that it used for internal testing and development only. The final published version of the program PubSoft registers in 2000 has a copyright notice that says "Copyright © 1998, 1999, 2000 by PubSoft, Inc." Although it was not required (see Chapter 3, *Copyright Notice*), PubSoft included the multiple year dates in the notice to make clear the copyright covers the earlier versions. PubSoft should include a letter like the following with its registration application:

Register of Copyrights
Library of Congress
Washington, D.C. 20559

Dear Register:

Enclosed is a copyright registration application for *Practical Publisher 1.0* submitted by PubSoft, Inc.

Please note that the deposit material for the program contains a copyright notice with multiple-year dates.

Practical Publisher 1.0 is not a derivative work or revised version for registration purposes. The multiple-year dates in the copyright notice refer to internal revisions that have not been published or registered.

I certify that the statements made in this letter are true.

Very truly yours,

Keith Stoke

Software Development Manager

Space 7 on Form TX

If you're filling out Form TX, skip this space. If you're filling out Form PA, skip to the instructions for Space 9, below.

Space 8 on Form TX: License for Handicapped

If you're using Form PA, instructions for Space 8 are covered below under Space 10.

The Library of Congress produces and distributes braille editions and recorded readings of registered works for the exclusive use of the blind and physically handicapped. Of course, this license doesn't apply to computer programs or any other machine-readable work, only printed text such as computer manuals and other written works.

If you wish to grant the library a license to copy and/or record your work for this purpose, check one of the boxes: a, for copies and phonorecords; b, for copies only; or c, for phonorecords. Most applicants give the blind and disabled a break and check one of these boxes.

Only a person who owns the right to reproduce and publish the work being registered can grant this license to the Library of Congress. If you're a transferee of one or more exclusive rights, but you don't own the right to reproduce and publish the work, skip this item completely.

The license is entirely voluntary and non-exclusive. You can terminate the license at any time by sending a written notice to the National Library Service for the Blind and Physically Handicapped (NLS), Library of Congress, 1291 Taylor Street NW, Washington. D.C. 20542.

Space 9 on Form TX (Space 7 on Form PA): Deposit Account and Correspondence

Deposit Account. If you plan to have 12 or more transactions per year with the Copyright Office, you may establish a money deposit account to which you make advance money deposits and charge your copyright fees against the account instead of sending a separate check each time. You must deposit at least $250 to open an account. For an application, obtain Circular R5 from the Copyright Office by calling 202-707-9100 or by downloading it from the Copyright Office Website at http://lcweb.loc.gov/copyright. If you already have a deposit account and wish to charge the registration fee to the account, state the account name and number.

Correspondence: Provide the name, address, area code and telephone number of the person the Copyright Office should contact if it has questions about your application. If the registration is being made by a corporation or other entity, list the name of the person in the organization who should be contacted. The Copyright Office makes calls between 8:00 a.m. and 5:00 p.m. eastern time; so give the number or numbers where the contact person can be reached at these times.

If you have a fax number, include that along with your regular phone number (remember to specify which is a fax). The Copyright Office may soon start corresponding by fax.

Space 10 on Form TX (Space 8 on Form PA): Certification

Check the appropriate box indicating your capacity as the person registering the work:

- Check the Author box if you are the person (or one of several people) named in Space 2. If there are several authors, only one need sign.
- Check the Other Copyright Claimant box if you are not named in Space 2 as the author, but have acquired all the author's rights.
- Check the Owner of Exclusive Right(s) box if you only own one or more—but not all—of the exclusive rights making up the entire copyright.
- Check the Authorized Agent of box if you are not signing for yourself as an individual, but as the authorized representative of the author, the copyright claimant who owns all the copyright rights or the owner of some exclusive rights. State the name of the person or organization on whose behalf you're signing on the dotted line following the box.

Copyright Tip

Check the Authorized Agent box if you, as an individual, are signing on behalf of a corporation, partnership or other organization that is the author, copyright claimant or holder of exclusive rights.

Type or print your name and date in the appropriate blanks, then sign your name on the line following "Handwritten signature."

Copyright Tip

If you are registering a published work, the Copyright Office will not accept your application if the date listed in the certification space is earlier than the date of publication shown in Space 3.

Space 11 on Form TX (Space 9 on Form PA): Return Mailing Address

Fill in your name and the return mailing address for your copyright registration certificate in the last box on the form. Make sure the address is legible, since the certificate will be returned to you in a window envelope.

Now that you've completed the form, you'll need to prepare your deposit, covered in Section D, just below.

D. How to Comply with Copyright Office Deposit Requirements

To register your work with the U.S. Copyright Office, you're required to submit (deposit) one or two copies of the work itself. When it comes to the registration of long programs, Copyright Office rules usually allow you to send a portion of the work instead of the whole thing.

Deposit requirements are designed to serve three primary functions:

- Deposits show the Copyright Office that your work is eligible for copyright protection (that it is an original work of authorship).

- Deposits show the Copyright Office that your work is adequately described on your application form.
- Deposits serve as an identifier for your work in the event a dispute arises involving your copyright.

Except where the software is embodied on a CD-ROM disk (see Section 4 below), you may not deposit floppy disks or other magnetic media (or computer chip(s) in the case of firmware). Rather, the Copyright Office wants a hard-copy printout of all or part of your code. There are four alternative types of deposits for you to choose from:

- a printout of all or part of your software source code (Section 1, below),
- a copy of part of the source code with any trade secrets blacked out so no one can read them (Section 2, below),
- a combination of source code and object code (Section 2, below), or
- object code only (Section 3, below).

These requirements are the same however software is distributed—whether in stores, by mail order or online over the Internet, commercial online services or BBS's. However, there are special requirements when software is contained on a CD-ROM.

Please read this entire section through at least once before making a decision as to what you wish to deposit. This material is potentially confusing, and you may well find yourself changing your mind several times.

Special Relief From Deposit Requirements

In some cases, you may be unwilling or unable to make a deposit in any of the forms described in this section. For example, if you need to register immediately for litigation purposes, it's possible that the required computer code may not be available. In this event, you may be able to deposit something else—for example, pictures of the screen displays for a computer game.

To get permission to file a special kind of deposit, you must request that the Copyright Office grant you special relief from their deposit requirements. Send a signed letter to the Chief of the Examining Division, Copyright Office, Library of Congress, Washington, D.C. 20559. Explain why you need special relief—for example, to preserve the confidentiality of your computer code, to avoid a severe financial burden, or because the normally required material is unavailable. Also explain exactly what you wish to deposit instead.

---

1. Depositing Straight Source Code

Your first alternative is to deposit all or part of your program source code. This is what most people do and what the Copyright Office prefers. The advantage to depositing source code is that it better identifies the nature of your original work of authorship than does object code.

Should you end up in litigation over your copyright, you'll want the best possible proof of the exact code you have copyrighted. A source code deposit may make it easier to prove copyright infringement.

Depositing your source code serves to register your object code as well even though the object code is not deposited. (*CGA Corp. v. Chance*, 217 U.S.P.Q. 718 (N.D. CA 1982).)

Under Copyright Office regulations (37 C.F.R. 202.70), you generally don't have to deposit your en-

tire program source code. This is fortunate, both from your standpoint and the Copyright Office's, since programs are often lengthy.

To satisfy the deposit requirement for program source code, you must deposit either:

- the entire program source code if the source is no more than 50 pages, or
- if the source code is longer than 50 printed-out pages, the first and last 25 pages.

A page isn't precisely defined, but in practice, standard 8½-inch by 11-inch paper is most often used.

There are no requirements as to the format or spacing of the code—that is, it may be single- or double-spaced.

As an alternative to a printout, you may deposit a microfiche of the identifying material. If you do this, deposit the entire program code or, if it's longer than 50 pages, microfiche the first and last 25 pages.

If the code contains a copyright notice, you must include the page or equivalent unit containing the notice. A photograph or drawing showing the form and location of the notice is acceptable. Whatever you do, it's always a good idea to sprinkle many copyright notices throughout the code.

If the deposit material does not give a printed title and/or version indicator, add the title and any indicia that can be used to identify the particular program.

Deposits and Trade Secrets

If you deposit the first and last 25 pages of your source code, you may wish to arrange the source code modules so that the most innovative and/or secret portions of the code do not appear in the first or last 25 pages. Copyright Office rules do not prevent this. You may also take out any comment statements that might help an infringer. The downside to this is that your deposit may not provide the best possible evidence of your work to prove copyright infringement. So there is a trade-off involved.

a. Revised programs

If the program you're registering is a revision of a previously registered program, and the revisions are uniformly (more or less) spread throughout the program, deposit the first and last 25 pages as indicated above and the page containing the copyright notice, if any.

If, on the other hand, the revisions are concentrated in a part of the program that isn't fairly represented by the first and last 25 pages requirement, you may deposit any 50 pages that are representative of the revised material in the new program together with the page containing the copyright notice.

b. Programs created in scripted language

For programs created in scripted language such as Hypercard, Supercard and JavaScript, the script is considered the equivalent of source code. Thus, the same number of pages of script are required as are required for source code.

2. Depositing Source Code with Trade Secrets Blacked Out or Depositing Source Code and Object Code

As discussed in Chapter 15, trade secret protection can be used in conjunction with copyright protection to protect the ideas, concepts and algorithms embodied in software. Source code is usually a software developer's or publisher's most closely guarded trade secret. Software is normally distributed in object code form only. The source code is usually kept locked away and shown only to employees and others who have agreed to keep it secret.

If you plan to keep your source code a trade secret, there's a danger that you'll compromise this status by using the source code as a registration deposit. Your deposit becomes a public record on file at the Copyright Office in Washington, D.C., and if you deposit source code, it could conceivably be studied by a competitor or pirate, and reproduced in an infringing program. This is not supposed to happen, but it has. In one well-known case, an attorney employed by Atari Games Corporation gained access to, and made a copy of, source code that Nintendo of America had deposited. The attorney accomplished this feat by falsely claiming the code was involved in litigation. (See Chapter 6, Section B2.) Using this information, Atari was able to create a key to open the ROM-based lock that controlled access to the Nintendo game system. Nintendo brought a copyright infringement suit against Atari for making the unauthorized copy of the code and won. (*Atari Games Corp. v. Nintendo of America, Inc.*, 980 F.2d 857 (Fed.Cir. 1992).) No one can say how many other times this has occurred.

To avoid revealing trade secrets in your deposit, Copyright Office rules permit you to deposit source code with any trade secrets blacked out, or a combination of source code and object code. Under these rules, you have the option of depositing:

- the first and last 25 pages of source code with up to 49% of the source code blacked out (in other words, you deposit 50 pages with only 26 being readable; this obviously helps you to protect source code against infringement); or
- the first and last ten pages of source code with no blacked out portions (this smaller deposit may, depending on the length of the program, or program package, pretty well frustrate pirates), or
- the first and last 25 pages of *object* code, plus any ten or more consecutive pages of source code with no blacked out portions (because object code is unreadable by humans, this should frustrate potential infringers), or
- for programs consisting of less than 50 pages, the entire source code with up to 49% of the code blacked out.

In all cases, the visible portion of the code must represent an "appreciable amount" of computer code.

If the code contains a copyright notice, you must include the page or equivalent unit containing the notice. A photograph or drawing showing the form and location of the notice is acceptable.

If the deposit material does not give a printed title or version indicator, add the title and any indicia that can be used to identify the particular program.

a. Revised programs

If you're depositing a revised program with the revisions contained in the first and last 25 pages, you may select any of the four options described just above.

If the revisions are not contained in the first and last 25 pages of code, your deposit must consist of either:

- 20 pages of source code containing the revisions with no blacked out portions, or
- any 50 pages of source code containing the revisions with up to 49% of the code blacked out.

3. Depositing Object Code Only

If you do not want to deposit any source code (even with portions blacked out), you may deposit object code only. Because object code is unreadable by most mortals, a deposit in this form won't likely be examined for ideas and code by a competitor. Also, if you're treating your work as a trade secret, an object code deposit doesn't reveal it.

However, depositing object code only has a down side. Because Copyright Office personnel can't read object code to determine whether it constitutes an original work of authorship, the Copyright Office registration will be made under the Office's "rule of doubt" and you'll receive a warning letter to that effect. The rule of doubt means the Copyright Office is unable to independently verify that your deposit is a work of original authorship.

Having your registration issued under the rule of doubt results in loss of one of the benefits of registration: the presumption that your copyright is valid. (*Freedman v. Select Information Sys.,* 221 U.S.P.Q. 848 (1984) (N.D. Ca. 1983).) This means that if you end up suing someone for copyright infringement, you will have to prove to the court that your software is an original work of authorship and otherwise qualifies for copyright protection. (See Chapter 13.) Usually this is not too difficult, but it will complicate matters. Loss of this presumption may be particularly damaging if you wish to obtain a quick pretrial injunction against an alleged infringer.

Programs Not Compiled Into Object Code

When you compile a program written in C or most other languages, the compiler translates the source code into machine code or processor instructions—this is what the Copyright Office terms object code. However, not all programs are compiled into object code. For example, programs written in the Java programming language are compiled into bytecode instead of machine code. The bytecode is then executed by a program called a bytecode interpreter. For programs such as Java, you may deposit the bytecode or similar intermediate code instead of your source code.

---

a. What to deposit

Deposit the same amount of object code as is required when depositing straight source code as described in Section 1, above. In other words, you must deposit either:

- The entire program object code; or
- If the object code is longer than 50 printed-out pages, the first and last 25 pages.

Make sure you deposit 50 pages of object code, and not the equivalent of 50 pages of source code translated into object code form.

If the code contains a copyright notice, you must include the page or equivalent unit containing the notice. A photograph or drawing showing the form and location of the notice is acceptable. Where the copyright notice is encoded within the object code so that its presence and content are not easily readable, the notice should be underlined or highlighted and its contents decoded.

If the deposit material does not give a printed title or version indicator, add the title and any indicia that can be used to identify the particular program.

b.   Letter to Copyright Office

All deposits consisting solely of object code must be accompanied by an assurance to the Copyright Office that the work contains copyrightable authorship. If you fail to include this assurance with your deposit, the Copyright Office will write you and state that since they can neither read your deposit nor verify that its subject material is copyrightable, you must either send human readable source code or a letter assuring the Copyright Office that your deposit contains copyrightable material. Obviously, it makes sense to anticipate this request.

The following letter will provide the needed assurance if you deposit object code.

**Sample Letter Declaring Your
Work Is Copyrightable**

April 1, 200X

Register of Copyrights

Library of Congress

Washington, D.C. 20559

Dear Register:

Enclosed is a copyright registration application for *Website Maker* submitted by Julia Youngster.

Julia Youngster is submitting the deposit in object code form in order to protect trade secrets that are contained in the computer code.

Website Maker as deposited in object code form contains copyrightable authorship.

I certify that the statements made in this letter are true.

Very truly yours,

Julia Youngster

---

4.   Special Deposit Requirements for Software Embodied on CD-ROMs

The Library of Congress wants to establish a collection of CD-ROMs, so a regulation was enacted in 1991 requiring applicants of works embodied on CD-ROMs to deposit the CD-ROM disk along with a printout of the program code.

CD-ROMs are often used for multimedia works—that is, works containing text, audiovisual elements like photos and video, and music or other sounds, in addition to software (usually operating software or software that produces screen displays).

A single copyright registration and deposit can cover all these elements—that is, the software plus the "content." These type of multimedia registrations and deposit requirements are discussed in detail in Chapter 10, *Multimedia Programs.*

However, a separate registration and deposit for the software used for a multimedia work embodied on a CD-ROM is required when the software:

- was previously published or was previously registered as an unpublished work, or
- was, or will be, sold or otherwise distributed separately.

a.   What to deposit

You must deposit one copy of the entire CD-ROM package. Everything that is marketed or distributed together must be deposited, whether or not you're the copyright claimant for each element. This includes:

- the CD-ROM disk(s),
- instructional manual(s), and
- any printed version of the work that is sold with the CD-ROM package—for example, where a book accompanies a CD-ROM.

In addition, you must deposit a printout of all or part of the source code or object code for the software you're registering as described in Sections D1–3 above.

5. Deposit Requirements for Computer Output Screens

You don't have to deposit identifying material for your screens unless you make specific reference to them in Space 2 (Nature of Authorship) of your registration form. (See Section C.) If you mention the screens, you *must* deposit them. Doing so will likely delay approval of your application, because the copyright examiner will have to examine the identifying material to see if the screens are copyrightable.

To deposit application software screens, use a printout, photograph, or drawing. These reproductions should be no smaller than 3" by 3" and no larger than 9" by 12". The Copyright Office will not accept the accompanying manual as a deposit for computer output screens, even if the screens are reproduced in it.

Where the authorship on the screens is predominately audiovisual (for example, an arcade game), a 1/2-inch VHS format videotape that clearly shows the copyrightable expression should be deposited. In the case of arcade games, you should deposit your "attract" and "play" modes together as part of a single registration in videotape form. For game screens, you should include any sound component, either as part of the videotape recording or separately on a cassette. Don't neglect this. The uniqueness of the sound that accompanies game programs has been helpful in establishing ownership of these types of works in several court decisions.

Even if you think your screen authorship is predominately audiovisual, don't deposit a videotape if the computer screens simply show the functioning of the program. Instead, deposit printouts, photos or drawings as described above.

As part of this type of registration, you should also explain your deposit in a letter.

Sample Letter

June 11, 20XX

Dear Chief Examiner:

Please find enclosed my deposit consisting of identifying material related to my computer program *Celestial Tease*. The material consists of videotape and photographs. These represent the output screens and accompanying sound from the above-mentioned program. I request you accept this material as a deposit accompanying my copyright registration.

Sincerely,

Crystal Star

Senior Programmer

When you submit identifying material for screen displays, the Copyright Office will examine them for copyrightability. To be copyrightable, a screen display must contain original authorship. (See Chapter 7 for detailed discussion.) The Copyright Office has expressed the view that menu screens and similar functional interfaces consisting of words or brief phrases in a particular format generally are not registrable.

If the Copyright Office determines all the displays are uncopyrightable, a new application omitting reference to the displays will be requested and the screen display identifying material will be removed from the deposit. Where some or most of the screen displays are uncopyrightable, a warning letter to that effect will be sent by the Copyright Office.

6. Deposit Requirements for Documentation

Documentation includes user manuals, training manuals, instruction sheets, textual flowcharts, film, slide shows and all other works that are used to support a program in some way. Written documentation can be anything from two pages stapled together to a bound, full-color 500-page book.

If you register your documentation separately (see Chapter 4, Section E3), you must deposit two copies of your entire work if it's in written, sound recording or graphic form.

If your documentation isn't registered separately and you include a reference to it on your registration form, you must deposit one copy of the documentation. If you don't refer specifically to the documentation, the deposit is optional.

Be sure any documentation you deposit contains the proper copyright notice. (See Chapter 3, *Copyright Notice*.)

7. Deposit Requirements for Online Works

Deposit requirements are different for online works such as Websites than for works published in the physical world. The Copyright Office gives you two deposit options:

• *Option 1:* Under the first deposit option, you must provide a computer disk containing the entire work clearly labeled with title and author information *and* a representative hard-copy sample of the work being registered.

If the work consists of less than five pages of text or graphics, or three minutes of music, sounds or audiovisual material, you must deposit a copy of the entire work along with a confirmation that it is complete.

If the work is longer, you must deposit five representative pages or three representative minutes. This identifying material must include the work's title and author, and a copyright notice, if any.

• *Option 2:* Alternatively, you may deposit a hard-copy version of the entire work. No computer disk is required in this case.

Your deposit should be in a format appropriate for the type of work being registered, for example, a hard-copy printout of text or graphics or an audio-cassette of music or sounds.

If a work is published both online and by distributing physical copies, you must deposit the physical copies, not the online materials. For example, if a work is published as a hardbound book and also transmitted online, two copies of the hardbound books must be deposited.

8. Full Term Retention of Deposit Option

Ordinarily, deposits are destroyed by the Copyright Office after five years, with the Copyright Office first making a copy of unpublished works that have been deposited.

If you wish, you may request full term retention of your deposit. Full term retention means that the Copyright Office will retain one copy of your deposit for 75 years from the date of publication. You must request full term retention in writing and pay a $365 fee.

Given the pace of developments in the software industry, most software won't have much value more than five years after it's registered. So, in most cases, there is no reason to seek full term retention of a software deposit.

Full term retention may be requested only by the person who made the deposit, the copyright owner or an authorized representative. You can make this request when you register the work or any time thereafter. There is no form for this purpose. Simply send a letter to the Chief, Information and Reference Division, Copyright Office, Library of Congress, Washington, D.C. 20559 stating that you desire full term retention of your deposit. Identify the deposit by title, author and, if you have already registered, Copyright Office registration number.

If you request full term retention of your deposit when you make your initial registration, include this request in a letter with your application along with the increased fee. You must also send the Copyright Office one additional copy of the entire deposit.

E. Mailing Your Application to the Copyright Office

By now, you have completed your application form and have your deposit ready to go. Make a photocopy of your application form and retain it in your records along with an exact copy of your deposit.

1. Application Fee

You must submit a check or money order for the nonrefundable application fee payable to the Register of Copyrights. Clip your check or money order to the application.

At this writing, the registration fee is $20. Application fees change from time to time, however, so call the Copyright Office at 202-707-3000 to double-check the current fees before mailing your application. Also, read the *Nolo News* for updates on fee changes. (See back of the book for information about requesting a free two-year *Nolo News* subscription.)

How to Make Sure the Copyright Office Received Your Application

The Copyright Office will not send an acknowledgment when it has received an application. The best way to know for sure that they got it is to send the application by certified or registered mail, return receipt requested. Allow three weeks for the receipt to be returned by the post office. The receipt will show exactly when the Copyright Office received the application. (If time is an important factor, see Section F, below, on expedited registration.)

---

2. Mail Single Package to Copyright Office

Put your application, deposit and check or money order for the appropriate application fee in a *single package*. If you send them separately, all the packages will be returned by the Copyright Office. But, if you send a deposit of a published work separately, the Copyright Office will turn it over to the Library of Congress rather than return it to you, so you'll get the application and fee back, but not the deposit.

If you're registering a published work, your application must be received by the Copyright Office after the publication date listed in Space 3 of your application. (See Section C, above.). Reason: A published work cannot be registered prior to the date of publication.

Mail your single package to:
Register of Copyrights
Copyright Office
Library of Congress
Washington, D.C. 20559

3. Registration Is Effective When the Application Is Received

Your registration is effective on the date the Copyright Office receives all three elements: application, deposit and application fee in acceptable form. This means you don't need to worry about how long it takes the Copyright Office to process the application and send you a certificate of registration. You'll be eligible to obtain statutory damages or attorney fees from anyone who copies your work while your application is being processed. (Remember, you can obtain such fees and damages only if the work was registered before the infringement occurred or within three months of publication; see Chapter 4, Section B.)

F. Expedited Registration

In a few special circumstances, you may request that your application be given special handling by the Copyright Office. Special handling applications are processed in five to ten days, rather than the normal 6 to 12 months or more. Special handling is available only if needed:

- for copyright litigation; under current law, a work must be registered before a copyright infringement suit may be filed (but this may change, see Chapter 4, Section B3, above); you'll need to have a certified copy of your registration certificate to show the court,
- to meet a contractual or publishing deadline, or
- for some other urgent need.

You must pay an additional $500 fee for special handling. You may complete the optional form reproduced in the tear-out Appendix at the end of this book or send a letter along with your application containing the same information: why there is an urgent need for special handling, if special handling is needed for litigation, whether the case has been filed already or is pending, who the parties to the litigation are or will be, in what court the action has been or will be filed; and certification that your statements are true.

If you're registering for litigation purposes, you'll need a certified copy of your registration certificate to submit to the court; so enclose an additional $8 fee and request that the Copyright Office provide you with a certified copy.

Mail the special handling form or letter, your application and deposit, and a *certified check or money order* payable to the Register of Copyrights for $528 (the $20 application fee, plus the $500 special handling fee, plus the $8 certification fee) all in one package to:

Library of Congress
Department 100
Washington, D.C. 20540

Write the words "Special Handling" on the outside of the envelope. But don't put the words "Copyright Office" on the envelope. ∎

After You've Mailed In Your Registration

This chapter is about what happens after you've sent in your copyright registration.

A. Dealing With the Copyright Office

The Copyright Office has an enormous workload: they handle over 600,000 applications per year. As this book went to press in late 1998, the Copyright Office was seriously understaffed and had a backlog of tens of thousands of applications. It can take anywhere from six months to one year or even longer for your application to be processed. (If you can't wait this long, you can get the Copyright Office to proecess your application on an expedited basis by paying an additional fee; see Chapter 5, Section F.) Be patient and remember that the registration is effective on the date it is received by the Copyright Office (assuming the forms were filled out properly), not the date you actually receive your registration certificate.

The Copyright Office will eventually respond to your application in one of three ways:

- If your application is acceptable, the Copyright Office will send you a registration certificate, which is merely a copy of your application with the official Copyright Office seal, registration date and number stamped on it. Be sure to retain it for your records.
- If your application contained errors or omissions the Copyright Office believes are correctable, a copyright examiner may phone you for further information. Or he may return the application or deposit with a letter explaining what corrections to make.
- If the Copyright Office determines that your work cannot be registered, it will send you a letter explaining why. Neither your deposit nor fee will be returned.

1. If You Don't Hear From the Copyright Office

If you don't hear anything from the Copyright Office within six months after your application should have been received, you may wish to write them and find out the status of your application. They may have lost the application, it may have never been received or they may be very far behind in their work. In your letter, identify yourself, the author and the copyright owner; give the date of your application and the form you used; and describe the work briefly. If the Copyright Office cashed your check, you'll know that they did receive the application. Include a copy of the canceled check with your letter. It will contain a number that will help the Copyright Office trace your application.

Copyright Tip

You'll have to pay the Copyright Office a fee if you want to find out about the status of an application fewer than 16 weeks after the Copyright Office received it. Call the Copyright Office at 202-707-3000 to ask about this.

2. Extent of Copyright Examiner's Review of Your Application

The Copyright Examiner will examine your deposit to see whether it constitutes copyrightable subject matter and review your application to determine whether the other legal and formal requirements for registration have been met.

a. The rule of doubt

As a matter of policy, the Copyright Office will usually register a work even if it has a reasonable doubt as to whether the work is copyrightable or whether the other requirements have been met. This is called the rule of doubt. The Copyright Office takes the view that determining a copyright's validity in such cases is a task for the courts. For example, the office would ordinarily register a new version of a previously registered software package under the rule of doubt, even though it had a reasonable doubt whether the new version contained enough new expression to be registrable.

When registration is made under the rule of doubt, the Copyright Office will ordinarily send the applicant a letter cautioning that the claim may not be valid and stating the reason.

b. Clearly unregisterable material

The Copyright Office will refuse to register a work that is definitely unprotectible. For example, the Copyright Office will not register a title, since titles are not copyrightable.

out to lunch again...

c. Presence of errors or omissions

The Copyright Office will not issue a certificate if the application contains errors or omissions or is internally inconsistent or ambiguous. Here are some of the more common errors:
- the application is not signed
- the application fee is incorrect or unpaid
- the nature of authorship is not adequately described
- the work's title is not contained on the deposit
- deposit does not match description of nature of authorship

- the publication date is not provided
- the Work Made for Hire box is checked, but the employer is not listed as the copyright claimant
- there is no statement as to how ownership was transferred where the copyright claimant is not the same as the author
- the date the application is signed is before the publication date in application.

The Copyright Office will ordinarily call you or send a letter asking you to fix technical errors such as these. Reread our discussion about how to complete the application form in Chapter 5, Section C, to help you make your corrections. Send your corrected application and any new deposit back to the Copyright Office in one package.

Be sure you respond within 120 days to any correspondence from the Copyright Office concerning your application. Otherwise, your file will be closed, your fee will not be returned to you, and you'll have to reapply by sending in a new application, deposit and fee.

3. Review of Copyright Office's Refusal to Register Application

If you think the Copyright Examiner has wrongfully refused to register your work, you may submit a written objection and request that the Copyright Office reconsider its action. The appeal letter should be addressed to the appropriate section of the Examining Division, Copyright Office, Washington, DC 20559. The first request for reconsideration must be received in the Copyright Office within 120 days of the date of the Office's first refusal to register, and the envelope containing the request should be clearly marked: FIRST APPEAL/EXAMINING DIVISION.

If the claim is refused after reconsideration, the head of the appropriate Examining Division section will send you written notice of the reasons for the refusal. After this, you may again request reconsideration in writing. This second appeal must be received in the Copyright Office within 120 days of the date of the Office's refusal of the first appeal, and be directed to the Board of Appeals at the following address: Copyright GC/I&R, P.O. Box 70400, Southwest Station, Washington, DC 20024.

The second appeal is handled by the Copyright Office Board of Appeals, which consists of the Register of Copyrights, the General Counsel and the Chief of the Examining Division. The Chair of the Board of Appeals will send you a letter setting out the reasons for acceptance or denial of your claim. The Appeals Board's decision constitutes the Copyright Office's final action. You may then bring a legal action to have a court review the Copyright Office's decision. In addition, you can bring a copyright infringement action notwithstanding the Copyright Office's refusal to register your work. You'll need to see a lawyer about this. (See Chapter 16, *Help Beyond This Book*.)

B. What the Copyright Office Does with Deposits

Whether or not your registration application is accepted, your deposit becomes the property of the U.S. government and will never be returned to you. The Library of Congress has the option of adding the deposit to its own collection. If the library chooses not to do so (which is usually the case), and your application is accepted, the Copyright Office will retain the deposit in its own storage facilities for five years. Due to a lack of storage space, the Copyright Office normally destroys all deposits of published works after five years. However, the Copyright Office may not destroy a deposit of an unpublished work without first making a copy of it.

1. Examining Deposits from Copyright Office Files

The Copyright Office is located in Washington, D.C., so anyone who wants to look at any records must go there. Direct copying from Copyright Office files by nonagency employees is prohibited by law. Because the Copyright Office stores great masses of informa-

tion, it normally takes from one to five days to even get access to a particular deposit.

To look at any specific deposit, a person normally needs:

- the registration number or the exact name of the work and author, and
- a signed, written statement as to why access is needed.

This written statement is placed in a file associated with the copyright deposit and is available to the copyright owner for examination.

When a deposit is retrieved, a Copyright Office employee is assigned to stay with the deposit at all times and to prevent the requester from taking notes or copying the deposit in any way. As a practical matter, this means that it's unlikely that your code will be directly copied from Copyright Office files. However, it won't stop an intelligent pirate from getting a pretty good overview of your approach.

If you suspect that your deposit has been copied, you may well want to have the Copyright Office conduct a search of your file for evidence of an examination of your deposit. The Copyright Office charges $20 an hour to conduct searches. Call the Copyright Office at 202-287-8700, explain that you want a search of your file to see whether it has been examined by anyone else, and ask what the charge will be. Then, mail this amount and a written request to have your file examined to:

Reference and Bibliography Section, LM-451
Copyright Office
Library of Congress
Washington, D.C. 20559

2. Obtaining Copies of Deposits From the Copyright Office

It's possible to obtain copies of deposits from the Copyright Office if any one of the following three conditions is met:

- Written authorization is received from the copyright claimant, the claimant's authorized agent or the owner of any of the exclusive rights. The owner of an exclusive right must also provide written documentation to support the exclusivity claim.

- A written request is received from an attorney representing either the plaintiff or defendant in pending or anticipated litigation involving the work. This request must be accompanied by an overall description of the dispute, a description of all parties involved in the dispute, the name of the court, a factual recounting of the case and an assurance that the reproduced deposit will only be used in connection with the specified litigation.
- A court order in pending litigation requires production of the work for submission as evidence.

If one of these conditions is met, and you also provide the other information necessary to locate the requested deposit, a reproduction of the deposit will be released from the Copyright Office for a fee to be determined on a case-by-case basis.

C. Library of Congress Deposit Requirement

Subject to various exceptions, the Copyright Act requires the copyright owner of any work published in the United States to deposit two copies of the best edition of the work with the Library of Congress in Washington, D.C. within three months after publication. Computer software that is published only in the form of machine-readable copies is specifically exempted from this deposit rule. However, the law apparently requires software publishers to deposit copies of their published documentation.

When you register with the U.S. Copyright Office, your Library of Congress obligations are fulfilled at the same time. It's only if you don't register with the Copyright Office that you might run afoul of this extra deposit rule. You need do nothing unless you receive a letter requiring you to deposit your published work for the Library of Congress archives. If you get such a letter, it will tell you how to comply with the deposit requirements and will include a telephone number to which you may direct inquiries.

The Library of Congress deposit requirement is seldom enforced and failure to comply with this requirement will in no way affect the validity (or protectability) of your copyright. However, you can be required to pay a $250 fine if you ignore the request (and an additional $2,500 fine can be imposed if you willfully or repeatedly fail to comply).

1. Donating Public Domain Software to the Library of Congress

Some software authors decide that they don't want their software to be protected by copyright. Instead, they dedicate it to the public domain, meaning anyone is free to use the software without the author's permission. Such software is sometimes called freeware. You cannot register such public domain software with the Copyright Office, but you may donate a copy to the Library of Congress for the benefit of its Machine-Readable Collections Reading Room. Doing so ensures that a copy of your work will be preserved for posterity and enables members of the public who use the reading room to become aware of your work.

To be eligible for donation, the software must contain an explicit disclaimer of copyright protection from the copyright owner. Send your computer disk(s) along with any documentation. If the documentation is on disk, you need to send a printout of the documentation. If the software is distributed in a box or other packaging, send the entire package. Along with this material, include a letter explaining that you're making a donation. Send donations to:

Gift Section, Exchange & Gift Division
Library of Congress
Washington, D.C. 20540

D. Corrections and Changes After Registration Is Completed (Supplemental Registration)

As discussed in Chapter 4, Section E, the same published work normally can only be registered once with the Copyright Office. However, a second supplemental registration may be necessary to augment your original basic registration if you later discover that you forgot something important, supplied the Copyright Office with the wrong information or important facts have changed. A special form, Form CA, is used for this purpose.

If you ever become involved in copyright litigation, your registration certificate (which is simply a copy of your basic registration application form stamped and returned to you by the Copyright Of-fice) will be submitted into evidence to prove the existence of your copyright. It could prove embarrassing, and possibly harmful to your case, if the certificate is found to contain substantial errors, is unclear or ambiguous or if important facts have changed since you registered. For this reason, you should file a supplemental registration to correct significant errors in your certificate or to reflect important factual changes.

Also, remember that your registration is a public record. By keeping your registration accurate and up-to-date you will make it easier for those searching the Copyright Office records to discover your work and locate you or your company. This may result in new marketing opportunities and help to prevent an infringement.

1. Corrections

A supplemental registration should be filed to correct *significant* errors that occurred at the time the basic registration was made, and that were overlooked by the Copyright Office. This includes:

- identifying someone incorrectly as the author or copyright claimant of the work,
- registering an unpublished work as published (or vice versa), or
- inaccurately stating the extent of the copyright claim.

Errors in these important facts could cast doubt upon the validity and duration of your copyright and could needlessly confuse and complicate copyright litigation. They will also confuse anyone searching the Copyright Office records. Correct them as soon as you discover them.

Supplemental Registration Not Needed to Correct Obvious Errors

It is not necessary to file a formal supplemental registration to correct obvious errors the Copyright Office should have caught when it reviewed your application. This includes, for example, the omission of necessary information, such as the names of the author or claimant, and obvious mistakes (like a publication date of 1095.) If, when you receive your registration certificate, you discover that such errors have been overlooked by the copyright examiner, simply notify the Copyright Office and the mistake will be corrected with no need for a supplemental registration and additional fee.

---

2. Changes and Amplifications

You should file a supplemental registration to:

- reflect important changes in facts that have occurred since the basic registration was made,
- provide additional significant information that could have been provided in the original application but was not, or
- clarify or explain information in the basic registration.

a. If you have changed your address

It's an excellent idea, although not legally necessary, for you to keep your address current in the Copyright Office's records. By doing so, you will make it easy for people who want to use your work to locate you and arrange for permission and compensation. The harder you are to locate, the more likely it is that your copyright will be infringed if someone else wants to use your work. You may file a supplemental registration to change your address.

b. If an author or copyright claimant was omitted

All the authors and copyright claimants must be listed in the registration (unless they are anonymous or pseudonymous; see the explanation in Chapter 5, Section C, above). This means a supplemental registration should be filed if an author or copyright claimant's name was omitted.

c. Change in claimant's name

A supplemental registration should be made where the name of the copyright claimant has changed for reasons other than a transfer of ownership.

d.   Change in title of the registered work

File a supplemental registration if you changed the title of the registered work without changing its content. However, if the content of the work is changed, a new registration will have to be made.

3.   When Supplemental Registration Cannot Be Used

Certain kinds of errors should not be corrected by supplemental registration. In addition, supplemental registration may not be used to reflect some kinds of factual changes.

a.   Changes in copyright ownership

Supplemental registration cannot be used to notify the Copyright Office of post-registration changes in ownership of a copyright, whether by license, inheritance or other form of transfer. A special recordation procedure is used for this. (See discussion in Chapter 12, *Transferring Software Copyright Ownership and Use Rights*.)

b.   Errors or changes in content of registered work

A supplemental registration cannot be filed to reflect changes or corrections to the content of a registered work. Where such changes are so substantial as to make the new work a new version, it must be registered separately with a new deposit. If the content changes are minor, there is no need to file a new registration, since the original registration will provide adequate protection. (See detailed discussion in Chapter 4, Section F, about when a new registration must be made to protect new material.)

c.   Failure to mention computer screens

As discussed in Chapter 4, Section E, a single registration for a computer program covers all the copyrightable content of the program, including screen displays. It is not necessary, although permissible, to specifically mention screen displays in the application or to deposit identifying material for them. (See Chapter 5, Section D.) Once you have registered your software, however, you cannot seek a supplementary registration to allow a separate claim in the screen displays.

4.   How to File a Supplemental Registration

Filing a supplemental registration is a straightforward procedure. Here's how to do it.

a.   When to file

You may file a supplemental registration any time during the existence of the copyright for a work that was published or registered after January 1, 1978. There is a time limit for works published or registered before that date. See a copyright attorney before filing a supplemental registration for a pre-1978 published work.

b.   Who may file

After the original basic registration has been completed, a supplemental registration may be filed by:
- any author or other copyright claimant in the work,
- the owner of any exclusive right in the work (see Chapter 4, Section D), or
- the authorized agent of any of the above.

c.   How to fill out a supplemental registration application form

Use the Copyright Office's official Form CA to file a supplemental registration. A copy of this form is contained in the tear-out Appendix at the end of this book.

Part A: Basic Instructions

Part A asks for five items of information regarding your original basic registration. This information must be identical to that which already appears on your basic registration, even if the purpose of filing Form CA is to change one of these items. Refer to your certificate of registration (the copy of your application mailed back to you by the Copyright Office) for this information.

- **Title of work:** Give the title as it appears in the basic registration, including any previous or alternative titles if they appear.
- **Registration number:** This is a six- or seven- digit number preceded by a two-letter prefix—for example, TX 1234567. It should be stamped on the upper right hand corner of your certificate of registration.
- **Registration date:** Give the year when the basic registration was completed.
- **Name of author(s) and copyright claimant(s):** Give the names of all the authors and copyright claimants exactly as they appear in the basic registration.

Part B: Correction

Part B should be completed only if information in the basic registration was incorrect at the time it was made. (See discussion in Section 1, above). Leave Part B blank and complete Part C instead if you want to add, update or clarify information rather than rectify an error.

Part B asks for four items of information:

- **Location and nature of incorrect information:** Give the line number and heading or description of the space in the basic registration where the error occurred—for example, "Line 2a… Name of Author."

- **Incorrect information as it appears in the basic registration:** Transcribe the erroneous statement in the basic registration exactly as it appears there.
- **Corrected information:** Give the information as it should have appeared.
- **Explanation of correction:** If you wish, add an explanation of the error or correction.

Part C: Amplification

Part C should be completed if you are filing the Form CA to amplify (add to) the information in your basic registration.

- **Location and nature of information to be amplified:** Where indicated, give the line number and heading or description of the space in the basic registration form where the information to be amplified (add to) appears.
- **Amplified information:** Provide a statement of the added, updated, or explanatory information as clearly and succinctly as possible—for example, "change nature of authorship statement from entire text of computer program to entire text of computer program and users' manual."
- **Explanation of amplification:** If you wish, add an explanation of the amplification.

Part D: Continuation

Part D is a blank space that should be used if you do not have enough space in Part B or C.

Part E: Deposit account and mailing instructions

If you maintain a deposit account with the Copyright Office, identify it in Part E. Otherwise, you will need to send a nonrefundable filing fee (currently $20) with your form. The space headed "Correspondence" should contain the name and address of the person to be consulted by the Copyright Office if there are any problems.

Part F: Certification

The person making the supplemental registration must sign the application in Part F and check the appropriate box indicating her capacity—that is, author, other copyright claimant, owner of exclusive rights or authorized agent.

Part G: Address for return of certificate

The address to which the Copyright Office should mail your supplemental registration certificate must be listed in Part G. Make sure the address is legible, since the certificate will be returned in a window envelope.

d. Filing form CA

Make a copy of the completed Form CA for your records. Attach the registration fee ($20 as of the date of this writing), either a check or money order payable to the Register of Copyrights, to the Form CA. No deposit is necessary for a supplemental registration. Send the form and payment to:

Register of Copyrights
Library of Congress
Washington, D.C. 20559

e. Effect of supplemental registration

If your supplemental registration application was completed correctly, the Copyright Office will assign you a new registration number and issue a certificate of supplementary registration under that number. The certificate is simply a copy of your Form CA with the new registration number, date and certification stamped on it. Be sure to keep it in your records.

The information in a supplementary registration augments, but does not supersede, that contained in the original basic registration. The basic registration is not expunged or canceled. However, if the person who filed the supplementary registration was the copyright claimant for the original registration (or his heir or transferee), the Copyright Office will place a note referring to the supplementary registration on its records of the basic registration. This way, anyone needing information regarding the registration will know there is a supplemental registration on file if an inquiry is made regarding the work. ■

Scope of Copyright Protection for Software

Perhaps the greatest difficulty with copyrights is determining to what extent a work is protected. This problem exists with all types of works of authorship—books, music, artwork—but it has proved particularly vexing for computer software. In this chapter we'll explore this difficult question. We can provide few final answers, but we do give some guidelines and examples to help you get a feel for the problems involved.

A. Three Prerequisites for Copyright Protection

Before we explore the scope of copyright protection for software, you must first understand that your software or other copyrightable works won't be protected at all unless they satisfy the following three fundamental prerequisites for copyright protection.

1. Fixation

The first requirement for copyright protection is that the work must be fixed in a tangible medium of expression. Any stable medium from which the work can be read back or heard, either directly or with the aid of a machine or device, is acceptable. For example, a work is protected when it is written or drawn on a piece of paper, typed on a typewriter or recorded on tape.

Copyright does not protect a work that exists in your mind but that you have not fixed in a tangible medium. Trade secrecy must be used to protect such unfixed works. (See Chapter 15.)

Copyright protection begins the instant you fix your work. There is no waiting period and it is not necessary to register with the Copyright Office; but important benefits are obtained by doing so (see Chapter 4). Copyright protects both completed and unfinished works, and works that are widely distributed to the public or never distributed at all.

When software is sufficiently "fixed" to qualify for copyright protection has been the subject of great controversy. It's clear that software satisfies the fixation requirement the moment it is stored on magnetic media such as disks or tapes; imprinted on devices such as ROMs, chips and circuit boards; or, of course, written down on paper.

But does fixation also occur when a program is loaded into computer RAM (volatile random access memory) or transmitted over the Internet? This is not so clear. Several courts have held that fixation does occur when a program is loaded from a permanent storage device into computer RAM. (*MAI v. Peak*, 991 F.2d. 511 (9th Cir. 1993).)

However, these cases involved situations where a program was retained in RAM for several minutes or even longer. It remains unclear whether transmitting a program or other material over the Internet counts as fixation. Such transmissions involve making several temporary copies of portions of the work ("data packets") and sending them over computer networks.

If such transmissions constitute fixation, simply browsing on the Internet could constitute a violation of copyright owners' exclusive rights to make copies of their protected online material. But many experts believe the copying involved in Internet transmissions is too temporary and ephemeral in nature to count as "copying" for copyright purposes. This issue has been the subject of international treaty negotiation, and may be the subject of legislation in the near future.

2. Originality

A work is protected by copyright only if, and to the extent, it is *original*. But this does not mean that it must be novel—that is, new to the world—to be protected. For copyright purposes, a work is original if it—or at least a part of it—owes its origin to the author. A work's quality, ingenuity, aesthetic merit, or uniqueness are not considered. In short, the Copyright Act does not distinguish between the most complex and innovative multimedia project and a high schooler's first efforts in BASIC. Both are protected to the extent they were not copied by the author—whether consciously or unconsciously—from other software.

Many works consist of some elements that are original and others that are copied. In this event, only the original elements will be protected (but, of course, the copied elements might be protected under someone else's copyright).

a. Independent creation a defense to copyright infringement

One effect of the originality requirement that has significant implications for the software industry is that so long as a work was independently created by its creators, it is protected even if other highly similar works already exist. In other words, a programmer cannot infringe upon a preexisting program she has never seen or otherwise been exposed to.

> **EXAMPLE:** Tom, a paleontologist at a midwestern university, writes a software program that helps identify and date fossils. Unbeknownst to Tom, Jane, a paleontologist in another part of the country, has written a program of her own that accomplishes the same task. Tom and Jane never had any contact with each other or each other's work.

Nevertheless, since they were designed to accomplish the same purpose, their programs closely resemble each other. However, since they were independently created, both programs are entitled to copyright protection despite the similarities.

This means that no matter how hard you work to create a program, someone else is perfectly free to create a similar program so long as he didn't copy it from you. We'll discuss the impact of this independent creation defense in more detail in Chapter 13.

3. Minimal Creativity

Finally, a minimal amount of creativity over and above the originality requirement is necessary for copyright protection. Works completely lacking creativity are denied copyright protection even if they have been independently created. For example, one court held that a programmer's minute variations on a standard communications protocol for fax machines were not sufficiently creative to be copyrightable. (*Secure Servs. Technology v. Time & Space Processing, Inc.* 722 F.Supp. 1354 (E.D. Va. 1989).)

In addition, there are some types of works that are usually deemed to contain no creativity at all. For example, telephone directory white pages are deemed to lack even minimal creativity and are therefore not protected by copyright. Other alphabetical or numerical listings of data in computer databases may also completely lack creativity. (See Chapter 9.)

Technically speaking, the amount of creativity required for copyright protection is very slight. However, as a practical matter, the more creative a work, the more copyright protection it will receive. This may be particularly true for software. Programs consisting primarily of standard programming techniques may receive little or no protection even if they are original, because the code will be judged to merge with the underlying ideas rather than qualify as protectible expression. In contrast, highly creative programs—programs unlike anything created before—receive full protection.

Copyright Does Not Protect Hard Work

In the past, some courts held that copyright protection extended to works lacking originality and/or creativity if a substantial amount of work had been involved in their creation. For example, these courts might have protected a telephone directory or similar alphabetical database if the author had personally verified every entry. However the Supreme Court has outlawed this sweat of the brow theory in *Feist Publications, Inc. v. Rural Telephone Service Co.,* 111 S.Ct. 1282 (1991). It is now clear that the amount of work expended to create a program or other work of authorship has absolutely no bearing on the degree of copyright protection it will receive. Copyright only protects fixed, original, minimally creative expressions, not hard work.

B. Nature and Extent of Copyright Protection for Software

Creating a new and useful computer program requires an investment of a great deal of time and intellectual labor. Understandably, programmers (and those that hire them) would like all the hard work they put into their creations to be protected by the copyright laws. In other words, they want to be able to own exclusive copyright rights for every element of their software. However, this is not the case. Copyright protection is limited in scope. This is because the copyright laws are intended to promote the advancement of knowledge, not to enable copyright owners to maximize their profits. Too much copyright protection for works of authorship would end up retarding, not promoting, this purpose.

All works of authorship—particularly computer programs—contain elements that are protected by copyright and elements that are not protected. Unfortunately, there is no system available to an interested party to precisely identify which aspects of a given work are protected by copyright. The Copyright Office makes no such determination when software is registered. The only time we ever obtain a definitive answer as to how much any particular program (or other work of authorship) is protected is when it becomes the subject of a copyright infringement lawsuit. In this event, a judge or jury determines the question. (See Chapter 13 for detailed discussion of infringement suits.) Of course, such litigation is usually very expensive and time consuming.

Since the late 1970s, federal courts all across the country have been deciding an ever-increasing number of software copyright infringement disputes. Their legal opinions are the only concrete guidance available on how and how much software is protected by the copyright law. Studying these opinions is the only means available, short of filing a lawsuit, to determine the extent to which a given work is protected. However, this is a difficult and complex area of the law subject to varying interpretations. Courts in different parts of the country sometimes disagree with each other on the extent of copyright protection for software.

All this means that studying these court decisions may not give a definitive answer to the question of how much a work is protected in your part of the country. At best an educated guess can be made. In many cases, this guess should be made by a copyright attorney who has had experience in deciphering the relevant court decisions. But keep in mind that even an attorney will often be unable to provide you with a definite "yes" or "no" answer.

The bottom line: There are few sure answers when it comes to copyright protection for software. This much is true: The more you stay away from someone else's creation, the better your chances of staying out of copyright trouble.

To appreciate the difficulties faced by the courts, attorneys, software copyright owners and programmers when assessing how much a particular program is protected by copyright, you must come to terms with these two basic rules of copyright law:

- Rule One: Copyright only protects "expressions," not ideas, systems or processes.
- Rule Two: The scope of copyright protection is proportional to the range of expression available.

Let's look at both rules and their ramifications for software in detail.

1. Rule 1: Copyright Only Protects "Expressions," Not Ideas, Systems or Processes

Copyright only protects the *expression* of an idea, system or process, *not the idea, system or process itself.* Ideas, procedures, processes, systems, mathematical principles, formulas or algorithms, methods of operation, concepts, facts and discoveries are not protected by copyright. (17 U.S.C. 102(b).) Remember, copyright is designed to aid the advancement of knowledge. If the copyright law gave a person a legal monopoly over her ideas, the progress of knowledge would be impeded rather than helped.

EXAMPLE: Grace writes a book about gardening that describes a revolutionary new method of growing vegetables with minimal amounts of water. The literal way in which Grace sets forth her ideas—that is, her *actual words*—are protected by copyright—no one can copy and publish them without her permission. But the *ideas, facts, processes and methods* contained in Grace's book are not protected. This means that any one is free to read Grace's book and employ her method for low-water gardening. In addition, anyone else is free to write his own book describing Grace's system—so long as he doesn't copy the literal expression contained in Grace's book.

This idea-expression dichotomy also applies to software. Consider the following real-life example:

EXAMPLE: While a student at the Harvard business school in the late 1970s, Daniel Bricklin conceived the idea of an electronic spreadsheet—a "magic blackboard" that recalculated numbers automatically as changes were made in other parts of the spreadsheet. Eventually, aided by others, he transformed his idea into *VisiCalc,* the first commercial electronic spreadsheet. The program, designed for use on the Apple II, sold like hotcakes and helped spark the personal computer revolution.

Of course *VisiCalc* was protected by copyright. Nevertheless, others were free to write their own original programs accomplishing the same purpose as *VisiCalc.* The copyright law did not give Bricklin et al. any ownership rights over the *idea* of an electronic spreadsheet, even though it was a revolutionary advance in computer programming. The copyright in *VisiCalc* extended only to the particular way *VisiCalc* expressed this idea—to *Visicalc's* actual code, its structure and organization, and perhaps to some aspects of its user interface.

Very soon, many competing programs were introduced. The most successful of these was *Lotus 1-2-3,* originally created by Mitchell Kapor and Jonathan Sachs. Building on Bricklin's revolutionary idea, Kapor and Sachs expressed that idea in a different, more powerful way. Designed for the IBM PC, *Lotus 1-2-3* took advantage of that computer's more expansive memory and more versatile screen display capabilities and keyboard. In short, *Lotus 1-2-3* did all that *Visicalc* did, only better. *VisiCalc* sales plunged and the program was eventually discontinued.

Of course, it's easy to say that copyright does not protect ideas, only expression. But what does this mean in the real world? Almost all computer programs embody systems or processes. When does the unprotectible system end and the protectible expression begin? In point of fact it can be very difficult to tell the difference between an unprotected idea, system or process and its protected expression. Nevertheless, let's look at what aspects of computer software have been found to constitute protectible expression by courts in recent years.

Legal Protection for Ideas, Processes And Systems

What if Bricklin in the above example had wanted to protect his idea or system of an electronic spreadsheet itself, not just *Visicalc?* He would have had to look to laws other than copyright. If the electronic spreadsheet had qualified as a patentable invention, it could have been protected under the federal patent law. In this event, Bricklin would have had a 17-year monopoly on its use. Anyone else seeking to write a program implementing the spreadsheet idea would have had to obtain Bricklin's permission or been liable for patent infringement. Bricklin did not apply for a patent, and it is far from clear whether, at the time, he could have obtained one had he done so. (See Chapter 15, *Other Legal Protections for Software*, for a discussion of software patents.)

---

a. Program documentation

Program documentation is protected by copyright, at least to some extent. It is classified as a literary work. This is true for both narrative program descriptions and schematic or logical diagrams of program functions such as flowcharts. Supporting documentation for end users—software manuals and instructions—are likewise protected.

However, copyright protection for software documentation (and similar highly technical written works) is limited. We've seen above that copyright never protects ideas themselves. This means that the ideas, methods, systems, procedures, processes, algorithms, principles, concepts, ideas or facts described, explained, illustrated or embodied in documentation are not copyrighted. Copyright only protects the particular way the ideas, facts and so forth contained in documentation are expressed. In other words, the actual words or drawings may be protected, but not their meaning.

Moreover, even the words or schematics contained in documentation may receive little protection. Where there are only a limited number of ways to describe a program's functions and/or structure in program documentation, that description may receive little or no protection because of the merger rule discussed in Section 2 below. In other words, if there is only one way, or a few ways, to flowchart the solution to a particular programming problem, that flowchart will not be protected by copyright. If this were not so, the first person to create the flowchart would effectively have a monopoly on the ideas expressed by the flowchart.

b. Program code is protected expression

A program's code clearly constitutes the programmer's expression of the ideas embodied in the program and, to the extent it is original, fixed and minimally creative, is protected by copyright.

This is true for source code (code written in high-level computer languages consisting of English-like words and symbols readable by humans, such as C++), object code (the series of binary ones and zeros read by the computer itself to execute a program, but not readable by ordinary humans) and microcode (instructions that tell a microprocessor chip how to work).

Subject to the limitations discussed under Rule 2 below, copyright protects both applications programs (programs that perform a specific task for the user, such as word processing, will and trust writing, patent drafting, bookkeeping or playing a video game) and operating systems programs (programs that manage a computer's internal functions and facilitate use of applications programs).

EXAMPLE: Franklin Computer Corp. manufactured a computer that was compatible with the Apple II. To achieve such compatibility, Franklin copied verbatim 14 separate programs comprising the Apple II's operating system. Apple sued Franklin for infringing on its copyright in these programs and won. The court held that operating system programs constitute protectible expression, not unprotectible methods, processes, systems or ideas. (*Apple Computer v. Franklin*, 714 F.2d 1240 (3rd Cir. 1983).)

Can Computer Languages Be Copyrighted?

No court has ruled on whether high-level computer languages like C++, FORTRAN or Pascal can themselves be protected by copyright. However, the Copyright Office apparently believes they cannot be protected since it refuses to register a work consisting solely of a computer language. The Copyright Office's view is supported by decades-old copyright cases involving telegraphic codes and stenographic systems. The courts in these cases held that the component elements of shorthand systems and telegraphic codes—that is, the individual coined words or symbols that form the vocabulary of the system—are not protected by copyright. But a particular arrangement of such symbols is protected if it meets the originality, fixation and minimal creativity requirements discussed above. (*Hartfield v. Peterson*, 91 F.2d 998 (2d Cir. 1937).) It seems likely, therefore, that anyone is free to write any program in any computer language. Although the language itself is not protected, a particular program written in that language is, just as the English language itself is not protected, but a poem written in English is.

c. Program structure, sequence and organization

There are many different ways to design a program, both in terms of its modular structure and dynamic behavior. A program's structure is an important factor determining its efficiency. Much of the expense and difficulty in creating a new program is often attributable to developing its structure, logic and flow, not in creating the literal program code. It is generally agreed by courts today that a program's structure, logic and flow can constitute protectible expression, even though these elements are not entirely visible and concrete, either in the program's code or screen displays.

> **EXAMPLE:** Whelan created a program written in the EDL computer language called *Dentalab* designed to automate the bookkeeping functions of dental offices. Jastrow created a very similar program in the BASIC language. He did not directly translate the *Dentalab* code into BASIC. Rather, he copied the way *Dentalab* instructed the computer to receive, assemble, calculate, hold, retrieve and communicate data, and the way data flowed sequentially from one program function to another. Whelan sued Jastrow for infringing on the copyright in her program and won. The court held that the protectible expression of a computer program includes "the manner in which the program operates, controls and regulates the computer in receiving, assembling, calculating, retaining, correlating and producing useful information either on a screen, print-out or by audio communication." (*Whelan v. Jastrow* 797 F.2d 1222 (3rd Cir. 1986).)
>
> The *Whelan* decision has been criticized by many legal experts and other courts, but it established the principle that copyright *can in theory* protect more than a program's literal code. Whether copyright *will* provide such protection in any given instance depends on the application of Rule 2 below.

d. Protection for user interfaces (look and feel)

The user interface of a computer program is the way a program presents itself to and interacts with the user. It consists principally of the sequence, flow and content of the display screens that appear on a computer's monitor (permitting the user to select various options and/or input data in a prescribed format) and the use of specific keys on the computer keyboard to perform particular functions. The look and feel of a program's interface can be very important to the user (a well-designed interface makes a program much easier to use) and therefore very valuable to the program's owner. It's possible to copy the way a user interface looks and works without copying any computer code.

After years of litigation involving some of the most famous software interfaces in the world it seems clear that copyright provides very little protection for most of the elements of a user interface. Anything less than slavish copying of an entire interface is likely not an infringement. As a result, developers need not go to the trouble of devising different words to convey simple menu commands and may use commands that are familiar to users of competing works.

The two most important cases involve the Macintosh interface and the Lotus 1-2-3 computer spreadsheet program.

Apple sued Microsoft, claiming that the user interface of Microsoft's Windows system violated Apple's copyright in the Macintosh user interface. Ultimately, all of Apple's claims were dismissed and the case was upheld on appeal. The trial court held that the "desktop metaphor" underlying the Macintosh user interface—suggesting an office with familiar office objects such as file folders, documents and a trash can—was an unprotectible idea. The court also ruled that most of the individual elements of the user interface at issue in the case were not protectible, either because Apple had licensed them to Microsoft, because they were not original or because of the factors discussed in Sections B1c, d and e above. However, the court also held the Macintosh interface might be protected as a whole, at least from virtually identical copying, even though its individual elements were not protected. In other words, although many of the individual elements of the interface were not protectible standing alone, they still formed part of a larger arrangement, selection or layout that was protected expression. (*Apple Computer, Inc. v. Microsoft Corp.*, 35 F.3d.1435 (9th Cir. 1994).)

Lotus Development Corp. sued Borland International, Inc., claiming that its *Lotus 1-2-3* spreadsheet program had been infringed by Borland's *Quattro* and *Quattro Pro* spreadsheet programs. In order to enable users familiar with *Lotus 1-2-3* to switch to *Quattro* without having to learn new commands or rewrite their Lotus macros, Borland included in its programs an alternate command menu structure that was a virtually identical copy of the *Lotus 1-2-3* menu command hierarchy. Borland did not copy any of Lotus's code. It copied only the words and structure of Lotus's menu commands. After losing at trial, Borland finally won on appeal. The Court of Appeal held that *1-2-3*'s command hierarchy was a method of operation that was not protected by copyright. The court stated that a software developer should be able to create a program that users can operate in exactly the same way as a competing program. (*Lotus Development Corp. v, Borland International, Inc.*, 49 F.3d 807 (1st Cir. 1995).) In the words of one copyright expert, this decision "safeguards interoperability between computer programs and allows users to port macros, which they themselves have composed, to competitive environments." (*Nimmer on Copyright*, Section 13.03[F][3][e].)

> ### Other Ways to Protect User Interfaces
>
> The copyright may not be the only means available to protect user interfaces. It may be possible to protect screen icons by obtaining a design patent. A design patent provides a 14-year monopoly on industrial designs that have no functional use. (See *Software Development: A Legal Guide*, by Stephen Fishman (Nolo Press) for discussion.)
>
> Another way interfaces might be protected is under the state and federal trademark laws. These laws protect a product's "trade dress"—that is, the image and overall appearance of a product—and also provide some protection against activity that misleads consumers about the origins of a product. (See *Trademark: How to Name a Business & Product*, by Kate McGrath and Stephen Elias (Nolo Press) for discussion.) However, as of this writing, the trademark laws have not provided the basis for any decision regarding the copying of a computer interface.

e. Video games

Computer games were the subject of many of the earliest copyright infringement cases involving software. For copyright purposes, a video game consists of two elements: the underlying software, which is protected like any other software; and a game's audiovisual elements (what happens on the computer screen and the sounds the game makes). These audiovisual elements in turn consist of two parts: the attract mode and the play mode. The attract mode consists of the visual and audio effects that occur when no player is using the game. The play mode refers to the visual and audio sequences that occur when a game is actually played.

Courts have held that the audiovisual elements of both a video game's attract and play modes are entitled to copyright protection separate and distinct from the underlying software. *(Midway Mfg. Co. v. Artic International, Inc.*, 704 F.2d 1009 (7th Cir. 1983).) But such protection may be limited through application of Rule 2 below.

2. Rule 2: The Scope of Copyright Protection Is Proportional to the Range of Expression Available

We've seen above that copyright *can* in theory protect program code, structure and even user interfaces, albeit to an unclear extent. But whether these elements *will* be protected in fact in any given instance depends on application of our second rule.

We said above that the copyright law only protects original works of authorship. Part of the essence of original authorship is the making of choices. Any work of authorship is the end result of a whole series of choices made by its creator. For example, the author of a novel expressing the idea of love must choose the novel's plot, characters, locale and the actual words used to express the story. The author of such a novel has a nearly limitless array of choices available.

However, the choices available to the creators of many works of authorship are severely limited. In these cases, the idea or ideas underlying the work and the way they are expressed by the author are deemed to "merge." The result is that the author's expression is either treated as if it were in the public domain (given no protection at all) or protected only against virtually verbatim or "slavish" copying.

If this were not so, the copyright law would end up discouraging authorship of new works and thereby retard the progress of knowledge.

> **EXAMPLE:** Data East USA created a video game called *Karate Champ* for the Commodore computer. Data East sued the creator of a competing karate video game called *World Karate Champ* for copyright infringement. Data East claimed that *World Karate Champ* had impermissibly copied the audiovisual elements of *Karate Champ*. Data East lost because of the merger doctrine.

The court found that the similarities between the two games—similar game procedures, common karate moves, a time element, a referee, computer graphics and bonus points—necessarily followed from the idea of creating a martial arts karate combat game: They were "inseparable from, or indispensable to… the *idea* of the karate sport." In other words, there were only a limited number of ways to express the idea of a karate video game for the Commodore computer. Anyone who wanted to create such a game would have no choice but to include these elements in the game.

As a result, the idea of a karate video game for the Commodore computer and its expression by Data East were deemed to merge, and Data East's game received very limited copyright protection. If this were not so, no one other than Data East could ever create a karate video game. *(Data East USA, Inc. v. Epyx, Inc.*, 862 F.2d 204 (9th Cir. 1988).)

The result of the merger doctrine is that the fewer choices a programmer has when setting out to create a given element of a piece of software, the less copyright protection that element will receive. Or, to put it another way: *The scope of copyright protection is proportional to the range of expression available to articulate the underlying ideas communicated by the program.*

In recent years, the courts have been finding that more and more elements of computer programs are not protectible because of the merger doctrine. The seminal court decision of *Computer Associates Int'l v. Altai, Inc.* (982 F.2d 693 (2d Cir. 1992)), identified the following constraints on the range of software expression (this list is not exclusive):

- elements dictated by efficiency,
- elements dictated by external factors, and
- standard programming techniques and program features.

a. Elements dictated by efficiency

Programmers usually strive to create programs that meet the user's needs as efficiently as possible. The desire for maximum efficiency may operate to restrict the range of choices available to a programmer. For example, there may only be one or two efficient ways to express the idea embodied in a given program, module, routine or subroutine. If a programmer's choices regarding a particular program's structure, interface or even source code are necessary to efficiently implement the program's function, then those choices will not be protected by copyright. In other words, no programmer may have a monopoly on the most efficient way to write any program. Paradoxically, this means that the better job a programmer does—the more closely the program approximates the ideal of efficiency—the less copyright protection the program will receive.

EXAMPLE 1: A court held that Lotus 1-2-3's basic spreadsheet screen display resembling a rotated "L" was not protected by copyright because there are only a few ways to make a computer screen resemble a spreadsheet; nor was the use of "+," "-," "*," and "/" for their corresponding mathematical functions; or use of the enter key to place keystroke entries into cells. The use of such keys was the most efficient means to implement these mathematical functions. (*Lotus Dev. Corp. v. Borland Int'l, Inc.* 799 F.Supp. 203 (D.Mass. 1992).)

EXAMPLE 2: Another court held that a cost-estimating program's method of allowing users to navigate within screen displays (by using the space bar to move the cursor down a list, the backspace key to move up, the return key to choose a function and a number selection to edit an entry) was not protectible. The court noted that there were only a limited number of ways to enable a user to navigate through a screen display on the hardware in question while facilitating user comfort. The court also found that the program's use of alphabetical and numerical columns in its screen displays was not protectible. The constraints of uniformity of format and limited page space (requiring either a horizontal or vertical orientation) permitted only a very narrow range of choices. (*Manufacturers Technologies, Inc. v. Cams*, 706 F.Supp. 984 (D.Conn. 1989).)

b. Elements dictated by external factors

A programmer's freedom of design choice is often limited by external factors such as:

- the mechanical specifications of the computer on which the program is intended to run,
- compatibility requirements of other programs which the program is designed to operate in conjunction with,
- computer manufacturers' design standards, and
- the demands of the industry being serviced.

EXAMPLE 1: Intel Corp. charged that NEC Corp. had unlawfully copied the microcode to Intel Corp.'s 8086/88 microprocessor chip to create compatible microprocessor chips of its own. (Microcode is a series of instructions that tells a microprocessor chip how to work.) NEC sued Intel to obtain a judicial declaration that it did not infringe on Intel's microcode. The court held that NEC had not committed infringement. Although some of the simpler microroutines in NEC's microcode were substantially similar to Intel's, the court held that machine constraints were largely responsible for the similarities; that is, NEC's programmers had very limited choices in designing their microcode to operate a chip compatible with Intel's 8086/88. Given these constraints, Intel's microcode was protected only against "virtually identical copying." (*NEC Corp. v. Intel Corp.* 10 U.S.P.Q.2d 1177 (N.D. Cal 1989).)

EXAMPLE 2: A cotton cooperative developed a program for mainframe computers called *Telcot* that provided users with cotton prices and information, accounting services and the ability to consummate cotton sales transactions. Former employee-programmers of the cooperative created a PC version of the cotton exchange program. The two programs were similar in their sequence and organization. The cooperative sued for infringement and lost. The court held that many of the similarities between the two programs were dictated by the externalities of the cotton market. The programs were designed to present the same information as contained in a cotton recap sheet, and there were not many different ways to accomplish this. (*Plains Cotton Cooperative Assoc. v. Goodpasture Computer Service, Inc.* 807 F.2d 1256 (5th Cir. 1987).)

EXAMPLE 3: Q-Co Industries created a program to operate a TelePrompTer. The program was written in BASIC and Atari to run on an Atari 800-XL. Hoffman created a program accomplishing the same purpose, written in another programming language and designed to run on the IBM PC. All four modules of Hoffman's program corresponded closely to four of the 12 modules contained in Q-Co's program. Q-Co sued for copyright infringement. The court held there was no infringement because "the same modules would be an inherent part of any prompting program." In other words, any programmer wishing to create a TelePrompTer program would have no choice but to include the four modules. (*Q-Co Industries, Inc. v. Hoffman*, 625 F.Supp. 608 (S.D.N.Y. 1985).)

c. Standard programming techniques and software features

Certain programming techniques and software features are so widely used as to be standard in the software industry. To create a competitive program, a software developer may have no choice other than to employ such techniques and features because users expect them. Courts treat such material as being in the public domain—it is free for the taking and cannot be owned by any single software author even though it is included in an otherwise copyrightable work.

EXAMPLE 1: The court in the *Apple v. Microsoft* case (see above) held that the following basic elements of the Macintosh user interface were unprotectible because they were common to all graphical user interfaces and were standard in the industry:

1. overlapping windows to display multiple images on a computer screen,
2. iconic representations of familiar objects from the office environment, such as file folders, documents and a trash can,
3. opening and closing of objects in order to retrieve, transfer or store information,
4. menus used to store information or control computer functions,
5. manipulation of icons to convey instructions and to control operation of the computer. (See *Apple Computer v. Microsoft Corp.*, 779 F.Supp. 133 (N.D.Ca. 1992).)

EXAMPLE 2: The owner of an outlining program called *PC-Outline* sued the owner of a competing program called *Grandview* for copyright infringement. *Grandview* had nine pull-down menus functionally similar to those of *PC-Outline*. Nevertheless, the court held that *Grandview* did not infringe on *PC-Outline*. The court reasoned that use of a pull-down menu was commonplace in the software industry. The court declared that a copyright owner cannot claim "copyright protection of an ... expression that is, if not standard, then commonplace in the computer software industry." (*Brown Bag Software v. Symantec Corp.*, 960 F.2d 1465 (9th Cir. 1990).)

C. Works Copyright Never Protects

There are some categories of works that copyright can never protect. Unless they are protected by some body of law other than copyright (patent or trademark law, for example), they are in the public domain freely available to anyone.

1. Purely Functional Items

Copyright only protects works of authorship. Things that have a purely functional or utilitarian purpose are not considered to be works of authorship and are not copyrightable. For example, there is no copyright protection for the purely functional aspects of machinery, refrigerators, lamps or automobiles. However, if the design of a useful article incorporates artistic features that are independent of the article's functional aspects, such features are protectible. For example, the decorative hood ornament on a Jaguar automobile is an artistic feature that is separable from any functional aspects of a Jaguar; therefore it is protectible.

Those elements of a computer program that are purely functional may also be denied copyright protection. For example, certain aspects of the Apple Macintosh graphical user interface were found by the court to be purely functional, the same as the dials, knobs and remote control devices of a television or VCR, or the button and clocks of a stove. These functional aspects included the ability to move a window partially off the screen, and the presence of menu items allowing a user to create a new folder within an existing folder.

2. Words, Names, Titles, Slogans, and Other Short Phrases

No matter how highly creative, novel or distinctive they may be, individual words and short phrases are not protected by copyright, and will not be registered by the Copyright Office (37 C.F.R. 202.1(a)). For this reason, the use of words and short phrases in the menus and icons of the Macintosh user interface—"Get Info" and "Trash," for example—were found not to be protectible.

The words and short phrases rule may be applied to source code, as well as to words. For example, a court has stated that a security code used with the *Genesis* video game system was "of such de minimis [minimal] length that it is probably unprotected under the words and short phrases doctrine." *(Sega En-*

terprises, Ltd. v. Accolade, Inc., No. 92-15655 (9th Cir. 1993).)

Names (whether of individuals, products or business organizations or groups), titles and slogans are also not copyrightable. However, these items may be protectible under the trademark laws. (See Chapter 15, *Other Legal Protections for Software.*)

3. Blank Forms Designed Solely to Record Information

In addition, blank forms designed solely to record information are not protected by copyright. The Copyright Office will not register such items. (37 C.F.R. 202.1(c).) According to the Copyright Office, this includes such items as time cards, graph paper, account books, bank checks, scorecards, address books, diaries, report forms and order forms.

This rule may also apply to computer screen templates designed to fit with electronic spreadsheets or database programs. If such templates are designed solely to record information, and do not convey information, they should not be protected.

However, it can be difficult in many cases to determine if a form is designed solely to record information. Even true blank forms—that is, forms consisting mainly of blank space to be filled in—may convey valuable information. For example, the columns or headings on a blank form may be interlaced with highly informative verbiage. Moreover, the configuration of columns, headings and lines itself may convey information.

4. Typeface Designs

The Copyright Office and courts have concluded that typeface designs—whether digital or analog—are industrial designs and are therefore not protected by copyright. The reasoning for this is that typeface styles or fonts are purely utilitarian. The Copyright Office, therefore, will not register a work consisting solely of a typeface design. However, copyright can protect typeface software (computer programs designed to produce fonts). In addition, some typefaces have been protected by design patents, including ITC Stone, Adobe Garamond and Adobe Minion.

5. Works for Which Copyright Has Expired

As discussed in Chapter 2, *Copyright Basics*, copyright protection does not last forever. When it expires the work enters the public domain. In effect, public domain works belong to everybody. Anyone is free to use them but no one can ever own them. However, copyright protection lasts so long—at least 50 years—that by the time the vast majority of software enters the public domain it will be worthless because of changes in technology.

The only software now in the public domain because of expiration of the copyright is software published before 1964 for which no renewal registration was filed with the Copyright Office during the 28th year after publication. Such software entered the public domain at the start of the 29th year after publication. For example, a program published in 1960 which was not renewed during 1988 entered the public domain on January 1, 1989. Of course, not much software was published before 1964, and what there was probably has little or no value today.

Note that this rule applies only to published software. Copyright protection for all unpublished software, whenever written, will last over 50 years.

6. Works Dedicated to the Public Domain

The author of a computer program or other copyrightable work is free to decide that he or she doesn't want it protected by copyright and may dedicate it instead to the public domain. By doing so, the author gives up all ownership rights in the work and permits anyone to copy or otherwise use the work without permission. There are no official forms to file to do this. The author merely needs to state clearly somewhere on the work that no copyright is claimed in the work. The Copyright Office will not register a work for which copyright has been expressly disclaimed. Without such registration, a copyright infringement suit cannot be filed.

Huge amounts of software have been dedicated to the public domain. For example, computer programming texts often contain code dedicated to the public domain that programmers are encouraged to copy. Much public domain software can also be found on the Internet and BBSs.

Freeware and Shareware Are Not In the Public Domain

Freeware is software that is made available to the public for free. Although it's free, freeware is not the same as public domain software because the author retains his or her copyright rights and can place restrictions on how the program is used. In contrast, authors who dedicate software to the public domain give up all their copyright rights. This means you can use their software any way you wish without restriction.

Shareware refers to a method of marketing software by making trial copies available to users for free. If the user wishes to keep the software, he or she is supposed to pay the shareware owner a fee. Shareware is fully protected by copyright and may be used only in the manner and to the extent permitted by the owner. ■

Derivative Works and Use of Preexisting Material

Most software is not created entirely from scratch. Rather, it is a mixture of new and preexisting material. For example, a programmer may create a new program by writing some new code and combining it with already existing code. If enough preexisting material is used, the new program may constitute a derivative work. Permission may be needed from the owner of the preexisting material to copy and distribute such a derivative work. This chapter explains how to recognize a derivative work and obtain maximum legal protection for such works.

A. Permission Required for Derivative Works Based on Someone Else's Prior Work

One of the five exclusive copyright rights that automatically come into existence the moment an original work of authorship is fixed in a tangible form is the exclusive right to prepare and distribute derivative works based on the work's protected expression. This means that, subject to the important exceptions discussed in Section D below, you cannot create and distribute a derivative work by using someone else's protected expression without obtaining their permission. If you do, you violate that person's copyright and would be subject to a copyright infringement suit.

Permission must be obtained from the owner of the exclusive right to prepare derivative works based on it. Usually the owner is the author or publisher but not always. In Chapter 12, *Transferring Software Copyright Ownership and Use Rights*, we discuss the ins and outs of dividing copyright ownership and obtaining permission to use someone else's work.

If you intend to create a derivative work from someone else's copyright work, be sure to get the copyright owner's permission to use the work *before* you go to the time and trouble of adapting it into a new work.

What Happens If You Fail to Get Permission?

A derivative work created without the necessary permission from the owner of the preexisting expression exists in a kind of legal limbo. The author of the derivative work cannot distribute it without infringing on the copyright in the preexisting material. But nobody else can use the derivative work without its creator's permission. Absent such permission, the derivative work is essentially worthless.

EXAMPLE: Lisa creates a Power Macintosh version of a Windows computer golf game. Lisa cannot distribute this program without infringing on the copyright in the original program. However, Lisa still owns the copyright in her Power Mac program. If anyone wanted to use it, they would have to get her permission, which of course she can't give without infringing the copyright in the original program.

B. What Is a Derivative Work?

A derivative work is "a work based upon one or more preexisting works." It includes any "form in which a work may be recast, transformed, or adapted." (17 USC Sec. 101.) To be derivative, a work must incorporate in some form a portion of the protected expression of a preexisting copyrighted work.

A derivative work stands on its own for copyright purposes and is entitled to its own copyright protection independent of the original work it was derived from.

A good example of a derivative work is a screenplay based upon a novel. For example, to create a film version of *War and Peace* the screenwriter would have to incorporate a substantial portion of the novel's plot, characters and dialog into the screenplay. But the screenwriter would also have to contribute original copyrightable work of his own, including organizing the material into cinematic scenes, editing the story down to film length, adding new dialog and camera directions. The end result would be a new work of authorship separately protected by copyright: a screenplay that is clearly different from *War and Peace*, yet clearly based upon or derived from it.

Other examples of derivative works would be an abridgment, condensation, sound recording, translation or any other form in which *War and Peace* or any other novel was recast, transformed or adapted.

Of course, all works are derivative to some extent. Authorship, whether of a novel or a computer program, is more often than not a process of transla-tion and recombination of previously existing elements—ideas, facts, discoveries, procedures, concepts, principles, systems and so forth. Rarely, if ever, does an author create a work that is entirely new. For example, writers of fiction often draw bits and pieces of their characters and plots from other fictional works they have read. The same is true of software authors. For example, it's likely that any spreadsheet program could be said to be derived to some extent from *VisiCalc*, the first computer spreadsheet.

However, a work is derivative for copyright purposes only if its author has taken a *substantial* amount of a previously existing work's *expression*. As discussed in detail in Chapter 7, *Scope of Copyright Protection for Software*, copyright only protects an author's expression of her ideas, facts, systems and discoveries, not the ideas, facts, systems and discoveries themselves. Thus, a new computer spread-

Computer disco

sheet would not be derivative of *VisiCalc* or *Lotus 1-2-3* unless its creators copied substantial portions of the protected expression in those programs—their computer code, structure, sequence and organization or the protected elements of the user interface.

How much is substantial? Enough so that the average intended user of the work would conclude that it had been adapted from or based upon the previously existing work. Enough so that, absent consent to use the material from the preexisting work, the second work would constitute an infringement on the copyright in the first work. This is, of course, a judgment call and in close cases opinions may differ as to whether one work is derivative of another.

EXAMPLE 1: Quaid Software created a program called *CopyWrite* that "unlocked" a copy protection program called *Prolok* manufactured by Vault Corp. In doing so, Quaid copied a 30-character source code sequence from *Prolok*. Vault Corp. sued Quaid for copyright infringement and lost. The court held Quaid had not copied enough code from *Prolok*—only 30 characters from over 50 pages of source code—for *CopyWrite* to be considered a derivative work of *Prolok*. (*Vault Corp. v. Quaid Software Limited*, 847 F.2d 255 (5th Cir. 1988).)

EXAMPLE 2: In the EDL computer language, Whelan created a program called *Dentalab* designed to automate the bookkeeping functions of dental offices. Jastrow created a very similar program in the BASIC language. He did not directly translate the *Dentalab* code into BASIC. Rather, he copied the way *Dentalab* instructed the computer to receive, assemble, calculate, hold, retrieve and communicate data; and the way data flowed sequentially from one program function to another. Whelan sued Jastrow for infringing on the copyright in her program and won. The court held that Jastrow's program was derivative of *Dentalab* because it so closely copied its structure, sequence and organization. (*Whelan v. Jastrow* 797 F.2d 1222 (3rd Cir. 1986))

The rest of this section will try to help you determine whether your work is a derivative work.

1. Altering an Original Work

Let's say you change an original software work by altering the code, adding additional code, or eliminating code. Have you created a derivative work? If the new work contains a substantial amount of material from the original work, the answer is "yes."

If you own the copyright in the original work, you're entitled to create any number of derivative works based upon it. But, even if you don't own the copyright in the original work, you may still be entitled to alter it solely for your personal use. (See Section D below for detailed discussion.) But you may not distribute or otherwise commercially exploit your derivative work without permission from the copyright owner of the original work.

EXAMPLE 1: The large accounting firm Gray & Grim licenses one copy of a new tax accounting program called *Lie-R-s*. Firm employees rewrite two program modules to improve the package's processing speed. The revised program is a derivative work. It would constitute copyright infringement for Gray & Grim to distribute this improved version of *Lie-R-s* without permission from the copyright owner of the original *Lie-R-s* (see Section A).

EXAMPLE 2: The publisher-copyright owner of *Lie-R-s* decides to make significant revisions in the package that will make it easier for small accounting firms to use. However, the publisher makes the revisions in a way that leaves the program basically intact. It markets this new version to small accounting firms under the name *White-Lie-R-s*. *White-Lie-R-s* is a derivative work based on the original *Lie-R-s*. The publisher should place a copyright notice on it and register it with the Copyright Office.

EXAMPLE 3: A Gray & Grim programmer who has used *Lie-R-s* decides to write her own tax accounting package. Although the new package accomplishes roughly the same tasks as *Lie-R-s*, and the programmer was inspired by some of its ideas, it's fundamentally different and uses no *Lie-R-s* code. This is a new and original work and, assuming the employee did the programming at work as part of her job, belongs to Gray & Grim as a work made for hire. The fact that she was inspired to write the new package by using *Lie-R-s* is of no legal significance.

a. Computer graphics

Digitized graphic images that are protected by copyright (for example, photographs, drawings) are commonly stored in computers. Such images can easily be combined and altered to create new graphics. As with text, any graphic that is based upon or recast from a preexisting image can be considered derivative of the earlier image and thus subject to its copyright. However, as with text, there is a point where the changes in the original image are so great, and the surviving portions of the original so minor, that the new image cannot be said to be recast or based upon the original. Instead, a new independently copyrightable work has been created.

EXAMPLE: Suzy uses an image digitizer and video camera to capture certain copyrighted art works in her computer. She then alters these works in several ways to produce related but different designs and produces a disk containing these designs that she sells as part of a clip-art package. One of the original artists recognizes his work in several of the designs and sues Suzy for copyright violation. If a judge is also able to see the connection between Suzy's designs and the original artwork, the artist will probably win. If, on the other hand, the resemblance only exists in the artist's eye, the artist will most likely lose.

b. New organization of existing material

A derivative work can be created simply by reorganizing existing material, without adding anything new. For example, you can create a derivative computer program by reversing the order of the routines, or putting them in alternating order, or making similar changes. Again, only the owner of the right to prepare derivative works (or someone who has obtained authorization from such owner) is authorized to do this.

2. Translations

A translation of a work from one language to another—whether a human or computer language—is a very common type of derivative work. It is usually necessary, therefore, to obtain permission from the copyright owner to translate a program into a new source code language.

3. Transferring Software From One Medium to Another

"Media" refers to whatever physically holds or carries computer code or output, such as the tape, disk, screen, printout or ROM on which software is housed. Changing the media in which an original work is fixed normally creates a derivative work consisting of the expression as fixed in the new media. And, regardless of what new media is used, a copyright infringement occurs if you don't first obtain permission from the owner.

4. Compare—Computer Output Is Not a Derivative Work

When you run a program on a computer in order to create something, that something is generally not a derivative work of the program. Rather, it is simply computer output that is owned by its creator. For example:

EXAMPLE 1: Pierre uses a computer graphics program to create a new wallpaper design. The design is not a derivative work of the graphics program.

EXAMPLE 2: Barbara uses a database program to create and manage a publishing company's sales and accounting information. The database is not a derivative work of the database program.

EXAMPLE 3: Art uses a spreadsheet program to create a number of spreadsheets for his business. The spreadsheets are not derivative works of the spreadsheet program.

Provided that the three requirements for copyright protection discussed in Chapter 2, *Copyright Basics*, are met (fixation, originality and minimal creativity), the design, database and spreadsheets are entitled to copyright protection in their own right. Such protection is totally independent of, and unrelated to, the particular programs used to create each item.

C. Protecting Derivative Works Where You Own the Prior Work

You don't need to get permission to create a derivative work if you already own the original work (or at least the right to prepare derivative works from and make copies of the original work). But there are steps you can take to give the new work maximum copyright protection.

First, the work should contain a proper copyright notice (see Chapter 3, *Copyright Notice*).

Second, as a general rule, if your derivative work contains a substantial amount of new code, or it's very valuable (no matter how minor your changes), it should be registered with the Copyright Office. The relationship between derivative works and copyright registration is discussed in more detail in Chapter 4, *Copyright Registration: The Basics*.

D. When You Don't Need Permission to Create a Derivative Work Based on Others' Prior Work

In the following instances it is not necessary to seek anyone's permission to create a derivative work of someone else's prior work.

1. Preexisting Material in the Public Domain

You don't need permission to create a derivative work based on expression that is in the public domain. Public domain material belongs to the world and anyone is free to use it in any way she wishes. We discuss the public domain in detail in Chapter 2, *Copyright Basics* and Chapter 7, *Scope of Copyright Protection for Software*.

Determining whether all or part of a computer program is in the public domain is far more difficult than for most other types of works because there are many different ways to legally protect software. Software may be protected not only by copyright (which is the focus of this book), but by patent, trademark and trade secret laws as well. We discuss these other protections for software in Chapter 15, *Other Legal Protections for Software*.

The fact that all or part of a program may not be protected by copyright doesn't mean it isn't protected by one or more of these other laws. For example, the ideas, discoveries, methods, procedures, processes, systems, concepts, principles, algorithms and facts embodied in software (or any other work) are not protected by copyright. But all these things could be protected by patents or under trade secret laws.

If you're not sure whether an item you want to use is in the public domain, seek legal assistance or get permission to use it from its owner.

Fair Use of Protected Expression

Even if a derivative work author uses someone else's protected expression, permission may not be required if the use constitutes a "fair use." Pursuant to the fair use privilege, an author may take a *limited* amount of the protected expression in preexisting works without the copyright owner's permission. Whether or not a use is fair is determined according to the facts and circumstances of the particular case. Courts consider the purpose of the use (whether for educational or commercial purposes, for example), the nature of the preexisting expression, the amount of preexisting expression taken, and whether the use reduces the value of the copyright owner's rights in the preexisting expression. As a general rule, questions regarding fair use almost always arise in the context of litigation where a person or business accused of infringing a copyright defends by saying, "No, I didn't infringe; my activity is protected by the fair use doctrine." Accordingly, we cover this subject in Chapter 13, *Software Copyright Infringement: What It Is, What to Do About It, How to Avoid It*.

---

2. Adaptations for Personal Use

Under Section 117 of the Copyright Act, the *lawful owner* of a copy of a computer program has the right to make a back-up copy for personal use. If the original copy is transferred, however, the copy must also be transferred with it or destroyed.

Section 117 also gives the lawful owner of a program copy the right to create an adaptation of the program provided that is "created as an essential step in the utilization of the computer program in conjunction with the [owner's] machine and in no other manner." In other words, the owner of a program copy may create her own derivative work so long as it is only for her own personal use. (*Foresight Resource Corp. v. Pfortmiller*, 719 F.Supp. 1006 (D.Kans. 1989).)

Under this adaptation right, the lawful owner of a program copy is entitled to create enhancements or otherwise alter the program from the one she lawfully purchased. She is completely within her legal rights, as long as she doesn't:

- Copy, distribute, display or perform the work itself for commercial purposes; or
- Sell the derivative copy or give it away.

EXAMPLE: The large accounting firm Gray & Grim buys one copy of a tax accounting program called *Lie-R-s*. Firm employees rewrite two program modules to improve the package's processing speed. So long as Gray & Grim uses this derivative work solely to improve the copies of *Lie-R-s* that it has legitimately purchased and uses in-house, no infringement of the copyright owner's exclusive right to prepare derivative works has occurred. However, if Gray & Grim distributes its derivative work to other accounting firms without the copyright owner's permission, the owner's copyright in the original work, which includes the exclusive right to make derivative works, would be infringed.

a. Who can exercise the adaptation right?

By its own terms, Section 117 applies only to "the owner of a copy of a computer program." Most courts have interpreted this language literally and have held that Section 117's back-up and adaptation rights apply only to owners of program copies, not licensees. In other words, a person who purchases a program copy outright may make back-ups and adaptations, but a person who licenses a copy may not exercise such rights unless they are granted in the license agreement. (*S.O.S., Inc. v. Payday, Inc.*, 886 F.2d 1081 (9th Cir. 1988).)

For various reasons, software owners often don't want their customers tinkering with their software. For example, a software publisher would usually prefer that a customer buy an enhanced feature from the publisher rather than create one himself. One of the principal reasons software is usually licensed rather than simply sold outright as books or records are, is to prevent the customer from exercising this adaptation right.

The mere act of licensing a program copy, rather than selling it outright, would appear to prevent the end user from exercising the Section 117 adaptation rights (provided that the license is valid). But, just to make sure, license agreements typically provide that the user cannot alter or adapt the software.

Assuming the license satisfies the basic principles of contract law (that is, it represents a true bargained-for agreement on the part of the user, involves some benefits on both sides, and isn't unduly oppressive), it's probably legal and binding according to its terms. See Chapter 12, *Transferring Software Copyright Ownership and Use Rights*, for more on this.

E. Derivative Works Compared with Compilations

A derivative work is not the same as a compilation. A "compilation" is a work created by selecting, organizing and arranging previously existing material in such a way that the resulting work as a whole constitutes an original work of authorship. Compilations differ from derivative works because the author of a compilation makes no changes in the preexisting material and need not add any new material of her own. Moreover, protectible compilations can be created solely from material that is in the public domain.

1. Fact Compilations (Databases)

A protectible fact compilation is created by selecting and arranging facts or other items that are in the public domain. Any computer databases consisting of data that are not individually protected by copyright is a fact compilation.

EXAMPLE: Trademark Research, Inc. compiles and publishes a computer database containing federal trademark registrations. The database is a fact compilation because the individual trademark records are in the public domain.

See Chapter 9, *Computer Databases*, for a detailed discussion.

2. Collective Works

A compilation may also be created by selecting and arranging into a single whole work preexisting materials that are separate and independent works entitled to copyright protection in their own right. Such compilations are called "collective works." Any computer database containing data or other materials that are protected by copyright is a collective work.

EXAMPLE: ScanSearch compiles a computer database containing the full text of selected articles on federal tax law. Each article is entitled to copyright protection in its own right. The database as a whole is also protected as a collective work.

Other examples of collective works include newspapers, magazines and other periodicals in which separately protectible articles are combined into a collective whole, and encyclopedias consisting of independently protectible articles on various topics.

See Chapter 9, *Computer Databases*, for a detailed discussion. ■

CHAPTER

9

Computer Databases

Acomputer database (or "automated database" in Copyright Office parlance) is a body of facts, data or other information assembled into an organized format suitable for use in a computer. For a computer database to be constructed, a computer must be told (programmed) where the information placed in it is stored and how that information can be retrieved upon request. Accordingly, when a database is actually constructed, it consists of:

- the data, and
- the database software—that is, the unique set of instructions that defines the way the data are to be organized, stored and retrieved.

In this chapter we'll discuss copyright protection for the data in computer databases. The database software is protected in the same manner and to the same extent as any other computer software. Accordingly, protection for database software is covered throughout the rest of the book.

We'll look first below at the nature and extent of copyright protection for database data and then show how to register a computer database with the Copyright Office.

A. Types of Computer Databases

The variety of information contained on computer databases is nearly endless and growing rapidly. However, for our purposes they can be classified into two types: published databases and unpublished databases.

1. Published Databases

Published databases are those that are made available to the general public. These include databases that are available on-line—that is, the database is housed on a computer in a remote location and end-users retrieve information from the database via telephone lines or computer networks. Examples include large commercial on-line information services such as *America Online, Lexis-Nexis* and *DIALOG*. On-line services such as these are actually collections of many databases provided by a variety of publishers and other sources. The services negotiate contracts with the owners of the databases for the right to distribute them, and pay royalties based primarily on how much the database is used. Costs to use such services are usually based on a subscription fee plus usage charges for actual use of particular databases.

Thousands of computer databases are also maintained by universities, research institutions, government agencies and large corporations. Many of these can be accessed via the Internet—a global network of networks linking together tens of thousands of regional, state, federal, academic and corporate computer networks.

Still other published computer databases are available on CD-ROM disks or other magnetic storage media. For example, a CD-ROM database containing over 2 million patents issued by the United States Patent and Trademark Office has recently been published. The user purchases or licenses such databases directly from the publisher and uses them directly on her own computer, rather than accessing them via an on-line service or computer network. This allows the database publisher to bypass the on-line service and market its product directly to end users.

2. Unpublished Databases

As the name implies, unpublished databases are those not available to the general public. These include all types of computer databases created and maintained by businesses—for example, a database containing customer ordering and payment information, or a computerized list of auto parts used by an auto parts store. Many individuals also have their own private databases; for example, containing tax information, or a list of personal property for identification and valuation purposes in the event of fire or theft.

B. When Is the Data in Computer Databases Protected by Copyright?

Not all databases are protected by copyright, and even those that are may enjoy very limited protection. Below we explain why this is so.

1. Databases Are Compilations or Collective Works

First, a little copyright law background. The individual bits of data contained in many databases are not entitled to copyright protection on their own. For example, names and addresses or numerical data may not qualify for copyright in their own right. But the way the database creator selected and arranged all these bits of data may constitute an original work of authorship protected by copyright (see below). In other words, the individual materials contained in a database may not be entitled to copyright protection, but the selection and arrangement of the entire database may be. This type of database is called a fact compilation.

However, many databases contain items that qualify for copyright protection on their own—for example, a database containing the full text of copyrighted articles. This type of database is a collective work. A collective work is a special type of compilation. It is a work created by selecting and arranging into a single whole work preexisting materials that are separate and independent works entitled to copyright protection in their own right. As with fact compilations, there may be copyright protection for the selection and arrangement of the materials making up a collective work.

Of course, some databases contain both protectible and unprotectible material, and are therefore both fact compilations and collective works.

2. Database Selection and Arrangement Constitutes Protected Expression

You may be wondering why any compilation should be protected by copyright. The author of a compilation does not really create anything new, he merely selects and arranges preexisting material; so what is there to protect? For example, say that you compile a computer database listing the 1,000 baseball cards you consider most desirable for collectors listed in order of desirability. What makes such a database protectible is the creativity and judgment you would have to employ in deciding which of the thousands of baseball cards in existence belong on your list of the 1,000 most desirable cards and in deciding what order the names should appear on the list. It is this selection and arrangement of the material comprising a compilation that constitutes protected expression.

The copyright in a protectible fact compilation or collective work extends only to this protected expression—that is, only to the compiler's selection and arrangement of the preexisting material, not to the preexisting material itself.

3. Minimal Creativity Required for Protection

A work must be the product of a minimal amount of creativity to be protected by copyright. This requirement applies to fact compilations as well as all other works. The data contained in a factual compilation need not be presented in an innovative or surprising way, but the selection and/or arrangement cannot be so mechanical or routine as to require no creativity whatsoever. If no creativity was employed in selecting or arranging the data, the compilation will not receive copyright protection.

In a landmark decision on fact compilations, the U.S. Supreme Court held that the selection and arrangement of white pages in a typical telephone directory fails to satisfy the creativity requirement and is therefore not protected by copyright. (*Feist Publications, Inc. v. Rural Telephone Service Co.* 111 S.Ct. 1282 (1991).) There are doubtless many other types of compilations that are unprotectible for the same reason.

Copyright Does Not Protect Hard Work

In the past, some courts held that copyright protected databases and other works that lacked originality and/or creativity if a substantial amount of work was involved in their creation. These courts might have protected a telephone directory, for example, if the authors had personally verified every entry. However, the Supreme Court outlawed this sweat of the brow theory in the Feist decision. It is now clear that the amount of work done to create a database or other work has absolutely no bearing on the degree of copyright protection it will receive. As discussed in detail in Chapter 7, *Scope of Copyright Protection for Software*, copyright protects only fixed, original, minimally creative expressions, not hard work.

The *Feist* decision caused great concern in the database industry because many databases would appear to involve no more creativity in their compiling than telephone book white pages. Does this mean they are not entitled to copyright protection? The answer is not entirely clear. However, database publishers should take heart from the Supreme Court statement in *Feist* that only a very minimal degree of creativity is required for copyright protection and that the vast majority of compilations should make the grade.

Nevertheless, for a database to be protected by copyright (and registrable by the Copyright Office), the selection, arrangement and/or coordination involved in its creation must rise to the level of original authorship.

Arguably, the *arrangement* of the data in databases is never minimally creative because it is the database software that arranges the data into the form requested by the searcher, not the compiler of the database. (But, of course, the software is entitled to separate copyright protection.) However, the *selection* of the data to be included in a database may pass the minimal creativity test, at least where less than all of the available information on a particular topic is included. For example, a database containing the titles of every article written on toxic waste disposal in the United States since 1980 would likely not qualify for protection. No creativity would be required to select the data in such a database. On the other hand, a database consisting of what the database's compilers consider to be the most useful and important articles on toxic waste would likely be entitled to protection. Creativity and judgment would have to be employed to select which articles to include in such a database.

Databases whose creation was dictated solely by mechanical or functional considerations will likely not be protectible. Examples of databases that likely lack copyright protection include:

- exhaustive lists or collections of all the data on a given topic—for example, an alphabetical list of all the parts contained in Ford automobiles.
- databases whose selection, arrangement and/or coordination was determined by external guidelines or rules—for example, a database containing the names and addresses of contributors to the Republican Party under 50 years of age who voted for Pat Buchanan in the 1996 presidential primaries and for Ross Perot in the general election and who subscribe to *Penthouse* magazine.
- databases that are so commonplace in their parameters that a great possibility exists that someone else would arrive at the same selection—for example, a database of physicians' phone numbers, names and addresses arranged according to their medical specialties.

One of the first post-*Feist* cases dealing with computer databases illustrates that the more "value-added" features a database publisher adds to the raw facts contained in a database, the more likely it will be copyrightable. The case involved a computerized database of state trademarks. The state trademark records were themselves in the public domain. However, the publisher added to each trademark record a code indicating the type of mark, modified the state records' description of the mark to conform to standard descriptions, divided the data into separate search fields, and added search indices to facilitate computer searches of the records. The court held that the publisher's "selection, coordination, arrangement, enhancement, and programming of the state trademark data" satisfied the originality and creativity requirements set forth in the *Feist* decision. (*Corsearch, Inc. v. Thomson & Thomson,* Guide to Computer L. (CCH) 46,645 (S.D.N.Y. 1992).) In other words, the database qualified for copyright protection.

4. Using Raw Data From Protected Databases

As discussed above, the copyright in a fact compilation extends only to the selection, coordination and arrangement of the data contained in the compilation and to any new expression the database author adds—for instance, instructions on how to use the database. The raw data itself is not protected. This is sometimes called a thin copyright.

Since the copyright in a fact compilation extends only to the compiler's selection and arrangement of the facts, the raw facts or data themselves are not protected by copyright. The Supreme Court has stated that the raw facts may be copied at will and that a compiler is even free to use the facts contained in another's compilation to aid in preparing a competing compilation. (*Feist Publications, Inc. v. Rural Telephone Service Co.* 111 S.Ct. 1282 (1991).) But the competing work may not feature the exact same selection and arrangement as the earlier compilation—provided that this selection and arrangement passes the minimal creativity test as described in the previous section.

This means that a database user may extract the individual bits of data from a fact compilation database without incurring liability for copyright infringement, but may not copy the entire database since this would involve copying the copyright owner's protected expression—that is, selection and arrangement. Thus, for example, the court held that the copyright in the state trademark database discussed above extended only to the publisher's "internally generated information and to its particular enhancements" to the state trademark records. The state trademark records themselves were not protected. Anyone could extract those records from the database and select and arrange them to create her own database without violating the publisher's copyright.

Copyright protection is greater where a database is a collective work—a work consisting of materials entitled to their own copyright protection. In this event, the database owner holds a thin copyright in the selection and arrangement of the entire database, and the items contained in the database may be protected individually. For example, each article contained in a full-text bibliographic database may be protected by copyright, as well as the selection and arrangement of the database as a whole.

Increased Protection for Databases in Europe: The EC Database Directive

The European Community (EC), which comprises most of the nations of Western Europe, enacted a final directive on the legal protection of commercial databases in early 1996. The Directive requires greater protection for databases than is available under U.S. law.

The Directive establishes two new sui generis (unique) rights for the makers of databases. It gives them the right to:

- prevent unauthorized extraction of all or a substantial part of the data from a database for commercial purposes, and

- prevent unauthorized re-utilization of all or part of the contents of a database for commercial purposes.

In other words, even if the data in a database lack sufficient creativity to qualify for copyright protection, the database maker can still prevent unauthorized extraction (copying) or use of the data. However, if the data in a database cannot be independently created, collected or obtained from other sources, the database maker may be required to grant licenses to those who wish to extract or use it.

These rights are to be available whenever a database maker has made a substantial investment in obtaining, verifying or presenting the contents of a database. They are to last for 15 years. However, if substantial changes are made to the content of a database, it receives a new 15-year term of protection.

Protection under the Directive is available only to nationals of members of the EC. Other countries will obtain such protection only if they offer comparable protection to databases of European nationals and if a bilateral agreement is reached. Current U.S. law does not provide comparable protection for databases, so U.S. residents will not enjoy the protection afforded by the Directive.

What all this means is that it may be illegal for you to extract the data from a database located in Europe, but perfectly legal to copy the same data from a database located in the U.S. However, legislation is being considered to amend U.S. law along the lines of the Directive.

C. Registering Contents of Computer Databases

If a computer database is protected by copyright, it should be registered with the Copyright Office for all the reasons discussed in Chapter 4, *Copyright Registration: The Basics*. Since most databases are frequently updated or revised, the Copyright Office has instituted a special group registration procedure whereby a database and all the updates or other revisions made within any three-month period may be registered in one application. This way, a database need only be registered a maximum of four times per year, rather than each time it is updated or revised.

Database Software Must Also Be Registered

The discussion below is only about how to register the selection and arrangement of the contents of a computer automated database. It does not cover registration of computer software designed to be used with databases to facilitate retrieval of the data. See Chapter 4, *Copyright Registration: The Basics*, for coverage of that topic.

---

1. Databases Qualifying for Group Registration

To qualify for group registration, a database must meet all of the following conditions:

- all of the updates or revisions must be fixed or published only in machine-readable copies,

- all of the updates or revisions must have been created or published within a three-month period, all within the same calendar year,

- all of the updates or revisions must be owned by the same copyright claimant (see Chapter 4, *Copyright Registration: The Basics*, Section E1 for more on copyright claimants),

- all of the updates or revisions must have the same general title, and
- the updates or revisions must be organized in a similar way.

2. Completing Form TX

Form TX must be submitted for a group database registration. Here's how to fill it out:

Space 1: Title

At the Title of this Work line, insert the following statement: "Group registration for automated database titled _____; published/unpublished (*choose one*) updates from _____ to _____." Give the earliest and latest dates for the updates included in the group registration. Remember, this time period must be three months or less, all within the same calendar year.

Use the Publication as a Contribution line to give the following information: The date (day, month, year) that is represented by the marked portions of the identifying material submitted as a deposit (see Section 3 below). Also indicate the frequency with which revisions are made—for example, "daily," "weekly," "monthly."

Space 2: Author(s)

You need to give the requested information about every author who contributed any appreciable amount of protectible material to the version of the work being registered. We're talking about the compilation/collective work authorship here, not the authorship of the individual articles or other works in the database. After the words "Nature of Authorship," give a brief general statement of the nature of the particular author's contribution to the work. Examples: "updates," "revisions," "revised compilation," "revised and updated text."

Space 3: Creation and Publication

Give the year in which the author(s) completed the group of updates or revisions being registered.

If the updates or revisions have been published, you must give the date (month, day, year) and nation of publication. This should be the *last* date on which revisions were added during the three-month period covered by the application. When is a database published? This is not exactly clear. For copyright purposes, "publication" means distributing or offering to distribute copies of a work to the public on an unrestricted basis. It is unclear whether on-line availability for the user constitutes publication. The Copyright Office leaves it up to the copyright owners to determine whether their database has been published.

Space 4: Claimants

Follow the instructions in Chapter 5, Section C on how to complete this space.

Space 5: Previous Registration

If the database has been previously registered, check the last box and give the previous registration number and date. If more than one previous registration has been made for the database, give the number and date of any one previous registration.

Space 6: Derivative Work or Compilation

Space 6 must be completed if the updates or the database and its updates contain a substantial amount of previously published, registered or public domain material. Leave Space 6 blank if the material contained in the database and its updates is entirely new and never before registered or published.

Preexisting Material (Space 6a): State "previously registered material," "previously published material," or "public domain data" for a new database that has not been previously registered or published, but that contains an appreciable amount of previously registered, published or public domain material.

For a previously published or registered database that has not been revised or updated periodically, describe the preexisting material as "previously published database" or "previously registered database," or "database prior to (*earliest date represented in the present group of updates*)."

Material Added to This Work (Space 6b): Describe the updates or revisions or new database being registered for the first time and specify the frequency of these updates or revisions—for example, "weekly updates," "daily revisions," or "revised compilation updated monthly."

Spaces 7 and 8

Leave these spaces blank. They're not applicable to computer databases.

Spaces 9, 10, 11: Fee, Correspondence, Certification, Return Address

Follow the instructions in Chapter 5, Section C on how to complete these spaces.

3. Deposit requirements for group registration

You must submit the following deposit with your registration application:

- *Identifying material:* Samples meeting the following requirements:
  - 50 representative pages of printout (or equivalent units if reproduced in microfilm) from a single-file database; or
  - 50 representative complete data records (not pages) from each updated data file in a multiple-file database.

    The printout or data records must be marked to show the copyrightable revisions or updates from one representative publication date (if the database is published) or from one representative creation date (if the database is unpublished) within the three-month period covered by the registration; or, alternatively, you may deposit a copy of the actual updates or revisions made on a representative date.

- *Descriptive statement:* In addition, you must submit a brief, typed descriptive statement providing the following information:
  - the title of the database
  - the name and address of the copyright claimant
  - the name and content of each separate file in a multiple-file database, including its subject, origin(s) of the data, and the approximate number of data records it contains
  - information about the nature, location, and frequency of the changes within the database or within the separate data files in multiple-file databases and
  - information about the copyright notice, if one is used, as follows:

- For a machine-readable notice, transcribe the contents of the notice and indicate the manner and frequency with which it's displayed—for example, at user's terminal only, at sign-on, continuously on terminal display or on printouts.
- For a visually perceptible notice on any copies of the work (or on tape reels or containers), include a photocopy or other sample of the notice.

4. Non-Group Registration

If your database doesn't qualify for group registration, or for some reason you do not wish to use that procedure, simply complete Form TX in the same manner as for any other compilation. You should deposit the first and last 25 pages of a single-file database. If the database consists of separate and distinct data files, deposit one copy of 50 complete data records (not pages) from each file, or the entire file, whichever is less. You must also include a descriptive statement for a multiple-file database containing the same information described in Section 3 just above.

If the database is fixed in a CD-ROM, deposit one complete copy of the CD-ROM package, any instructional manual, and a printed version of the work which is fixed on the CD-ROM if such an exact print version exists. The deposit must also include any software that is included as part of the package. A print-out of the first and last 25 pages of the software source code is acceptable. If the software contains trade secrets, other deposit arrangements can be made. See the discussion in Chapter 5, Section D, above.

D. Using Contracts to Protect Databases

Given the limitations on copyright protection for computer databases, and the fact that some databases are probably not even entitled to these protec-

tions, the database industry has been placing increasing reliance on the use of contracts to prevent unauthorized use of databases. These include form contracts as well as negotiated agreements tailored for individuals or institutions. They may appear in traditional print, in shrink-wrap form, on a computer screen as part of software or online or in a combination of these formats.

Samples of numerous database agreements can be found in Contracts in the Information Industry III, published by the Information Industry Association; 202-986-0280; www.infoindustry.org.

1. Terms of Use

Though terms vary from company to company and from product to product, database contracts typically contain provisions restricting access and specifying conditions of use. These agreements limit users' ability to use the contents of databases in ways that the law would otherwise allow.

> **EXAMPLE:** A Dun & Bradstreet online license for its database provides: "You are granted a nonexclusive, nontransferable limited license to access and use for research purposes the Online Services and Materials from time to time made available to you … are prohibited from downloading, storing, reproducing, transmitting, displaying, copying, distributing, or using Materials retrieved from the Online Services. You may not print or download Materials without using the printing or downloading commands of the Online Services."

Other agreements used for databases in CD-ROM format make explicit reference to fair use. For example, a Lexis-Nexis contract for CD-ROMs allows users to "create a printout of an insubstantial portion of material retrieved from the Licensed Databases," and reproduce them "to the extent permitted under the fair use provisions of the Copyright Act."

Terms may be more restrictive for particularly valuable or sensitive information. Dun & Bradstreet, for example, has strict practices for its sensitive information, such as information relating to bankruptcy filings. For these products, it restricts third party distribution and exercises extreme caution in its licensing practices. By keeping direct control over distribution, the company is always in a position to recall or expand earlier data. It also conducts thorough background checks on potential patrons and extends licenses only to those who are creditworthy and risk-free.

2. Limitations on Contracts

Despite their usefulness, there are important practical limitations on the effectiveness of database contract restrictions. Most significant is the privity requirement for enforcing a contract—that is, a contract may only be enforced against a person who has agreed to it. A contract is not enforceable against third persons who never agreed to it. For example, the contract accompanying a CD-ROM database product binds only the initial contracting parties; it would not bind third parties who come into possession of the CD-ROM. Once such a CD-ROM leaves a database owner's possession, the owner has no practical way of preventing third parties from obtaining it. ∎

CHAPTER

Multimedia Programs

Multimedia programs combine text with visual images (both still photos and video and film clips) and sound (including music, ordinary speech and dramatic performances). Software is usually included to enable the user to search, retrieve and manipulate the material.

Multimedia programs often present some difficult copyright problems. Below we examine the copyright aspects of obtaining permission to use third-party content in multimedia programs. We also discuss in detail the Copyright Office registration and deposit requirements for such works.

A. Obtaining Permissions for Multimedia Works

Many multimedia programs consist, at least in part, of preexisting materials. This poses special copyright problems. Consider this example: AcmeSoft, a large software publisher, plans to publish a multimedia history of the Persian Gulf War on a CD-ROM disk. AcmeSoft wants the disk to contain a variety of preexisting materials about the Gulf War, including:

- text from several articles and books
- photos from books, magazines and other sources
- video clips from many television programs
- raw feeds from news reporters
- music to be used as background to the images and text, and
- third-party application software programs to support graphics, sound and animation.

AcmeSoft intends to incorporate hundreds of separate items into its multimedia package. This sounds like a fine idea for a multimedia product. However, AcmeSoft must overcome a substantial legal obstacle before it can publish the work: It must obtain permission to use at least some—and probably most—of the preexisting material. Obtaining such permission can involve tracking down many different copyright owners and negotiating licenses to use their material. This can be very time consuming and expensive. Indeed, some software developers have discovered that the multimedia works they had in mind are not economically feasible in today's marketplace because the legal and licensing costs are too high.

1. When Copyright Permissions Are Needed

Whether permission is needed to include any given item in a multimedia work depends first, of course, on who owns it. Review the detailed discussion of copyright ownership in Chapter 11, *Initial Copyright Ownership*, and Chapter 12, *Transferring Software Copyright Ownership and Use Rights.*

Generally, permission is not needed to use materials specially created for a multimedia work, whether by employees or third parties. The developer will automatically own materials created by employees within the scope of their employment and will routinely obtain an assignment of copyright rights from nonemployees (or have them sign work made for hire agreements). For sample employment and independent contractor agreements, refer to *Software Development: A Legal Guide*, by Stephen Fishman (Nolo Press).

However, permission may be needed to use preexisting materials created by nonemployees (or by employees before they became employees). But even in this event, permission will not be needed if the material is (1) in the public domain, or (2) the use of the material clearly constitutes a fair use.

We discuss the public domain in Chapter 2, *Copyright Basics.*

Fair use is discussed in detail in Chapter 13, *Software Copyright Infringement: What It Is, What to Do About It, How to Avoid It.*

To reiterate this important point, if a preexisting work is protected by copyright and the intended use cannot qualify as a fair use, permission must be obtained to include it in a multimedia work.

I SEE MANY MEDIUMS IN YOUR FUTURE.

2. Obtaining Multimedia Permissions

With the notable exception of the music industry, which has had a collective system for granting permissions and collecting royalties in place for many decades, obtaining permission to use copyrighted materials in a multimedia project is a difficult, time-consuming and often chaotic process.

Obtaining multimedia permissions can be especially hard because, for a variety of reasons, many copyright owners are reluctant to grant any multimedia permissions. Some have decided against granting permissions for the time being because of uncertainty about how much such rights are worth. Others fear they will lose control over unauthorized copying if their works are distributed in electronic form. And still others intend to launch their own multimedia ventures and don't want to help potential competi-

tors. Some owners will grant permission, but only for exorbitant amounts of money (there are no standard rates for such permissions).

Securing a multimedia permission, then, can require a good deal of persistence, salesmanship and creative negotiating. A two-step process should be followed:

1. Find out who owns the rights that are needed.
2. Negotiate and have signed a written release or multimedia license agreement.

Reference

Refer to Chapter 13 of *Software Development: A Legal Guide* by Stephen Fishman (Nolo Press), for a detailed discussion of how to obtain permission to use text, photographs, film and video, drawings and other artwork and music. A sample multimedia license agreement is also included in that book.

B. Copyright Notice for Multimedia Works

Where a multimedia work consists of both written material and a computer disk, both should contain their own copyright notice. The computer disk should have a label containing a notice. In addition, it's a good idea to include a notice on the title screen on the computer when the disk is activated, or in an about or credit box. Alternatively, the notice could be displayed on screen continuously when the disk is used. (See Chapter 3, *Copyright Notice*, for detailed discussion.)

C. Copyright Registration for Multimedia Works

For all the reasons discussed in Chapter 4, *Copyright Registration: The Basics*, multimedia works can and should be registered with the Copyright Office. It is always permissible to register each element of a multimedia work separately—manual, text, photos, video, etc. However, it may not be necessary to do

so. An entire multimedia work can be registered at one time on one registration form for one $20 fee provided that:

- the copyright claimant is the same for all elements of the work for which registration is sought (the claimant is the original author of the item being registered or the person or entity to whom all the author's rights have been transferred; see Chapter 4, Section E1 for detailed discussion), and
- all such elements are published together as a single unit—that is, they are distributed together as part of a single multimedia package (usually in the same package).

An example will help make these rules clear. Assume that AcmeSoft in the example in the above section has finished developing its multimedia history of the Persian Gulf War. The multimedia package consists of a CD-ROM disk containing text, photos, video and music; and a printed manual explaining how to use the CD-ROM. Let's assume that AcmeSoft employees wrote the manual and some of the text on the CD-ROM. AcmeSoft employees also compiled all the materials together on the CD-ROM—that is, they chose which preexisting and new text, photos, videos and music to use, how much of each item to use and where to place each item in the multimedia work.

AcmeSoft is the copyright owner of the manual, which was written by its employees. AcmeSoft employees also wrote some of the text on the CD-ROM. All the other material on the CD-ROM was licensed by AcmeSoft—that is, it obtained permission to copy and distribute it on the CD-ROM from the copyright owners. AcmeSoft does not own the copyright in any of these individual bits of text, photos, video or music. However, AcmeSoft does own a compilation copyright in the multimedia work—that is, a copyright in the selection, arrangement and coordination of all the material on the CD-ROM disk, which was performed by AcmeSoft employees.

This selection, arrangement and coordination constitutes a work of authorship if it is original and minimally creative. (See Chapter 9, *Computer Databases*, for detailed discussion of copyright protection for compilations.) This compilation copyright extends to all the material on the CD-ROM, both new and preexisting, both owned by AcmeSoft and licensed from third party copyright owners.

AcmeSoft may register all the elements to which it claims copyright ownership—the manual, the CD-ROM text it owns and the compilation copyright covering the selection and arrangement of all the CD-ROM material—on a single application for a single fee. Why? Because the copyright claimant for all the elements of the multimedia work for which protection is sought by AcmeSoft is the same: AcmeSoft; and all these elements are being published together as a single unit at the same time.

What about registering all the individual bits of preexisting text, music, photos and video that AcmeSoft licensed? That's the province of the copyright owner of each individually licensed item. AcmeSoft may not register such material since it is not the copyright claimant (owner). But note that this preexisting material will end up being deposited with the Copyright Office by AcmeSoft when it deposits the whole CD-ROM (see below). However, this deposit will not result in registration of such material since AcmeSoft is not the copyright claimant in this example.

1. Which Form to Use

Form PA is usually used for registration of multimedia works. Form PA is used to register any multimedia work containing an audiovisual element—photos, video, film clips, etc. A multimedia work consisting solely of text is registered on Form TX. If a multimedia work does not contain any audiovisual elements, but does contain sounds in which sound-recording authorship is claimed, Form SR is used.

2. Filling Out Form PA

We discuss how to fill out Form PA and Form TX in detail in Chapter 5, *The Registration Process.* Following are the significant differences when registering a multimedia work on either form.

Space 1: Nature of This Work

State "audiovisual work" in the Nature of this Work box in Space 1.

Space 2: Name of Author

State only the name of the author(s) for the elements of the work for which copyright is claimed in this registration. If preexisting materials have been licensed from third parties, don't mention their names in Space 2. In our example above, AcmeSoft would be listed as the author in Space 2. The third parties from whom AcmeSoft licensed the material included in the work are not the authors of the work AcmeSoft is applying to register, and AcmeSoft's copyright does not cover their work.

Nature of Authorship. The elements of the multimedia work in which original authorship is claimed should be listed here. AcmeSoft in our example above could state "compilation and editing of preexisting text, photographs, video clips, film clips and music plus new original text."

Or, more broadly, if you are entitled to claim copyright in an audiovisual work, artwork on computer screens and the text of a computer program, all embodied on a CD-ROM, Space 2 of your application would read: "audiovisual work, artwork on computer screens and text of computer program."

If your CD-ROM claim consists solely of an original compilation of preexisting facts and data, the authorship in Space 2 would be described as "original compilation of preexisting data." Note that this nature of authorship statement is appropriate only where the applicant claims no authorship in the preexisting data, where the CD-ROM contains no computer program authorship the applicant is entitled to claim copyright in, and where the work is not marketed with a print manual. In this situation, you should submit a cover letter along with your application explaining what original selection, arrangement or ordering is present—that is, explaining what work was involved in selecting and arranging the preexisting material on the CD-ROM. Such selection and arrangement must rise to the level of original authorship to be copyrightable and therefore registrable. (See detailed discussion of compilation copyrights in Chapter 9, *Computer Databases.*)

Space 6: Derivative Work or Compilation

If a multimedia work contains preexisting material such as photos, video and film clips, preexisting text, or music, Space 6 must be completed. If the work contains all new material, Space 6 can be left blank.

Space 6a must be filled in if the multimedia work is a derivative work; it is left blank if the work is just a compilation. As discussed in detail in Chapter 8, *Derivative Works and Use of Preexisting Material,* a derivative work is a work that is created by adapting and recasting preexisting material into a new work of authorship. Most multimedia works containing preexisting material are derivative works—the preexisting material is edited and combined with other preexisting materials and new material to form a new original work of authorship. It's not necessary to individually list every preexisting work included in the multimedia work; a general description is sufficient. For example, AcmeSoft in our example above could state "previously published text, film and video footage, graphics and music."

Space 6b: Material Added to This Work

Space 6b calls for a description of the new material added to the preexisting material in which copyright is claimed. You can simply repeat what you stated in the Nature of Authorship box in Space 2 above.

3. Deposit Requirements

The Copyright Office has imposed special deposit requirements for multimedia works. One complete copy of the best edition of a multimedia work first published in the United States must be deposited with the Copyright Office. Everything that is marketed or distributed together must be deposited, whether or not you're the copyright claimant for each element. This includes:

- the ROM disk(s),
- instructional manual(s), and
- any printed version of the work that is sold with the multimedia package (for example, where a book is sold with a CD-ROM).

Multimedia works used on computers typically contain software that enables the user to operate the CD-ROM or other storage medium and access, search and retrieve the data and produce screen displays. The deposit must include identifying material for any such software in which copyright is claimed by the applicant. (But if the software is simply licensed from a third party, no such deposit is necessary.)

The software deposit must consist of a printout of the program source code or object code. However, the entire program need not be deposited. Instead, the applicant may deposit a printout of the first and last 25 pages of the source code. Or, if the program contains trade secrets, the applicant has the option of depositing:

- the first and last 25 pages of source code with the portions containing trade secrets blacked out, or
- the first and last ten pages of source code with no blacked out portions, or
- the first and last 25 pages of object code, together with any ten or more consecutive pages of source code with no blacked out portions, or
- for programs consisting of less than 25 pages, the entire program with the trade secret portions blacked out. (See Chapter 5, *The Registration Process*, for detailed discussion of software deposit requirements.)

The Copyright Office wishes multimedia applicants to inform it as to whether the operating software is part of the multimedia work, and where it is embodied—for example, on a CD-ROM disk or other medium.

The Copyright Office has experienced some difficulty in viewing a number of CD-ROM products that have been deposited because it doesn't have the proper equipment. When this occurs, the Copyright Examiner will require the applicant to make a supplemental deposit of identifying material. For example, it might require a supplemental deposit of a video tape showing the audiovisual elements in which authorship is claimed. ■

Initial Copyright Ownership

Computer software, documentation, and other works of authorship that satisfy the criteria for copyright protection discussed in Chapter 2, *Copyright Basics*, are protected automatically upon creation. At that same moment, the author or authors of the work become the initial owner(s) of the copyright in the work. This chapter is about determining who these authors—and initial owners—are.

There are several basic ways to author software and thereby become its initial owner.

- An individual may independently author the software.

- An employer may pay an employee to author the software, in which case the employer is an author under the work made for hire rule.

- A person or company may hire an independent contractor (not an employee) to create software on its behalf.

- Two or more individuals or entities may collaborate to become joint authors.

We discuss each of these types of authorship (and initial ownership) in turn.

A. Independent Authorship by an Individual

Software created by a single self-employed individual is initially owned by that individual.

> **EXAMPLE:** Lucy is a self-employed freelance programmer. She writes a program that helps investors analyze stock market data. Lucy created the program on her own time—that is, not on anyone's behalf. Lucy owns all the copyright rights in the program.

An individual copyright owner may exercise any of her copyright rights herself. For example, she may reproduce and sell her work herself, or authorize others to do so. She may also transfer her ownership in whole or in part to others. (See Chapter 12, *Transferring Software Copyright Ownership and Use Rights*.) An individual copyright owner can do whatever she wants with her copyright in the United States; she is accountable to no one.

Impact of Community Property Laws on Copyright Ownership

In states that have community property laws, property that is acquired while people are married is usually considered to belong to both spouses equally. This means that individual software authors who reside in California, Nevada, New Mexico, Idaho, Arizona, Texas, Louisiana, Washington and Wisconsin may be required to share ownership of their copyrights with their spouses. (See discussion in Chapter 12, *Transferring Software Copyright Ownership and Use Rights*.)

B. Ownership of Works Created by Employees (Works Made for Hire)

Today, probably the majority of software is created by employees, not self-employed programmers working on their own behalf. Copyrightable works created by an employee within the scope of employment are owned by the employer. Such works are called works made for hire. Not only is the employer the owner of the copyright in a work made for hire, it is considered to be the work's author for copyright purposes. This is so whether the owner is a human being or a business entity, such as a partnership or corporation. As the author, the employer is entitled to register the work with the Copyright Office, exercise its copyright rights in the work such as distributing it to the public, permit others to exercise these rights or sell all or part of its rights. The employee—the actual creator of the work—has no copyright rights at all. All she receives is whatever compensation the employer gives her.

This result is considered to be an obvious and natural consequence of the employer-employee relationship. It's assumed that an employee understands and agrees to this when she takes a job. Thus, an employer doesn't have to tell an employee that it will own copyrightable works she creates on the employer's behalf; the employee is supposed to know this without being told. Likewise, the employer need not have the employee sign an agreement relinquishing his copyright rights—he doesn't have any to relinquish.

> **EXAMPLE:** John is hired to work as a programmer for AcmeSoft, Inc. John is AcmeSoft's employee. He is assigned to a project to develop a new database program. All of John's work on the program will be work made for hire to which AcmeSoft owns all the copyright rights. AcmeSoft need not tell John this or have him sign a copyright transfer agreement.

At first glance, this all sounds very straightforward. It would seem that both the hiring firm and the worker should always know who owns any copyrightable works created by the worker. However, things are not always so simple. In fact, it can be very difficult to know for sure who owns software created by workers for hiring firms. This is because there are problems in determining:

- just who is an employee, for copyright ownership purposes, and
- when a work is created within the scope of employment.

1. Problem 1: Who Is an Employee?

A person is an employee for copyright ownership purposes if the person or entity on whose behalf the work is done has the right to control the manner and means by which the work is created. If the hiring firm does not have the right to control the worker, he is not an employee for copyright purposes; rather, he is an independent contractor and a whole other set of ownership rules apply as discussed in Section C below.

The requisite right of control is present, and the worker will be considered an employee, where the hiring firm has the right to direct the way the worker performs, including the details of when, where and how the work is done.

It makes no difference what the parties call themselves or how they characterize their relationship. If the person or entity on whose behalf the work is done has the right of control, the person hired is an employee and any protectible work he creates within the scope of his employment is a work made for hire. It also makes no difference whether the control is actually exercised. All that matters is that the hiring firm has the right to exercise such control. (CCNV v. Reid, 109 S.Ct. 2166 (1989).)

When a legal dispute arises as to whether the creator of a protectible work is an employee, the courts are supposed to examine a variety of factors to determine if the hiring firm has the right to control the worker. The rules are ambiguous and given to highly subjective interpretation. Thus, if a dispute later arises, it is always possible that a judge could decide the programmer an employer thought was an employee was actually an independent contractor. The consequences could be disastrous for the employer and quite surprising for the worker. (See Section E below.)

**Factors Considered In
Determining Employee Status**

Here is a list of some of the factors the Supreme Court has said judges might consider in determining if a hiring firm has the right to control a worker. As stated above, if the right to control is present, the worker is an employee; if not, he is an independent contractor. This is not an exclusive list, and no single factor is determinative:

- the skill required to do the work (highly skilled workers are less likely to perform their work under a hirer's direct control)

- the source of tools and materials used to create the work (workers who supply their own equipment are less likely to be under a hirer's control)

- the duration of the relationship (long-term relationships indicate control by the hiring firm and employee status)

- whether the person who pays for the work has the right to assign additional projects to the creative party

- who determines when and how long the creative party works

- the method of payment (paying by the hour indicates an employment status, payment by the job indicates the worker is an independent contractor)

- who decides what assistants will be hired, and who pays them

- whether the work is in the ordinary line of business of the person who pays for the work (if yes, the hiring party will more likely control the worker)

- whether the creative party is in business for herself

- whether the creative party receives employee benefits from the person who pays for the work

- the tax treatment of the creative party.

However, legal decisions in recent years make clear that two of the factors listed in the sidebar above are of prime importance in determining whether a worker is an employee for copyright ownership purposes:

- whether the hiring firm pays the worker's Social Security taxes, and

- whether the hiring firm provides the worker with employee benefits.

Obviously, if a company (or individual) hires someone and pays their Social Security taxes and gives him employee benefits, the company (and worker) must believe that the worker is an employee. Why else would the hiring firm incur these expenses? A hiring firm that pays such expenses for a worker will almost always treat him like an employee and have the right to control his work.

In one important decision, the court held that a part-time programmer employed by a swimming pool retailer was not the company's employee for copyright purposes and the programmer was therefore entitled to ownership of a program he wrote for the company. The court stated that the company's failure to provide the programmer with health, unemployment or life insurance benefits, or to withhold Social Security, federal or state taxes from his pay was a "*virtual admission*" that the programmer was an independent contractor. These factors were so important they outweighed other factors that indicated a right of control by the pool company, such as the fact that the company could assign the programmer additional projects. (*Aymes v. Bonelli*, 980 F.2d. 857 (2d Cir. 1992).)

Another reason the tax treatment of the worker is so important is fairness. It is manifestly unfair for a hiring firm to treat a worker like an independent contractor for tax purposes (and thereby avoid paying payroll taxes and employee benefits) and then turn around and claim he is an employee for copyright ownership purposes (and thereby claim that his copyrightable creations are works made for hire). Simply as a matter of fairness, a worker must be treated consistently for both tax and copyright purposes.

All the other courts that have considered this question have reached the same result as Aymes v. Bonelli. No court has allowed a hiring firm to treat a worker as an independent contractor for tax purposes and an employee for copyright purposes.

The moral for hiring firms: If a hiring firm doesn't pay a worker's Social Security taxes or provide him with benefits available to other employees, the firm should assume he is an independent contractor for copyright ownership purposes. See the following section for a discussion of what this means in practical terms.

Given the track record of the courts, a hiring firm can probably safely assume that a formal salaried employee for whom the firm pays Social Security taxes and provides employee benefits would be considered an employee for copyright purposes. When anything short of a formal, salaried employment relationship is involved, there is always the risk it will not be deemed an employment relationship for copyright purposes. See Section 3 below for what hiring firms should do in this event.

What should software workers do? A worker should always clarify her employment status before beginning any job. If you're supposed to be an employee, you should be put on the hiring firm's payroll and classified and treated as an employee for tax, salary, job benefit and all other purposes. If you're going to be an independent contractor, you should have the firm sign a written independent contractor agreement that states what it is you're supposed to do, how and how much you will be paid and who will own the copyright in your work. If you are going to transfer ownership of your work to the hiring firm, try to make the transfer contingent on payment as provided under the agreement. For a sample independent contractor agreement, refer to *Software Development: A Legal Guide* by Stephen Fishman (Nolo Press).

2. Problem 2: When Is a Work Created Within the Scope of Employment?

Even when it is clear that an employment relationship exists, serious disputes can arise as to whether an employee who creates a copyrightable work did so within the scope of employment. For example, many people employed in the software industry are moonlighters—they create software or other copyrightable works on their own time, using their own equipment, alone or with others. If such work is closely related to an employee's job duties, the employer may claim an ownership interest in it, while the employee insists that he is the sole owner.

Where such a dispute arises, the courts look to the common law of agency relationships to determine whether a work was created within the scope of employment. Under these rules, an employee's work is created within the scope of employment if it:

- is the kind of work the employee is paid to perform, and
- occurs substantially within work hours at the work place, and
- is performed, at least in part, to serve the employer. (*Miller v. CP Chemicals, Inc.,* 808 F.Supp. 1238 (D.S.C. 1992) (a case based on the Restatement of Agency).)

These rules are ambiguous and given to highly subjective and inconsistent interpretations. Consider these real-life examples where opposite results were reached in cases involving similar fact situations:

EXAMPLE 1: Miller was a supervisor who worked at CP Chemical's quality control lab. He created a program for making mathematical computations needed for in-process adjustments to one of CP's products. Miller was paid by the hour and created the program primarily at home on his own computer during off hours, and without any overtime pay. Nevertheless, the court held that the program was created within the scope of Miller's employment and was therefore owned by CP Chemicals, not Miller. The court held that the first and third factors listed above favored CP Chemicals, while only the second favored Miller. The court reasoned that "the ultimate purpose of the development of the computer program was to benefit CP by maximizing the efficiency of the operation of the quality control lab." (Miller v. CP Chemicals, Inc., 808 F.Supp. 1238 (D.S.C. 1992).)

EXAMPLE 2: While employed by Avtec Systems, Pfeiffer created a computer program for managing and presenting satellite data. The court held that the program was not created within the scope of Pfeiffer's employment, and was therefore not a work for hire owned by Avtec. This was so even though the program performed many of the same functions found in other programs used by Avtec and by Pfeiffer during his employment by Avtec. The court found that the majority of Pfeiffer's work on the program was done on his own time and his own computer in furtherance of a personal hobby, and not to satisfy any specific work obligations for Avtec. (Avtec Systems, Inc. v. Pfeiffer, 805 F.Supp. 1312 (E.D.Va. 1992).)

The result of all this is that an employee (or ex-employee) might be able to legitimately claim that he should own the copyright in his contribution to a software project because he was not hired or paid to create that work. As you might expect, such disputes can get messy and very expensive, particularly if the software involved is quite valuable.

3. What Employers Should Do About Problems 1 and 2

The best policy for companies and individuals who employ others to create software or any other copyrightable works is to have all creative (or potentially creative) employees sign employment agreements. Such an agreement should:

- Make clear that the employee's job duties include creating, or contributing to the creation of, software and other copyrightable works;
- Provide that any software or copyrightable works the employee creates as part of his job are works made for hire to which the company owns all the copyright rights; and
- Provide that if for some reason such works are determined not to be works made for hire, the employee assigns in advance (transfers) to the employer all his copyright rights in such works.

A signed document like this will help convince a court that creating software or other copyrightable works was part of the employee's job. And the assignment provision will serve as a back-up in case a court determines the work made for hire rule does not apply.

Not only should new employees assign their copyright rights to their employers, but existing employees should do so as well if they haven't already. See *Software Development: A Legal Guide* by Stephen Fishman (Nolo Press) for a detailed discussion and sample employment agreements.

4. Copyright Concerns for Moonlighting Employees

Employees of software companies who create software or other copyrightable works on their own time need to be very careful. As discussed above, an employer owns the intellectual property rights in software created by an employee within the scope of her employment. Moreover, an employer may even have certain rights over works created outside the scope of employment if the employee used the employer's resources (for example, did a substantial amount of the work during business hours or used the employer's equipment). If an employee creates a valuable work on her own time, an unscrupulous employer might try to assert ownership over it by claiming that the work was within the scope of employment or the employee used its resources.

To avoid potential problems, if you plan to do software-related work on your own, make sure you inform your employer and obtain written acknowledgment that the employer will not have an ownership interest in such work. For obvious reasons, it's a lot easier to get that acknowledgment before you do the work than after.

EXAMPLE: Art Acres is hired by AcmeSoft to help develop communications software. On his own time, Art decides to develop a computer game. Art's work on the game is in no way connected with his work for AcmeSoft, nor could the game be competitive with any of AcmeSoft's products. However, just to make sure there will be no problems, Art informs his boss about his plans and gets AcmeSoft to sign the following agreement:

March 1, 200_

Bill Fates
President
AcmeSoft, Inc.
1000 Main St.
Seattle, WA 90002

Dear Bill:

This letter is to confirm the understanding we've reached regarding ownership of my computer game program, tentatively titled *You Are What You Eat.*

You acknowledge that my program will be written on my own time and shall not be written within the scope of my employment with AcmeSoft, Inc.

It is expressly agreed that I shall be the owner of all rights in the program, including the copyright. Furthermore, AcmeSoft, Inc., will sign all papers necessary for me to perfect my ownership of the entire copyright in the work.

If this agreement meets with your approval, please sign below to make this a binding contract between us. Please sign both copies and return one to me. The other signed copy is for your records.

Sincerely,

Art Acres

Art Acres

I agree with the above understanding and represent that I have authority to make this agreement and to sign this letter on behalf of AcmeSoft, Inc.

Bill Fates

Bill Fates

Date: March 2, 200_

C. Ownership of Works Created by Independent Contractors

Subject to the important exceptions discussed in Section C1 below, works created by independent contractors (nonemployees) are not works made for hire, that is, the independent contractor, *not the hiring party*, owns the copyright in what she creates. This means that the hiring party must always require independent contractors to sign written agreements assigning their copyright ownership to the hiring party. To be effective, such an agreement must be signed *before* the independent contractor begins work on the project. (*See Software Development: A Legal Guide*, by Stephen Fishman (Nolo Press) for sample independent contractor agreements.)

EXAMPLE 1: AcmeSoft hires Dana, a freelance programmer, to help code a new version of an accounting program. Dana is not AcmeSoft's employee. AcmeSoft has Dana sign an independent contractor agreement before commencing work. The agreement contains a provision whereby Dana assigns to AcmeSoft all his ownership rights in the work he will perform on the accounting program. Dana completes his work and his relationship with AcmeSoft ends. Because of the signed agreement, AcmeSoft owns all the copyright in Dana's work.

EXAMPLE 2: Assume instead that AcmeSoft hires Dana, but fails to have him sign an independent contractor agreement transferring his ownership rights. When Dana completes his work he, not AcmeSoft, will own the copyright in the code he created for AcmeSoft. This is so even though AcmeSoft paid for it! (See Section E below for detailed discussion.)

1. When Works Created by Independent Contractors Are Works Made for Hire

Certain types of works created by independent contractors are considered to be works made for hire to which the hiring party automatically owns all the copyright rights—provided that:

- the hiring party and independent contractor both sign an agreement *before* the work is created stating that the work shall be a work made for hire, and
- the work falls within one of the following work for hire categories:
  - a contribution to a collective work (a work created by more than one author such as an anthology)
  - a part of an audiovisual work
  - a translation
  - "supplementary works" such as forewords, afterwords, supplemental pictorial illustrations, maps, charts, editorial notes, bibliographies, appendixes and indexes
  - a compilation
  - an instructional text
  - a test and test answer materials
  - an atlas

User manuals and other software documentation (whether printed or on-line) written by independent contractor technical writers would probably fall within the instructional text, supplementary work and/or collective work categories. This means that such works can be works made for hire if the independent contractor signs an agreement to that effect before starting work.

> **EXAMPLE:** AcmeSoft, Inc. hires Alberta, a freelance technical writer, to write the user manual for its new small business accounting software. AcmeSoft has Alberta sign an agreement before she commences work stating that her work on the manual shall be a work made for hire. When Alberta finishes her work, the manual will be considered a work made for hire to which AcmeSoft owns all the copyright rights. Indeed, AcmeSoft will be considered the author for copyright purposes. Alberta will have no copyright ownership interest whatsoever in the manual.

2. Does Software Fall Within a Work Made for Hire Category?

Unfortunately for software companies, most of the work made for hire categories set out above don't seem to have much application to computer programs themselves (but merely to their written documentation). A computer program might arguably constitute a collective work, compilation or even an audiovisual work, but no court has so ruled. Moreover, in 1982 the Copyright Office officials stated that in their opinion none of the work made for hire categories applied to software. For this reason, until the question is conclusively resolved by court or congressional action, persons who hire independent contractors to create, or contribute to the creation of, computer programs should never rely on the work made for hire rule but rather should obtain an assignment of rights as discussed in Section B3 above.

Caution

Many software companies have independent contractors who work on software projects sign agreements stating that their work shall be a work made for hire. Such an agreement will not make the contractor's work a work made for hire unless it falls within one of the categories listed above. At best, it might be viewed as an assignment of the contractor's copyright rights. (See the discussion in Section E.)

Special Rules for California

California law provides that a person who commissions a work made for hire is considered to be the employer of the creator of the work for purposes of the workers' compensation, unemployment insurance and unemployment disability insurance laws. (Cal. Labor Code Section 3351.5(c); Cal. Unemployment Insurance Code Sections 621, 686.) No one is entirely sure what impact this has on persons or entities who commission works made for hire. Neither the California courts nor state agencies have addressed the question. However, it may mean that the commissioning party has to obtain workers' compensation coverage for the creative party and might be liable for any injuries she sustains in the course of her work. It might also mean that special penalties could be assessed against a commissioning party who willfully fails to pay the creative party any monies due her after she is discharged or resigns. These potential requirements and liabilities are one reason why it might be desirable for those commissioning work in California not to enter into work made for hire agreements, and instead have the creator assign the desired copyright rights to the commissioning party in advance.

Assignments Can Be Terminated After 35 Years

One theoretical disadvantage of using an assignment of rights as opposed to a work made for hire agreement is that an assignment can be terminated by the author or her heirs 35 to 40 years after it is made. (See Chapter 12, *Transferring Software Copyright Ownership and Use Rights*, for a detailed discussion.) However, this disadvantage is essentially meaningless because little or no software can be expected to have a useful economic life of more than 35 years.

D. Jointly Authored Works

Given the time and expense involved in creating new software, joint authorship has become common in the software industry. Two or more companies or individuals (or combinations of companies and individuals) will agree to jointly contribute to the creation of new software. When such a work is completed, it is normally jointly owned by its creators—that is, each contributing author shares in the ownership of the entire work.

A joint author's life is not as simple as that of an individual copyright owner. There may be restrictions on what each joint author can do with its ownership share, and joint authors must account to each other for any profits they receive from commercial exploitation of the joint work.

1. When Is a Work Jointly Authored?

A work is jointly authored automatically upon its creation if (1) two or more authors contributed material to the work; and (2) each of the authors prepared his or her contribution with the intention that it would be combined with the contributions of the other authors as part of a single unitary work. We'll refer to such works as "joint works."

The key to determining whether a work is a joint work is the authors' intent at the time the work is created. If the authors intended that their work be absorbed or combined with other contributions into an integrated unit, the work that results is a joint work. It is not necessary that the authors work together or work at the same time. Indeed, it is not even necessary that they know each other when they create their respective contributions.

> **EXAMPLE:** Peter and Mary agree to create a new computer game. Peter designs the game and Mary does the actual computer coding. When the game is completed, it will be jointly owned by Peter and Mary because they intended that their respective contributions be combined to form one integrated work—a new computer game.

a.   How much material must a person contribute to be a joint author?

The respective contributions made to a joint work by its authors need not be equal in terms of quantity or quality. But to be considered a joint author, a person must contribute more than a minimal amount of work to the finished product.

Most courts require that a person's contribution be separately copyrightable in its own right for him or her to be considered a joint author. A person who merely contributes ideas or other unprotectible items is not entitled to an ownership interest in the work's copyright unless the parties expressly agree to it, preferably in writing.

As the following real-life example illustrates, simply describing to a programmer what a program should do is not sufficient to become a joint author. Such a description will be viewed as a mere idea, not copyrightable expression.

> **EXAMPLE:** Ross and Wigginton decide to collaborate to develop a computer spreadsheet program. They agreed that Ross would write the computational component of the program (the engine) and Wigginton design the user interface. Ross provided Wigginton with a handwritten list of potential commands that should be incorporated in the user interface. The two later went their own ways and Wigginton's interface was combined with another engine component and marketed by Ashton-Tate. Ross filed suit, claiming that Wigginton's interface was a joint work. The court held that the interface was not a joint work because Ross's list of commands was not separately copyrightable. The court stated that the list was merely an unprotectible idea, telling Wigginton what tasks Ross believed the spreadsheet interface should perform. (Ashton-Tate Corp. v. Ross, 916 F.2d 516 (9th Cir. 1990).)

 Copyright Tip

It is always a good idea for collaborators to have a written agreement setting forth their respective interests in the work to be written. This way, if one contributor is found not to be a joint owner of the work because he did not contribute protectible expression to it, he would still be entitled (as a matter of contract law) to the ownership interest stated in the collaboration agreement. (See Section 2 below for further discussion of collaboration agreements.)

b.   Employees are not joint authors

An employee who contributes copyrightable work to a joint work is not a joint author. As discussed above, copyrightable works created by employees within the scope of employment are owned by the employer; indeed the employer is deemed author of such a work made for hire. Thus, the employer would be the joint author, not the employee.

EXAMPLE: Simon and Sally agree to jointly create a computer arcade game. Simon hires Suzy, a skilled programmer, to aid him in coding the game. The code Suzy creates is a work made for hire owned by Simon, Suzy's employer. Suzy is not a joint author of the game, only Simon and Sally are.

c. Joint authors need not be human beings

A joint author doesn't have to be a human being. A corporation, partnership or other business entity can also be a joint author. For example, two software companies can agree to jointly develop new software. This type of strategic partnering is now common.

EXAMPLE: Sunnydale Software, Inc. and AcmeSoft, Inc. agree to jointly develop a new software package designed to enable dairy farmers to automate milk production. Sunnydale and AcmeSoft employees work together to design, code and test the new software. The software package, called Milkrun, is a joint work that is also a work made for hire. The joint authors are Sunnydale and AcmeSoft.

2. Joint Authors' Collaboration Agreement

A written collaboration agreement is not legally required to create a joint work; an oral agreement is sufficient. However, as Samuel Goldwyn supposedly once said, "an oral agreement isn't worth the paper it's printed on." It is vital that joint authors draft and sign a written agreement spelling out their rights and responsibilities. This avoids innumerable headaches later on.

A collaboration is like a marriage—no two are the same. It is not, therefore, a good idea to simply fill in the blanks on a form agreement. Rather, prospective joint authors need to think carefully about the form their relationship should take and custom draft an agreement that suits their particular needs. To get a feel for the most important points such an agreement should cover, see the chapter on custom software development in *Software Development: A Legal Guide*, by Stephen Fishman (Nolo Press).

3. Joint Authors' Rights and Duties in the Absence of a Collaboration Agreement

The drafters of the Copyright Act realized that not all joint authors would be prudent enough to enter into a written (or even oral) agreement setting forth their ownership interests, rights and duties. To avoid chaos, they made sure that the act contained provisions governing the most important aspects of the legal relationship between joint authors who fail to agree among themselves how their relationship should operate. You might think of these provisions as similar to a computer program's "default settings" that control the program when the user fails to make his own settings.

a. Ownership interests

Unless they agree otherwise, joint authors each have an undivided interest in the entire work. This is basically the same as joint ownership of a house or other real estate. When a husband and wife jointly own their home they normally each own a 50% interest in the entire house, that is, they each have an undivided one-half interest. Similarly, joint authors share ownership of all five exclusive rights that make up the joint work's copyright.

b. Right to exploit copyright

Unless they agree otherwise, each joint author has the right to exercise any or all of the five copyright rights inherent in the joint work: any of the authors may reproduce and distribute the work or prepare derivative works based upon it (or display or perform it). Each author may do so without the other joint authors' consent.

c. Right to license joint work

Unless they agree otherwise, each joint author may grant third parties permission to exploit the work—on a nonexclusive basis—without the other joint authors' consent. This means that different authors may grant nonexclusive licenses of the same right to different persons!

> **EXAMPLE:** Manny, Moe and Jack are joint authors of a Power Macintosh utility program. Manny gives software publisher A the nonexclusive right to distribute the program in North America. Moe gives the same right to Publisher B, and Jack to Publisher C. The result, perfectly legal, is that three publishers have the right to publish the program at the same time.

Copyright Tip

Anyone who wishes to purchase an exclusive right in a joint work should require signatures by all the authors to ensure that they all agree to the transfer. (See Chapter 12, *Transferring Software Copyright Ownership and Use Rights*, for a detailed discussion.)

d. Right to transfer ownership

Finally, unless they agree otherwise, each author of a joint work may transfer her entire ownership interest to another person without the other joint authors' consent. Such person then co-owns the work with the remaining authors. But a joint author can only transfer her particular interest, not that of any other author.

EXAMPLE: DataBest, Inc. and Bellevue Software are joint authors of psychiatric testing software. Databest decides to sell its ownership interest in the software to AcmeSoft, Inc. Since Databest and Bellevue have not agreed among themselves to restrict their transfer rights in any way, Databest may transfer its interest to Acmesoft without Bellevue's consent (but Databest could not transfer Bellevue's ownership interest to AcmeSoft without its consent). When the transfer is completed, AcmeSoft will have all the rights Databest had as a joint author.

e. Duty to account for profits

Along with these rights, each joint author has the duty to account to the other joint authors for any profits received from his use or license of the joint work. All the joint authors are entitled to share in these profits. Unless they agree otherwise, the profits must be divided among the authors according to their proportionate interests in the joint work. (Note, however, that such profits do not include what one author gets for selling his or her share of the copyright.)

> **EXAMPLE 1:** Recall our example above where Manny, Moe and Jack were joint authors of a utility program. Manny licenses the program to a large software publisher for an 8% royalty. Since there are three joint authors, they are each entitled to a one-third share of the royalty.

> **EXAMPLE 2:** Bill and Lee are joint authors of a text-based computer adventure game. Bill writes a screenplay based on the game and sells it for $10,000. Lee is entitled to one-half of the $10,000.

It may not seem fair that a joint author—who goes to the time and trouble of exploiting the copyright in the joint work by getting it published or creating derivative works based upon it—is required to share his profits equally with the other joint authors, who did nothing. This is still another reason why it's wise to enter into a collaboration agreement.

f. What happens when joint authors die?

Absent a joint tenancy with right of survivorship agreement, a deceased individual joint author's heirs would acquire her share in the joint work. The other joint authors do not acquire a deceased owner's share (unless, of course, the deceased owner willed it to them, or the author died without a will and another joint author was related to her and inherited her interest under the general inheritance laws).

E. What Happens If a Hiring Firm Fails to Obtain Ownership of Works It Pays For?

Our discussion above should make clear that it's quite possible for a company or person to hire another person to create or contribute to the creation of software, pay for the work, and yet end up not owning the copyright in that person's work product. This can happen in a variety of ways:

- A worker the hiring firm thought was an employee turns out to be an independent contractor,
- The work performed by the employee was outside his or her scope of employment,
- The hiring firm fails to obtain a written assignment of copyright rights in advance from an independent contractor, or
- The hiring firm has an independent contractor sign a work for hire agreement, but the work does not fall within one of the work for hire categories enumerated in Section C1 above.

Whenever any of these things happen there are three possible consequences:

1. The creator of the work will be considered the sole copyright owner, or
2. The creator and hiring party will be considered to be joint authors and share ownership, or

3. The hiring party will be considered the sole copyright owner.

1. The Creator of the Work Owns the Copyright

First of all, unless the hiring firm can obtain an ownership interest by claiming joint authorship or by virtue of some written document (see below), the worker will solely own all of the copyright rights in her work product.

> **EXAMPLE 1:** The law firm of Dewey, Cheatum and Howe hires Sally, a freelance systems analyst and programmer, to design and code custom case management software for the firm. Sally is not Dewey's employee and signs no document transferring her ownership rights in her work to Dewey. Sally completes the program and is paid in full. Sally is also the sole copyright owner of the case management software. This means that Sally may sell the software to others, reproduce it, create derivative works from it or otherwise exercise her copyright rights in the software.

a. Hirer has nonexclusive license to use work

However, all will not be lost for the hiring firm. At the very least, a company or person who pays an author to create a protectible work has a nonexclusive license to use it as intended. (*Avtec Systems, Inc. v. Pfeiffer*, 805 F.Supp. 1312 (E.D.Va 1992).) This seems only fair, considering that the hiring party paid for the work. A person with a nonexclusive license in a work may use the work, but may not prevent others from using it as well. Nonexclusive licenses may be implied from the circumstances; no express agreement is required. (See detailed discussion of nonexclusive licenses in Chapter 12, *Transferring Software Copyright Ownership and Use Rights.*)

> **EXAMPLE 2:** Since Dewey in Example 1 paid Sally to create the case management software, it would have a nonexclusive license to use the software. But this would not prevent Sally from allowing others to use the software as well.

2. Joint Work Created

The best thing that could happen from the hiring firm's point of view would be for it to be considered a joint author of the work. This way, it would share ownership with the other creator(s). However, as discussed in Section D above, for a person or company to be considered a joint author, it must contribute actual copyrightable expression to the finished work. Simply describing how a program should function or contributing other ideas or suggestions is not sufficient.

> **EXAMPLE 3:** Assume that Sally in the examples above was aided by Dewey's employees. The employees contributed not only ideas, but actually helped design the program, contributing work that was separately copyrightable in its own right (flowcharts, for example). In this event, the software would probably constitute a joint work and would be jointly owned by Sally and Dewey. (See Section D above for a detailed discussion of joint works.)

3. Hiring Party Is Sole Copyright Owner Under Work Made for Hire Contract

As discussed in Section C above, many companies use form agreements with independent contractors that state that the contractor's work will be a work made for hire. But such an agreement will be effective only if the contractor's work falls within one of the work for hire categories enumerated in Section C1 above. Software may not fall into any of these categories. This means that the contractor's work will not be deemed a work made for hire even though he signed the agreement.

EXAMPLE 4: Assume that Dewey in the example above had Sally sign a contract stating that the case management software would be a work made for hire. Unfortunately for Dewey, such software does not come within one of the nine categories of specially commissioned works. This means that regardless of what the contract said, the work is not a work made for hire and Sally is the author and initial owner of the copyright.

However, it is possible that a court would interpret the work made for hire contract as a transfer by Sally to Dewey of all her copyright rights in her work. Sally would still be the initial owner and author, but Dewey would still end up owning all the copyright rights in the work—that is, Dewey would have the exclusive right to use and reproduce it, create derivative works based upon it, and so on. But it's also possible that a judge would rule the contract unenforceable and simply award Dewey a nonexclusive license. ■

12

Transferring Software Copyright Ownership and Use Rights

opyrights, as we've discussed, are a form of intellectual property. And like other forms of property, the rights that accompany copyright ownership can be sold or otherwise transferrred to another party. In Chapter 2, *Copyright Basics*, we discussed the rights that accompany copyright ownership. Here is a brief recap.

A software author automatically becomes the owner of a complete set of exclusive rights in any protected work he or she creates. These include the right to:

- reproduce the protected work,
- distribute copies of the work to the public by sale, rental, lease or otherwise (but this right is limited by the first sale doctrine which permits the owner of a particular copy of a work to sell, lend or otherwise dispose of the copy without the copyright owner's permission; but the right to rent software is limited by a special provision of the Copyright Act discussed in Section B3d below),
- prepare derivative works using the work's protected expression (that is, adapt new works from the original work), and
- perform and display the work publicly.

These rights are exclusive because only the owner of one or more particular rights that together make up copyright ownership may exercise it or permit others to do so. For example, only the owner of the right to distribute a program may sell it to the public or permit others—a publisher, for instance—to do so.

A. Overview of How Copyright Ownership Rights Are Transferred to Others

A transfer of copyright ownership rights must be in writing to be valid. There are two basic types of copyright transfers: exclusive licenses and assignments. Although these terms are often used interchangeably, there are some differences.

1. Licenses

A license is a grant of permission to do something. For example, when you get a driver's license the government gives you permission to drive a car. A copyright owner can give others permission to exercise one or more of the owner's exclusive rights listed above. Such a permission is also usually called a license. Licenses fall into two broad categories: exclusive and nonexclusive licenses.

a. Exclusive licenses

When a copyright owner grants someone an exclusive license it means that person (called the licensee) is the only person entitled to exercise the rights covered by the license. As mentioned, since the licensor is granting the licensee the exclusive right to exercise the rights covered by the license, an exclusive license is considered to be a transfer of copyright ownership. If you have the exclusive right to use something, you own it; that's what ownership is.

> **EXAMPLE:** AcmeSoft, a small software developer, creates a multimedia program on the history of World War II. Since it lacks the resources to effectively market the program itself, AcmeSoft grants an exclusive license to distribute the program in the United States to Scrivener & Sons, a well-established book publisher seeking entry into the electronic book market. Granting such an exclusive license means that only Scrivener may distribute the program in the U.S.; Scrivener owns this right. But AcmeSoft retains all its other copyright rights not covered by the license. For example, it retains the right to market the program outside the U.S. and to create derivative works based upon it (for example, a computer game).

A copyright owner's exclusive rights can be divided and subdivided and transferred to others in just about any way imaginable: by geographical area, computer platform, operating system, hardware, time or virtually any other way. Taking advantage of this sort of flexibility is often at the heart of a successful plan for getting a product protected by copyright distributed and sold in the marketplace.

EXAMPLE 1: AcmeSoft, a small start-up software developer, develops a new program and gives Behemoth Distribution, Inc., a software distribution company, an exclusive license to distribute the program for use on PCs in the United States. AcmeSoft also gives CDS, Inc., another distributor, the right to bundle the program with personal computers in Europe. (This type of exclusive license is called an exclusive territorial license.) Finally, AcmeSoft grants an exclusive license to DigiTek, Inc., a mainframe computer manufacturer, to bundle the program with its mainframes worldwide.

EXAMPLE 2: Jason grants Gameland an exclusive license to sell the Windows version of his computer game, *Kill or Die,* in the United States for three years. He grants Nintendo an exclusive license to sell a Nintendo version of the game throughout the world. He licenses the right to create a movie from the game (a derivative work) to Repulsive Pictures. He retains all his other rights and produces and sells a Macintosh version of the game himself.

Exclusive Licensee's Rights

Again, the holder of an exclusive license becomes the owner of the transferred right(s). As such, unless the exclusive license provides otherwise, she is entitled to sue anyone who infringes on that right while she owns it, and is entitled to transfer her license to others. She may also record the exclusive license with the Copyright Office; this provides many valuable benefits. (See discussion in Section F below.)

---

b. Nonexclusive licenses

A nonexclusive license gives someone the right to exercise one or more of a copyright owner's rights, but does not prevent the copyright owner from giving others permission to exercise the same right or rights at the same time. A nonexclusive license is not a transfer of ownership; it's a form of sharing.

Nonexclusive licenses (like all other licenses) can be restricted in all sorts of ways. Thus, you can grant a nonexclusive license to use (or sell your program for use) on one particular microcomputer in one country (or county) for a set period of time.

Except in cases where custom software is created for a single customer, software licenses with end users normally take the form of nonexclusive licenses. This way, the software owner can give any number of end users the right to use the software.

EXAMPLE: AcmeSoft creates a hot new program for identifying and locating lost cats. It grants nonexclusive licenses to dozens of fire departments and animal shelters throughout the country. These licenses give these end users the right to copy and use the program. Since these licenses are nonexclusive, there is no limit on the number AcmeSoft can grant.

We discuss nonexclusive licenses with end users in detail in Section C below.

As with exclusive licenses, nonexclusive licenses may be limited as to time, geography, media or in any other way. They can be granted orally or in writing. The much better practice, however, is to use some sort of writing; this can avoid possible misunderstandings and gives the nonexclusive licensee certain priority rights discussed in Section F4, below.

2. Assignments

The word "assignment" means a transfer of all the rights a person owns in a piece of property. So whenever a person or entity transfers all the copyright rights it owns in a work of authorship, the transaction is usually called an "assignment" or sometimes an "all rights transfer." An assignment must be in writing to be valid. When such a transaction is completed, the original copyright owner no longer has any ownership rights at all. The new owner—the assignee—has all the copyright rights the transferor formerly held (this may or may not be the entire bundle of copyright rights in the work).

Software publishers will often insist on such an assignment from a software author before publishing his work.

EXAMPLE: Otto develops a new Power Macintosh utility program and asks PubSoft, a large software publisher, to publish and distribute it. PubSoft agrees to do so, but only if Otto signs a publishing agreement assigning to PubSoft the entire copyright in the program. Otto signs the agreement. The result is that PubSoft, and only PubSoft, may copy and distribute the work or permit others to do so, or exercise any other part of the bundle of rights that make up the copyright in the work (such as creating a derivative work based on it—for example, revising the program for use on PCs). Otto has relinquished these rights. For all practical purposes, PubSoft now owns the copyright instead of Otto. However, PubSoft is obligated to pay Otto for these rights as set forth in the publishing agreement.

A software developer who creates an expensive custom software system for a single client may also assign all its copyright rights to the client, giving the client sole ownership of the system. For a detailed discussion of custom software development agreements and sample forms, refer to *Software Development: A Legal Guide,* by Stephen Fishman (Nolo Press).

EXAMPLE: Apollo Software develops a sophisticated scheduling program for the Acme Moving Company. Prior to creating the software, Apollo signed a development agreement with Acme containing a provision assigning all its copyright rights in the software upon its completion and acceptance by Acme and payment of Apollo's fee. When the software is accepted and paid for, Acme becomes the sole copyright owner.

Right to Terminate Copyright Transfers After 35 Years

We've all heard sad stories about authors or artists who sold their work for a pittance when they were young and/or unknown, only to have it become extremely valuable later in their lives or after their death. In an effort to protect copyright owners and their families from unfair exploitation, the Copyright Act gives individual authors or their heirs the right to terminate any transfer of their copyright rights 35 to 40 years after it was made. This special statutory termination right may be exercised only by individual authors or their heirs, and only as to transfers made after 1977. This termination right can never be waived or contracted away by an author. The owner of a work made for hire, whether an individual or a business entity such as a corporation or partnership, has no statutory termination rights.

EXAMPLE: Art, a teenaged video game enthusiast, creates a new and exciting computer arcade game in 1980. He sells all his rights in the game to Fun & Gameware for $500 the same year. The game becomes a best-seller and earns Fun & Gameware millions. Art is entitled to none of these monies, but he or his heirs can terminate the transfer to Fun & Gameware in the year 2015 and get back all rights in the game without paying Fun & Gameware anything.

This statutory termination right may be important to visual artists (painters and sculptors, for example), but, the fanciful example above aside, it probably doesn't mean much in the software world. Given the pace of development in the software industry, it is likely that little or no software will have any economic value 35 years after its creation.

B. Sales of Software Copies to End Users

Book and magazine publishers, record companies, photographers and artists and most other copyright owners usually sell their works outright to end users. The transaction works like this: Say you want to buy a book; you walk into a bookstore or call the publisher directly; you pay your money and you are sold a copy of the book. You now own the copy of the book.

Software copyright owners are also free to simply sell copies of their software, that is, sell floppy disks, CD-ROMs or digital copies of the software, to end users.

Today, however, virtually all software is licensed to end users rather than sold outright as books are. (We discuss software licenses in Section C.) But to understand why software owners prefer to license their work to end users, you must first understand what rights the purchaser of a copy of a copyrighted work has. Software licenses are used to take away most of these rights.

Note carefully that a software user doesn't have any of the ownership rights discussed below unless the software license grants him such rights or the license turns out to be legally invalid.

1. What Is a Copy?

For copyright purposes, a "copy" is defined as any material object in which a work of authorship is "fixed." Software transferred to CD-ROMs, floppy disks, hard disks and other media certainly qualifies as a "copy." Thus, a person who downloads a program to a hard disk from the Internet receives a "copy" of the program, just as person who buys the same program on a CD-ROM does.

Software contained in computer RAM may also qualify as a copy, so long as it stays in RAM for at least several minutes. Thus, copying occurs where a person downloads a program to RAM and uses it, even if it is never saved to a permanent storage medium such as a hard disk.

However, simply transmitting a computer program over the Internet probably doesn't involve making copies, even though temporary copies are stored in the RAM of various node computers on the Internet. These RAM copies likely exist for too short a time to be copies for copyright purposes. However, this is not a settled question.

2. Sales of Copies Do Not Transfer Copyright Ownership

Ownership of a copyright and ownership of a material object in which the copyrighted work is embodied—such as a computer disk—are entirely separate things. This means the sale or gift of a copy or copies of a program or other protected work does not operate to transfer the copyright owner's exclusive rights in the work. A copyright owner's exclusive rights can only be transferred by a written agreement. For example, a person who buys a CD-ROM or floppy disk containing a computer program owns that CD-ROM or disk, but acquires no copyright rights in the program copy contained on the disk.

3. Rights of Owners of Software Copies

The fact that a person who purchases a copy of a computer program acquires no copyright rights does not mean, however, that the purchaser has no rights at all. On the contrary, there are a number of things the purchaser can do with his copy.

a. Unlimited use rights

First, a software copy purchaser can use the program copy any way he wants. He can run it on any single computer he chooses, in any location, for any purpose. If he so chooses, a purchaser is free to use a program copy or copies to operate a service bureau and perform data processing for third parties. Or, he can permit third parties to use the software on a time-sharing basis. This is so even though these third parties might otherwise buy the program themselves from the copyright owner.

b. Right to copy the program into computer RAM

Of course, to utilize a program on a computer it is necessary to copy it from a permanent storage medium such as a floppy disk into the computer's memory (also known as RAM or random access memory). Such copying is specifically permitted by Section 117 of the Copyright Act, which provides that "the owner of a copy of a computer program … [may] make or authorize the making of another copy… of that computer program provided that such new copy… is created as an essential step in the utilization of the computer program in conjunction with a machine and that it is used in no other manner." But courts have held that this provision does not permit permanent copies to be made on computer disks or other permanent storage mediums. *(Allen-Myland, Inc. v. IBM Corp.*, 746 F.Supp. 520 (E.D.Pa. 1990).)

Of course, in the real world, end users usually copy the original copy of a program onto their computer's hard disk. This hard disk copy is what is then loaded into computer RAM. This copying onto a hard disk is apparently not allowed by Section 117. But making one copy of a lawfully possessed program onto a hard disk for use in one computer almost certainly constitutes a fair use of the original copy and is almost certainly permissible. (See Chapter 13 for a discussion of fair use.)

c. Right to make archival copies

Because the magnetic media upon which computer programs are normally stored can easily be damaged and the program rendered unusable, it is highly advisable to make a back-up or archival copy of a program on a floppy disk and store it in a safe place. Section 117 of the Copyright Act provides that program owners may make permanent copies of their programs "for archival purposes only." This means they can only be used internally and cannot be made accessible to third parties.

d. Right to sell or give away the program

A software copy purchaser also has the right to sell his copy of the program to anyone he chooses, for any price he desires, without getting the copyright owner's permission. Or, the purchaser may give away his copy.

e. Adaptation right

Section 117 of the Copyright Act also permits a program owner to modify and adapt the program for his own personal use. For example, he can upgrade it himself and thereby avoid having to purchase upgrades from the software publisher or other copyright owner. (See Chapter 8 for detailed discussion of this adaptation right.)

f. Reverse engineering

Finally, a software purchaser is free to reverse engineer the program. That is, figure out how it works. Reverse engineering can take many forms. One form of reverse engineering is decompiling a program's unreadable object code into readable code. Whether or not such decompilation is permissible or is a copyright infringement has been hotly debated. But some courts have held that decompilation is permissible under some circumstances when the information is used to create a noncompetitive product. (See Chapter 13.)

In any event, a purchaser of a software copy can use the information gained from reverse engineering not involving decompilation in any way he wishes. For example, he might create a competing program and go into competition with the seller of the original program.

4. Things Owners of Software Copies Can't Do

Since the purchaser of a copy of a program acquires no copyright rights, he can't exercise any of the copyright owner's exclusive rights listed at the beginning of this chapter.

a. No copies other than back-up and RAM copy

A purchaser can't make any copies of the program other than archival copies and a copy loaded into a single computer's RAM as mentioned above. If the purchaser sells or gives away the program, he must destroy these copies or give the permanent archival copies to the new owner.

Of course a purchaser can't make copies of a program and sell them, give them away or otherwise distribute them.

b. Copy can only be used on a single computer at a time

A single program copy can only be used on a single computer at a time. This means, for example, that if a purchaser owns a desktop computer and a laptop, and wants to use his program on both, legally he must buy two copies. Similarly, a purchaser cannot load a program onto his hard disk and then give his CD-ROM or floppy disk to someone else to run simultaneously on another computer.

Nor is it permissible for a program owner to make RAM copies for use in more than one machine simultaneously. For example, it would be impermissible for a user to insert a CD-ROM or floppy disk in his computer, load a program into RAM and then hand the CD-ROM or floppy disk to another user who would load the program into RAM on another computer.

c. No running the software on computer networks

Computers are often interconnected with each other through cables or phone lines. A local area network (or LAN) connects together two or more computers that are located nearby (usually in the same office or building). Typically, all the personal computers hooked up on the network can access or use programs or files from any disk drive or other storage device on any other computer on the network. In most networks, a file-server computer manages the transfer and flow of data on the network. If a user of one computer on the network wants to use a program contained on a storage device somewhere else on the network (either on the file-server or another computer), the program is downloaded from the storage device to the user's computer where it resides in RAM while in use. In effect, the user is loading the program into his computer's RAM from a hard disk or other storage device on somebody else's computer on the network. This way a single copy of a program located on a storage device on a single computer can be used by any number of computers.

Without permission from the copyright owner, the purchaser of a copy of a computer program may not use the program on a network. Remember, the purchaser may load a program into the RAM of only a single computer at a time. The multiple copies typically used in networks, although located only in volatile RAM, are not permissible without the copyright owner's permission. Persons or companies that want to use software on a network usually obtain a network/multi-user license from the copyright owner; or, in the case of mass-marketed software intended to be used in networks, such licenses are already included in the package (see Section C below).

d. No software rentals or lending

Software developers and publishers have long feared that letting users lend or lease their software to the public would cause software piracy to increase (a potential pirate could simply rent a software package and copy it). After years of lobbying by the software industry, Congress added a special provision to the Copyright Act in 1990 expressly forbidding the owner of a copy of a computer program from renting, leasing or lending the copy to the public for "direct or indirect commercial advantage." (17 U.S.C. 109.)

However, there are four exceptions to this rental and lending prohibition:

- First, nonprofit libraries may lend software to the public for nonprofit purposes provided that the library affixes a copyright warning to the packaging of each copy lent.
- The rental prohibition also doesn't apply to "a computer program embodied in or used in conjunction with a limited purpose computer that is designed for playing video games." In other words, it is permissible to rent video game cartridges.
- The prohibition does not apply to "a computer program … embodied in a machine or product" that "cannot be copied during ordinary operation or use." For example, it is permissible to rent computer hardware that contains computer programs, such as operating systems, in ROM (read-only memory).
- Finally, the transfer of possession of a lawfully made copy of a computer program from one nonprofit educational institution to another or to faculty, staff and students does not constitute "rental, lease or lending for direct or indirect commercial purposes" and thus is not prohibited.

e. No derivative works

Other than making an adaptation for her personal use, the purchaser of a copy of a program may not make any derivative works based on the copy without the copyright owner's permission. See Chapter 8 for detailed discussion.

C. License Agreements With End Users

Most software owners prefer to license their programs rather than sell copies outright. Instead of owning the copy of the software they pay for, end users merely acquire permission to use it. A written license agreement defines the nature and extent of that permission. The person or company granting such a license is usually called the licensor, and the user-customer is called the licensee.

Unlike a purchaser of a copy of a program who, as discussed in the previous section, can do almost anything he wants with his copy (except infringe on the copyright owner's exclusive rights), a software licensee's use rights are carefully restricted by the license agreement.

Why should this be so? The answer is simple: money. Software owners believe that license agreements help them preserve their market share, obtain the maximum return on each transaction and help safeguard their intellectual property rights. All of this adds up, at least in theory, to greater profits.

This section provides an overview of the basic types of software licenses: those actually negotiated with and signed by end users, and preprinted shrink-wrap or click-wrap licenses used with mass-marketed software.

1. Negotiated License Agreements

Negotiated license agreements are those actually agreed upon and signed by the user. They are actual enforceable contracts. Such licenses take a variety of forms. However, they typically include provisions that effectively take away most of the rights that a purchaser of a copy would have (see the discussion at Section C2 above). Such licenses may include provisions:

- limiting use of the software to a particular computer with a particular serial number,
- limiting use of the software to a particular model of computer,
- limiting use of the software to computers with a particular processing capacity,
- limiting use of the software to computers at a particular physical location,
- limiting use of the software to a specified number of concurrent users,
- limiting use of the software to a particular application within the licensee's business,
- prohibiting use of the software to perform processing for third parties or even for other divisions of the licensee's business,
- prohibiting transfer or sublicensing of the license without the licensor's prior written consent,
- prohibiting the use of the software on a computer network,
- prohibiting copying of the software for all but adaptation and archival purposes,
- prohibiting modification of the software,
- prohibiting the licensee from allowing a service bureau to operate on the licensee's behalf,
- prohibiting the licensee from reverse engineering, disassembling or decompiling the software, and
- prohibiting the licensee from using the software to run and publish test results of the software without the licensor's consent.

(For a sample negotiated license you can adapt for your use, see *Software Development: A Legal Guide*, by Stephen Fishman (Nolo Press).)

a. Types of end user licenses

Software licenses take a variety of forms:

- *Single user/CPU licenses:* This is a license giving permission to use the software on a single CPU/computer by a single user. The software may only be run on the computer designated in the license. Most single user licenses are for mass-marketed software. However, negotiated licenses are drafted and signed for some high-end programs. These other types of licenses all allow the user to make multiple copies of the software.

- *Site licenses:* As the name implies, a site license is a grant of permission to use software at a particular location. The location can be a single office address or an entire corporate division.

- *Enterprise licenses:* Rather than defining the scope of the licensee's use in terms of a physical location, enterprise licenses are based on the licensee's identity and the types of uses the licensee intends to make with the software. This approach leads to great flexibility regarding pricing. For example, the license price can be linked to the licensee's overall computing capacity or indexed to any other measure, such as the user's annual revenues. Many of the major software companies are experimenting with enterprise licenses.

- *Network/multi-user licenses:* These licenses permit the licensee to use the software on a computer network. Such licenses typically identify a series of computer/operating system combinations on which the software may be installed. The hardware platforms must be owned, leased to or under the sole control of the licensee. Such licenses do not limit the number of computers on which the software may be installed, but may limit the number of users of the programs.

b. Software licensees' rights

Negotiated end user licenses are normally nonexclusive licenses. As discussed in Section B1b above, the holder of a nonexclusive license acquires none of the licensor's exclusive copyright rights. All he has are the use rights granted in the license agreement. The licensor is free to enter into other nonexclusive licenses with as many other customers as it chooses.

One question that has arisen is whether a software licensee has the right to make archival copies and adaptations as provided in Section 117 of the Copyright Act. (See Section B2b above.) By its own terms, Section 117 applies only to "the owner of a copy of a computer program." Most courts have interpreted this language literally and held that Section 117's back-up and adaptation rights apply only to program owners, not licensees. In other words, a person who purchases a program copy outright may make back-ups and adaptations, but a person who licenses a copy may not exercise such rights unless they are granted in the license agreement. (*S.O.S., Inc. v. Payday, Inc.*, 886 F.2d 1081 (9th Cir. 1988).) However, a few courts have held that Section 117 really applies to any rightful possessor of a program copy, and thus applies to licensees as well to purchasers. (For example, see *Foresight Resources Corp. v. Pfortmiller*, 719 F.Supp. 1006 (D.Kan. 1989).)

One court has even held that a licensee cannot load licensed software into computer RAM unless permitted by the license. This meant that the licensee could not permit a third party maintenance company to service its computers because doing so required that the licensed operating system be loaded into RAM by the maintenance company. The court held that the operating system software license didn't allow this and that a licensee has no right under Section 117 to make a RAM copy of a program without the owner's permission; only software copy owners had this right. (*MAI Systems Corporation v. Peak Computer Inc.*, 991 F.2d 511 (9th Cir. 1993).)

The moral of the *MAI Systems* case is that a licensee should make sure that any rights it may wish to exercise are specifically authorized by the software license. If a licensee wants to be able to hire third parties to maintain the software, it should insist that the license agreement include language permitting this. Blanket prohibitions on any use of the software other than for internal information processing by the licensee may prove very onerous.

2. Shrink-Wrap Licenses for Mass-Marketed Software

Of course it's not practical to negotiate and sign license agreements for mass-marketed software that is purchased and used by thousands or even millions of end users. Software developers and publishers typically have no contact in advance with the people who purchase their products from computer stores, mail-order houses, bookstores and other retail outlets. This would seem to mean that copies of mass-marketed software must be sold to the public, rather than licensed—the same as copies of books, for example.

However, software publishers really want to license their software, not sell it. So they developed the shrink-wrap license agreement. If you've ever bought a mass-marketed software package, you've probably seen a shrink-wrap license. They may be printed on an envelope inside the package in which the program disks are sealed or, in rare cases, printed in bold type on the outside of the software package under the clear plastic shrink-wrap. Some shrink-wrap licenses appear on the computer screen when the software is first installed. Their purpose is to attempt to turn what would otherwise be a simple consumer purchase of a copy of a computer program into a licensing transaction.

a. Contents of shrink-wrap licenses

As with negotiated end user licenses, shrink-wrap licenses attempt to take away or restrict most of the rights a purchaser of a software copy would have. They typically include the following provisions:

- **Agreement clause.** An agreement clause usually provides that by opening the software package or the envelope containing the program diskettes, the user agrees to the terms of the license. If the user doesn't want to agree to the license, he is told to return the software for a full refund *before* opening the package.
- **Title retention clause.** The main purpose of using the shrink-wrap license is for the publisher to retain

ownership of the copy of the software stored on the disk. The user just gets a nonexclusive license to use the program, subject to various restrictions. This means the user does not have any of the rights of a software copy owner discussed in Section B2 above.

- **Use restrictions.** The user is normally permitted to load and use the software only on one computer at a time. The user is usually permitted to make backup copies (at least one) and load the software into computer RAM (but only on one computer at a time).
- **No transfers.** The user is barred from selling, sublicensing, loaning or giving away his copy of the software to any other person.
- **Anti-rental clause.** Shrink-wrap licenses almost always contain a provision prohibiting the user from renting or leasing the software to the public. But, as discussed in Section B3d above, this is already prohibited by the Copyright Act.
- **No reverse engineering.** The user is also barred from reverse engineering, decompiling or translating the software.
- **No adaptations.** The user is not permitted to modify or adapt the software in any way, even for her own personal use. As discussed in Section B2e, above, this is a right a software purchaser has. This means that if the user wants an upgrade she has to get it from the publisher; she can't create it herself.
- **Warranty disclaimer.** A warranty disclaimer is also usually included. It typically provides that, except for the program diskettes being free from defects, the publisher makes no other warranties of any kind. In other words, the software is provided "as is."

(For a sample shrink-wrap license you can adapt for your use, see *Software Development: A Legal Guide*, by Stephen Fishman (Nolo Press).)

b. Are shrink-wrap licenses enforceable?

For years, copyright experts have questioned whether shrink-wrap licenses are legally enforceable. One of the requirements for an enforceable contract is a meeting of the minds. That is, the parties must knowingly agree on all the material terms of the contract. There would appear to be no meeting of the minds between most consumers of mass-marketed software and software publishers. Most consumers don't bother to read the shrink-wrap licenses before buying and opening the package. The vast majority undoubtedly assume that when they buy a software package in a store they own it, just as when they buy a book in a bookstore.

Because of such doubts, the software industry lobbied state legislatures in the mid-1980s to change existing state contract laws to permit enforcement of such licenses. Only two states ultimately enacted such laws—Illinois and Louisiana. The Illinois law was repealed in 1988 and a federal court held that most of the key provisions of the Louisiana law were invalid because they were preempted (superseded) by the federal copyright law. (*Vault Corp. v. Quaid Software Ltd.*, 847 F.2d 255 (5th Cir. 1988).)

However, shrink-wrap licenses received a huge shot in the arm in 1996, when for the first time a federal court ruled they were enforceable. This all happened when Matthew Zeidenberg bought a CD-ROM containing 95 million business telephone listings from ProCD. He downloaded the listings into his computer from the CD-ROM and made them available on his Website, averaging over 20,000 "hits" per day. Zeidenberg did not commit copyright infringement because phone listings are in the public domain. However, he did violate the terms of the shrink-wrap license that came with the CD-ROM. The license barred purchasers from copying, adapting or modifying the work. The license was contained in written form inside the box the CD-ROM came in. It was also splashed on the computer screen when the user started up the software. Zeidenberg had to agree to the license terms by clicking on an "I agree" box before he could access the data on the CD-ROM.

The court held that the license was an enforceable contract. ProCD had offered to form a contract with Zeidenberg—ProCD would allow him to use the CD-ROM subject to the terms of the enclosed li-

cense agreement in return for his payment. ProCD had invited Zeidenberg to accept the terms of the contract by conduct—clicking on the "I agree" icon and using the software after having had an opportunity to read the license agreement. Zeidenberg had accepted and a valid contract was formed. Since Zeidenberg violated the terms of license, he was liable to ProCD for damages. (*ProCD v. Zeidenberg*, 86 F.3d 1447 (7th Cir. 1996).)

For a shrink-wrap license to be enforceable, however, the software licensor should take the following steps to alert the purchaser-licensee to the existence of the license prior to the sale:

- place a prominent notice on the outside packaging of the software stating that the purchaser will be bound by a shrink-wrap license
- when the purchaser first starts up the software, include an "I agree" routine in which the purchaser is required to scroll through the license terms and must then click on an "I agree" box or type in the words "I agree" before the software can be used, and
- give the purchaser the right to return the software and receive a full refund of the purchase price if he or she doesn't agree to the terms of the license.

Do Shrink-Wraps Subject Software Publishers to State Taxes?

We said above that shrink-wrap licenses cost software publishers nothing; but this may not necessarily be true. Some tax experts fear that shrink-wrap licenses may have a tax cost for software publishers because licensing personal property like software in a state may subject a software publisher to state income tax liability. No such liability would exist where software is sold outright because federal law prohibits states from imposing income taxes on the sale of personal property in the state (15 U.S.C. 381-384). In addition, some local taxing authorities have asserted that the publisher, rather than the end user, is liable for personal property tax on licensed software since the publisher still owns the copy of the software subject to the tax. Consult a tax expert for more information.

---

3. Click-Wrap Licenses

"Click-Wrap" licenses serve the exact same function as shrink-wrap licenses except they are used for software that is distributed to end users over the Internet and commercial online services. The user downloads the software directly into his or her computer over phone lines, so there is no package or physical written license agreement the user can read. Instead, the user is asked to read the terms of the license on the computer screen and then click on an "accept" button to initiate the software download.

A click-wrap license may be easier to legally enforce than a shrink-wrap license because the user must take an active step—clicking on an accept button—to accept the license terms.

Moreover, the customer can be required to agree to the license before paying for the software. This avoids one of the principal legal objections to shrink-wraps: that they are not supported by consideration. Consideration is the value or quid pro quo that each

party to a contract is supposed to receive from the other party in exchange for entering into the contract. Unless a contract provides some consideration for each party, the law will not usually recognize it as binding.

When a software consumer buys a software package containing a shrink-wrap license in a store or by mail order he or she gives consideration—the purchase price—and receives consideration in return—the software. The consumer assumes at this point that he or she owns the software copy. When the consumer then opens the software package he or she is supposed to enter into what seems a new agreement with the developer—the shrink-wrap license. The consumer is asked to provide consideration by giving up some of the ownership rights he or she would otherwise have, but gets no new consideration from the developer in return, since he or she already has the software. This can be avoided in an online transaction where the consumer must read and agree to the click-wrap license before purchasing the software.

(For a sample click-wrap license you can adapt for your use, see *Software Development: A Legal Guide*, by Stephen Fishman (Nolo Press).)

D. Effect of Bankruptcy on Software Licenses

The federal bankruptcy laws are intended to give insolvent debtors an opportunity to reorganize and/or discharge their debts and gain a fresh start. When an insolvent debtor files for bankruptcy, all its assets and any contracts or licenses it has made come under the control of the federal bankruptcy court. To help give the debtor a fresh start and to avoid loss of the estate's resources, the debtor or bankruptcy trustee (an official appointed by the bankruptcy court to administer the debtor's affairs) has the power under the Bankruptcy Code to reject (terminate), with court approval, any executory (outstanding) contracts. In most cases where this occurs, the injured party is left with an unsecured claim against the bankruptcy estate. Depending upon the financial condition of the debtor, such a claim may be valuable; but in many cases it is worthless.

Almost all software licenses would probably be considered executory and thus subject to rejection by a licensor-debtor or bankruptcy trustee. However, a special provision of the Bankruptcy Code (Section 365(n)) gives licensees of intellectual property (including software) certain rights that most other bankruptcy creditors don't have. If the debtor-licensor or trustee elects to reject a software license, the licensee has the option of either:

- treating the license as terminated by the rejection and pursuing any legal remedies the licensee may have (that is, filing a claim for damages against the estate), or
- retaining its rights under the license for the term of the license (and any contractually permitted extensions of the term).

If the licensee elects to retain its rights under the license, the debtor or bankruptcy trustee must allow it to exercise those rights. But the licensor must continue to pay any royalty amounts due under the license agreement. License royalties must be paid even though the bankruptcy filing relieves the licensor from any obligation to perform maintenance services under the license agreement. However, if the parties entered into a source code escrow agreement, the licensee is entitled to obtain a copy of the program source code from the source code escrow holder so it can perform maintenance on its own (or hire someone else to do it).

> **EXAMPLE:** Goniff Airlines enters into a nonexclusive license with BagSoft to use a software package designed to automate airline baggage handling. BagSoft then files for bankruptcy and elects to reject the license with Goniff. The airline can accept the rejection and simply file a claim for damages against BagSoft in the Bankruptcy Court, or it can elect to retain its rights under the license. That is, Goniff can continue to use the software for the full license term, provided it continues to make any royalty payments to BagSoft as they become due. Goniff elects to take the latter course because it wants to continue to use the software.

E. Marriage, Divorce and Software Copyright Ownership

This section is for individuals who already own software copyrights, or who may own software copyrights in the future because of software they will create. Like everybody else, individuals who own software copyrights get married and get divorced. A copyright is an item of personal property that must be given to one spouse or the other, or somehow shared, upon divorce. Every state has a set of laws about how property acquired or created by married persons is owned and divided upon divorce. These laws vary greatly from state to state. This section highlights some basic principles. You'll need to consult an attorney to answer specific questions about how the laws of your state operate.

1. Copyrights as Community Property

Nine states have community property laws: Arizona, California, Idaho, Louisiana, Nevada, New Mexico, Texas, Washington and Wisconsin (in all but name). Under these state laws, unless they agree otherwise, a husband and wife automatically become *joint owners* of most types of property they acquire during their marriage. Property acquired before or after marriage is separately owned.

A court in the most populous community property state—California—has held that a copyright acquired by one spouse during marriage is community property jointly owned by both spouses. (*Marriage of Worth*, 195 Cal. App.3d 768, 241 Cal. Rptr. 135 (1987).) This means that if you are married and reside in California (or later move there), any work you have created or will create automatically would be owned jointly by you and your spouse *unless you agree otherwise in writing* (see below). This amounts to a transfer of copyright ownership by operation of state marital property law.

> **EXAMPLE:** Emily and Robert are married and live in California. Emily writes a computer program. Under the federal Copyright Act, Emily becomes the sole owner of the program the moment it's created. But at that same moment, under California's community property law, Robert automatically acquires an undivided one-half interest in the copyright (unless they agree otherwise).

Courts in the eight other community property states have yet to consider whether copyrights are community property. No one knows whether they will follow California's lead. If you're married and reside in Arizona, Idaho, Louisiana, Nevada, New Mexico, Texas, Washington or Wisconsin, the most prudent approach is to assume that the copyright in any protectible work you create during marriage is community property. However, check with a family law or copyright lawyer familiar with the laws of your state before taking any action.

The following discussion briefly highlights the effect of according copyrights community property status in California.

a.   Right to control copyrights

Normally, *either* spouse is entitled to sell community personal property (which would include a copyright) without the other's consent. But the profits from such a sale would themselves be community property (that is, jointly owned). The rule is different, however, as to gifts: Neither spouse can give away community property without the other's consent. However, a special provision of California law (Civil Code Section 5125(d)) provides that a spouse who operates a business has the primary management and control of that business and its assets. In most cases, a married freelance programmer or software engineer would probably be considered to be operating a business and would therefore have primary management and control over any work he or she creates (the business's assets).

This means that a married freelance programmer may transfer all or part of the copyright in a work he or she creates during marriage without his or her spouse's consent and/or signature on any contract. However, the programmer is legally required to give his or her spouse prior written notice of such transfers (but failure to do so only results in giving the nonauthor spouse the right to demand an accounting of the profits from the transfer).

b.   When a spouse dies

Under California law (Probate Code section 201.5) each spouse may will a one-half interest in their community property to whomever they choose; this would include, of course, their interest in any community property copyright. If a spouse dies without a will, the surviving spouse acquires all the deceased spouse's community property.

c.   Division of copyrights at divorce

When a California couple gets divorced, they are legally entitled to arrange their own property settlement, jointly dividing their property as they wish. If, however, they can't reach an agreement and submit the dispute to the court, a judge will divide the community property equally. A judge would have many options as to how to divide community property copyrights—for instance, she could award all the copyrights to one spouse and give the other cash or other community property of equal value; if there were, say, ten copyrights of equal value, she could give five to one spouse and five to the other; or the judge could permit each spouse to separately administer their one-half interest in all the copyrights.

d. Changing marital ownership of copyrights by contract

Property acquired during marriage by California residents does not *have* to be community property. Spouses are free to agree either before or during marriage that all or part of their property will be separately owned. Such an agreement must be in writing and signed by the spouse giving up their community property interest. In some cases, it is desirable for the spouse giving up their community property interest to first consult a lawyer. This is something a husband and wife must discuss and decide on their own; we're not advising you to take any particular action.

2. Equitable Distribution States

All states other than the nine community property states listed above and Mississippi employ equitable distribution principles when dividing property at divorce. Equitable distribution is a principle under which assets (including copyrights) acquired during marriage are divided equitably (fairly) at divorce. In theory, equitable means equal, or nearly so. In some equitable distribution states, however, if a spouse obtains a fault divorce, the "guilty" spouse may receive less than an equal share of the marital property. Check with a family law attorney in your state for details.

F. Recording Copyright Transfers With the Copyright Office

The Copyright Office does not make or in any way participate in transfers of copyright ownership. But the office does *record* transfer documents after they have been signed by the parties. When a transfer document is recorded, a copy is placed in the Copyright Offices files, indexed and made available for public inspection. This is similar to what happens when a deed to a house or other real estate is recorded with a county recorder's office. Recordation of transfer documents is not mandatory, but it results in so many valuable benefits that it is almost always a good idea.

The Difference Between Recordation and Registration

As described in detail in Chapter 4, *Copyright Registration: The Basics*, copyright registration is a legal formality by which an author or other copyright owner fills out a registration application for a published or unpublished work and submits it to the Copyright Office along with one or two copies of the work. If the copyright examiner is satisfied that the work contains protected expression and the application is completed correctly, the work is registered—that is, assigned a registration number, indexed and filed in the Copyright Office's records and the copies retained for five years.

Recordation does not involve submitting copies of a work. Recordation simply means that the Copyright Office files a document so that it is available for public inspection. As mentioned above, this can be any document relating to copyright. It can be for a work that is published, unpublished, or even not yet created. A good way to distinguish the two procedures is to remember that computer programs themselves are registered, while contracts or other documents relating to the copyright in a program are recorded.

---

1. Why Record a Copyright Transfer?

Because a copyright is intangible and can be transferred simply by signing a piece of paper, it is possible for dishonest copyright owners to rip off copyright purchasers.

EXAMPLE: Carol signs a contract transferring the exclusive right to publish and distribute her computer game, The Goniff, to Scrivener & Sons. Scrivener fails to record the transfer with the U.S. Copyright Office. Two months later, Carol sells the same rights in the game to Fun & Gameware. Gameware had no idea that Carol had already sold the same rights to Scrivener. Carol has sold the same property twice! As a result, if Scrivener and Gameware both publish the game, they'll be competing against each other (and they'll both probably be able to sue Carol for breach of contract, fraud and other causes of action).

Recordation of transfer documents protects copyright transferees from these and other abuses by establishing the legal priorities between copyright transferees if the transferor makes overlapping or confusing grants (see Section 3 below). Recordation also establishes a public record of the contents of transfer documents. This enables prospective purchasers of copyright rights to search the Copyright Office's transfer records to make sure that the copyright seller really owns what she's selling. (This is similar to the title search that a homebuyer conducts before purchasing a house.) Finally, recordation of a transfer document for a registered work gives the entire world constructive notice of the transfer; constructive notice means everyone is deemed to know about the transfer, whether or not they really do.

Things would be much better for Scrivener & Sons in our example above if it had recorded the copyright transfer from Carol. In that event, the transfer to Scrivener would have priority over Fun & Gameware and would be deemed the only valid transfer. This would mean that as the sole copyright owner, only Scrivener would have the right to distribute the computer game.

2. What Can Be Recorded?

Any document pertaining to a copyright can be recorded with the Copyright Office. Of course, this includes any document transferring all or part of a copyright—whether it be an exclusive license or assignment. It also includes nonexclusive licenses, wills, powers of attorney in which authors or other copyright owners give others the power to act for them and other contracts dealing with a copyrighted work.

You can record a document without registering the underlying work it pertains to, but important benefits are obtained if the work is registered. You can even record a document for a work that doesn't exist because it has yet to be written, such as a publishing contract.

It's a very good idea to record any document that affects a transfer of copyright ownership. Also record any document that contains information you want the world at large to be aware of—for example, a change of the copyright owner's name. Documents pledging a copyright as collateral or security for a loan should also be recorded.

3. Effect of Recordation on Copyright Conflicts

So what happens when an unethical (or awfully forgetful) software author or owner transfers the same copyright right(s) to different persons or entities? The rules of priority for copyright transfers may be summarized as follows:

- As between two conflicting transfers of exclusive rights to a work that has been *registered with the Copyright Office*, the first transfer is always entitled to priority over the later transfer if it was recorded first.
- But, even if the second transfer is recorded first, the first transfer is still entitled to protection if it's recorded *within one month* after it is signed (two months if signed outside the U.S.).
- However, if the first transfer is recorded more than one month after it's signed (or not recorded at all), the transfer that is recorded first is entitled to protection (even if it was the second one granted). (This rule does not apply if the second transfer was a gift or bequest—that is, inherited through a will.)
- But the later transfer is entitled to protection only so long as it was made in good faith and without knowledge of the earlier transfer.

A subsequent transferee will always lose out to a prior transferee who records first because such recordation gives the later transferee (and everyone one else in the world) constructive notice of the prior transfer—that is, the second transferee is deemed to know about the earlier transfer whether or not he really did. This means that the second transferee cannot claim that he recorded the later transfer without knowledge of the earlier transfer.

EXAMPLE 1: AcmeSoft creates a program which it registers with the Copyright Office. AcmeSoft sells the exclusive right to distribute the program in North America to Gullible Distribution Company. One week later, AcmeSoft sells the same rights to Dummies, Inc. Assume that Gullible recorded its transfer agreement from AcmeSoft on August 2. Dummies records its transfer agreement on August 3. Who is entitled to distribute AcmeSoft's program? Gullible is. The first transfer is always entitled to priority if the work has been registered and the first transfer is recorded first.

EXAMPLE 2: Assume that the two sales occurred on July 1 (to Gullible) and July 8 (to Dummies) and that Dummies, Inc. records its transfer agreement from AcmeSoft on July 10. Dummies did not know about the prior transfer from AcmeSoft to Gullible and acted in good faith. Gullible did not record its transfer agreement until July 30. Who has the exclusive right to distribute AcmeSoft's program? Still Gullible. Since Gullible recorded its transfer agreement within 30 days of the July 1 transfer, it prevails over Dummies regardless of when Dummies recorded.

EXAMPLE 3: Assume the same facts as in Example 2 except that Gullible waited until August 15 to record, while Dummies recorded in good faith on July 10. Who prevails? Dummies. Since Gullible waited more than 30 days to record, the first transferee to record prevails regardless of when the transfer itself was made.

EXAMPLE 4: Assume the same facts as in Example 3, except that Dummies actually knew about AcmeSoft's prior transfer to Gullible (AcmeSoft told them). In this event, Gullible would prevail regardless of when it recorded.

Transfers of Unregistered Works

What happens if conflicting transfers are made of a work that has not been registered? Until the work is registered, no transferee has legal priority over any other transferee. As a result, it makes no sense to record a document without registering the underlying work.

EXAMPLE: Jason, a freelance programmer, creates a utility program for the Power Macintosh. Jason knows nothing about copyright law and fails to register his program with the Copyright Office. He later signs a contract with XYZ Software giving it the exclusive right to distribute the program in the United States. One week later, he signs a similar agreement with ABC Software. Who has the right to distribute the program? They both do until the program is registered and transfer a document recorded. But the first one to register and record will have priority over the other. The entity without priority may not distribute the utility program, but can probably sue Jason for breach of contract, fraud and other causes of action.

---

4. Priority When a Copyright Transfer and a Written Nonexclusive License Conflict

What happens if a copyright owner grants Party A a nonexclusive license to exercise some of his copyright rights, but later transfers those same rights (or all his exclusive copyright rights) to Party B? B now owns the rights A has a nonexclusive license to use.

May A continue to rely on the nonexclusive license or must he seek a new nonexclusive license from B? Luckily for nonexclusive licensees, there is a special statute giving them priority over later conflicting transfers of ownership. As long as a nonexclusive license is (1) in writing, and (2) signed by the licensor, it prevails over a conflicting transfer if:

- the license was taken before the conflicting transfer was signed or
- the license was taken in good faith before recordation of the transfer and without notice of it.

EXAMPLE 1: WidgetCo obtains a written nonexclusive license to use a program owned by AcmeSoft. A week later, AcmeSoft sells all its copyright rights in the program to Behemoth Software. WidgetCo may continue to use the program; it need not obtain Behemoth's permission to do so. Its written nonexclusive license has *priority* over AcmeSoft's subsequent transfer to Behemoth.

EXAMPLE 2: Change facts: Assume that AcmeSoft transferred all his copyright rights in the program to Behemoth. However, before Behemoth records the transfer agreement, AcmeSoft grants the nonexclusive license to WidgetCo. AcmeSoft does not tell WidgetCo about the prior transfer to Behemoth and it knows nothing about it. WidgetCo's nonexclusive license still has priority.

5. How to Record Transfer Documents (or Other Documents Pertaining to Copyright)

To record a document with the Copyright Office, you must complete and sign the Copyright Office Document Cover Sheet form and send it to the Copyright Office along with the document and recordation fee.

If the work involved hasn't already been registered with the Copyright Office, it should be at the same time the document is recorded. It's possible to record without registering, but important priority

rights are obtained if the work is registered. (Of course, you can't register if the work is not yet in existence.)

a. Step 1: Complete the Document Cover Sheet

First, complete and sign the Document Cover Sheet. A tear-out copy of the form is included in the Appendix to this book. You can obtain additional copies by calling the Copyright Office Forms Hotline at 202-707-9100. Here's how to fill out the form.

Space 1: Name of Parties to Document

In Space 1, you must name all the parties to the document you are recording. The document will be indexed under their names. Under "Party 1," list the name of the assignor or grantor—that is, the name of the person making a transfer of copyright rights (a work's author, for example). Under "Party 2," list the name of the assignee or grantee—that is, the name of the person receiving the transfer of copyright rights (a publisher, for example). If you don't have enough space to list all the parties involved, use a white 8½ inch by 11 inch sheet of paper to list them.

Space 2: Description of Document

Check the box that best describes the document you're recording. This will usually be the first box, "Transfer of Copyright."

Space 3: Title(s) of Work(s)

List here the titles, registration numbers (if any) and authors of all the works covered by the document being recorded. Use additional white sheets if you can't fit them all in on the form.

Space 4: Completeness of Document

A document being recorded with the Copyright Office should be complete on its own terms. At a minimum, it should contain (1) the names and addresses

DOCUMENT COVER SHEET
For Recordation of Documents
UNITED STATES COPYRIGHT OFFICE

DATE OF RECORDATION
(Assigned by Copyright Office)

Month   Day   Year

—————————Do not write above this line.—————————

Volume _____ Page _____

Before you complete this form, please read the instructions on the reverse side. If additional space is needed, use white 8½ x 11 inch paper.

Volume _____ Page _____

Attachments to Cover Sheet? Yes ❑ No ❑ If so, how many?_____

REMITTANCE _____

To the Register of Copyrights:
Please record the accompanying original document or copy thereof.

FUNDS RECEIVED ¡ _____

1 Name of the Party or Parties to the Document Spelled as They Appear in the Document.

Party 1: (assignor, grantor, etc.)_____

Party 2: (assignee, grantee, etc.)_____

2 Description of the Document:
❑ Transfer of Copyright
❑ Security Interest
❑ Change of Name of Owner

❑ Termination of Transfer(s) [Section 304]
❑ Shareware
❑ Life, Identity, Death Statement [Section 302]

❑ Transfer of Mask Works
❑ Other _____

3 Title(s) of Work(s), Author(s), Registration Number(s), and Other Information to Identify Work.
Title   Author(s)   Registration Number   Registration Date/Year

4 ❑ Document is complete by its own terms.
❑ Document is not complete. Record "as is."

5 Number of titles in Document: _____

6 Amount of fee enclosed or authorized to be charged to a Deposit Account _____ .

7 Deposit account number _____
Deposit account name _____

8 Date of execution and/or effective date of accompanying document _____
(Month)   (Day)   (Year)

9 Affirmation:* I hereby affirm to the Copyright Office that the information given on this form is a true and correct representation of the accompanying document. This affirmation will not suffice as a certification of a photocopy signature on the document.
(Affirmation *must* be signed.)

10 Certification:* Complete this certification in addition to the Affirmation if a photocopy of the original signed document is submitted in lieu of a document bearing the actual signature.
I certify under penalty of perjury under the laws of the United States of America that the accompanying document is a true copy of the original document.

Signature _____

Date _____

Phone Number _____ Fax Number _____

Signature _____

Duly Authorized Agent of: _____

Date _____

MAIL RECORDA-TION TO

Name▼
Number/Street/Apt▼
City/State/ZIP▼

YOU MUST:
• Complete all necessary spaces
• Sign your cover sheet in Space 9
SEND ALL 3 ELEMENTS IN THE SAME PACKAGE:
1. Two copies of the Document Cover Sheet
2. Fee in check or money order payable to *Register of Copyrights*
3. Document
MAIL TO:
Documents Unit, Cataloging Division
Copyright Office, Library of Congress
Washington, D.C. 20559-6000

*Knowingly and willfully falsifying material facts on this form may result in criminal liability. 18 U.S.C.§1001.

September 1996

☆ U.S. COPYRIGHT OFFICE WWW FORM: 1997

of the copyright owner(s) and person(s) or entity acquiring the copyright right(s); and (2) a description of the rights that are being transferred. The transfer document must also be signed by the transferor.

The Copyright Office will not examine your document to see if it meets these requirements. It will be recorded whether it does or not. However, if it doesn't, it may not be legally effective to establish a priority in case of conflicting transfers.

If your document meets these requirements, check the first box in Space 4. If not, and you want it recorded anyway, check the second box instructing the Copyright Office to record it as is.

Space 5: Number of Titles in Document

List in Space 5 the number of titles covered by the document. This will determine the recordation fee.

Space 6: Fee

State the amount of the recordation fee in Space 6. As of November 1994, the Copyright Office charges a $20 fee to record a transfer document covering one to ten titles. For additional titles, there is an added charge of $10 for each group of up to ten titles—for example, it would cost $30 to record 11–20 titles, $40 to record 21–30 titles and so forth.

Space 7: Deposit Account

If you have a deposit account with the Copyright Office and want the fee charged to it, give the account number and name in Space 7.

Space 8: Date of Execution

State in Space 8 the date the document being recorded (not the Cover Sheet) was signed or became effective.

Space 9: Affirmation

The person submitting the document being recorded or her representative must sign where indicated in Space 9.

Space 10: Certification

You are supposed to submit one copy of the *original* transfer document *signed by the transferor*. If this is not possible, and you need to record a photocopy of the original document instead, Space 10 must be completed. Leave it blank if you submit the original.

To submit a photocopy in lieu of the original document, one of the parties to the document or his or her authorized representative must sign and date Space 10. By doing so, the signer certifies under penalty of perjury that the copy is a true copy of the original document.

Address

Finally, include at the bottom of the form the address where the Copyright Office should send the Certificate of Recordation.

b. Step 2: Send Your Recordation Package to the Copyright Office

You need to send all the following to the Copyright Office in one package:

- The original signed Document Cover Sheet and one copy,
- The proper recordation fee in a check or money order payable to the Register of Copyrights (unless you have a deposit account), and
- The document to be recorded.

Send your package to:

Documents Unit, LM-462
Cataloging Division
Copyright Office
Library of Congress
Washington, D.C. 20559

Within six to eight weeks you should receive a Certificate of Recordation from the Copyright Office showing that your transfer document (or nonexclusive license) has been recorded. The original signed transfer document (or nonexclusive license) will be returned with the certificate.

G. Searching Copyright Office Records for Conflicting Transfers

You wouldn't buy a house or other real estate without conducting a title search. Likewise, you shouldn't spend a substantial sum to purchase all or part of a software copyright without searching the Copyright Office's records to make sure the transferor owns what he's selling.

Take careful note, however, that such searches are not foolproof. As discussed above, under the priority rules, a transferee who records within one month after the transfer is signed (two months if signed abroad) has priority over all subsequent transfers even if they were recorded earlier. Thus, a person who received a transfer less than one month before you (two months if the transfer document was signed outside the U.S.) will have priority over you even if she records *after* you, provided that she records within one month after the transfer to her.

1. Searching Copyright Office Records

You can have the Copyright Office search its records for you to determine whether any work was registered, whether any transfers of ownership were recorded and the names and addresses of the persons named in such documents (which won't necessarily be current). The Copyright Office charges $20 an hour for this service. Call the Reference & Bibliography Section at 202-707-6850 and ask for an estimate of how long they think your particular search will take. Then, fill out the search request form located in the Appendix to this book, and send it and your check in the amount of the estimate payable to the Register of Copyrights, to:

Reference & Bibliography Section, LM-451
Copyright Office
Library of Congress
Washington, D.C. 20559

Instead of having the Copyright Office conduct the search, you can have a professional search firm conduct the search for you. This will probably cost much more than having the Copyright Office do the search—fees range from $100 to $300—but you will get much faster service. Search firms usually report back in two to ten working days, while it usually takes the Copyright Office one or two months to conduct a search.

Copyright Search Firms

There are several copyright search firms, located primarily in the Washington, D.C. area:

Copyright Council
2121 Crystal Dr., Ste. 704
Arlington, VA 22202
703-521-1669

Government Liaison Services, Inc.
3030 Clarendon Blvd., Ste. 209
Arlington, VA 22201
800-642-6564 or 703-524-8200

Thomson & Thomson Copyright Research Group
500 E St., S.W., Ste. 970
Washington, D.C. 20024
800-356-8630
(This is the largest and best-known search firm.)

XL Corporate Services
62 White St.
New York, NY 10013
800-221-2972 or 212-431-5000

Finally, you can search the Copyright Office records yourself. The Copyright Office's records are open to the public at its headquarters located in the James Madison Memorial Building, 101 Independence Ave. S.E., Washington, D.C. The Office is open from 8:30 a.m. to 5:00 p.m. Monday through Friday.

Some of these records are available on the Internet. The Internet address is "locis.loc.gov"; the password is "Copyright Information."

H. Copyright Office Computer Shareware Registry

Shareware is a term that describes a special way of marketing copyrighted computer software. Under a shareware system of marketing, the copyright owner of a program permits end users to obtain a copy and use it for free. If the user decides he wants to keep the program, he is supposed to register with the author and pay a fee. Of course, the shareware author has no way of forcing the user to pay the fee. For this reason, shareware authors often only provide free copies of crippled or incomplete versions of their software. To get the complete version, the user must pay the fee. Shareware is usually obtained from computer bulletin boards, the Internet or from commercial on-line services like CompuServe and America Online. Some shareware is also sold through catalogs.

The Copyright Office has established a shareware registry that is intended to provide a means for shareware authors to notify the public about the licensing terms for their shareware programs. Shareware authors may record with the registry copies of their licenses or similar agreements. These records are maintained in a system separate from other recorded documents. End users can access these agreements to see how much a shareware author is charging for a program and what the other licensing terms are.

This may sound like a good idea in theory, but in practice it's probably a lot easier for end users to get information regarding shareware license terms direct from the shareware author, rather than attempting to access the shareware registry in Washington, D.C. Perhaps for this reason, the shareware registry has not proved very popular with shareware authors.

In any event, if you want to record a license or similar document pertaining to shareware with the shareware registry you should submit a copy which should be clearly designated as a "Document Pertaining to Computer Shareware." The Copyright Office encourages submission of a copy of the document on an IBM-PC compatible disk in addition to a hard copy of the document. You must also pay a $20 recording fee for a document covering no more than one shareware title. An additional $10 must be paid for each group of up to ten additional titles. Send this material to:

Documents Unit, LM-462
Cataloging Division
Copyright Office
Library of Congress
Washington, D.C. 20559 ■

Software Copyright Infringement: What It Is, What to Do About It, How to Avoid It

opyright infringement is where the rubber hits the road in the copyright law. It concerns how authors and other copyright owners enforce their legal rights. However, the right to bring copyright infringement suits is a two-edged sword: You may have the right to sue others, but others may also have the right to sue you. Consequently, this chapter is divided into two parts. Part I discusses how to avoid being sued for copyright infringement. Part II provides an overview of infringement lawsuits from the plaintiff's point of view.

Part I.   Avoiding Copyright Infringement

Many programmers and software developers have been sued for copyright infringement or threatened with such suits. Others are fearful of being sued. This fear is understandable. Unfortunately, in the litigation-happy United States the answer to the question "Can I be sued?" is always yes. You can be sued by anyone at any time for anything. The only way a programmer or developer can be absolutely sure he or she will never be accused of copyright infringement is to never develop and sell any new software.

Even if you don't copy other people's software you can still end up getting sued if, because of factors like coincidence and external constraints, your software turns out to be similar to someone else's. So if you want to stay in the software business, being sued one day is a risk you'll have to take. Obviously, however, the less you copy from others the less risk there will be.

A. Things You Should Never Do

The clearest cases of software copyright infringement involve direct copying of computer code, particularly where you copy all or most of a program. If you're caught doing these types of copying you likely won't have a legal leg to stand on should the copyright owner elect to sue you for infringement. Indeed, your best course would probably be to seek to settle the case as cheaply as possible without going to court.

Creating derivative works without permission and going beyond the restrictions contained in software license agreements also usually present clear cases of copyright infringement.

It goes without saying that you should never become involved in these types of copyright infringement. The risks will usually be greater than the rewards. See Section I for a detailed discussion of the many unpleasant legal consequences of copyright infringement.

1. Wholesale Unauthorized Copying of Computer Code

A simpler caption for this section would be software piracy. It means copying all or most of a program's code without permission. Subject to important limitations discussed in Section B1 below, copyright protects source code (code written in high-level computer languages consisting of English-like words and symbols readable by humans, such as C++ and Java), object code (the series of binary ones and zeros read by the computer itself to execute a program, but not readable by ordinary humans), microcode (instructions that tell a microprocessor chip how to work) and other forms of computer code such as Java bytecode.

Copyright protects both applications programs (programs that perform a specific task for the user, such as word processing, will and trust writing, accessing the World Wide Web, bookkeeping or playing a video game) and operating systems and utility programs (programs that manage a computer's internal functions and facilitate use of applications programs).

Wholesale copying or software piracy takes a variety of forms, including:

- *Creating "new" software from old.* Creating a "new" program by copying a substantial amount of the protected expression in a preexisting program is a classic example of software piracy.

- *End user piracy by companies and individuals.*

  EXAMPLE: AcmeSoft, Inc., a large software developer, makes 100 unauthorized copies of a well-known HTML editor program and distributes them to its employees.

- *Counterfeiting published software.*

  EXAMPLE: Fly By Night Software, Inc., a software distributor, makes 50,000 unauthorized copies of the popular computer arcade game, *Kill or Die*, and distributes them throughout the world.

- *Online piracy.* This includes uploading and downloading computer programs to and from the Internet and computer BBSs without the copyright owners' permission.

What About Copying Only a Small Amount of Code?

Copying only a small portion of a program's code could constitute copyright infringement. Then again, it might not. Because of the various factors discussed in Section B1 below, a particular routine or subroutine or other piece of code may enjoy little or no copyright protection. In this event, copying it wouldn't be an infringement. On the other hand, if the code is protected, copying only a small amount could be an infringement, particularly if it is a highly creative or important example of the programmer's art. Copyright infringement has been found to exist where only 14 lines of source code out of a total of 186,000 lines were copied verbatim. (*SAS Inst., Inc. v. S&H Computer Sys., Inc.*, 605 F.Supp. 816 (M.D.Tenn. 1985).) You'll usually be better off not copying other people's code.

---

2. Creating Unauthorized Derivative Works

Copyright infringement is not limited to the crude wholesale copying described in the previous section. It can take a more subtle form—creating "new" software from old, for example, by transferring a chunk of code to the new program and subsequently modifying it. If such a "new" program contains a substantial amount of copyrighted material from an existing program, it may constitute a derivative work. You need to obtain permission to create a derivative work from someone else's software. (See Chapter 8 for a detailed discussion of derivative works.)

3. Going Beyond Software License Restrictions

Yet another form of copyright infringement is going beyond the restrictions in software license agreements. Today, most software is licensed rather than sold outright. License agreements typically contain many restrictions on what a licensee may do with his or her copy. (See Chapter 12.) For example, software licensees are typically barred from using the software on a local area network (LAN). You must obtain a special license for this sort of use. Using a program on a LAN in violation of a license agreement constitutes copyright infringement.

One of the most hotly contested disputes involving software license restrictions concerns the use of computer manufacturers' licensed software by competing third-party computer maintenance firms (often called independent service organizations or ISOs). In the best known case of its kind, a computer manufacturer called MAI Systems licensed its operating system and diagnostic software to its customers. The license agreements provided that only the purchasers could use the software. MAI sued an ISO called Peak Computer, Inc., for copyright infringement when it used MAI software to perform routine maintenance on MAI computers. MAI claimed that illegal copying beyond the bounds of its license agreements took place when Peak Computer loaded MAI's operating software into computer RAM.

The court agreed, holding that a licensee cannot load licensed software into computer RAM unless permitted by the license. This meant that the licensee could not permit a third party ISO to service its computers because doing so required that the licensed operating system be loaded into RAM by the ISO. (*MAI Systems Corporation v. Peak Computer Inc.*, 991 F.2d 511 (9th Cir. 1993).)

This issue has been the source of much litigation over the past five years, with most, but not all, courts agreeing with *MAI Systems.* A bill submitted in Congress to overturn the decision failed to pass. If you're an ISO, it's advisable to review your customers' license agreements and seek permission before using a computer manufacturer's licensed software.

B. Things You May Be Able to Do

Many copyright protections for computer software are limited in scope. You may be free to copy or otherwise use those software elements that are unprotected by copyright. Additionally, copying of protected material may be permissible under the fair use doctrine. Finally, the copyright laws never prevent you from independently creating new software, even if it's similar to software already in existence.

Be Careful. The following discussion provides an overview of a complex area of law subject to varying interpretations. Even if you and the author of this book believe that a particular software element is unprotected by copyright, the copyright owner might disagree and take legal action against you if you copy it. Before you do any serious copying of someone else's work, it's advisable to seek advice from an experienced computer lawyer. (See Chapter 16.)

1. Using Software Elements Unprotected by Copyright

Many software elements are not protected by copyright and may be freely copied by anyone unless they are protected by another form of intellectual property such as trade secrecy, patent law or trademark law. (See Chapter 7 for a detailed discussion.)

2. Creating Similar Works Independently

So long as a program or other work is independently created, it is entitled to copyright protection even if other similar works already exist. This means that if a programmer can prove he or she independently created the program, he or she cannot be guilty of infringing on a preexisting program, even if it is very similar to that program.

Of course, proving that a program was independently created can be difficult. The creators of the program must be able to show they did not have access to the preexisting program; or, even if they could have had access to it, they never saw it. One approach taken by some software developers who wish to create programs similar to and/or compatible with preexisting software is the use of clean room procedures to establish independent creation. Clean room procedures are used to isolate the persons who actually develop the software. In some cases such persons are denied access to any information about the preexisting software. In other cases they may be given only information about the preexisting program's purpose or functions.

The important decision *Computer Associates v. Altai*, 982 F.2d 693 (2d Cir. 1992) shows that clean room procedures can really work and serve as a good defense to copyright infringement claims. Here's what happened in that case: Altai hired a programmer formerly employed by CAI to create a job scheduling program. Unbeknownst to Altai, the programmer used substantial chunks of CAI code to create Altai's software. When Altai learned what happened, it decided to create a clean version of its scheduling program. Altai hired eight new programmers to create the new version. They were denied access to the infringing version of the software and forbidden to talk to the programmer who created that version. The new programmers were only provided with a specification developed from an earlier noninfringing version of the software. It took about six months to create the new program. It accomplished everything the prior version did, but used none of CAI's code. Altai was sued for copyright infringement by CAI, but the court held that this version of the program did not infringe on CAI's copyright.

For clean room procedures to be effective, great care must be taken not to give the clean room personnel information protected by copyright. For example, an overly specific description for a user interface might contain protected expression which, if used, could taint the clean room. Before implementing a clean room procedure of your own, you should consult with a knowledgeable software attorney.

3. Copying Within the Bounds of Fair Use

The Copyright Act contains several exceptions to the general rule that copyright rights are exclusive to their owners. These exceptions are generally referred to as fair use.

If a particular use of a copyrighted item comes within the legal definition of fair use, the copyright owner's permission isn't necessary, nor is the user required to pay the owner compensation for the use. Often, whether a particular act is or isn't fair use is a major issue in a copyright infringement case, with the defendant claiming, "I didn't infringe your copyright, I only made fair use of it."

The Copyright Act contains several broad categories of what constitutes fair use. A more specific description is found in the congressional committee report that accompanied the act as it was being considered by Congress. According to this report, examples of when unauthorized copying of a copyrighted work is considered fair use include:

- quotations or excerpts in a review or criticism for purposes of illustration or comment
- quotation of a short passage in a scholarly or technical work for illustration or clarification of the author's observation

- use in a parody of some of the content of the work parodied
- summary of an address or article, with brief quotations, in a news report
- reproduction by a library of a portion of a work to replace part of a damaged copy
- reproduction by a teacher or student of a small part of a work to illustrate a lesson
- reproduction of a work in legislative or judicial proceedings or reports, and
- incidental and fortuitous reproduction, in a newsreel or broadcast, of a work located at the scene of an event being reported.

As you may glean from these examples, fair use has historically been used to allow the media broad latitude in reporting on items of public interest, even if they're otherwise subject to copyright protection. Fair use has also been important to educational, scientific and political pursuits. Note also that, with the exception of uses by the for-profit press and mass media, most of these examples involve nonprofit uses of copyrighted material. Authors of works created primarily for financial gain usually have had a difficult time successfully invoking the fair use privilege. This seemed to mean that the fair use doctrine had relatively limited application to the commercial software industry.

However, fair use law underwent a major change with the Supreme Court's highly publicized decision in the so-called "Pretty Woman" case. In that case the Court held that a parody of the song "Pretty Woman" by the rap group 2 Live Crew was a fair use. (*Campbell v. Acuff-Rose Music, Inc.* 114 S.Ct. 1164 (1994).) But the decision has broad implications for creators of all types of works, not just song parodies. Perhaps the most important aspect of the decision is the Supreme Court's ruling that a commercial use of copyrighted material may be a fair use if the new work is more than a mere duplication of the original, what the court terms a transformative use (see Section a, below). This may mean that the fair use privilege can apply to at least some for-profit commercially motivated software. All the ramifications of the Supreme Court's decision are unclear, and will have to be resolved by the lower courts.

a.   Four factors considered in fair use analysis

Four primary factors are considered to determine whether an unauthorized use is a fair use, rather than copyright infringement:

- *The character and purpose of the use.* The test here is to see whether the subsequent work merely serves as a substitute for the original or "instead adds something new, with a further purpose or different character, altering the first with new

expression, meaning, or message." (*Campbell v. Acuff-Rose Music, Inc.*, 114 S.Ct. 1164 (1994).) The Supreme Court calls such a new work transformative. This is the most significant fair use factor. The more transformative a work, the less important are the other fair use factors, such as commercialism, that may weigh against a finding of fair use. Why should this be? It is because the goal of copyright to promote human knowledge is furthered by the creation of transformative works. "Such works thus lie at the heart of the fair use doctrine's guarantee of a breathing space within the confines of copyright." (*Campbell v. Acuff-Rose Music, Inc.*)

- *The nature of the copyrighted work.* Legal, scientific, historical and other factual works are more often subject to the fair use defense than fanciful works like novels or movies.

- *The amount and substantiality of the portion of the copyrighted work used in relation to the entire work.* Using a small part of a large work is more likely to be considered fair use than if most of the work is used. Similarly, a part of a work that is somewhat tangential to the whole will qualify as fair use more easily than a portion of core importance.

- *The effect of the use on the potential market for the copyrighted work, and/or the work's value.* The fact that the use actually competes with the copyrighted work (for example, creating a competing program) weighs against fair use. However, the more transformative the subsequent work, the less important this factor is. In other words, if a software author borrows some copyrighted material to create a new and better work, the fact that it may harm the market for the previous work will not necessarily bar a finding of fair use.

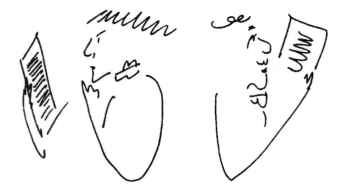

b. Making archival copies is a fair use

Congress has specifically authorized two fair uses that relate to computer programs. A person who purchases a computer program has the right to copy or adapt the program if the copy or adaptation is either:

1. "An essential step in the utilization of the computer program in conjunction with a machine and that it is used in no other manner"—in other words, the purchaser has to copy the program from a floppy disk to his hard disk or adapt the program to get it to work on his computer; or

2. The copy or adaptation is for archival purposes only (a single back-up copy) and is made and kept only by the person who owns the legally purchased copy. (17 U.S.C. 117.)

This limited right to make a back-up or archival copy is not really very generous. Since the copy is for back-up purposes only, it cannot be used on a second computer. This means, for example, that if you own a desktop computer and a laptop, and want to use your word processor on both, legally you must buy two copies. In an effort to make their customers happy, some large software publishers are now including provisions in their license agreements permitting their customers to use a program on two different computers.

c. Reverse engineering as a fair use

Reverse engineering is the process of taking a product or device apart and reducing it to its constituent parts or concepts to see how it works. Reverse engineering has long been used by manufacturers of all types of products to help them create new products. Reverse engineering is perfectly legal so long as it doesn't violate another's patent or copyright rights.

Computer hardware may be reverse engineered by unscrewing the box and looking inside. The best way to reverse engineer a computer program is usually to read the source code. To prevent competitors from reading their valuable source code, software owners normally distribute their programs in object code form only while the source code is kept locked

away. However, it is possible, though often difficult, to reverse engineer object code by translating it into human-readable assembly language which programmers then read to understand the object code. This process is called decompilation or disassembly.

The information gained by reverse engineering can be put to a variety of uses, each with a different economic effect on the owner of the original program. For example, the information can be used to develop a competitive product. In other cases, decompilation can be used to create a program that is functionally compatible—a clone program. Decompilation can also be used to help develop a program that is not competitive, but complementary to the original program—for example, creating a video game cartridge to run on a video game system like Nintendo or Genesis.

Decompilation and disassembly involve the making of at least a partial reproduction or derivative work of the object code. Typically, a copy of the original program is made on a disk; decompiler software is then used to load the program into computer memory; the copy is then transformed into human-readable form, which is then fixed on disk and/or paper.

Both source and object code may be protected by copyright and a copyright owner has the exclusive right to copy and create derivative works from his protected material. Does this mean that decompilation and disassembly constitute copyright infringement? In 1992, two courts said "no," and apparently gave the green light to decompilation, at least under certain circumstances.

The most important of these cases involved Sega Enterprises, manufacturer of the Genesis video game system. (*Sega Enterprises, Ltd. v. Accolade, Inc.*, 977 F.2d 1510 (9th Cir. 1992).) Accolade, Inc., wanted to manufacture a video game cartridge to be used with the Genesis system. Rather than pay Sega for a license to do so, Accolade reversed engineered the Genesis system. It disassembled the object code stored in commercially available read-only memory (ROM) chips in Sega's games to learn the requirements for creation of a Genesis-compatible game cartridge. This process required that Accolade make unauthorized copies of Sega's code for study and analysis (called intermediate copies). Sega sued Accolade for copyright infringement, claiming that Accolade's copying violated its copyright. Sega lost.

The federal appeals court held that disassembly of object code is a fair use if:

1. it is the *only* means available to obtain access to the unprotected elements of a computer program—ideas, functional principles and so forth (see Section B1), and

2. the copier has a legitimate reason for seeking such access.

In applying the fair use factors discussed above, the court found "the purpose and character of the use" to be noncommercial, despite the fact that the copying was being done to create competing game cartridges. The court reasoned that the interim copies were not themselves sold. The court also said that the copying would not harm the market for Sega's video games because consumers might easily purchase both Sega-made and Accolade-made game cartridges. The court also stressed that, if disassembly like Accolade's were prohibited, Sega would in effect enjoy a monopoly over the unprotected ideas and functional principles contained in its code, since the only way to obtain access to those ideas was through disassembly.

d.   Limitations on decompilation as a fair use

The Sega case did not create a blanket rule permitting all decompilation. Rather it demonstrated that decompilation may be a permissible fair use when necessary to develop compatible or complementary programs that do not cause the copyright owner economic harm. If a copyright owner can establish that decompilation of its object code has or will cause it economic harm, a court should conclude that the decompilation was not a fair use.

Furthermore, decompilation can be a fair use only when it is the *only* available means to study the unprotected elements of a program. Often, there are means available other than decompilation to study such elements—simply studying the screen display

will reveal the ideas and concepts of many programs. The Sega court stated that the need for disassembly "arises, if at all, only in connection with operations systems, system interface procedures, and other programs that are not visible to the user when operating."

The fair use factors discussed above are subject to varying interpretations and it is often difficult to predict the outcome of any particular case. This fact is illustrated by another court decision on fair use, involving decompilation of security system source code for the Nintendo video game system by Atari Games. (*Atari Games Corp. v. Nintendo of America, Inc.*, 980 F.2d 857 (Fed.Cir. 1992).) The court reached the same legal conclusion as the Sega decision—decompilation can be a fair use in the proper circumstances. But the court held that Atari's decompilation was not a fair use because it obtained the Nintendo source code from the Copyright Offices under false pretenses. Atari's bad faith and lack of fair dealing obviated a finding of fair use.

The question of whether a use qualifies as a fair use must always be decided on a case-by-case basis. For these reasons, anyone wishing to reverse engineer any program to create a new product should first consult with a qualified software attorney.

C. Protecting Against Infringement Claims

To protect yourself against infringement claims, you must not only avoid committing copyright infringement yourself, but guard against infringement by your employees, independent contractors and other people you deal with.

1. When You Can Be Held Liable for Infringement

Unfortunately, you don't have to commit copyright infringement yourself to be held liable. You can be held legally responsible for infringements carried out by your employees, consultants and others you deal with.

a. Employers Liable for Infringement by Employees

A copyright infringer's employer (whether a corporation, partnership or individual) will be held liable for any infringing acts by employees within the scope of employment. This is based on the general legal principle that an employer has the right to supervise and control employees' activities and is therefore responsible for their wrongful acts. Because an employer has the right to control the work-related activities of an employee, it will be held liable for an employee's infringement even though it didn't actually know about or condone it at the time. Indeed, liability may be imposed even if the employer instructed the employee not to commit the infringement. The reasoning behind this is that the employer should have used its right of control to prevent the infringement.

b. Hirers of independent contractors

You don't have to be an employer of someone to be held liable for their infringement. The hirer of an independent contractor may be liable for the contractor's infringement if the hirer actively participated in, materially contributed to or furthered the hired party's infringing acts.

Liability may also be imposed if a contractor had a direct financial interest in the infringing activities and the right to supervise the contractor or at least police his or her conduct.

c. Corporate officers and partners

The president and other officers of a corporation may be held personally liable for infringement by the corporation if the officer caused the infringement, participated in it or benefited financially from it.

Partners in a partnership may also be held personally liable for infringement by their fellow partners if they participated in it, benefited from it or arranged it.

d. Employee liability

An employee who commits infringement on his or her own initiative will be held liable. However, liability usually will not be imposed where an employee is ordered to commit an infringement by the employer. But the employer would of course be liable.

e. Anyone who induces an infringement

In addition, any person who induces, causes or helps another to commit copyright infringement may be held liable as a contributory infringer and subjected to the same penalties as the person who actually committed the infringement.

Owners of online services and BBSs can be held liable for contributory infringement when users use their systems to commit copyright infringement, even if the owners didn't know about or authorize it. Similar cases have been brought against Internet access providers.

> **EXAMPLE:** Users of a BBS uploaded and downloaded copies of copyrighted Sega computer video games. Sega sued the BBS's sysops (systems operators) for copyright infringement and won. The court held that although there was no evidence the sysops were themselves posting the Sega games on the board, they knew the games were there, knew they were being uploaded and downloaded, and encouraged the process. They were therefore liable as contributory copyright infringers. (*Sega Enterprises v. Maphia*, 30 U.S.P.Q.2d 1921 (N.D. Ca. 1994).)

2. Preventing Illegal Copying in the Software Development Process

As discussed in detail in Chapter 7, many elements of computer software are not protected by copyright and can therefore be copied at will unless they are protected by some other body of law, such as the federal patent law. But exactly what these uncopyrightable elements are in any given instance can be very hard to know because the legal decisions in this area are not always clear or consistent. So before you do this type of copying, you may want to consult with a computer law attorney.

a. Keep good records

It is also very important for software programmers and developers to keep meticulous records of the entire development process, from the initial idea stage to coding, debugging and testing. This includes copies of storyboards and prototypes, interim versions, flowcharts and internal memoranda documenting the many decisions that must be made in the course of software development. Documentation like this will help prove that your work was original and not copied from others, which is an absolute defense to all copyright infringement claims.

b. Registering software under development

If you're especially concerned about being sued for copyright infringement, you may wish to register your software with the Copyright Office while it's still under development. The advantage of this is that you deposit a copy of the software with the Copyright Office as part of the registration process. This copy is kept on file at the Copyright Office. The existence of this registered copy can serve as proof that you didn't copy from someone else. If your software was deposited before the software you are alleged to have copied was created, then you couldn't have copied it.

c. Don't indemnify clients for infringement claims

Another thing a developer can do to help reduce his or her exposure is to refuse to indemnify customers for infringement claims. Indemnification means the developer promises to defend the customer in court if it is sued for infringement and to pay any damages awarded. Indemnification provisions have been commonly included in software development agreements in the past; but, in light of the risks involved, more and more developers are refusing to agree to them or insist on limiting their exposure. (For a detailed discussion, see *Software Development: A Legal Guide*, by Stephen Fishman (Nolo Press), Chapter 17.)

Insurance Coverage for Infringement Claims

Your business may be insured for intellectual property infringement claims and not even know it. The Comprehensive General Liability Insurance (CGL) policies typically obtained by businesses may provide such coverage. Several courts have held that the advertising injury provision included in many CGL policies covers infringement claims. However, not all CGL policies provide such coverage, particularly those written after 1986. You should ask your insurance broker whether your policy provides this coverage. If the broker doesn't know, you may need to consult with an insurance attorney who represents policyholders. If your CGL policy doesn't cover infringement claims, you may be able to obtain such coverage by purchasing a rider to your policy that covers such claims.

---

3. Preventing Illegal Copying in the Workplace

The Business Software Alliance, a software publishers' trade organization, estimates that 30% of all software used in the U.S. is pirated. Much of this copying occurs in the workplace. For the past several years a vigorous and effective campaign against workplace software piracy has been waged by the two largest software industry trade groups: the Software Publishers Association (SPA) and Business Software Alliance (BSA).

SPA and BSA investigators are actively seeking out companies that routinely make illegal copies and both organizations maintain toll-free hotlines to which people can report violations (this is often done by disgruntled employees or ex-employees).

Once evidence of illegal copying is obtained, the SPA or BSA will send the company a cease and desist letter asking the company to voluntarily destroy the illegally copied software and buy legal copies. The SPA or BSA will also often seek permission to have its investigators conduct an audit of the company's computers. If illegally copied software is found during an audit, they ask the company to pay twice—once for the illegal copies, which are destroyed, and a second time to buy legal replacement copies.

If a company does not cooperate voluntarily with the SPA or BSA, they or the company whose software has been copied will take the violator to court or even seek to have it criminally prosecuted by the government. In one case, a $500,000 criminal fine was imposed. Initially, the SPA only went after large Fortune 500 companies; but in recent years it has focused on smaller companies as well.

Since it can be held liable for copyright infringement engaged in by its employees, any company that uses software should have an established policy forbidding employees from making unauthorized copies of software or otherwise committing copyright infringement on the job. Here are some of the steps the SPA advises a company to take to ensure that illegal copying is not taking place:

- First, the company should designate someone to serve as a software manager. This person will be responsible for implementing the company's software policy and maintaining records.
- Conduct an inventory of all the software the company is using. Illegal copies should be destroyed and legal copies purchased.
- Establish clear procedures for purchasing and registering new software.
- Maintain a software log listing each software package the company owns and the computer it runs on.

- Conduct periodic audits of the company computers to ensure they contain no illegal software. Software is commercially available that can scan hard drives on networked computers to see what applications they are running. The SPA also can provide a free inventory program called SPAudit. You can download a copy from the SPA's Web page at www.spa.org; or obtain a copy by calling 202-452-1600.
- Establish an employee education program stressing that copyright infringement will not be tolerated.
- Maintain a library of the company's software licenses.

A wealth of information on these issues can be obtained from the SPA's Website at www.spa.org/piracy/info.htm. The SPA can also be contacted at 800-388-7478.

D. What to Do If You're Accused of Copyright Infringement

What should you do if you're accused of copyright infringement? First, see how serious the claim is. If it's minor—for example, a photographer claims you used one of her pictures in your latest multimedia work without permission—the matter can usually be settled very quickly for a small amount of money. This kind of thing happens all the time. There is no need to see a lawyer (who'll probably charge you at least $150 per hour) to deal with this type of minor annoyance. Have the copyright owner sign a letter releasing you from liability in return for your payment. (See Section G4 for an example of a settlement letter.).

On the other hand, if you receive a letter from a copyright owner or owner's attorney alleging a substantial claim—for example, that your popular spreadsheet program is an unauthorized derivative work and its sale should be halted immediately—it's probably time to find a copyright lawyer. If, even worse, you are served with a court complaint (a document initiating a lawsuit), you must act quickly because you may have as little as 20 days to file an answer (response) in court. If you don't respond in time, a judgment can be entered against you. Finding a lawyer is discussed in Chapter 16.

Even if the case is serious, don't despair. The fact is, many infringement suits are won by the defendant, either because the plaintiff did not have a valid claim to begin with or because the defendant had a good defense. This chapter is not a substitute for a consultation with an experienced attorney; rather, it is designed to give you an idea of some of the things you need to discuss when you see an attorney.

If a substantial claim is involved, the decision whether to settle the case or fight it out in court should only be made after consulting with an attorney who is familiar with the facts of your particular case. However, in making this decision you need to carefully weigh the following factors:

- how likely is it that the plaintiff will prevail
- how much the plaintiff is likely to collect if the plaintiff does win
- the costs of contesting the case, not only in terms of money, but also in terms of the time it will take, and the embarrassment and adverse publicity it will generate, and
- how much the plaintiff may be willing to settle for.

Typically, a copyright infringement plaintiff will seek a preliminary injunction (a court order) soon after the lawsuit is filed stopping you from continuing the infringing activity. A hearing will be held at which the judge must determine whether it's likely the plaintiff would prevail at trial and would be irreparably harmed if an injunction doesn't issue. Most often, infringement cases are settled on the basis of such a hearing's outcome. That is, if the plaintiff obtains an injunction, the defendant will usually agree to settle the case on terms favorable to the plaintiff. If an injunction doesn't issue, the plaintiff may drop the case entirely or accept a settlement favorable to the defendant.

In cases where a settlement can't be reached, you may be able to have the suit dismissed very quickly by filing what's called a summary judgment motion.

Under this procedure the judge examines the plaintiff's claims and decides whether there is any possibility he could prevail if a trial were held. If not, the judge will dismiss the case. Of course, you must pay a lawyer to file a summary judgment motion, but, if successful, it will cost far less than taking the case to trial. Summary judgment motions are frequently used—and are frequently successful—against plaintiffs who bring patently frivolous infringement suits. Moreover, if the plaintiff's claim was clearly frivolous or brought in bad faith, the judge might order the plaintiff to pay all or part of your attorney fees.

On the other hand, if the plaintiff does have a valid claim, paying an attorney to fight a losing battle will only compound your problems. Valid claims should be settled whenever possible. If the plaintiff was able to obtain a preliminary injunction from a federal judge, he or she probably has a valid claim.

1. Defenses to Copyright Infringement

Even if there are substantial similarities between the plaintiff's work and your work, you will not necessarily be found guilty of infringement. The similarities may simply be the result of coincidence; in this event there is no liability. But, even direct copying from the plaintiff's work may be excused if it constitutes a fair use or there is another valid defense.

Possible defenses to an infringement action include many general legal defenses that often involve where, when and how the lawsuit was brought, who was sued, and so on. We obviously can't cover all of this here. This section is limited to outlining the major defenses that are specific to copyright infringement actions. Again, if you find yourself defending a serious copyright infringement action, retain a qualified attorney.

a. Material copied was not protected by copyright

Many elements of computer programs are not protected by copyright at all or are given very limited protection. (See Chapter 7.) Most courts require that these elements be eliminated from consideration when the plaintiff's software is compared with the allegedly infringing software to determine whether they are substantially similar. This means that if you've only copied or paraphrased these unprotected elements, you won't be found to have committed copyright infringement.

b. The use was authorized

In some cases, you may not be an infringer at all, but a legal transferee. For example:

- You might legitimately claim to have received a license to use the plaintiff's work, and that the work the plaintiff claims to infringe on his copyright falls within that license. For instance, Programmer A orally tells Programmer B he can copy his work, then later claims never to have granted the permission.
- Conflicting or confusing licenses or sublicenses are granted and you claim to be the rightful owner of the right(s) in question.
- You received a transfer from the plaintiff and weren't restricted in making further transfers, and transferred the copyright to individuals unknown to the original owner.

c. Statute of Limitations

A plaintiff can't wait forever to file an infringement suit. As discussed in Section H4, the statute of limitations is three years from the time the infringement should reasonably have been discovered (but applying this rule can be extremely tricky). If the plaintiff waited too long, you may be able to have the case dismissed.

d. Other Defenses

Some of the other possible defenses to copyright infringement include such things as:

- the notion that if the plaintiff is guilty of some serious wrongdoing himself or herself—for example, falsifying evidence—he or she cannot complain about your alleged wrongs
- the notion that the plaintiff waited so long to file suit that it would be unfair to find the defendant guilty of infringement—"it is inequitable for the owner of a copyright, with full notice of an intended infringement, to stand inactive while the proposed infringer spends large sums of money on its exploitation, and to intervene only when his speculation has proved a success. Delay under such circumstances allows the owner to speculate without risk with the other's money; he cannot possibly lose, and he may win." (*Hass v. Leo Feist, Inc.*, 234 Fed. 105 (S.D.N.Y. 1916).)
- The idea that the copyright owner knew of your acts and expressly or impliedly consented to them.

2. Collecting Your Attorney Fees If You Prevail

If the plaintiff (the person who sues you for infringement) loses his or her suit, the court has discretion to award you all or part of your attorney fees. In the past, many courts would award such fees to a defendant only if they found that the plaintiff's suit was frivolous or brought in bad faith. But these courts would not use this criterion when making fees awards to plaintiffs. In 1994 the Supreme Court held that this approach was incorrect and that attorney fees must be awarded to plaintiffs and defendants in an evenhanded manner. In other words, the same criteria must be applied to both plaintiffs and defendants. (*Fogerty v. Fantasy, Inc.*, 114 S.Ct. 1023 (1994).)

What this means is that if you defeat your accuser in court, you have a good chance of getting an award against him or her for some or all of your attorney fees. The actual amount you'll be awarded, if any, is up to the judge. However, such an award will be useless unless the plaintiff has the money or insurance to pay it.

Part II.   Suing Others for Copyright Infringement

The other side of the copyright infringement equation involves suing others for infringing on your protected work. When a copyright dispute arises, there are often several self-help steps a copyright owner can take. These generally amount to telling the infringer to stop the infringing activity and/or pay for the infringement. When push comes to shove, however, there is only one remedy with teeth in it: to ask a federal court to order the infringing activity halted and to award a judgment for damages. Because this type of litigation is procedurally complex, an attorney skilled in copyright litigation is required. (See Chapter 16.)

This discussion is not intended as a substitute for a good copyright attorney. Rather, its aim is to:

- help you recognize when copyright infringement has occurred
- suggest some steps you—as a software author or other copyright owner—might take on your own to deal effectively with infringement without resorting to lawyers and the courts
- tell you what to expect in the event of a court action, and
- help you estimate what damages and other types of court relief are potentially available to you in an infringement suit.

E. What Is Software Copyright Infringement?

In Chapter 2, a copyright was described as a bundle of five exclusive rights. These include the right to reproduce, distribute, prepare derivative works based upon, perform and display a protected work. Subject to important exceptions discussed in Section B, these rights cannot be exercised by anybody but the copyright owner unless the owner's permission is ob-

tained. If copyright rights are exercised without the owner's permission, the copyright is said to be infringed.

Software copyright infringement usually involves the unauthorized exercise of a copyright owner's exclusive rights to reproduce and/or distribute the work and/or prepare derivative works based on it. However, the display and performance rights can be violated as well. For example, simply using a program might violate a copyright owner's display rights.

Courts generally use the word copying as shorthand for violation of any of these exclusive copyright rights (not just the reproduction right). Thus, a copyright owner must prove copying by the defendant to win an infringement suit.

F. How to Know Whether You Have a Valid Infringement Claim

When a civil copyright infringement action is filed, the person bringing the action (called the plaintiff) must prove certain facts in order to prevail. This is called the burden of proof. While a detailed discussion of court procedure is beyond the scope of this book, here are the major things you must establish to prove infringement:

- you are the lawful owner of all or part of a work protected by a valid copyright
- one or more of the copyright rights you own has been infringed, and
- the person, partnership or corporation being sued has actually done the infringing act or contributed to it (called a contributory infringer).

Once you've proven infringement, the next step is to establish what remedies you're entitled to. If you can show that the infringer profited from the infringement, or negatively affected your profits, you may be able to recover these profits (what the infringer gained or what you lost) from the infringer, subject, of course, to any defenses the infringer may have (discussed in Section D1). Or you may be eligible to elect to receive statutory damages instead of your actual damages caused by the infringement (see Section I2b). In addition, the judge has discretion to award you attorney's fees (see Section I4). Finally, you can have the court order the infringer to stop future infringement and destroy all existing copies.

Let's look at these proof requirements one at a time:

1. Ownership of a Work Protected by Copyright

The question of infringement does not even arise unless the work allegedly infringed is protected by copyright. This means that the work must meet the three prerequisites for copyright protection discussed in detail in Chapter 3; that is, the work must be:

- *Fixed in a tangible medium of expression.* A work is sufficiently fixed if it exists on paper, on disk, or even just in computer RAM.
- *Independently created.* You cannot sue someone for copying software or other materials that you copied from others.
- *Minimally creative.* The work you believe has been infringed upon must have been the product of a minimal amount of creativity. The vast majority of software easily satisfies this requirement; but some databases may not.

Timely Registration Creates Presumption of Validity of Copyright and Ownership

As long as your work is registered within five years of the date of first publication, it is presumed to be protected by a valid copyright and the persons named in the registration certificate are presumed to be the lawful copyright owners. This is one of the greatest benefits of copyright registration. It means that you do not have to go to the time and trouble of proving that your work is original (which can be very hard to prove) or that you actually created it. Rather, it's up to the alleged infringer to try to prove that the work was not original or that your copyright is invalid for some other reason, or that you are not really the owner of the copyright.

---

2. Infringement of Your Copyright Rights

As a practical matter, most cases of software copyright infringement involve a violation of the owner's exclusive right to make copies. That is, someone copies all or part of somebody else's program without the owner's permission. For purposes of illustration, this discussion assumes that is the case here. Although the focus here is on the right to make copies, the principles discussed relative to copying also apply to all copyright rights that make up the entire bundle of rights (such as the exclusive right to display the work or create derivative works based on it).

To prevail in an infringement lawsuit, the plaintiff must prove that an infringement actually occurred. If someone is caught with an exact copy of a copyrighted work, or is seen copying it, the plaintiff has what is aptly called a smoking gun. The infringing villain has been caught red-handed.

Unfortunately, this type of evidence usually isn't available. Most infringers are smart enough to attempt to disguise their copying. Where source code is involved, for example, it is easy for an infringer to use a text editor to disguise its origin by rearranging lines or blocks of code, changing variable names or altering certain sequences of operations. Moreover, there are rarely any witnesses to copyright infringement. Infringement usually happens behind closed doors and the participants rarely admit their involvement.

This means that in most cases you must prove two things to establish infringement:

- that the claimed infringer had access to your work, and
- that the infringing work is *substantially similar* to your work.

If these are proven, copying is *inferred* because there is no other reasonable explanation for the similarities. However, the defendant can rebut (defeat) the inference by proving independent creation—that is, that his or her work was created without copying your work. Let's take a closer look at these two infringement criteria.

a. Access

To prove access, you must show that the alleged infringer had the opportunity to view and copy your software. This requirement is easy to show if the work is mass-marketed. It may be more difficult if the work has only been accessible to a very few people or the source code has been protected as a trade secret. Problems can develop, for example, when software that is very narrowly distributed under a license agreement is pirated. In one legal decision, access was established when a marketing firm changed clients and showed a copy of the former client's product to the new clients, resulting in copyright infringement. (*Synercom Technology, Inc. v. University Computing Company*, 462 F.Supp. 1003 (1978).)

Salting Code to Prove Copying

The best evidence of infringement is to produce a smoking gun in the hands of the infringer. In the software business, this usually means catching the pirate with a program that is somehow instantly identifiable as being the plaintiff's. Since even the most stupid pirate will probably be smart enough to remove the plaintiff's copyright notice if one is used, the wary programmer should bury nonfunctional and idiosyncratic symbols somewhere in the code or salt it with intentional nonharmful errors or unnecessary codings. The idea is to subtly brand the program so it can easily be identified in the event it is copied by someone else.

---

b. Substantial similarity

Proving substantial similarity is usually the crux of any copyright infringement case. Assuming the alleged infringer had access to your work, the similarities between your work and his must be compared to see if copying may reasonably be inferred. The similarities must be such that they can only be explained by copying, not by factors such as coincidence, independent creation or the existence of a prior common source for both programs.

Today, the first step most courts take is to filter out the unprotectible elements of the plaintiff's program before comparing it with the allegedly infringing program. Under this filtration test, those elements of the plaintiff's program that are not protected by copyright are identified and eliminated from consideration. This includes, for example, ideas, elements dictated by efficiency or external factors or taken from the public domain. (See Section B1.) After this filtration process is completed, there may or may not be any protected program elements left. If there are, this core of protected expression is compared with the allegedly infringing program of the defendant to see if there has been impermissible copying. (*Computer Associates International, Inc. v. Altai, Inc.* 982 F.2d 692 (2d Cir. 1992); *Gates Rubber Co. v. Bando Ltd.*, 9 F.3d 823 (10th Cir. 1993).)

The defendants in most software copyright infringement actions will doubtless claim that any alleged similarities relate only to elements of the plaintiff's program that should be filtered out as unprotectible. This filtration test can make it very difficult for plaintiffs to win infringement cases. Indeed, it makes it difficult for plaintiffs and their attorneys to know whether they have a good infringement case in the first place, since opinions can and will naturally differ as to what elements should and should not be filtered from the infringement analysis.

The clearest cases of copyright infringement involve wholesale copying of your computer code as described in Section A1 above. You'll likely have far more difficulty proving infringement when you allege that nonliteral elements of your program have been copied—that is, things other than computer code such as the user interface. (See Chapter 7.)

The bottom line is that it is virtually impossible for even the most experienced software attorney to predict with confidence whether a nonliteral infringement claim will succeed. In effect, plaintiffs who bring these cases enter a crap shoot: You pay your money and take your chance.

Good Records May Help Win Infringement Cases

Good records of the development process may be crucial for success by infringement plaintiffs where the filtration test discussed above is used. Software developers should get in the habit of keeping meticulous records from the initial idea stage of development, through coding, debugging, testing and the revision process. This should include copies of storyboards and prototypes, interim versions, flowcharts and internal memoranda documenting the many decisions that must be made in the course of software development. Documentation like this may prove very useful if the defendant claims that important elements of your work should be filtered out of the infringement analysis because they were in the public domain, dictated by external factors or efficiency and so forth. If your documentation shows that the disputed elements were the result of creative thinking and problem-solving on your part, not merely the result of standard programming techniques, they should not be filtered out.

G. Self-Help Remedies for Copyright Infringement

If you suspect your copyright has been infringed, you should discuss your problem with a copyright attorney, even if you plan to try to settle or compromise with the infringer without court action. A preliminary conference shouldn't be expensive. However, whether you see an attorney at this stage or not, there are some preliminary things you can safely do on your own.

1. Determine Scope of the Problem

Your first step is to make a common sense assessment of how large the problem is. Who is the infringer? What are the infringer's motives? How much infringement is occurring?

If you believe your copyright has been infringed by an ex-employee who created a program substantially similar to your own without authorization, the possible ways of dealing with the infringement are different than if you're dealing either with an unauthorized posting on the Internet or with an international pirate based in Taiwan. In one situation (the Internet), a cease and desist letter (Section G3) might be sufficient, whereas in another (the international pirate), nothing short of a large-scale lawsuit will probably work. And something in between may be the correct approach for the infringement by the ex-employee.

2. Collect Information About Your Copyright Registration

It is a good idea to make sure your copyright records are complete in the event a visit to a lawyer is necessary to stop the infringer. Hopefully, you've registered your copyright and have retained copies of all filed documents and correspondence with the Copyright Office. You should also have retained copies of all copyright transfers you've made.

Because you're human, however, one or more of these documents may have slipped through your fingers. If so, you'll need to obtain a copy of the missing documents from the Copyright Office. Fortunately, Copyright Office records are public records. This means that any member of the public can obtain copies of the information, application, deposit, other documents relating to registration or ownership. However, you must provide the Copyright Office with specific information, including:

- The type of record you're interested in (for instance, the correspondence between the Copyright Office and the copyright owner, a copy of the deposit, a certificate of registration).
- Whether you require certified or uncertified copies (you would want certified copies in case you need to introduce them in a lawsuit).
- Complete identification of the record, such as the type of work (program, novel, manual, etc.), the complete registration number, the year or approximate year of registration, the complete title of the work as it appears on the application, the author, including any pseudonym by which the author may be known, the claimants, and the volume and page number where the document is recorded if you're seeking a copy of an assignment, any exclusive license, or other recorded contract.

- Any additional information that may be required for the specific record you want. For instance, obtaining copies of deposits requires that you comply with some additional conditions.
- $4 for each certification requested and $4 for additional copies of the application. The fees for all other requests will be added up by the Copyright Office on a case-by-case basis.
- Your telephone number and address, so the Copyright Office can contact you for additional information.

If you don't provide the year or the title of the work, a search of the records may be required for verification of your request. The fee for this search is $20 per hour.

Mail your request to:

Certification and Documents Section
LM-402
Copyright Office
Library of Congress
Washington DC 20559

DEAR COPYRIGHT OFFICER:
I AM WRITING REGARDING.

3. Cease and Desist Letter

Once you've mailed your request for any missing copyright records, you may want to send the alleged infringer a cease and desist letter. This sort of letter serves several functions:

- First, it lets the infringer know that you believe she is infringing your copyright.
- Second, it dates your discovery of the infringing activity, should more serious action be warranted later. This is important for purposes of the statute of limitations on copyright infringement lawsuits discussed below.
- Third, it tells the infringer that you have every intention of stopping her.
- Fourth, and perhaps most important, it gives the infringer a chance to explain her conduct and

perhaps offer a satisfactory compromise, before you've spent a lot of money initiating a lawsuit. Even if you're sure you're right, it doesn't hurt to listen to the other person's story. In addition, by giving the infringer a chance to respond, you may find out a lot about how he or she plans to defend a court action.

Here is what is normally covered in a cease and desist letter:

- who you are, including your business address and telephone number, or, if you want to protect your privacy, some way to contact you—such as a P.O. box
- the name of your work, date of first publication, and the copyright registration certificate number, if your work is registered
- the nature of the activity you believe to be an infringement of your copyright
- a demand that the infringer cease and desist from the activity, and
- a request for a response within a stated period of time.

Your letter can threaten legal action, but you're probably wiser not to at this stage. The specter of courts and lawyers usually does little but make the other person paranoid, defensive and unwilling to cooperate.

If you act as if your lawsuit is only hours away, the answer to your letter is likely to come from the infringer's lawyer. Once two lawyers are involved, the chances of any compromise settlement are greatly reduced, as lawyers, by the very nature of their profession, usually get paid more to fight than to compromise.

When you draft your letter, remember that you may end up wanting to use it in court. Accordingly, avoid being cute, nasty, tentative or overly dramatic. The following example contains about the right tone and level of information.

Sample Cease and Desist Letter

> January 1, 200X
> Ms. Oleo Oboe, President
> Oboe, Inc.
> 567 Symphony Drive
> Anywhere, USA 11111
>
> Dear Ms. Oboe:
>
> I recently became aware of your manufacture and sale of a CD-ROM called *100 Best Java Applets*. I am the owner of the copyright in a Java Applet entitled *Java 1-2-3*, copyright registration No. 22222222. I believe that your CD-ROM contains a copy (or a substantial copy) of *Java 1-2-3*. Since I have not authorized you or your company to make or sell copies of *Java 1-2-3*, it follows that you're infringing my copyright by doing so.
>
> This letter is to demand that you and Oboe, Inc., immediately cease and desist from the manufacture and sale of *Java 1-2-3*, on the CD-ROM *100 Best Java Applets* or by any other means. In addition, I request reasonable compensation for the copies you have already sold and your remaining inventory.
>
> Please respond to this letter by January 15, 20XX.
>
> Sincerely,
>
> *Carl Jones*
>
> 123 Action Street
> Hollywood, CA

Cease and desist letters should be sent by certified mail, return receipt requested. If the infringer refuses to accept your letter, arrange to have it delivered personally, by someone who isn't involved in the dispute and who'll be available to testify that the letter was delivered to the party, if that should become necessary.

What you do next depends on the response you receive, as well as the nature of the infringer and the infringing conduct. Reasonable and routine solutions to many infringements include:

- payment for profits previously made on the infringing work

- making the infringement legal through a license under which you're paid an agreed-upon fee for all future copies, and
- getting the infringer to agree to stop future infringements.

Mediation as an Alternative to Litigation

One low-cost alternative to filing a lawsuit is getting the other party to agree to mediation. In mediation, the parties to a dispute work with a mediator to attempt to reach an amicable settlement. Mediation is informal. Typically, the mediator either sits the parties down together and tries to provide an objective view of their disputes, or shuttles between the parties as a cool conduit of what may be red-hot opinions. A good mediator may be able to lead the parties to a mutually satisfactory resolution that will obviate time-consuming and expensive litigation. Mediation is nonbinding—that is, either side can still file a lawsuit if it wants to. The mediator can be a lawyer, but doesn't have to be. Many organizations provide mediation services, including the American Arbitration Association, which has offices in most major cities. In most cases, however, mediation is a realistic alternative only where the parties are located near each other. It's not likely that either party would want to incur substantial travel expenses to take part in such an informal, nonbinding procedure. For further information on mediation, refer to *Mediate Your Dispute*, by Peter Lovenheim (Nolo Press).

---

4. Settlement Letter

Any compromise settlement should be in writing, and signed by all parties. At this point, you should definitely get the help of a lawyer with experience in the area.

Here is a sample of the way the *Java 1-2-3* dispute might be settled:

Sample Settlement Letter

Ms. Oleo Oboe, President

Oboe, Inc.

567 Symphony Drive

Anywhere, USA 11111

Dear Ms. Oboe:

This letter embodies the terms and conditions to settle all outstanding disputes between Oboe, Inc., and Carl Jones and to authorize Oboe, Inc., to market the computer program, *Java 1-2-3*.

Carl Jones and Oboe, Inc., hereby agree:

1. Oboe, Inc., will pay Carl Jones the sum of $10,000 for copies of *Java 1-2-3* sold up to the date of our agreement, January 20, 20XX.

2. Oboe, Inc., will place the following copyright notice on all copies of *Java 1-2-3* sold from January 20, 20XX, until termination of our Standard Resellers Agreement: © copyright Carl Jones 20XX.

3. Oboe, Inc., will execute and be bound by the terms of our Standard Resellers Agreement attached hereto.

4. Carl Jones agrees that this agreement completely settles the matter in dispute between Carl Jones and Oboe, Inc., and releases Oboe, Inc., from any further liability for the sale of *Java 1-2-3* prior to January 20, 20XX.

Carl Jones

123 Acton Street

Hollywood, CA

H. Nuts and Bolts of Infringement Lawsuits

If you can't satisfactorily resolve the matter yourself (perhaps through mediation and/or with a short consultation with a copyright lawyer), you have two alternatives: forget about it, or hire a lawyer and bring an infringement suit in federal court. The following is an overview of the nuts and bolts of a copyright infringement suit. It is intended to give you a general idea of what you can expect from copyright litigation, not as a substitute for further research or a consultation with an experienced copyright attorney. See Chapter 16 for a guide to further research and ways to find a copyright attorney.

1. Who Can Sue

A person or entity who files an infringement suit is called the plaintiff. The plaintiff must be someone who owns the copyright rights at issue, or holds an exclusive license to them. This will typically be the creator of the software or a person or entity to whom the creator has transferred ownership—for example, a software publisher.

> **EXAMPLE:** DynoSoft, Inc., a software publisher, purchases the exclusive right to publish in the United States a computer game called *Life or Death*. DynoSoft discovers that a pirated version of the game is being sold in the U.S. by CopySoft, Inc. DynoSoft is entitled to sue CopySoft for copyright infringement.

a. Copyright registration prerequisite to suit

A civil lawsuit based on a claim of copyright infringement of a U.S. copyright cannot be brought unless and until the copyright has been registered with the U.S. Copyright Office. Registration can occur after an infringing act and you can still sue for that infringement. However, if you registered prior to the infringement (or within three months of publication), you're eligible for special statutory damages, attorney fees and certain other procedural benefits that are not available if you waited to register until after the infringement began. (See Chapter 4.)

Registration is not required where a resident of a foreign country that has signed the Berne copyright convention files an infringement suit in the U.S. See Chapter 14 for a list of Berne signatory countries.

Copyright registration can take anywhere from three to six months or even longer. However, if you need to register immediately so that you can sue, there is an expedited procedure by which registration can be accomplished in a much shorter period. You must pay an extra fee and follow the procedure set out in Chapter 4, Section K.

2. Criminal Liability for Infringement

Willful copyright infringement for financial gain has long been a federal crime, punishable by imprisonment, fines or both. However, as a practical matter this didn't mean much because the federal authorities rarely bothered to prosecute copyright infringers. They just didn't view copyright infringement as a high priority crime justifying allocation of limited law enforcement resources.

This has changed, at least with regard to infringement of computer software, an activity software publishers claim costs them billions of dollars every year. The U.S. Justice Department and FBI have been actively going after software pirates, particularly those who use the Internet. The FBI has established a computer crime squad headquartered in San Francisco. In 1997, it raided home and offices in eight cities, seizing computers it alleged were being used in nationwide computer piracy rings that used the Internet and BBSs.

In the best known case of its kind, the U.S. Attorney attempted to prosecute an MIT student who set up a computer bulletin board to dispense copyrighted software for free. The case was ultimately dismissed because the infringer didn't earn any money from his actions. (*United States v. LaMacchia*, 871 F.Supp. 535 (D.Mass. 1994).)

In response to this defeat, Congress has amended the copyright law to permit criminal prosecutions of those who commit copyright infringement, even if they don't do so for financial gain. Two different types of copyright infringement can now result in criminal liability:

a. Willful infringement not for financial gain

First, it is now a federal crime to willfully reproduce or distribute by electronic or any other means one or more copyrighted works with a total retail value of $1,000 or more within any 180-day period. This is so even though the infringer earns no money or other financial gain from the infringement.

There is a sliding scale of penalties that can be imposed against people convicted of violating this law:

If the copyrighted works involved have a total retail value of more than $1,000 but less than $2,500, a violator can be imprisoned for up to one year and/or fined up to $100,000.

If the offense consists of the reproduction or distribution of 10 or more copies of one or more copyrighted works with a total retail value of $2,500 or more, the violator can be imprisoned for up to three years and fined up to $250,000. Jail time can be increased to six years in the case of a second offense.

This provision was specifically designed to apply to people who use the Internet or electronic bulletin boards to copy and distribute pirated software, but who don't charge users for the copies or otherwise financially benefit from the infringement.

b. Willful infringement for financial gain

The criminal penalties are greater if a person willfully commits copyright infringement for financial gain. "Financial gain" includes receipt, or expectation of receipt, of anything of value, including the receipt of other copyrighted works.

If less than 10 unauthorized copies are made, or the copied works have a retail value of less than $2,500, violators can be imprisoned up to one year and/or fined up to $100,000.

If the offense consists of reproducing or distributing during any 180-day period, at least 10 copies of one or more copyrighted works, with a retail value of more than $2,500, violators can be jailed for up to five years and/or fined up to $250,000. Jail time can be increased to 10 years in the case of a second or subsequent offense.

3. Who Is Liable for Infringement

Although a primary goal may be simply to stop an infringer from distributing any more copies of an infringing software, you are also entitled to collect damages from those liable for the infringement. You may also be able to receive special statutory damages, which is an important right when your actual damages are very small or difficult to prove, and at-

torney fees as well. (See Section I below for a detailed discussion of damages.)

Who may be liable for such damages and fees? Quite simply, *everybody* who participates in or contributes to copyright infringement.

4. How Much Time You Have to Sue: Statute of Limitations

There are strict time limits on when copyright infringement suits may be filed. If you fail to file in time, the infringer may be able to have your suit dismissed, even though you have a strong case.

The general rule is that an infringement suit must be filed within three years after the date the copyright owner should reasonably have discovered the infringing act occurred. This is usually plenty of time. However, in some cases, it can reasonably take the copyright owner a long time to discover that the infringement took place, especially where the infringer attempted to conceal the act of infringement. For this reason, if more than three years have passed since the infringing work was first published, don't jump to the conclusion that your suit is barred by the statute of limitations. Again, see a copyright attorney.

Seek Legal Help. In cases where you have not discovered the infringement fairly promptly after it has occurred, statute of limitations questions can be tricky. It's wise to see a knowledgeable copyright lawyer about the proper application of the limitations period to your particular case.

I. What You Can Get If You Win: Remedies for Copyright Infringement

Once you've proven the elements of infringement discussed in Section F above, the next step is to establish what remedies you're entitled to. The potential remedies include:

- *Injunctive relief.* This typically consists of a court order requiring the infringer (the defendant) to stop the infringing activity and destroy all remaining copies of the infringing work.
- *Actual damages and infringer's profits.* The plaintiff is entitled to be compensated for the value of lost sales (often difficult to prove) and for other monetary losses resulting directly from the infringement. The plaintiff is also entitled to collect the amount of the defendant's profits from the infringement.
- *Statutory damages.* If the plaintiff's work was timely registered and she so chooses, she is entitled to receive special statutory damages provided in the copyright law (statute) instead of actual damages and other economic damages.
- *Attorney fees.* A copyright owner may also be awarded attorney fees by the judge.

We'll examine each remedy in turn. Again, this isn't a complete description of the legal procedures involved, but is designed to give you an overview of the available remedies.

1. Injunctive Relief

An injunction is a court order telling someone to stop doing something. In a copyright infringement action, the order usually is simply for the defendant to stop the infringing activity. This is commonly a quick, effective remedy because, in many cases, it is possible to get positive action from the court long before the actual trial is held to decide who wins.

Indeed, it is possible to get a temporary restraining order (TRO) almost immediately with very short notice to the defendant. A TRO may last ten days at most. A hearing must then be held on whether the judge should issue a preliminary injunction. A preliminary injunction operates between the time it is issued and the final judgment in the case. This interim court order is available when it appears likely to a federal judge, on the basis of written documentation and a relatively brief hearing at which the lawyers

for each side present their view of the dispute, that (1) the plaintiff will most likely win the suit when the trial is held, and (2) the plaintiff will suffer irreparable injury if the preliminary injunction isn't granted. Ordinarily, irreparable injury is presumed to exist where someone infringes upon a copyright owner's exclusive rights. (*Apple Computer, Inc. v. Franklin Computer Corp.,* 714 F.2d 1240 (3rd Cir. 1983).)

If the judge grants the preliminary injunction, the plaintiff must post a bond in an amount determined by the judge. If the injunction is later found to have been wrongfully granted, the defendant can collect from the bond the damages and costs he incurred due to the injunction.

Once a preliminary injunction is granted, it remains in effect pending a further determination of whether infringement occurred at the formal trial. In theory, a trial will probably be held one or two years later. In fact, the parties often fashion a settlement based on the results of the preliminary injunction hearing.

If a settlement is not reached and a full-scale trial occurs, the same issues raised in the preliminary injunction hearing (and possibly additional issues) will be litigated in more detail. If the plaintiff again prevails, the preliminary injunction will be converted into a permanent one, either including the same terms and orders or different ones, depending on what the plaintiff proves at trial. If the plaintiff loses, the preliminary injunction (if one was granted) will be dissolved and the defendant can go back to doing what it was doing before, plus be compensated for the consequences of the lawsuit by the issuer of the bond that was required for the preliminary injunction.

2. Damages

If you win a copyright infringement suit, you usually have the right to collect money (called damages) from the infringer.

a.   Actual damages and infringer's profits

Actual damages are the lost profits and/or other losses sustained as a result of the copyright infringement. In other words, actual damages are the amount of money that the plaintiff would have made but for the infringement. This may include compensation for injury to plaintiff's reputation due to the infringement and for lost business opportunities (often difficult to prove). To obtain actual damages, the plaintiff must prove in court that the alleged losses actually occurred. This may not be too difficult where the plaintiff can prove (through witnesses, software audits, business records or other means) that the defendant has committed software piracy. It should be easy to show how much each unauthorized copy cost the plaintiff.

Proving damages may be much more difficult where the defendant has copied from the plaintiff's work to create a competing product. How does the plaintiff prove that its sales have been hurt by the competition? Evidence that sales of plaintiff's software immediately went down when the defendant's infringing competing product was introduced to the market might be the best means to establish damages in this situation.

As stated above, the plaintiff is also entitled to recover the amount of the defendant's profits from the infringement to the extent they exceed the plaintiff's recovery for her lost profits.

> **EXAMPLE:** Plaintiff is awarded $10,000 for lost sales due to defendant's infringement. The defendant earned $15,000 in profits from the infringement. Plaintiff is entitled to $5,000 of defendant's profits.

To establish the defendant's profits, the plaintiff is required only to prove the defendant's gross revenue from the infringing work. The defendant's business records (obtained by the plaintiff through formal "discovery" procedures) would usually be presented for this purpose. The defendant must then prove what its actual net profit from the infringement was—that is, the defendant must produce records or witnesses to show the amount of expenses deductible from the infringing work's gross revenues (such as production and distribution costs in the case of published infringing software) and the amount of profit, if any, attributable to the noninfringing material in the defendant's work (often difficult to prove).

b.   Statutory damages

Statutory damages are set by the copyright law and require no proof of how much the loss was in monetary terms. However, statutory damages are only available if the work was timely registered—that is, before the infringement began or within three months of publication. Statutory damages are awarded at the judge's discretion and don't depend on having to prove a loss in any specific amount due to the infringement. You have to decide whether you want statutory damages or your actual damages and the defendant's profits. You can't collect both.

Statutory damages fall within the following range:

- Absent a finding that the infringer acted either willfully or innocently, between $500 and $20,000 for all the infringements by a single infringer of a single work, no matter how many infringing acts there were. If multiple separate and independent works were infringed, statutory damages may be awarded for each work.
- If the court finds that the infringer acted willfully—that is, knew he or she had no legal right to the material he used, but took it anyway—it may increase the amount of statutory damages up to $100,000.
- But if the court finds that the infringer acted innocently—that is, he or she used the copyrighted material sincerely believing he had the right to do so—the judge has discretion to award as little as $200. However, if the work to which the infringer had access contained a valid copyright notice, the infringer may not claim to have acted innocently. This is why it is always a good idea to include a valid copyright notice on your software (even though a notice is not legally required for works published after March 1, 1989). (See Chapter 3.)

3. Seizing the Infringing Software

Another civil remedy for copyright infringement consists of an impound and destroy order from the court. This tells the federal marshal to go to the infringer's place of business (or wherever the infringing material is located) and impound any infringing works. If the plaintiff wins, the court may order the sheriff to destroy the infringing material. To obtain such an order, however, the plaintiff must post a bond at a value at least twice the reasonable value of the infringing software.

Seizure can happen at any time after the suit has been filed. It's usually done as soon as a complaint is filed, but before the defendant is served with a copy of the suit. This way, the defendant learns he or she has been sued only when the marshal comes to the defendant's premises to impound the infringing software.

This is an extremely effective remedy because it deprives the defendant of the infringing software . The defendant can only get it back if the plaintiff is defeated at trial.

4. Attorney Fees and Costs

If your suit is successful and you timely registered your copyright, the court may also order the defendant to pay your attorney fees and other costs of going to court, such as filing fees. However, this is not required. It's up to the judge to decide whether to make such an award and how much it should be (the amount must be reasonable). The criteria some courts use to decide whether to award attorney fees include whether the defendant acted in bad faith, unreasonably or was otherwise blameworthy. Many courts will be especially likely to award fees to a plaintiff whose actions helped to advance the copyright law or defend or establish important legal principles.

The cost of bringing an infringement suit can be very high, easily tens of thousands of dollars. If for no other reason than to have the opportunity of recovering your attorney fees should you have to bring an infringement suit, you should always timely register your work with the Copyright Office.

If the plaintiff loses his or her suit, the court has discretion to award the defendant all or part of his attorney fees. In the past, many courts would award such fees to a defendant only if they found that the plaintiff's suit was frivolous or brought in bad faith. But these courts would not use this criterion when making fees awards to plaintiffs. In 1994 the Supreme Court held that this approach was incorrect and that attorney fees must be awarded to plaintiffs and defendants in an evenhanded manner. In other words, the same criteria must be applied to both plaintiffs and defendants. (*Fogerty v. Fantasy, Inc.*, 114 S.Ct. 1023 (1994).)

⚠ Plaintiffs Should Only File Legitimate Infringement Cases. You should never file a copyright infringement case in order to get even with somebody even though you know you don't have a good case. Likewise, don't file clearly frivolous claims in the hope the defendant will pay you something merely to get you off his or her back and avoid having to pay for expensive litigation. In either instance, you will not only lose your case, but the judge will likely order you to pay all or part of the defendant's attorney fees. ■

International Software Copyright Protection

The United States dominates the worldwide software industry like few others. According to the Business Software Alliance (an industry trade association), U.S. publishers hold 75% of the global market for prepackaged software and about 60% of the market for custom software and software-related services.

Obviously, American software developers and publishers need to be concerned about protecting their products abroad. Copyright is the primary vehicle for international protection of software. Most foreign countries provide at least some copyright protection for software; and, because of recently enacted international trade agreements discussed below, the level of international copyright protection for software is growing. This doesn't mean that international software piracy isn't a major problem, far from it. But the overall picture is improving.

In this chapter we provide an overview of international copyright law, focusing on software copyright protection in Western Europe, Japan and Canada. We also discuss some affirmative steps you can take to protect your software outside the U.S.

The topic of international copyright protection in general, and software protection in particular, is an exceedingly complex one. We probably won't answer all your questions, but the information in this chapter should help you when you see a copyright attorney for specific legal assistance.

A. Overview of International Copyright Protection

There is no single body of international copyright law. Each country has its own copyright law that applies within its own borders. Thus, the protection afforded to software and other copyrighted works by the U.S. copyright laws ends at the United States borders. However, through a series of international treaties and trade agreements, almost all nations have agreed to give each other's citizens at least the same copyright protection they afford to their own citizens and to provide certain minimum protections for copyrighted works in general and software in particular.

As a result, whenever you create any software that is entitled to copyright protection in the U.S. you automatically receive copyright protection for the software in almost all the countries of the world. There is no need to file an application to obtain copyright protection in a foreign country—unlike the requirement for foreign filings to obtain patent and trademark protection in other countries. International copyright protection is automatic, free and essentially painless.

This section first discusses the five major international copyright and trade treaties providing for international copyright protection and then covers copyright protection for software in Western Europe, Canada and Japan.

The following chart show which of the world's nations are members of the most important of these treaties.

Members of Berne Convention, U.C.C. and GATT

Country	Berne Convention	U.C.C.	GATT	Country	Berne Convention	U.C.C.	GATT
Albania	✔			El Salvador	✔	✔	✔
Algeria		✔		Fiji	✔	✔	✔
Andorra		✔		Finland	✔	✔	✔
Argentina	✔	✔	✔	France	✔	✔	✔
Armenia		✔		Gabon	✔		✔
Australia	✔	✔	✔	Gambia	✔		✔
Austria	✔	✔	✔	Germany	✔	✔	✔
Azerbaijan		✔		Ghana	✔	✔	✔
Bahamas	✔	✔		Greece	✔	✔	✔
Bahrain			✔	Guatemala		✔	✔
Bangladesh		✔	✔	Guinea-Bissau	✔		
Barbados	✔	✔	✔	Haiti		✔	✔
Belarus		✔		Honduras	✔		✔
Belize		✔	✔	Hungary	✔	✔	✔
Benin (Dahomey)	✔			Iceland	✔	✔	✔
Bolivia	✔	✔	✔	India	✔	✔	✔
Bosnia	✔	✔		Indonesia			✔
Botswana			✔	Ireland	✔	✔	✔
Brazil	✔	✔	✔	Israel	✔	✔	✔
Burkina Faso	✔		✔	Italy	✔	✔	✔
Bulgaria	✔	✔		Jamaica	✔		✔
Burundi			✔	Japan	✔	✔	✔
Cambodia		✔		Jordan	✔	✔	
Cameroon	✔	✔	✔	Kazakhstan		✔	
Canada	✔	✔	✔	Kenya	✔	✔	✔
Central African Republic	✔		✔	Korea (South)			✔
Chad	✔		✔	Kuwait			✔
Chile	✔	✔	✔	Laos		✔	
China	✔	✔	✔	Lebanon	✔	✔	
Colombia	✔	✔	✔	Lesotho	✔		
Costa Rica	✔	✔	✔	Liberia	✔	✔	
Côte d'Ivoire	✔		✔	Libya	✔		
Croatia	✔	✔		Liechtenstein	✔	✔	
Cuba		✔	✔	Lithuania	✔		
Cyprus	✔	✔	✔	Luxembourg	✔	✔	✔
Czech Republic	✔	✔	✔	Madagascar	✔		✔
Denmark	✔	✔	✔	Malawi	✔		✔
Dominican Republic	✔	✔	✔	Malaysia		✔	✔
Ecuador	✔	✔		Maldives			✔
Egypt	✔		✔	Mali	✔		✔

Members of Berne Convention, U.C.C. and GATT (Cont.)

Country	Berne Convention	U.C.C.	GATT	Country	Berne Convention	U.C.C.	GATT
Malta	✔	✔	✔	Singapore			✔
Mauritania	✔		✔	Slovakia	✔	✔	
Mauritius	✔		✔	Slovenia	✔	✔	✔
Mexico	✔	✔	✔	South Africa	✔		✔
Moldova		✔		Spain	✔	✔	✔
Monaco	✔	✔		Sri Lanka	✔	✔	✔
Morocco	✔	✔	✔	Suriname	✔		✔
Mozambique			✔	Sweden	✔	✔	✔
Namibia	✔		✔	Switzerland	✔	✔	✔
Netherlands	✔	✔	✔	Tanzania			✔
New Zealand	✔	✔	✔	Thailand	✔		✔
Nicaragua		✔	✔	Tobago	✔	✔	✔
Niger	✔	✔	✔	Togo	✔		✔
Nigeria	✔	✔	✔	Tunisia	✔	✔	✔
Norway	✔	✔	✔	Turkey	✔		✔
Pakistan	✔	✔	✔	Turkmenistan		✔	
Panama		✔		Uganda			✔
Paraguay	✔	✔	✔	Ukraine		✔	
Peru	✔	✔	✔	United Kingdom	✔	✔	✔
Philippines	✔		✔	United States	✔	✔	✔
Poland	✔	✔	✔	Uruguay	✔	✔	✔
Portugal	✔	✔	✔	Uzbekistan		✔	
Romania	✔		✔	Vatican City	✔	✔	
Russia	✔	✔		Venezuela	✔	✔	✔
Rwanda	✔	✔	✔	Yugoslavia	✔	✔	
Senegal	✔	✔	✔	Zambia	✔	✔	✔
				Zimbabwe	✔		✔

1. The Berne Convention

The world's first major international copyright convention was held in Berne, Switzerland, in 1886. The resulting agreement was called the Berne Convention for the Protection of Literary and Artistic Works, or the Berne Convention for short. One hundred countries have signed the Berne Convention, including almost all major industrialized countries. These countries include the United States (as of March 1, 1989), most of western Europe, Japan, Canada, Mexico and Australia. (See the chart above for a complete list of Berne member countries.)

The basic protections for literary, artistic and scientific works under the Berne convention are discussed below.

a. Principle of national treatment

Every country that has signed the Berne Convention must give citizens or permanent residents of other Berne countries at least the same copyright protections that it affords its own nationals; this is known as national treatment. As a U.S. citizen or permanent resident, any protectible work you create or publish after March 1, 1989 (the date the U.S. joined the Berne Convention), is entitled to national treatment in every country that has signed the Berne Convention.

> **EXAMPLE:** AmeriSoft, a U.S. software developer, creates a German-English translation program. AmeriSoft publishes the program both in the U.S. and Germany. AmeriSoft subsequently discovers that unauthorized copies of the program are being made and sold by a small German publisher. Since the U.S. and Germany have both signed the Berne Convention, if AmeriSoft sues the German publisher for copyright infringement in the German courts, it will be entitled to the same treatment as any German citizen who brought such a suit.

b. No formalities

No formalities, such as notice and registration, may be required by a Berne country for basic copyright protection. However, some Berne countries offer greater copyright protection if a copyright is registered or carries a particular type of notice. For example, in Japan and Canada (as well as in the U.S.), registration provides a means of making your work a public record and may thus be helpful in case of an infringement action (see discussion in Sections 7 and 8 below). Other countries have certain procedural requirements that must be followed before foreign works may be distributed within their borders, such as customs rules, censorship requirements or other regulations. Compliance with these types of formalities should be taken care of by a foreign attorney or agent hired by a software publisher.

c. Minimal protections required

Every Berne country is required to offer a minimum standard of copyright protection in their own country to works first published or created by nationals of other Berne countries. This protection must include:

- Copyright duration of at least the author's life plus 50 years
- Authorization for governmental seizure of infringing goods as a remedy for copyright infringement
- Granting authors the following exclusive rights in their works:
  - translation,
  - performance in public,
  - broadcasting their works,
  - reproducing their works,
  - motion pictures, and
  - creating adaptations and arrangements from a protected work
- The granting of moral rights to authors. Moral rights are rights an author can never transfer to a third party because they are considered an extension of his or her being. Briefly, they consist of the right to:
  - claim authorship,
  - disclaim authorship of copies,
  - prevent or call back distribution under certain conditions, and

- object to any distortion, mutilation or other modifications of the author's work injurious to her reputation.

    The right to prevent colorization of black and white films is an example of a moral right. Moral rights are generally of most concern to visual artists and, despite the Berne Convention requirement, are not recognized in the U.S. except for artists.

- Some provision allowing for fair dealing or free use of copyrighted works. This includes material used in quotations for educational purposes, for reporting current events, and so forth. (In the United States, this is called fair use, and is discussed in detail in Chapter 13.)

The Berne Convention and Works Created Before March 1, 1989

As mentioned earlier, the United States was a latecomer to the Berne Convention. It did not join until March 1, 1989. The Berne Convention does not apply to a work first published in the U.S. before that date unless the work was also published in a Berne country at the same time (that is, within 30 days of each other). This is called simultaneous publication. Before 1989, American book publishers (and some software publishers) often had their works published simultaneously in the U.S. and Canada and/or Great Britain (both Berne countries) so that they could receive the protection of the Berne Convention. This fact was usually indicated on the same page as the work's copyright notice.

2. The Universal Copyright Convention

Another important international copyright treaty is the Universal Copyright Convention (U.C.C.). The United States joined the U.C.C. on September 16, 1955; it applies to all works created or originally published in the U.S. after that date. Where a country has signed both the U.C.C. and Berne Conventions, the Berne Convention has priority over the U.C.C. Since the U.S. has joined the Berne Convention, the U.C.C. is relevant to works by American nationals only (1) in countries that have signed the U.C.C. but not the Berne Convention (about 20 countries in all, most notably Russia and South Korea); and (2) to works first published in the U.S. before March 1, 1989, that were not simultaneously published in a Berne country.

The U.C.C. is very similar to the Berne Convention. It requires member countries to afford foreign authors and other copyright owners national treatment. The U.C.C. also requires that each signatory country provide adequate and effective protection of the rights of foreign authors and other foreign copyright owners of literary, scientific and artistic works.

Unlike the Berne Convention, the U.C.C. does not require member countries to dispense with formalities as a prerequisite to copyright protection. But an author or copyright owner of a work first published in one U.C.C. country can avoid complying with another U.C.C. country's formalities (registration, deposit, payment of fees, etc.) simply by placing the following copyright notice on all published copies of the work: © [Your name] [Date of first publication]. Compliance with the U.S. requirements for a valid copyright notice discussed in Chapter 4 also constitutes compliance with the U.C.C. notice requirement. This is one very good reason to always affix a valid copyright notice to your published work.

3. The WIPO Copyright Treaty

The Berne Convention was last revised in 1971, and neither it nor the U.C.C. specifically provided for copyright protection for software or digital technolo-gies. A copyright convention discussing protection for such technologies was held in 1996 by the World Intellectual Property Organization (WIPO), a United Nations agency headquartered in Geneva, Switzerland, that is responsible for administering the various international intellectual property treaties.

In late 1996 the U.S. and several other countries signed the WIPO Copyright Treaty (WCT). The WCT has yet to be ratified by the U.S. Senate and has not yet taken effect. However, approval seems likely. The treaty requires no significant changes in U.S. copyright law.

The WCT has also been signed by Belgium, Bolivia, Burkina Faso, Chile, Finland, Germany, Ghana, Greece, Hungary, Indonesia, Israel, Italy, Kazakhstan, Kenya, Luxembourg, Monaco, Mongolia, Namibia, Nigeria, Spain, Togo, the United Kingdom, Uruguay and Venezuela.

a. Protection for digital works

As written, existing international copyright agreements protect authors by giving them the right to control the production and distribution of physical copies. But, of course, there are no physical copies on the Internet and digital networks. By far the most significant aspect of the WCT is that it requires member countries to give copyright protection to works in digital form. This means, for example, that unauthorized copying of a program posted on a Website can constitute copyright infringement.

b. Software protections

The WCT provisions concerning software are very similar to those already enacted as part of the GATT trade agreement. (See Section 4.) Specifically, the WCT provides that:

- Computer programs are protected by copyright as literary works within the meaning of the Berne Convention. (See Section A1.) Such protection applies to computer programs "whatever may be the mode or form of their expression." This means that both source code and object code are protected as literary works.
- In addition, the WCT gives software owners the right to prohibit the commercial rental of their

works to others. However, this does not apply "where the program itself is not the essential object of the rental"—for example, one may rent a car that includes a computer program.

- The WCT also requires member countries to provide effective legal remedies against anyone who removes or alters electronic Rights Management Information (RMI) from copyrighted digital works— that is, electronically stored information regarding who owns the copyright in a digital work.

4. International Trade Agreements: GATT and NAFTA

The Berne Convention, U.C.C. and WIPO Copyright Treaty all sound good on paper. The problem with them, however, is they have few enforcement teeth. Because of this serious inadequacy, important protections for intellectual property, particularly software, were included in two international trade agreements: the GATT and NAFTA.

a. GATT and intellectual property rights

The General Agreement on Tariffs and Trade is called GATT for short. GATT is a multinational treaty signed by 117 nations dealing with tariffs and other international trade matters. It is, quite simply, the most important international trade agreement in history. Most of the world's trading nations are parties to GATT, including the U.S. GATT was ratified by the U.S. Senate in 1994.

For our purposes, what is most important about GATT is that it includes a special agreement on intellectual property called Trade Related Aspects of Intellectual Property Rights (TRIPS for short). TRIPS requires each member country to agree, as a minimum, to enact national copyright laws giving effect to the substantive provisions of the Berne Convention discussed above. However, moral rights, which are generally not recognized in the U.S., were expressly left out of TRIPS. This means that the U.S. cannot be subject to GATT dispute settlement procedures over the scope of moral rights.

Specifically with respect to software, TRIPS:
- provides that computer programs (whether object code or source code) are literary works within the meaning of the Berne Convention and are therefore entitled to full copyright protection and national treatment in all Berne countries, and
- requires GATT member countries to grant software owners the right to prohibit commercial rental of their computer programs (except if the program is not an essential object of the rental—for example, the copyright owner of the computerized electronic system that controls many automobile functions could not prohibit car rentals because the car, not the computer program, is the object of the rental).

But, perhaps most important of all, TRIPS requires all GATT member countries to provide significant penalties for copyright infringement. These must include injunctive relief (including preliminary injunctions that can be obtained to stop infringing activities before trial) and adequate monetary damages. In addition, member countries must adopt procedures for excluding infringing software and other goods at their borders upon application by U.S. or other copyright owners to their customs services.

GATT also includes mechanisms for enforcement of country-to-country disputes regarding implementation of these requirements. The entity responsible for handling disputes under GATT is the World Trade Organization, a new international agency based in Geneva—similar to the World Bank. Special GATT remedies (for example, withdrawal of tariff concessions) may be imposed for violation of GATT rules.

The only bad thing about the GATT/TRIPS agreement from software publishers' point of view is that it will not take effect immediately in many countries. Developing countries and countries in transition from centrally planned to market economies (primarily countries that were part of the former Soviet Union or Warsaw Pact members) will not have to comply until the year 2000. What are termed "least developed countries" need not comply until 2006.

b. NAFTA

The North American Free Trade Agreement (NAFTA for short) was approved by Congress in November 1993 and became effective on January 1, 1994. As the name implies, NAFTA is a treaty between Canada, Mexico and the U.S. Its primary purpose is to eliminate tariffs and other trade barriers between the three countries. However, NAFTA also contains important provisions regarding intellectual property protection for software. These provisions are very similar to those of the GATT/TRIPS agreement above.

First, NAFTA provides that all types of computer programs are literary works within the meaning of the Berne Convention above, and requires each country to protect them as such. NAFTA provides for the unrestricted transfer of copyright rights by contract and protects licensees' rights.

Like the GATT/TRIPS agreement, NAFTA requires that adequate damages and injunctive relief be provided for copyright infringement. NAFTA also provides for criminal penalties in cases of willful software piracy on a commercial scale, including fines, imprisonment and seizure and/or destruction of infringing goods. (NAFTA Article 1717.)

Perhaps most importantly, member countries are required to enforce the rights granted under NAFTA at the border—that is, prevent the importation or export of infringing goods.

5. Protections in Countries Not Covered by Treaties

There are some countries that have not signed any of the copyright treaties discussed above and that are not a party to trade agreements such as GATT. These include some countries in which copyright piracy is widespread, such as Taiwan. The United States has entered into bilateral (country-to-country) copyright treaties with some of these countries, including Taiwan, Indonesia and Singapore. Under these treaties, works by U.S. citizens are afforded copyright protection in the country involved. In addition, many countries afford foreign authors and their works copyright protection if the foreign author's country of origin provides similar treatment. This means it is possible for your work to be protected in a country that has not signed any of the multinational conventions or entered into a bilateral copyright treaty with the U.S.

However, some countries have no copyright relations with the U.S. and provide no protection for U.S. authors' works. These include Afghanistan, Bahrain, Bhutan, Ethiopia, Iran, Iraq, Mongolia, Nepal, Oman, Qatar, San Marino, Saudi Arabia, Sierra Leone, Tonga, United Arab Emirates and Yemen.

6. Software Protection in the European Community (EC)

The European Community (EC for short) comprises most of the nations of Western Europe, including Belgium, Denmark, France, Germany, Greece, Ireland, Italy, Luxembourg, the Netherlands, Portugal, Spain and the United Kingdom. The EC is in the process of being transformed into a single integrated market without internal frontiers in which the free movement of goods, services, people and capital will be ensured. The EC is the largest trading block in the world, with over 340 million consumers, and the largest market for software outside the U.S.

All EC countries are also members of the Berne Convention and GATT. U.S. software copyright owners are therefore entitled to the same copyright protection in an EC country as citizens of that country.

The EC is much like a supranational government, with its own parliament, courts and executive body. The EC passes and implements various types of legislation. In 1991, the EC adopted the Council Directive on the Legal Protection of Computer Programs (often referred to as the EC Software Directive). The purpose of the directive was to harmonize legal protection for software throughout the EC and provide computer software with a level of copyright protection comparable to that provided for such works as books, films and music recordings.

The EC Software Directive generally mirrors U.S. software copyright law; but there are a few differences which are noted below.

a. What is protected?

The directive mirrors U.S. law regarding what software is protected. It requires that all computer programs be protected as literary works within the meaning of the Berne Convention. So long as it is original—that is, the author's own intellectual creation—any program will be protected by copyright. Both source and object code are protected, as well as software embodied in semiconductor chips. Preparatory design materials—for example, specifications and flowcharts—are also protected. (EC Software Directive Art. 1(1).)

b. Scope of protection

As under U.S. law, protection applies only to the expression and not to the "ideas and principles which underlie any element of a computer program, including those which underlie its interfaces." (EC Software Directive Art. 1(2).) Whether, and to what extent, a program's look and feel and/or sequence, structure and flow will be protected is up to each EC country's courts.

c. Exclusive copyright rights

As under U.S. law, the owner of the copyright in a computer program has the exclusive right to:

- reproduce the program by any means
- translate, adapt, arrange or otherwise alter the program, and
- distribute the program to the public in any form. (EC Software Directive Art. 4.)

As under U.S. law, once a copy of a program is sold, the copyright owner loses all control over further distribution of that copy, except that the owner's permission must be obtained to rent or lease the program copy to the public.

Furthermore, in the absence of an express prohibition in a software license or other contract, a lawful owner of a program or a program copy may reproduce, translate or otherwise alter the program if necessary to use the program for its intended purpose or to correct program errors. For example, the user may load the program onto computer RAM for use in his computer. (EC Software Directive Art. 5(1).)

It is also permissible for a lawful user of a program to make a back-up copy of the program. (EC Software Directive Art. 5(2).)

d. Copyright ownership

Software copyright ownership under the directive mirrors U.S. law. The exclusive copyright rights in programs created by an employee "in the execution of his duties or following the instructions given by his employer" are owned by the employer unless otherwise provided by contract. (EC Software Directive Art. 2(3).)

Programs created by a number of individuals are jointly owned. (EC Software Directive Art. 2(2).)

The drafters of the directive omitted a provision which provided that the rights to a commissioned work automatically vest in the commissioning party. This means that a person or company that hires an independent contractor—that is, a nonemployee—to create software must enter into an agreement with the contractor to acquire his copyright rights. This is generally the same as under U.S. law.

e. Formalities

Unlike in the U.S., there is no system of copyright registration in the EC. It is not necessary for a copyright owner to comply with any formalities (copyright notice or registration) to obtain or maintain copyright protection within the EC. However, it is advisable to include a copyright notice on any published work distributed in the EC. Including a notice on your work ensures that it will be protected if it finds its way to a country that belongs to the U.C.C. but not the Berne Convention. There are about 20 such countries, most notably Russia.

f. Reverse engineering

Reverse engineering is the process of examining or taking apart a product to see how it works. This is permitted under U.S. copyright law and under the EC Software Directive. The directive seeks to aid standardization and interoperability of software, particularly computer interfaces. Therefore, the directive provides that a person having a right to use a copy of a computer program is entitled to "observe, study or test the functioning of the program" to understand its underlying principles and ideas. Such observation, study or testing is limited to the acts of normal use of the program—that is, it may be done while loading, displaying, running or storing the program. This provision does not permit any alteration or decompilation of the program. (EC Software Directive Art.5(3).) But see Section g just below.

g. Decompilation

Where reverse engineering alone does not provide sufficient information to "achieve the interoperability of an independently created computer program with other programs," the user may decompile the program under certain limited circumstances. Decompilation means using a decompiler to translate an object code copy of a program (which is unreadable by humans) into human-readable assembly language.

The question whether decompilation of software should be allowed was the most hotly debated issue during the deliberations over the directive. As enacted, the directive permits decompilation for the purposes of ascertaining sufficient information to permit the interoperability of hardware and software, but not to permit creation of competitive products.

Decompilation is allowed only if the following three conditions are met:
- First, decompilation of the code must be indispensable to obtain the interface information necessary

to make software interoperable with the decompiled program. Therefore, such interface information must not have been readily available to the person wishing to make an interoperable program.
- Second, decompilation may be performed only by a person who has a license or some other right to use the software or a person acting on his behalf.
- Finally, decompilation is restricted to those parts of the original program necessary to achieve interoperability. This means that only the interface may be decompiled, not the entire program. (EC Software Directive Art. 6(1).)

The directive specifically bars information obtained from decompilation from being used for the development of competing substantially similar programs. Furthermore, such information cannot be given to others except when necessary for the interoperability of an independently created program. (EC Software Directive Art. 6(2)(c).)

U.S. copyright law does not contain any counterpart to the EC Software Directive's limited decompilation right. However, U.S. courts have held that decompilation may be a fair use of a copyrighted program where it is necessary to gain access to elements of a program that are not protected by copyright—that is, ideas and other unprotected expression. (See Chapter 13.)

The upshot of all this is that U.S. companies that import software into the EC may find other companies decompiling their programs to create interoperable programs.

7. Software Copyright Protection in Japan

Japan accounts for about 20% of the worldwide computer market. It is a member of the Berne Convention and GATT. U.S. software copyright owners are therefore entitled to the same copyright protection in Japan as Japanese citizens.

a. Protection for software

Computer programs that are original or creative are expressly protected by the Japanese copyright law. Protection begins automatically upon creation. However, protection does not extend to programming languages, rules (an interface or protocol permitting one computer to interact with another), or algorithms. Both source code and object code are protected. (Japanese Revised Copyright Law, Arts. 2, 10.)

b. Exclusive rights

Under Japanese law a copyright owner has the exclusive right to reproduce, translate, adapt, perform or publicly exhibit the copyrighted work. The owner also has the exclusive right to rent copies of the work—that is, third parties cannot rent copies without getting the owner's permission. (Japanese Revised Copyright Law, Arts. 21–27.)

In addition, copyright owners are granted certain moral rights. These include the:

- right to make a work public—that is, to publish an unpublished work
- right to claim authorship—that is, the right to be recognized as author of a work and to determine the way the author's name should be used on a work or not to disclose the name
- right to integrity of one's work—that is, the right to prevent a work from being distorted, mutilated, or otherwise modified against the author's will. (Japanese Revised Copyright Law, Arts. 18–20.)

c. Exceptions to exclusive rights

Japanese law recognizes that the possessor of a copy of a computer program will often have to modify the program to get it to work on his computer. The owner of a copy of a program may make copies or adaptations of the program if and to the extent necessary for using use the program or protecting against its destruction. However, the owner must dispose of such copies if he transfers possession of the original copy of the program. (Japanese Revised Copyright Law, Arts. 20(2), 47.)

d. Software ownership

A work created by a single author is initially owned by that author. Works created by two or more authors are jointly owned. No single joint author may exercise the copyright rights in the joint work or transfer his ownership interest without the other joint authors' consent (which cannot be unreasonably withheld). (Japanese Revised Copyright Law, Art. 65.)

A program created by an employee at the employer's instruction and within the scope of employment is a work made for hire to which the employer owns the entire copyright, including any moral rights. (Japanese Revised Copyright Law, Art. 15.)

However, the Japanese work made for hire rule does not extend to works created by independent contractors. The copyright in a program created by an independent contractor is owned by the contractor unless the contractor transfers her rights to the hiring party. For this reason, companies hiring independent contractors in Japan to do programming should obtain an assignment of their copyright rights. Such an assignment should be in writing and contain a specific assignment of the rights to prepare and control derivative works (such rights are not transferred unless specifically indicated).

An independent contractor's moral rights, including the rights of integrity and authorship discussed above, may not be transferred or assigned to others. This means, for example, that an independent contractor-programmer could conceivably prevent a hiring firm from modifying software the contractor created for the firm, developing derivative works based upon it, or distributing it without identifying the contractor as the author, because such acts would violate his moral rights. To avoid this problem, hiring firms should obtain a contractor's affirmative consent in writing to carry out these and any other acts that might otherwise be barred by moral rights.

e. Formalities—copyright notice and registration

Since Japan is a Berne Convention signatory, it is not legally necessary to comply with any formalities to obtain or maintain a copyright. However, as in the United States, copyright notices are generally used on published works. Although not mandatory, a copyright notice prevents a defendant in an infringement suit from seeking to limit damages by arguing that the infringement was innocent.

Japan also has a nonmandatory copyright registration procedure. A special registry called the Program Register was established in 1986 for registration of computer programs. A foundation called the Software Information Center administers the Program Register. Registration provides certain evidentiary benefits in the event a copyright infringement suit is filed; for example, it establishes the date of creation and publication of the work. However, these benefits have rarely proved important in practice.

Copyright transfers may also be registered with the Copyright Register administered by the Director General of the Cultural Affairs Agency. It is important to register any assignment or transfer of copyright, since it will not be enforceable against any third party (that is, any person not covered by the transfer) unless it is registered. (Japanese Revised Copyright Law, Art. 77.)

f. Copyright infringement

A person who exercises any of an author's exclusive rights without the author's consent is guilty of copyright infringement. Japanese law specifically provides that a person who uses a pirated copy of a computer program is liable for copyright infringement if he or she was aware the copy was pirated. (Japanese Revised Copyright Law, Art. 113(2).)

Civil remedies for infringement include monetary damages, injunctions, seizure and destruction of infringing goods. Criminal penalties including imprisonment and fines may also be imposed on infringers.

8. Software Copyright Protection in Canada

Canada is a member of the Berne Convention, GATT and NAFTA. U.S. software copyright owners are therefore entitled to the same copyright protection in Canada as Canadian citizens.

a. Protection for software

Computer programs are protected as literary works so long as they are original and "expressed, fixed, embodied or stored in any manner." (Canadian Copyright Act, Sec. 2.) As under U.S. law, a minimum amount of creativity must have been required to create the software, but it need not be novel or inventive. It makes no difference whether a program is expressed as object or source code, or is embodied on computer chips, disks or any other form. Both application and operating system programs are protected.

b. Exclusive rights

A copyright owner has the exclusive right to reproduce, publish, adapt, translate or perform a protected work. (Canadian Copyright Act, Sec. 3(1).) In addition, Canadian law grants software authors certain "moral rights." These include the:

- right of integrity (permitting the software author to prevent modifications to software by the owner of a copy under certain circumstances), and
- right of paternity (the right to be recognized as author of the software). (Canadian Copyright Act, Sec. 5.)

c. Exceptions to exclusive rights

There are two important exceptions to a software copyright owner's exclusive rights:

- the owner of a copy of a program may alter or adapt it to the extent necessary for personal use, and
- the owner of a copy may make one copy of the program to serve as a back-up. (Canadian Copyright Act, Sec. 27(2).) Such copies must be destroyed if the copier ceases to be the lawful owner of the original program.

d. Software ownership

A work's author is its initial copyright owner. A work created by two or more authors is jointly owned by all of them. However, to qualify as a joint author, a person must contribute actual expression, not mere ideas. (Canadian Copyright Act, Sec. 13(1).)

Works created by employees within the course of employment are works made for hire to which the employer is considered the author and initial copyright owner. (Canadian Copyright Act, Sec. 13(3).)

However, the copyright in works created by independent contractors is owned by the contractor, not the hiring party. (*Goldner v. C.B.C.*, (1971) 7 C.P.R.(2d) 158 (Fed.Ct.).) This means that when a software consultant creates a program to a client's order, the consultant retains the copyright in the work and may recreate it and use it for other clients unless copyright is later transferred to the first client or such later use would violate any duty of confidentiality toward the client. As in the U.S., then, it is necessary for persons hiring Canadian independent contractors to create software to have them sign a written agreement transferring their copyright rights to the hiring party.

e. Copyright notice

Since Canada is a member of the Berne Convention, no formalities need be complied with to obtain copyright protection. It is not necessary to place a copyright notice. However, as discussed in Chapter 4, it is wise to do so anyway to obtain copyright protection in those countries that have signed only the U.C.C. copyright convention (notably, Russia and South Korea).

f. Copyright registration

Copyright registration is completely optional. Unlike in the U.S., it is not necessary to register to file a copyright infringement suit in Canada. The benefits of registration are much more limited than in the U.S. A person who registers a work in Canada receives a registration certificate from the Canadian Copyright Office. The certificate serves as evidence that your work is protected by copyright and that you—the person registered—are the owner. This means that in the event of a legal dispute, you do not have to prove ownership; the burden is on your opponent to disprove it. This will prove modestly beneficial if you ever sue someone for copyright infringement in Canada. It may be particularly helpful if you need to obtain a quick court injunction against a copyright pirate to stop an infringing activity.

To register, a completed application form and fee must be sent to the Canadian Copyright Office, which is part of the Department of Consumer and Corporate Affairs in Ottawa. It is not necessary to send a copy of the work being registered. You may obtain a copy of the application form by contacting the Canadian Copyright Office at:

Canadian Intellectual Property Office (CIPO)
Industry Canada
50 Victoria Street
Place du Portage, Phase I
Hull, Quebec
K1A 0C9
819-997-1936

The fee for registration is $35 in Canadian dollars. U.S. and other foreign applicants should pay by money order payable in Canadian funds. Registration is valid for as long as the copyright for the work exists. Once you register your copyright, you do not have to pay any additional fees to maintain or renew it.

Documents transferring copyright rights may also be registered with the Copyright Office upon production of the original document, a certified copy and payment of a fee. Registration is not mandatory, but gives a transfer certain priority rights over unregistered transfers.

g. Software infringement

A software copyright is infringed under Canadian law whenever a person exercises any of a software copyright owner's exclusive rights without receiving authorization. (Canadian Copyright Act, Sec. 27(1).)

Copyright infringement occurs where a substantial part of a protected work (in terms of quality) is taken or copied. However, as in the U.S., a Canadian copyright only protects the form or expression of a work, not the underlying ideas it contains. Thus, copyright does not protect a program's algorithm, only the particular way a program is written to express or implement an algorithm. (*Systems informatises Solartronix v. College d'enseignement general et professional de Jonquiere,* (1990) 38 C.P.R. (3d) 143 (Que. S.C.).)

Canada has a wide range of penalties for copyright infringement, including monetary penalties, injunctions, destruction of infringing copies and criminal penalties.

h. Fair use

Canadian law recognizes the concept of fair use (called fair dealing): "any fair dealing with any work for the purposes of private study, research, criticism, review, or newspaper summary" is not a copyright infringement. (Canadian Copyright Act, Sec. 27(2)(a).) However, this provision is narrowly construed by Canadian courts.

B. Strategies to Prevent International Software Piracy

Software piracy is not limited to the United States; it occurs around the world. The Software Publishers Association estimates that in one recent year the software publishing and distribution industries lost more than $12.8 billion due to software theft. The dollar loss was largest in the United States ($2.25 billion) with an estimated piracy rate of 35%. But the software piracy rate is thought to be much greater in most foreign countries: an estimated 80% in Japan, for example. The rates of piracy are even greater in less developed nations. According to the SPA, 99% of the software used in Pakistan, Thailand and Indonesia is pirated; 94% in China; 83% in Brazil; and 84% in Taiwan.

International copyright and trade agreements, and foreign copyright laws, may look good on paper but, of course, they don't prevent software piracy unless they are enforced. U.S. software owners can't rely on foreign governments to protect their rights for them. Indeed, some (particularly developing) countries look on piracy as a cheap and easy way to gain access to new technology. Following are some steps an American software owner can take to prevent, or at least reduce, piracy abroad.

1. Join a Software Trade Association

It is usually not economically feasible for an American software company to take direct action on its own to enforce its copyrights outside the U.S. Litigation costs are too high, the prospects of success are too dim and it's too difficult to find the pirates in the first place.

Realizing that some sort of joint action was required, the software industry has formed two trade associations that are waging an effective war against software piracy both in the U.S. and abroad. These are the:

- Software Publishers Association, 1730 M Street, NW, Suite 700, Washington, D.C. 20037, 202-452-1600; www.spa.org.

- Business Software Alliance, 2001 L Street NW, Suite 400, Washington, D.C. 20036, 202-872-5500.

These organizations have substantial budgets to fight software piracy worldwide. Any company that sells software abroad should seriously consider joining either or both.

The Software Publishers Association (SPA), the oldest and largest software trade association, was originally formed to fight piracy in the United States. However, it has recently begun an international antipiracy campaign, specifically targeting Singapore, Korea, Taiwan, France, Mexico, Brazil, Australia, and Italy. Membership in the SPA is open to any software publisher. Members ranges from game manufacturers to mainframe manufacturers. Costs of membership are based on the size and revenue of the company.

The Business Software Alliance is active in the U.S. and 55 other countries and has brought hundreds of lawsuits since 1988. Full membership in the Alliance is very expensive and is usually limited to large software publishers. However, smaller companies are allowed to become regional members at a lesser cost. For example, if a company has a piracy problem in Europe, it can get a European membership.

These trade organizations engage in a variety of activities, including:

- education—for example, the SPA is currently using lectures and videos to educate the public in Western Europe that software piracy is illegal;

- piracy investigations—both organizations employ private investigators to help discover piracy and maintain toll-free hotlines to which people can report piracy (this is often done by disgruntled corporate employees);

- intellectual property audits—when the SPA or Alliance learns that a company is engaging in piracy, it will seek to audit the company's computer equipment to find and destroy the pirated software and require the company to buy legal copies;

- lawsuits—the SPA and Business Software Alliance will sue infringers who refuse to cooperate with audits; the Alliance has filed over hundreds of such lawsuits around the world since 1988;

- lobbying—both organizations actively lobby both the U.S. and foreign governments to enact and enforce strong copyright laws.

2. Consider Technical Solutions

Technical solutions to software piracy such as copy-protection devices have proved to be so unpopular in the United States that they have been abandoned by most software publishers. However, consumers in many foreign countries do not object to copy protection schemes.

Other technical approaches to prevent piracy include:

- placing a unique serial number on every software copy; this costs almost nothing and makes it easy to prove piracy has occurred—that is, if multiple software copies used by a company all have the same serial number illegal copying must have occurred;

- building things into software packaging that are difficult for counterfeiters to reproduce—for example, holograms;

- employing hardware locks that tie software to a particular piece of hardware;

- including network limiting features in software that prevent a user from using more than one copy of a program with the same serial number on a network.

3. Seek Trade Sanctions by the U.S. Government

Perhaps the most powerful method to prevent foreign software piracy is for the U.S. government to impose trade sanctions on countries where piracy is rampant. The U.S. Trade Representative, a federal agency located in Washington, D.C., is empowered under federal law to investigate whether any foreign country is violating the rights of the United States under any trade agreement or is otherwise restricting American commerce.

Under current law (Section 301 of the Omnibus Trade and Competitiveness Act of 1988; 19 U.S.C. 2411 et seq.), if the Trade Representative determines that a country is acting improperly, it has broad authority to impose import duties or other import restrictions on the country's goods or services. However, if and when the U.S. formally joins GATT, the Trade Representative will have to use the special GATT procedures for addressing trade violations (where another GATT country is involved), rather then acting unilaterally.

The Trade Representative can conduct investigations on its own. But, if you think a country is behaving improperly, you can petition the Representative to conduct an investigation requesting that action be taken under Section 301. The Trade Representative is required to respond within 45 days with a decision whether an investigation will be conducted.

The U.S. Trade Representative is also an excellent resource for information concerning foreign countries' trade practices and policies and the United States' rights under international trade agreements.

4. Preventing Infringing Software from Entering the United States

It is against U.S. law for anyone to import pirated software into the United States. (17 U.S.C. 602.) The U.S. Customs Service is supposed to prohibit infringing goods from entering the country. However, as a practical matter, customs officials cannot carefully scrutinize every work of authorship being imported to see whether it does or doesn't infringe an existing U.S. work. Indeed, even if they had the time, it would be impossible to determine whether a particular imported software infringed protected copyright.

Accordingly, the burden of enforcing the prohibition against infringing works falls squarely on the shoulders of the copyright owner. There are two ways to do this:

a. Recordation with Customs Service

Under the U.S. Customs Act, a copyright owner may record her work with the U.S. Customs Service. (19 C.F.R. Part 133 Subpart (D).) Once this is done, any imports that are either pure copies or are highly similar to yours may be held up until you have a chance to go into court and obtain a court order preventing importation. Unfortunately, the chances of the infringing work being spotted and you being notified are relatively slim. However, the procedure for registering is relatively easy and you've nothing to lose.

b. Initiating an International Trade Commission complaint

Under the Customs Act, it's possible to seek an order having a work excluded from the U.S. on the ground its importation would be an unfair act or would constitute an unfair method of competition. (19 U.S.C 1337.) Copyright infringement meets this test.

Finally, to get a work excluded you must also prove that:

- It's produced in another country;
- It has a tendency to destroy an industry existing in the U.S. (in practice, this qualification is much easier than it looks);
- The industry being destroyed must be efficiently and economically operated (also almost always found to be the case).

For the most part, any major importation of works that are clearly piratical or that substantially infringe a domestic U.S. work will qualify for exclusion under this law. One well-known example of this happening is when Apple Computers, Inc. prevented the importation of Pineapple Computers. (*Apple Computers, Inc. v. Formula International, Inc.* (725 F.2d 521 (1983).)

To utilize this law, the copyright owner must file a formal complaint with the United States International Trade Commission. The case is heard by an Administrative Law Judge who's empowered to grant immediate relief and, ultimately, to either ban the works entirely or only a portion. As with infringement cases (covered in Chapter 13), it would be unwise to attempt this procedure without the assistance of a skilled attorney.

5. Suing for Copyright Infringement

Generally, suing foreign copyright infringers is not economically feasible for a single software company. However, in some cases of large-scale piracy it may be worthwhile, particularly if you can get other software publishers to join you to help pay the cost.

The first thing to do is consult with an experienced American copyright attorney. Even if the infringement occurred in another country, you may be able to sue the infringer in the United States. In this event, an American court would apply the copyright law of the foreign country, not American law. If you have to file suit abroad, you'll need to hire a copyright attorney in the foreign country involved to represent you. Your American copyright attorney should be able to refer you to an experienced copyright lawyer in the country involved.

Before you go to the expense of filing suit, however, be sure to have your attorney explain to you what remedies (for instance, monetary damages, injunctions) you will be entitled to if the suit is successful. Remember, you'll only be entitled to the same treatment that a citizen of the country involved would receive.

Some (particularly developing) countries still do not impose meaningful penalties on copyright infringers. This means it is not economically worthwhile to bring infringement suits against infringers in some countries.

C. Protection in the United States for Foreign Nationals' Software

We now examine software copyright protection in the United States from the point of view of non-U.S. citizens.

1. Protection for Nationals of Berne Countries

If you're a citizen or permanent resident (that is, a national) of a country that is a member of the Berne Convention (see list of Berne countries above), you are entitled to full copyright protection in the U.S. so long as your work was first created or published on or after March 1, 1989 (the date the U.S. joined the Berne Convention). This is true regardless of where the work was first created or published.

> **EXAMPLE 1:** Pierre, a French citizen and resident, creates a computer program in 2000. Since France joined the Berne Convention in 1887, the work is entitled to protection in the U.S. pursuant to the Berne Convention.

> **EXAMPLE 2:** Assume that Pierre had published another program way back in 1988. Since this was before the U.S. joined the Berne Convention, the program could not be protected in the U.S. under that convention. Pierre would have to look to the U.C.C. for protection (see below).

2. Protection Under the U.C.C.

What if your work does not qualify for protection under the Berne Convention because it was first created or published before March 1, 1989 or because you are a citizen or permanent resident of a country that is not a member of the Berne Convention? Your published or unpublished work will still be entitled to full protection in the U.S. if your country is a member of the Universal Copyright Convention and the work is published with the proper copyright notice (see Section A2, above). This is true regardless of where the work was first created or published.

> **EXAMPLE:** Pierre the French citizen in Example 2 above who was not entitled to copyright protection in the U.S. for a program published in 1988, is entitled to full U.S. protection under the U.C.C. (to which France belongs) provided that his program was published with the proper copyright notice.

3. First Publication Rule

Regardless of what country you are a citizen of or permanently reside in, if your work is first (or simultaneously) published on or after March 1, 1989 in any country that is a member of the Berne Convention, you are entitled to full copyright protection in the United States under the Berne Convention. Similarly, if your work was first published with a valid copyright notice prior to March 1, 1989 in a country that is a member of the U.C.C., you are entitled to full copyright protection in the U.S. pursuant to the U.C.C.

4. Compliance with U.S. Copyright Formalities

Neither U.S. citizens or noncitizens need place a copyright notice on their published work for it to be protected by copyright. However, it is a good idea to use a copyright notice anyway on all software published in the U.S. See Chapter 3, *Copyright Notice*, for detailed discussion.

Unlike the case with U.S. citizens, a non-U.S. citizen need not register her work before filing suit in the U.S. for copyright infringement. However, as discussed in Chapter 4, *Copyright Registration: The Basics*, important advantages are gained under U.S. copyright law if a published or unpublished work is registered with the Copyright Office. Therefore, registration is advised for all foreign authors of software and other protectible works. ∎

Other Legal Protections for Software

This book has focused on copyright protection for computer software. Copyright has been and remains the primary vehicle by which most software is protected. However, to obtain the maximum possible protection for software, it is usually necessary to supplement copyright protection with one or more of the other legal protections available for software. These are:

- **Trade secret laws.** These protect information that is both maintained as a proprietary secret and provides its owner with a competitive advantage in the marketplace.
- **Patent laws.** These laws protect novel and nonobvious inventions.
- **Trademark laws.** These laws protect original names, symbols and slogans that are used to distinguish goods and services in the marketplace.

Although this chapter provides an overview of how patent, trademark and trade secret legal protection doctrines relate to copyright law, you may wish to refer to *Software Development: A Legal Guide*, by Stephen Fishman (Nolo Press) for more specific and practical information about these other ways to protect your computer-related creative work.

What Is "Intellectual Property"?

Intellectual property is a generic term used to describe products of the human intellect that have economic value. Examples include such works as books, music, movies, photographs, artwork, certain inventions, industrial processes and chemical formulae. Among the many computer-related items properly classifiable as intellectual property are computer programs, computer output, hardware inventions (for example, a new type of disk controller), computer-related names (for example, Microsoft, Apple, *Lotus 1-2-3*), object code, source code and many databases.

A. Trade Secret Law

The simplest way to protect any intellectual property is to keep it secret. What your competitors don't know about, they can't use or benefit from. You can protect any type of valuable information this way. In the software field, trade secrecy can be used to:

- Protect ideas that offer a business a competitive advantage, thereby enabling you to get a head start on the competition;
- Keep competitors from knowing that a program is under development and from learning its functional attributes;
- Protect source code, software development tools, design definitions or specifications, manuals and other documentation, flow diagrams and flowcharts, data structures, data compilations, formulas and algorithms embodied in software;
- Protect valuable business information such as marketing plans, cost and price information and customer lists.

But, sooner or later, you'll probably have to reveal your secrets to somebody. Most likely, some or all of your employees will have to know about them, as well as nonemployee consultants and even users of your products. Does this mean that people such as these can tell competitors about your secrets? The answer is "no." This is where the law of trade secrecy comes in. It prevents employees and others who have a confidential relationship with you from revealing your trade secrets to third party competitors without your permission. If they do, you can sue both them and the competitor and get a court to order the third party not to use the information and even pay you damages.

EXAMPLE: Space Age Robotics Inc. (SARI) has spent three years developing a computer security system that visually recognizes a small group of people and responds only to their voice commands. SARI has been in a race with its chief competitor, Universal Systems, Inc. which has been working around the clock to build a similar system. Having solved most of the bugs in the system, SARI plans to make a product announcement in about a month. Universal Systems hires Fred, SARI's chief engineer, at twice what SARI paid him. After Fred leaves, SARI discovers that a number of confidential documents dealing with the security system are missing from his old office. SARI is convinced that Universal hired Fred and agreed to pay him such a high salary only because he will disclose SARI's trade secrets. Sari immediately files a trade secret infringement action against Universal and Fred and obtains a court order preventing Fred from disclosing SARI's trade secrets to Universal until the trade secret action is tried. When SARI's case against Universal and Fred is tried, SARI wins and the court grants SARI an injunction prohibiting Fred from disclosing any confidential information about SARI's security system to Universal or anyone else for one year (the time the court concludes it would have taken Universal to perfect its own system independently).

Trade secrecy is one of the most important weapons in a software owner's arsenal. Although this book has focused on copyright protection for software, the copyright laws cannot single-handedly prevent your product from being wrongfully exploited by others. One important reason for this is that copyright only protects a programmer's *expression* of the ideas embodied in a program, not the ideas themselves. Copyright does not protect ideas, systems, facts, methods, discoveries or algorithms. (See Chapter 7, *Scope of Copyright Protection for Software*.)

There are no such limitations on trade secrets. That is, an idea *can* be a protected trade secret. When dealing with trade secrecy there is no need to make the often Jesuitical distinctions between idea and expression that courts make in the copyright realm. Stated simply, trade secrecy can protect everything copyright can protect *and* everything copyright cannot protect (provided the requirements discussed in this section are satisfied)

You may be asking: Why bother with copyrights at all, why not just use trade secrecy? There are six good reasons why trade secrecy should not be relied upon alone to protect software:

• A trade secret owner may enforce its trade secret rights only against people who are bound by a *duty of confidentiality* not to disclose or use the information (for example, employees and others who sign confidentiality agreements), and people who steal or otherwise acquire the trade secret through improper means. In contrast, copyright rights are enforceable against everyone in the United States.

• Basic copyright protection is extended to your work automatically, without the necessity of your engaging in any procedures. Whether you want it or not, and whether or not you treat your work as a trade secret, you get copyright protection as soon as you fix it in some tangible form. If you treat your work as a trade secret, you qualify for both types of protection.

• Trade secret protection only protects secrets as long as they remain secret. If your work is somehow made public and you lose your trade secret, you'll want to fall back on copyright protection.

• Maintaining a trade secret can be expensive and time-consuming. Copyright protection costs almost nothing (only $20 to register with the Copyright Office).

- Copyright protection is available in almost all countries under international treaties, while trade secret protection is iffy or nonexistent in many parts of the world.
- Since secrecy is required for trade secret protection, such protection is not well suited for mass-marketed products like mass-marketed software.

Sources of Trade Secret Protection

Unlike copyrights and patents, whose existence is provided and governed by federal law that applies in all 50 states, trade secrecy is not codified in any federal statute. Instead, it is made up of individual state laws. Nevertheless, the protection afforded to trade secrets is much the same in every state. This is partly because some 42 states have based their trade secrecy laws on the Uniform Trade Secrecy Act (UTSA), a model trade secrecy law designed by legal scholars. (For a text of the UTSA and a list of those states adopting it, refer to volume 14 of the *Uniform Laws Annotated*, published by West Publishing Co.)

---

1. What Are Trade Secrets?

A trade secret is any formula, pattern, physical device, idea, process, compilation of information or other information that (1) is not generally known, (2) provides a business with a *competitive advantage*, and (3) is treated in a way that can reasonably be expected to prevent the public or competitors from learning about it, absent improper acquisition or theft.

A trade secret can be a formula, a scientific or technical design, a process, a procedure or a significant improvement to any one of these. It can also be an idea, an expression of an idea, a machine design or any other secret that gives an economic edge to the holder.

a. No protection for generally known information

Information that is public knowledge or generally known in the software industry cannot be a trade secret. Things that everybody knows cannot provide anyone with a competitive advantage. However, information comprising a trade secret need not be novel or unique. All that is required is that the information not be a matter of public knowledge. Most software qualifies as a trade secret. Computer programs usually contain at least some elements or combination of elements that are different from other programs and not generally known. Thus, for example, trade secret protection has been extended to accounts receivable programs, database management software, time-sharing systems and communications programs even though similar software already existed.

b. Reasonable secrecy must be maintained

Software or other information qualifies as a trade secret only if precautions are taken to keep it secret. Absolute secrecy is not required—it is not necessary to turn your office into an armed camp. A trade secret owner's secrecy precautions need only be *reasonable under the circumstances*. What precautions are reasonable will vary from case to case, depending on the size of the company, the nature and value of the information and other factors. These measures commonly include:

- Locking up documents and disks containing trade secrets when not in use;
- Restricting physical access to the areas where secret material exists;
- Taking reasonable computer security measures, such as using passwords;
- Conducting exit interviews with employees who are leaving employment and advising them of their confidentiality obligations;
- Conducting audit trails and transaction logs regarding the trade secret to document who has viewed the secret, when and for what purpose;

- Requiring all persons with access to the trade secret to sign nondisclosure or confidentiality agreements in which they agree to treat the information as a trade secret;
- Including a notice on all materials that "this information is considered a trade secret."

For a detailed discussion of how to implement a trade secret protection plan for software, refer to *Software Development: A Legal Guide*, by Stephen Fishman (Nolo Press), Chapter 7.

2. Enforcing Your Trade Secrets

A trade secret owner may enforce her rights by bringing a trade secret infringement action in court. Such suits may be used to (1) prevent another person or business from using the trade secret without proper authorization, and (2) collect damages for the economic injury suffered as a result of the trade secret's improper acquisition and use. All persons responsible for the improper acquisition, and all those who have benefited thereby, are typically named as defendants in trade secret infringement actions.

Among the most common situations that give rise to infringement actions are:

- Where an employee having knowledge of a trade secret changes employment and discloses the secret to her new employer in violation of her duty of confidentiality,
- Improper use or disclosure of trade secrets made in violation of a nondisclosure agreement—for example, by a contractor or licensee, or
- A theft of trade secrets occurring through industrial espionage.

To prevail in a trade secret infringement suit, the plaintiff (person bringing the suit) must show that the information alleged to be secret is actually a trade secret (see Section A.1 above) and that the information was either improperly acquired by the defendant (if accused of making commercial use of the secret) or improperly disclosed (or likely to be so) by the defendant (if accused of leaking the information).

3. Using Trade Secrecy in Conjunction with Copyright Protection

Trade secrecy and copyright are not incompatible. Indeed, they are typically used in tandem to provide the maximum legal protection available for most programs (patents provide far greater protection than either trade secrets or copyright, but are available only for a small minority of software; see Section B). Typically, trade secrecy is most important during a software product's development phase.

a. Development phase

As discussed in Chapter 2, *Copyright Basics*, the copyright laws grant a copyright owner the exclusive right to copy, initially distribute, adapt or display protected expression, but not ideas. The moment a program or other information is fixed in a tangible medium of expression (typed into a computer, saved on disk or other media, written down, etc.) it is protected by the federal copyright laws to the extent it is original (independently created). However, provided that secrecy is maintained, trade secret protection can continue. Because an item is automatically protected by copyright upon its fixation, rather than when it is first published, there usually is a substantial time period during which both trade secret and copyright protection apply. This is because a program is usually tested and modified for some time after it is first fixed, but before it is distributed. As long as it is maintained as a trade secret during this period, the program enjoys both trade secret and copyright protection.

b. Distribution phase

Hopefully there will come a time when you want to sell your creative work. Once a program is distributed, however, it will lose trade secret status unless steps are taken to preserve secrecy. This includes distributing the program only in object code form and having each person who receives the work sign a license restricting disclosure of the secrets it contains. Of course, it is impossible to have the purchasers of mass-marketed programs all sign licenses. Pre-printed shrink-wrap or click-wrap licenses must be relied upon to establish a duty of nondisclosure for mass-marketed software. (See Chaper 12.)

B. Software Patents

A patent provides its owner with a statutory 14- to 20-year monopoly to make, sell and use an invention. Thousands of software and software-related patents have been issued, and thousands more are in the application stage. Anyone who develops software needs to be aware of what patents are and how the patenting process works, so that they can tell whether their innovation qualifies for a patent, or whether they might be infringing someone else's patent. We provide a brief overview below; for a detailed discussion, refer to *Patent It Yourself,* by David Pressman (Nolo Press).

1. Patentability of Software

When first faced with applications for patents on software-based inventions in the 1950s, the United States Patent and Trademark Office (PTO) routinely rejected the applications on the grounds that software consists of mathematical algorithms (that is, a series of mathematical relationships, like differential equations). Mathematical algorithms were considered a law of nature, or pure thought. Patents cannot be granted for a law of nature or mental process. For example, no one can legally have a patent on the use of "1 + 1 = 2" because it would create too huge (and fundamental) a monopoly. Thus, software by itself was considered to be nonpatentable.

However, in 1981 the Supreme Court held that an algorithm may be patentable if it works in connection with a specific apparatus—that is, a physical structure of some type—and is described that way in the patent claims (the precise statements in the

patent application that describe the parameters of the invention). *(Diamond v. Diehr,* 450 U.S. 171 (1981).) This cleared the way for patentability of software-based inventions.

Note carefully that patents don't issue on software itself, rather, they issue on inventions that use software to produce a useful result (software-based inventions). Software-based inventions that have qualified for a patent often involve software connected to and running hardware components, such as a computer controlling a rubber molding press, a computer attached to a machine that receives seismic activity data, and a computer attached to a machine that receives an electric signal that represents the electrical activity of the human heart. The essence of these inventions is found in the functional combination of their software and hardware.

2. Which Software-Based Inventions Qualify for a Patent?

Most software doesn't qualify for patent protection. This is because to qualify for a patent an invention must be novel and nonobvious at the time of creation (35 USC Sections 102, 103). The test for determining novelty is fairly easy to meet. To be novel, an invention (invention includes improvements of existing inventions) must be different in some important way from previous inventions and developments in the field, both patented and nonpatented.

In addition to being novel, an invention must have a quality referred to as nonobviousness. Translated into regular English, this means that the invention would have been surprising or unexpected to someone who is familiar with the field of the invention. In deciding whether an invention is nonobvious, the PTO may consider all previous developments in the field (called prior art) that existed when the invention was conceived. As a general rule, an invention is considered nonobvious when it does one of the following:

- solves a problem that people in the field have been trying to solve for some time,

- does something significantly faster than was previously possible, or
- performs a function that could not be performed before.

Most software-based inventions are rejected at least in the first instance by the PTO because they can't pass the nonobviousness test.

3. The Patent Process

To obtain a patent, one must submit a detailed application and fee to the PTO. The application must contain:

- specialized sentence fragments called patent claims, that is, statements that recite the novel features of your invention,
- a detailed description of the invention, which must be consistent with the patent claims and specific enough to allow someone to build the invention, and
- detailed drawings of the invention.

Once the application is received, the PTO assigns it to an examiner who is supposed to be knowledgeable in the technology underlying the invention. The examiner is responsible for deciding whether the application meets all the technical requirements for obtaining a patent, and assuming it does, what the scope of the patent should be. Usually, back and forth communications—called patent prosecution in the jargon of the patent world—ensue. Eventually, if all the examiner's objections are overcome, the invention is approved for a patent.

It usually takes between one and a half to three years to obtain a patent. Many applications (about 50%) either are rejected by the U.S. Patent and Trademark Office, or abandoned by the applicant.

As mentioned, if a patent is issued, you'll be granted the right to exclude others from making, selling or using your invention for 17 years. This means no one can copy your idea or your product, or use it in any way. The protection is all encompassing.

Many inventors hire an attorney to help them patent their work. However, Nolo Press offers two excellent products on doing your own patent:

- a book, *Patent It Yourself*, by David Pressman (Nolo Press), and
- software based on the book, also called *Patent It Yourself*.

Order information is in the back of this book.

4. Enforcing a Patent

Should you receive a software-based patent, your program and its unique, novel approach cannot be used by others without your permission. In other words, independent creation, which is sufficient to beat a claim that a copyright or trade secret has been infringed, isn't good enough to defend against a charge of patent infringement. As long as you patent it first, it's yours and yours alone for 14 to 20 years, depending on the type of invention..

However, patents are not self-enforcing, and the U.S. government will not help you enforce yours. Patents are a little like hunting licenses. If someone uses your invention as described in your patent without your permission you have the right to sue them in federal court. Patent suits are among the most expensive of all forms of litigation. However, the potential rewards can be enormous if a patent suit is successful (treble damages may be recovered in the case of willful infringement).

It is very common for a company or person accused of patent infringement to agree to license (pay for the use of) the invention rather than face the uncertainties and expenses of litigation. However, some accused infringers elect to fight and seek to have the patent overturned in court. Many software experts believe that the Patent Office has issued a number of software-related patents that should have been rejected on grounds of failure to satisfy the nonobviousness test. Such patents are particularly likely to be subject to court challenge.

C. Trademark Law and Software

This section provides a brief overview of trademarks. Before selecting or registering a trademark you should read *Trademark: How to Name a Business and Product* by Kate McGrath and Stephen Elias (Nolo Press).

1. What Is a Trademark?

A trademark is any visual mark that accompanies a particular tangible product, or line of goods, and serves to identify and distinguish it from products sold by others and to indicate its source. A trademark may consist of letters, words, names, phrases or slogans, numbers, colors, symbols, designs or shapes.

> **EXAMPLE:** The word and numbers Lotus 1-2-3 is a trademark that identifies a particular electronic spreadsheet program as the product of the Lotus Development Corp. and distinguishes it from all similar programs.

The word trademark is also a generic term used to describe the entire broad body of state and federal law that covers how businesses distinguish their products and services from the competition. Each state has its own set of laws establishing when and how trademarks can be protected. There is also a federal trademark law called the Lanham Act (15 U.S.C. 1050 *et seq.*) that applies in all 50 states. Generally, state trademark laws are relied upon for marks used only within one particular state, while the Lanham Act is used to protect marks for products that are sold in more than one state. The state and federal trademark laws protect distinctive trademarks (see below) from unauthorized use by others.

a. Trade names

A trade name is the formal name of a business or other organization. For example, Apple Computer Inc. and Lotus Development Corporation are trade names. Every business has a trade name. A trade name is used to identify a business for such purposes as opening bank accounts, paying taxes, ordering supplies, filing lawsuits and so on. However, a trade name may become a trademark (or service mark) when it is used to identify individual products or services sold in the marketplace. Businesses often use shortened versions of their trade names as all or part of a trademark: a good example is the trademark *Lotus 1-2-3*.

Trade names, whether the name of a corporation, partnership or sole proprietorship must be registered with the appropriate state or local authorities. Each state has its own business license requirements requiring that trade names be registered with city, county or state offices. See *Trademark: How to Name a Business and Product*, by Kate McGrath and Stephen Elias (Nolo Press), Chapter 3.

Other Types of Marks

Trademarks are the type of mark of most interest to software developers and owners, since software is a product. However, there are other more specialized marks, including:

Service marks. Marks that are used to identify services, rather than products, are called service marks. Example: The word "Citibank" is a service mark for banking services. The rules for determining when and how servicemarks qualify for protection are the same as for trademarks.

Collective marks. A symbol, label, word, phrase or other identifying mark used by members of a group or organization for goods they produce or services they render is called a collective mark. Example: The symbol showing the handing of a floppy disk from one person to another used by members of the Association of Shareware Professionals. Only members of the group or organization are entitled to use the collective mark.

Certification marks. A mark used for the express purpose of certifying various characteristics or qualities of products and services manufactured by others is called a certification mark. Example: The Good Housekeeping Seal of Approval.

2. How Trademark Law Protects Software

As mentioned in Chapter 7, *Scope of Copyright Protection for Software*, copyright law doesn't protect names, titles or short phrases. Neither do the patent or trade secrecy laws. This is where trademark protection comes in. Under both federal and state trademark laws a manufacturer, merchant or group associated with a product or service can obtain protection for a word, phrase, logo or other symbol used to distinguish that product or service from others. If a competitor uses a protected trademark, the trademark holder can obtain a court injunction and money damages. Accordingly, trademark law can be used to protect a program's name—for example, *Lotus1-2-3* or *Microsoft Word*. In short, it's the public association with the product name that can be protected under trademark law.

Trade Dress Protection

The overall appearance and image of a product or its packaging is known as its "trade dress." Trade dress may include product shapes, designs, colors, advertising and graphics, and, under the law, may be treated in the same manner as a more traditional trademark.

As with other types of trademarks, trade dress can be registered with the PTO, and receive protection from the federal courts. To receive protection:

- the trade dress must be inherently distinctive, unless it has acquired secondary meaning (becomes associated with a product in the public's mind through long and continuous use), and
- the subsequent use of the trade dress by another person or entity (called the junior user) must cause a likelihood of consumer confusion.

For trade dress to be considered inherently distinctive, one court has required that it "must be unusual and memorable, conceptually separable from the product and likely to serve primarily as a designator of origin of the product." (*Duraco Products Inc. v. Joy Plastic Enterprises Ltd.*, 40 F.3d 1431 (3d Cir. 1994).)

Functional aspects of trade dress cannot be protected under trademark law. Only designs, shapes or other aspects of the product that were created strictly to promote the product or service are protectible trade dress.

Trade dress protection can be important to software developers and publishers in three ways:

- It can be used to protect the distinctive design of the packaging used to sell software.
- Some trademark experts believe that trade dress protection may be available for graphical user interfaces (GUIs). As discussed in Chapter 13, little or no copyright protection is available for GUIs, so trade dress may be the only way to protect them. However, no court has yet ruled that such protection is available.
- Trade dress protection may also be available to protect the nonfunctional and distinctive design of Web pages.

This is a very complex area of trademark law. If you wish to seek trade dress protection for a GUI, you should obtain guidance from an experienced trademark lawyer.

---

3. Federal Protection for Trademarks

The first person who uses a trademark on a product sold across state or national lines, or files an application declaring an intent to use such a trademark within 6 months, is entitled to have his trademark protected under the federal trademark statute, known as the Lanham Act. The owner of such a trademark can apply to have the mark placed on a federal trademark register (below).

a. Trademark registration

A trademark is registered by filing an application with the United States Patent and Trademark Office (USPTO) in Washington, D.C. Registration is not mandatory, and a company will obtain rights in a mark in the states in which it is actually used under both federal and state law. However, federal registration provides many important benefits. These include:

- The mark's owner is presumed to have the exclusive right to use the mark nationwide.

- Everyone in the country is presumed to know that the mark is already taken (even if they haven't actually heard of it).
- The trademark owner obtains the right to put an ® after the mark (see sidebar below).
- Anyone who begins using a confusingly similar mark after your mark has been registered will be deemed a willful infringer, which means you can collect large damages and pay for your lawsuit.
- The trademark owner obtains the right to make the mark incontestable by keeping it in continuous use for five years (this substantially reduces others' ability to legally challenge the mark).

To qualify for registration, a trademark must actually be used in commerce (but not solely within one state's borders), be sufficiently distinctive to reasonably operate as a product identifier and not be confusingly similar to an existing federally registered trademark.

b. Intent to use registration

If you seriously intend to use a trademark on a product in the near future, you can reserve the right to use the mark by filing an intent to use registration. If the mark is approved, you have six months to actually use the mark on a product sold to the public. If necessary, this period can be increased by six-month intervals to up to 24 months if you have a good explanation for the delay. No one else can use the mark during this interim period. You should promptly file an intent to use registration as soon as you have selected a trademark for a forthcoming product.

For detailed discussion of trademark registration, see *Trademark: How to Name a Business and Product,* by Kate McGrath and Stephen Elias (Nolo Press).

Trademark Notices

The owner of a trademark that has been registered is entitled to use a special symbol along with the trademark notifying the world of the fact of registration. Use of trademark notices is not mandatory, but makes it much easier for the trademark owner to collect meaningful damages in case of infringement. It is also a powerful deterrent against use of the mark by others. The most commonly used notice for trademarks registered with the USPTO is an "R" in a circle—®—but "Reg. U.S. Pat. & T.M. Off." may also be used. The "TM" superscript—™—may be used to denote marks that have been registered on a state basis only or marks that have not yet officially been registered by the U.S. Patent & Trademark Office.

---

4. Enforcing Trademark Rights

The owner of a valid trademark has the exclusive right to use the mark on its products. Depending on the strength of the mark and whether and where it has been registered, the trademark owner may be able to bring a court action to prevent others from using the same or similar marks on competing or related products.

Trademark infringement occurs when an alleged infringer uses a mark that likely causes consumers to confuse the infringer's products with the trademark owner's products. A mark need not be identical to one already in use to infringe upon the owner's rights. If the proposed mark is similar enough to the earlier mark to risk confusing the average consumer, its use will constitute infringement.

Determining whether an average consumer might be confused is the key to deciding whether infringement exits. The answer to this question depends primarily on whether the products or services involved are related (that is, sold through the same marketing channels) and, if so, whether the marks are sufficiently similar to create a likelihood of consumer confusion.

If a trademark owner is able to convince a court that infringement has occurred, she may be able to get the court to order the infringer to stop using the infringing mark and obtain monetary damages (money) from the infringer. Depending on whether the mark was registered, such damages may consist of the amount of the trademark owner's losses caused by the infringement or the infringer's profits. In cases of willful infringement, the courts may double or triple the damages award.

EXAMPLE: PlaySoft develops a computer arcade game and markets the program under the name *Boing*. PlaySoft registers this mark with the U.S. Patent & Trademark Office. One year later, Badd Software, Inc. markets an arcade game of its own under the name *Boing*. PlaySoft sues Badd for using a mark confusingly similar to its own on a similar product. PlaySoft is able to convince a judge that a strong likelihood exists that consumers will be confused by Badd's use of the *Boing* mark (it is not necessary to show actual confusion, although it is common to do so). The judge orders Badd to stop using the mark on its arcade game. ∎

Help Beyond This Book

opefully, this book provides you with most of the information you need about software law and contracts. But you may need additional help, either in the form of more advanced legal resources or an attorney's advice.

Section A introduces you to resources that contain comprehensive information on each area of intellectual property law. Section B gives some tips for finding a lawyer specializing in copyright law.

A. Further Information on Intellectual Property Law

If you have any questions about intellectual property law (copyright, trade secret, patent or trademark law) that have not been answered by this book, a three-step process is suggested.

- If you have access to the World Wide Web, check one or more of the sites listed below to see if there is an article or other discussion answering your question.
- If you need more in-depth information, take a look at one or more discussions by experts in the field to get a background and overview of the topic being researched. You will already have obtained a basic background from this book and will be looking for additional details on a particular topic. You'll probably need to go to a law library to find these materials.
- If you need still more information, read the law itself (cases and statutes) upon which the experts base their opinions. The accompanying sidebar discusses how to research case law in more detail.

1. Using the Law Library

Many law libraries are open to the public and can be found in most federal, state and county courthouses. Law school libraries in public universities also routinely grant access to the public. In addition, it is also

often possible to use private law libraries maintained by local bar associations, large law firms, state agencies or large corporations if you know a local attorney or are willing to be persistent in seeking permission from the powers that be.

Law libraries may seem intimidating at first. It may be helpful to know that most librarians have a sincere interest in helping anyone who desires to use their library. While they won't answer your legal questions, they will often put your hands on the materials that will give you a good start.

After you locate a law library, your approach to legal research should proceed along these lines:

Legal Research: How to Find and Understand the Law, by Stephen Elias and Susan Levinkind (Nolo Press), or another basic legal research guide, can help you understand legal citations, use the law library, and understand what you find there.

Researching Court Decisions

Throughout this book, legal treatises and law review articles are referred to in citations like this: *Apple Computer v. Franklin*, 714 F.2d 1240 (3rd Cir. 1983). This identifies a particular legal decision and tells you where the decision may be found and read. Any case decided by a federal court of appeals is found in a series of books called the Federal Reporter. Older cases are contained in the first series of the Federal Reporter or "F." for short. More recent cases are contained in the second series of the Federal Reporter or "F.2d" for short. To locate the *Apple v. Franklin* case, simply find a law library that has the Federal Reporter, Second Series (almost all do), locate volume 714 and turn to page 1240.

Opinions by the federal district courts (these are the federal trial courts) are in a series called the Federal Supplement or "F.Supp." For example, a case that appears in the Federal Supplement is *Lotus Dev. Corp. v. Paperback Software Int'l.*, 740 F.Supp. 37 (D. Mass. 1990).

Cases decided by the U.S. Supreme Court are found in three publications, any of which is fine to use: United States Reports (identified as "U.S."), the Supreme Court Reporter identified as "S.Ct.") and the Supreme Court Reports, Lawyer's Edition (identified as "L.Ed."). Supreme Court case citations often refer to all three publications—for example, *Diamond v. Diehr*, 450 U.S. 174, 101 S.Ct. 1048, 96 L.Ed. 187 (1985).

2. Copyright Law

The first place to go for more information on copyright law is *The Copyright Handbook: How to Protect and Use Written Works,* by Stephen Fishman (Nolo Press). This book discusses copyright protection for writings, but the principles are applicable to software as well. It also has a chapter on copyright on the Internet.

a. Internet resources

If you have access to the Internet's World Wide Web you can find valuable information about copyright by using any of the following sites:

- The U.S. Copyright Office at lcweb. loc.gov/ copyright. This site offers regulations, guidelines, forms and links to other helpful copyright sites.
- Findlaw at www.findlaw.com. This search engine offers a comprehensive list of copyright resources on the Web. Click intellectual property under the topic heading on the home page and click copyright from the subcategory list on the intellectual property page.
- Law Journal Extra Copyright Law Center at www.ljx.com/copyright. This site offers articles, recent copyright cases and links to further copyright information on the Web.
- Kuesterlaw at www.kuesterlaw.com. The Jeffrey R. Kuester law firm provides an online reference service that will lead you to other copyright resources on the World Wide Web.

b. Legal treatises

Software copyrights are discussed in many outstanding legal treatises.

- *Scott on Computer Law*, by Michael D. Scott (Prentice Hall Law & Business). This two-volume treatise contains a detailed discussion of copyright protection for software, including copyright protection in foreign countries.
- *Software, Copyright, & Competition*, by Anthony Lawrence Clapes (Quorum Books), gives one lawyer's view on how software should be protected by the copyright law.
- *Nimmer on Copyright*, by Melville and David Nimmer (Matthew Bender), is the leading treatise on all aspects of copyright law. This four-volume work covers virtually every legal issue concerning U.S. and foreign copyright law. Its coverage of computer software has recently been expanded, but it is not concerned exclusively with software, like the two treatises cited above.

- *The Law and Business of Computer Software*, edited by D.C. Toedt III (Clark Boardman Callaghan), contains a useful article providing a country-by-country analysis of international copyright protection for software.
- *International Copyright Protection*, edited by David Nimmer and Paul Geller (Matthew Bender), provides exhaustive coverage of copyright protection in other countries.

c.   Law review articles

If you have a very unusual copyright problem that is not covered by books on copyright and/or computer law, or you have a problem in an area in which the law has changed very recently, the best sources of available information may be law review articles. You can find citations to all the law review articles on a particular topic by looking under "copyright" in the Index to Legal Periodicals or Current Law Index. A key to the abbreviations used in these indices is located at the front of each index volume. Substantial collections of law reviews are usually kept in large public law libraries or university libraries.

A number of articles dealing with copyright are available on the World Wide Web. Many are listed on the Findlaw site at www.findlaw.com/01topics/23intellectprop/01copyright/publications.html.

d.   Statutes

The primary law governing all copyrights in the United States after January 1, 1978, is the Copyright Act of 1976. A copy of the complete Copyright Act is located on the World Wide Web at www.law.cornell.edu/usc/17/overview.html.

The United States Copyright Office has issued regulations which implement the copyright statutes and establish the procedures which must be followed to register a work. These regulations are located on the World Wide Web at www.law.cornell.edu/copyright/regulations/regs.overview.html.

e.   Court decisions

There are several ways to find court decisions on a particular legal issue. This book, legal treatises and law review articles contain many case citations. In addition:

- The United States Code Annotated and United States Code Service both cite and briefly summarize all the decisions relevant to each section of the Copyright Act of 1976. These are located just after each section of the Act.
- Federal Practice Digest (West Publishing Company) provides short summaries of copyright law decisions under the term "copyright." The digest contains a detailed table of contents and a very detailed subject matter index at the end of the set.

To understand how court decisions are named and indexed, see instructions in the sidebar, above.

After you find the name of a decision you want, you'll need to obtain a copy. You can get copies of many recent decisions from the World Wide Web. The Findlaw site at www.findlaw.com contains links to sites containing legal decisions. For older decisions, you'll need to go to a law library.

For the most recent information available on copyright, consult the Copyright Law Reporter, a weekly loose-leaf service published by Commerce

Clearing House (CCH). It contains the full text or summaries of recent copyright-related court decisions and relevant discussions of new developments in copyright law. The first volume of the set contains easy-to-follow instructions on how to use this valuable resource.

If you have Web access, recent copyright decisions can also be found at the Law Journal Extra Copyright Law Center at www.ljx.com/copyright.

3. Patent Law

The first source to consult if you have any questions about patent law is *Patent It Yourself*, by David Pressman (Nolo Press). This book explains in detail how the patent system works and how to prepare and file a patent application yourself.

a. Internet resources

If you have access to the Internet's World Wide Web you can find valuable information about patent law by using any of the following sites:

- Findlaw at http://www.findlaw.com. This general purpose legal search engine is a good place to start for researching patent law. Click on intellectual property in the topics section of the home page and then click on the patent subcategory when the intellectual property page appears. From there you can find patent statutes, regulations, the Manual of Patent Examination Procedures (MPEP), other PTO materials and articles of general interest.
- Kuesterlaw at http://www.kuesterlaw.com/. This site, maintained by an Atlanta, Georgia, intellectual property law firm, also is an excellent springboard for finding patent statutes, regulations, court cases and articles on recent patent law developments, such as software patents and the provisional patent applications.
- The U.S. Patent and Trademark Office at http://www.uspto.gov. This is the place to go for recent policy and statutory changes and transcripts of hearings on various patent law issues. You may also use this site to conduct a search of the first pages of patents (that include the patent abstracts) for patents issued since 1971.
- IBM Patent Search Site at http://patent.womplex.ibm.com. This site offers free patent searching for patents issued since 1971.
- The Shadow Patent Office at http://www.spo.eds.com/. This site, operated by Electronic Data Systems, lets you search recently issued patents for free and also offers an excellent patent search service (for patents back to 1972) for a per-search fee.
- Software Patent Institute at http://www.spi.org. This site lets you search for previous software developments that may affect whether a particular software item qualifies for a patent.

b. Legal treatises

Legal treatises on patents include:
- *Patent Law Fundamentals*, by Peter Rosenberg (Clark Boardman Callaghan), is the best legal treatise for patent law. This publication is generally considered by patent attorneys to be the bible of patent law. Because it is written for attorneys, it might be somewhat difficult sledding for the nonlawyer. However, if you first obtain an overview of your topic from the Pressman book, you should do fine.
- *Patent Law Handbook*, by C. Bruce Hamburg (Clark Boardman Callaghan), is another useful book. A new edition of this book is issued every year.

c. Law review articles

As mentioned earlier, law review articles are an excellent way to keep abreast of recent legal developments. By looking under "Patents" in the Index to Legal Periodicals or Current Law Index, you will find frequent references to articles on current patent law developments. A key to the abbreviations used in these indexes is located at the front of each index volume. Substantial collections of law reviews are usually located in large public law libraries or university libraries.

A number of useful articles can be found through the Findlaw and Kuesterlaw sites mentioned above.

d.   Statutes

The basic U.S. Patent Law is located in Title 35, United States Code, Section 101 and following. This can be found in the United States Code Annotated (U.S.C.A.) or United States Code Service, Lawyers Edition (U.S.C.S.). A copy of the complete Patent Law is located on the World Wide Web at www.law.cornell.edu/usc/35/i_iv/overview.html.

e.   Court decisions

You'll find citations to relevant court decisions in Patent Law Fundamentals or a law review article. In addition, the U.S. Code Annotated and U.S. Code Service both refer to and briefly summarize all the decisions relevant to each section of the patent law. You can also find short summaries of patent law decisions in West Publishing Company's Federal Practice Digest under the term "patent."

To understand how court decisions are named and indexed, see instructions in the sidebar, above.

After you find the name of a decision you want, you'll need to obtain a copy. You can get copies of many recent decisions from the World Wide Web. The Findlaw site at www.findlaw.com contains links to sites containing legal decisions. For older decisions, you'll need to go to a law library.

Recent patent law court decisions can be found at the Law Journal Extra Patent Law Center at www.ljx.com/patents/.

4.   Trade Secret Law

There isn't quite as much information available on trade secrets as on the other areas of intellectual property.

a.   Internet resources

If you have access to the Internet's World Wide Web you can find valuable information about trade secrets by using the Trade Secret Home Page [www.execpc.com/~mhallign/]. This site provides discussions of recent developments and general background information on trade secrets. Also visit Findlaw [www.findlaw.com], a general-purpose legal search engine. Click on intellectual property in the topics section of the home page and then click on the trade secret subcategory when the intellectual property page appears. From there you can find appropriate statutes and discussions of trade secret principles.

b.   Treatises

Treatises on trade secret law include:

- *Milgrim on Trade Secrets*, a comprehensive treatment of trade secret law published by Matthew Bender as Volume 12 of its Business Organizations series, is probably the most complete resource regarding trade secret issues, especially if you have a specific or detailed question.
- *Trade Secret Law Handbook*, by Melvin F. Jager (Clark Boardman Callaghan), contains mini-discussions of most trade secret-related concepts, a number of sample agreements and licenses, as well as references to cases and statutes where appropriate.
- *Trade Secrets*, by James Pooley (Unacom), is an excellent book written for nonlawyers. You will find this book more accessible than the treatises cited above. It does not contain the extensive

citations to primary resource materials (cases and statutes) that the Milgrim and Jager books have, but it does include sample trade secret agreements.

c. Law review articles

Law review articles are often a good place to find information about recent software protection developments. Look under "Trade Secret" in the Index to Legal Periodicals or Current Law Index. A key to the abbreviations used in these indexes is located at the front of each index volume. Substantial collections of law reviews are usually located in large public law libraries or university libraries.

d. Statutes

There is no national trade secret law; instead, it consists of individual laws for each state. For direct access to state statutes governing trade secrets, look under "Trade Secret," "Proprietary Information," or "Commercial Secret" in the index accompanying the statutes of the state in question.

In addition, the Uniform Trade Secrets Act, a model statute designed by legal scholars, has been adopted in one version or another by some 46 states.

e. Court decisions

For summaries of cases involving trade secret principles, consult the West Publishing Company state or regional digests under "Trade Regulation," "Contracts," "Agency" and "Master and Servant."

To understand how court decisions are named and indexed, see instructions in the sidebar, above.

After you find the name of a decision you want, you'll need to obtain a copy. You can get copies of many recent decisions from the World Wide Web. The Findlaw site at www.findlaw.com contains links to sites containing legal decisions. For older decisions, you'll need to go to a law library.

5. Trademark Law

Before consulting any of the resources cited below, first read *Trademark: How to Name Your Business & Product*, by Kate McGrath and Stephen Elias (Nolo Press). This guide provides an overview of trademark law and explains how to select and register a trademark and conduct trademark searches.

a. Internet resources

If you have access to the Internet's World Wide Web you can find valuable information about trademarks by using any of the following sites:

- Nolo Press at http://www.nolo.com. Nolo Press offers self-help information about a wide variety of legal topics, including trademark law. (See the Intellectual Property topic in the Legal Encyclopedia, which incidentally includes selected entries from this part of the book.)
- Findlaw at http://www.findlaw.com. This search engine offers an excellent collection of trademark-related materials on the Web, including trademark statutes, regulations, classification manuals and articles of general interest. Click the intellectual property link in the topics section on the Findlaw home page and then click trademark in the subcategory section on the intellectual property page.
- GGMARK at http://www.ggmark.com/. This site, maintained by a trademark lawyer, provides basic trademark information and a fine collection of links to other trademark resources.
- Sunnyvale Center for Invention, Innovation and Ideas at http://www.sci3.com. This site, maintained by the Sunnyvale Center for Innovation, Invention and Ideas (a Patent and Depository Library), provides information about their excellent, low-cost trademark search service conducted by the Center's librarians.
- Micropatent at http://www.micropat.com/trademarkwebindex.html. This site, maintained by Micropatent, lets you do your own search of the federal trademark register for $20 a day (text)

and $30 a day (text and images). You can get a lot of searching done within a 24-hour period if you're adequately prepared.

- Kuesterlaw at http://www.kuesterlaw.com/. This site, maintained by an Atlanta, Georgia, intellectual property law firm, also is an excellent springboard for finding trademark statutes, regulations, court cases and articles on such recent trademark law developments as domain name disputes.

- Law Journal Extra Trademark Law Center at www.ljextra.com/trademark/ contains recent trademark decisions, articles and links to many other trademark sites.

- U.S. Patent and Trademark Office at http://www.uspto.gov. The U.S. Patent and Trademark Office is the place to go for recent policy and statutory changes and transcripts of hearings on various trademark law issues.

b. Treatises

For truly in-depth information on trademarks, consult the following treatises:

- *Trademarks and Unfair Competition*, by J. Thomas McCarthy (Clark Boardman Callaghan), is the most authoritative book on trademark law. This multi-volume treatise discusses virtually every legal issue that has arisen regarding trademarks.

- *Trademark Registration Practice*, by James E. Hawes (Clark Boardman Callaghan), provides a detailed guide to trademark registration.

- *Trademark Law—A Practitioner's Guide*, by Siegrun D. Kane (Practicing Law Institute), contains practical advice about trademark disputes and litigation.

c. Law review articles

You can find law review articles on trademark law by looking under "trademark" or "unfair competition" in the Index to Legal Periodicals or Current Law In-

dex. A key to the abbreviations used in these indexes is located at the front of each index volume. Substantial collections of law reviews are usually located in large public law libraries or university libraries. You can also find a number of articles on the Web. You can access many articles on the Web through the Findlaw and Kuesterlaw sites mentioned above.

d. Statutes

The main law governing trademarks in the United States is the Lanham Act, also known as the Federal Trademark Act of 1946 (as amended in 1988). It is codified at Title 15, Chapters 1051 through 1127, of the United States Code. You can find it in either of two books:

- United States Code Annotated (U.S.C.A.), or
- United States Code Service, Lawyers Edition (U.S.C.S.).

All law libraries carry at least one of these series. To find a specific section of the Lanham Act, consult either the index at the end of Title 15, or the index at the end of the entire code.

A copy of the complete Lanham Act is located on the World Wide Web at www. law.cornell.edu/uscode/15/ch22.html.

e. Court decisions

You'll find citations to relevant court decisions in *Trademarks and Unfair Competition* or a law review article. In addition, the U.S. Code Annotated and U.S. Code Service both refer to and briefly summarize all the decisions relevant to each section of the Lanham Act. You can also find short summaries of trademark law decisions in West Publishing Company's Federal Practice Digest under the term "trademark."

To understand how court decisions are named and indexed, see instructions in the sidebar, above.

After you find the name of a decision you want, you'll need to obtain a copy. You can get copies of many recent decisions from the World Wide Web.

The Findlaw site at www.findlaw.com contains links to sites containing legal decisions. For older decisions, you'll need to go to a law library.

Recent patent law court decisions can be found at the Law Journal Extra Trademark Law Center at www.ljx.com/trademark/.

B. Finding a Lawyer

If you're faced with a problem you cannot or do not want to handle yourself, you may need to see a lawyer. Copyright is part of a larger specialty known as intellectual property law, which also includes patents and trademarks. Many lawyers who advertise as intellectual property lawyers can competently handle all three types of cases. But some are primarily patent attorneys who don't put much effort into the copyright side of their practice. If you are shopping for a copyright lawyer, do your best to find someone who specializes primarily in copyrights.

Finding a good copyright lawyer is no different from finding any other professional to help your business. The best way is first to get a good grasp on the problem yourself. Reading this book will help you do that. Then, always ask for referrals from friends or colleagues in your industry. If you have a general business lawyer who handles corporate, debt collection and similar matters for your company, ask her for a referral as well. Your county bar association may also be able to refer you to someone. If all else fails, look in your local yellow pages under Computer Law and Patent, Trademark & Copyright. ■

Sample Forms

1 Unpublished computer program created by a single author; not a work made for hire

FORM TX
For a Literary Work
UNITED STATES COPYRIGHT OFFICE

REGISTRATION NUMBER

_____ TX _____ TXU _____

EFFECTIVE DATE OF REGISTRATION

_____

Month _____ Day _____ Year _____

DO NOT WRITE ABOVE THIS LINE. IF YOU NEED MORE SPACE, USE A SEPARATE CONTINUATION SHEET.

1 **TITLE OF THIS WORK ▼**

Birdbrain

PREVIOUS OR ALTERNATIVE TITLES ▼

PUBLICATION AS A CONTRIBUTION If this work was published as a contribution to a periodical, serial, or collection, give information about the collective work in which the contribution appeared. **Title of Collective Work ▼**

If published in a periodical or serial give: **Volume ▼**   **Number ▼**   **Issue Date ▼**   **On Pages ▼**

2 **a** **NAME OF AUTHOR ▼**

Basilio Chan

DATES OF BIRTH AND DEATH
Year Born ▼   Year Died ▼
1960

Was this contribution to the work a "work made for hire"?
☐ Yes
☒ No

AUTHOR'S NATIONALITY OR DOMICILE
Name of Country
OR { Citizen of ▶ USA
Domiciled in ▶ USA

WAS THIS AUTHOR'S CONTRIBUTION TO THE WORK
Anonymous? ☐ Yes ☒ No
Pseudonymous? ☐ Yes ☒ No

If the answer to either of these questions is "Yes," see detailed instructions.

NATURE OF AUTHORSHIP Briefly describe nature of material created by this author in which copyright is claimed. ▼

NOTE

Under the law, the "author" of a "work made for hire" is generally the employer, not the employee (see instructions). For any part of this work that was "made for hire" check "Yes" in the space provided, give the employer (or other person for whom the work was prepared) as "Author" of that part, and leave the space for dates of birth and death blank.

b **NAME OF AUTHOR ▼**

DATES OF BIRTH AND DEATH
Year Born ▼   Year Died ▼

Was this contribution to the work a "work made for hire"?
☐ Yes
☐ No

AUTHOR'S NATIONALITY OR DOMICILE
Name of Country
OR { Citizen of ▶
Domiciled in ▶

WAS THIS AUTHOR'S CONTRIBUTION TO THE WORK
Anonymous? ☐ Yes ☐ No
Pseudonymous? ☐ Yes ☐ No

If the answer to either of these questions is "Yes," see detailed instructions.

NATURE OF AUTHORSHIP Briefly describe nature of material created by this author in which copyright is claimed. ▼

c **NAME OF AUTHOR ▼**

DATES OF BIRTH AND DEATH
Year Born ▼   Year Died ▼

Was this contribution to the work a "work made for hire"?
☐ Yes
☐ No

AUTHOR'S NATIONALITY OR DOMICILE
Name of Country
OR { Citizen of ▶
Domiciled in ▶

WAS THIS AUTHOR'S CONTRIBUTION TO THE WORK
Anonymous? ☐ Yes ☐ No
Pseudonymous? ☐ Yes ☐ No

If the answer to either of these questions is "Yes," see detailed instructions.

NATURE OF AUTHORSHIP Briefly describe nature of material created by this author in which copyright is claimed. ▼

3 **a** **YEAR IN WHICH CREATION OF THIS WORK WAS COMPLETED**   This information must be given ◀ Year in all cases.

20XX

b **DATE AND NATION OF FIRST PUBLICATION OF THIS PARTICULAR WORK**
Complete this information ONLY if this work has been published.
Month ▶ _____ Day ▶ _____ Year ▶ _____ ◀ Nation

4 **COPYRIGHT CLAIMANT(S)** Name and address must be given even if the claimant is the same as the author given in space 2. ▼

Basilio Chan
123 1st St.
Berkeley, CA 94700

TRANSFER If the claimant(s) named here in space 4 is (are) different from the author(s) named in space 2, give a brief statement of how the claimant(s) obtained ownership of the copyright. ▼

See instructions before completing this space.

APPLICATION RECEIVED

ONE DEPOSIT RECEIVED

TWO DEPOSITS RECEIVED

FUNDS RECEIVED

DO NOT WRITE HERE
OFFICE USE ONLY

MORE ON BACK ▶ • Complete all applicable spaces (numbers 5-11) on the reverse side of this page.
• See detailed instructions.   • Sign the form at line 10.

DO NOT WRITE HERE
Page 1 of _____ pages

1

Unpublished computer program created by a single author; not a work made for hire (back)

DO NOT WRITE ABOVE THIS LINE. IF YOU NEED MORE SPACE, USE A SEPARATE CONTINUATION SHEET.

PREVIOUS REGISTRATION Has registration for this work, or for an earlier version of this work, already been made in the Copyright Office?

☐ Yes ☒ No If your answer is "Yes," why is another registration being sought? (Check appropriate box) ▼

a.☐ This is the first published edition of a work previously registered in unpublished form.

b.☐ This is the first application submitted by this author as copyright claimant.

c.☐ This is a changed version of the work, as shown by space 6 on this application.

If your answer is "Yes," give: **Previous Registration Number** ▼ _____ **Year of Registration** ▼ _____

5

DERIVATIVE WORK OR COMPILATION Complete both space 6a and 6b for a derivative work; complete only 6b for a compilation.

a. Preexisting Material Identify any preexisting work or works that this work is based on or incorporates. ▼

b. Material Added to This Work Give a brief, general statement of the material that has been added to this work and in which copyright is claimed. ▼

6

See instructions
before completing
this space.

—space deleted—

7

REPRODUCTION FOR USE OF BLIND OR PHYSICALLY HANDICAPPED INDIVIDUALS A signature on this form at space 10 and a check in one of the boxes here in space 8 constitutes a non-exclusive grant of permission to the Library of Congress to reproduce and distribute solely for the blind and physically handicapped and under the conditions and limitations prescribed by the regulations of the Copyright Office: (1) copies of the work identified in space 1 of this application in Braille (or similar tactile symbols); or (2) phonorecords embodying a fixation of a reading of that work; or (3) both.

a☒ Copies and Phonorecords   b☐ Copies Only   c☐ Phonorecords Only

8

See instructions.

DEPOSIT ACCOUNT If the registration fee is to be charged to a Deposit Account established in the Copyright Office, give name and number of Account.

Name ▼ _____   **Account Number** ▼ _____

9

CORRESPONDENCE Give name and address to which correspondence about this application should be sent.   Name/Address/Apt/City/State/ZIP ▼

Basilio Chan
123 1st St.
Berkeley, CA 90000

Area Code and Telephone Number ▶ 510-555-1234

Be sure to
give your
daytime phone
◀ number

CERTIFICATION* I, the undersigned, hereby certify that I am the

Check only one ▶

☒ author
☐ other copyright claimant
☐ owner of exclusive right(s)
☐ authorized agent of _____

of the work identified in this application and that the statements made by me in this application are correct to the best of my knowledge.

Name of author or other copyright claimant, or owner of exclusive right(s) ▲

10

Typed or printed name and date ▼ If this application gives a date of publication in space 3, do not sign and submit it before that date.

Basilio Chan   Date ▶ 1/2/XX

☞   Handwritten signature (X) ▼

**MAIL
CERTIFI-
CATE TO**

Name ▼
Basilio Chan

Number/Street/Apt ▼
123 1st St.

City/State/ZIP ▼
Berkeley, CA 94700

**Certificate
will be
mailed in
window
envelope**

11

*17 U.S.C. § 506(e): Any person who knowingly makes a false representation of a material fact in the application for copyright registration provided for by section 409, or in any written statement filed in connection with the application, shall be fined not more than $2,500.

May 1995—300,000   ☆U.S. COPYRIGHT OFFICE WWW FORM: 1995

2 Published work made for hire; computer program and documents registered together

FORM TX
For a Literary Work
UNITED STATES COPYRIGHT OFFICE

REGISTRATION NUMBER

TX _____ TXU _____

EFFECTIVE DATE OF REGISTRATION

Month _____ Day _____ Year _____

DO NOT WRITE ABOVE THIS LINE. IF YOU NEED MORE SPACE, USE A SEPARATE CONTINUATION SHEET.

1 TITLE OF THIS WORK ▼

Orchid 1-2-3

PREVIOUS OR ALTERNATIVE TITLES ▼

PUBLICATION AS A CONTRIBUTION If this work was published as a contribution to a periodical, serial, or collection, give information about the collective work in which the contribution appeared.   **Title of Collective Work ▼**

If published in a periodical or serial give: Volume ▼   Number ▼   Issue Date ▼   On Pages ▼

2

a NAME OF AUTHOR ▼
Micro Weird, Inc.

DATES OF BIRTH AND DEATH
Year Born ▼   Year Died ▼

Was this contribution to the work a "work made for hire"?
☒ Yes
☐ No

AUTHOR'S NATIONALITY OR DOMICILE
Name of Country
OR { Citizen of ▶ USA
Domiciled in ▶

WAS THIS AUTHOR'S CONTRIBUTION TO THE WORK
Anonymous?   ☐ Yes ☒ No
Pseudonymous? ☐ Yes ☒ No

If the answer to either of these questions is "Yes," see detailed instructions.

NATURE OF AUTHORSHIP Briefly describe nature of material created by this author in which copyright is claimed. ▼

NOTE
Under the law, the "author" of a "work made for hire" is generally the employer, not the employee (see instructions). For any part of this work that was "made for hire" check "Yes" in the space provided, give the employer (or other person for whom the work was prepared) as "Author" of that part, and leave the space for dates of birth and death blank.

b NAME OF AUTHOR ▼

DATES OF BIRTH AND DEATH
Year Born ▼   Year Died ▼

Was this contribution to the work a "work made for hire"?
☐ Yes
☐ No

AUTHOR'S NATIONALITY OR DOMICILE
Name of Country
OR { Citizen of ▶
Domiciled in ▶

WAS THIS AUTHOR'S CONTRIBUTION TO THE WORK
Anonymous?   ☐ Yes ☐ No
Pseudonymous? ☐ Yes ☐ No

If the answer to either of these questions is "Yes," see detailed instructions.

NATURE OF AUTHORSHIP Briefly describe nature of material created by this author in which copyright is claimed. ▼

c NAME OF AUTHOR ▼

DATES OF BIRTH AND DEATH
Year Born ▼   Year Died ▼

Was this contribution to the work a "work made for hire"?
☐ Yes
☐ No

AUTHOR'S NATIONALITY OR DOMICILE
Name of Country
OR { Citizen of ▶
Domiciled in ▶

WAS THIS AUTHOR'S CONTRIBUTION TO THE WORK
Anonymous?   ☐ Yes ☐ No
Pseudonymous? ☐ Yes ☐ No

If the answer to either of these questions is "Yes," see detailed instructions.

NATURE OF AUTHORSHIP Briefly describe nature of material created by this author in which copyright is claimed. ▼

3

a YEAR IN WHICH CREATION OF THIS WORK WAS COMPLETED   This information must be given
20XX ◀ Year in all cases.

b DATE AND NATION OF FIRST PUBLICATION OF THIS PARTICULAR WORK
Complete this information ONLY if this work has been published.
Month ▶ 4   Day ▶ 1   Year ▶ 20XX
USA ◀ Nation

4
COPYRIGHT CLAIMANT(S) Name and address must be given even if the claimant is the same as the author given in space 2. ▼
Micro Weird, Inc.
666 Dreary Lane
Marred Vista, CA 90000

See instructions before completing this space.

TRANSFER If the claimant(s) named here in space 4 is (are) different from the author(s) named in space 2, give a brief statement of how the claimant(s) obtained ownership of the copyright. ▼

APPLICATION RECEIVED

ONE DEPOSIT RECEIVED

TWO DEPOSITS RECEIVED

FUNDS RECEIVED

DO NOT WRITE HERE
OFFICE USE ONLY

MORE ON BACK ▶ • Complete all applicable spaces (numbers 5-11) on the reverse side of this page.
• See detailed instructions.   • Sign the form at line 10.

DO NOT WRITE HERE
Page 1 of _____ pages

2   Published work made for hire; computer program and documents registered together (back)

	FORM TX
EXAMINED BY _____	
CHECKED BY _____	
☐ CORRESPONDENCE Yes	FOR COPYRIGHT OFFICE USE ONLY

DO NOT WRITE ABOVE THIS LINE. IF YOU NEED MORE SPACE, USE A SEPARATE CONTINUATION SHEET.

5

PREVIOUS REGISTRATION Has registration for this work, or for an earlier version of this work, already been made in the Copyright Office?
☐ Yes ☒ No If your answer is "Yes," why is another registration being sought? (Check appropriate box) ▼
a.☐ This is the first published edition of a work previously registered in unpublished form.
b.☐ This is the first application submitted by this author as copyright claimant.
c.☐ This is a changed version of the work, as shown by space 6 on this application.
If your answer is "Yes," give: **Previous Registration Number** ▼   **Year of Registration** ▼

6

DERIVATIVE WORK OR COMPILATION Complete both space 6a and 6b for a derivative work; complete only 6b for a compilation.
a. Preexisting Material Identify any preexisting work or works that this work is based on or incorporates. ▼

b. Material Added to This Work Give a brief, general statement of the material that has been added to this work and in which copyright is claimed. ▼

See instructions before completing this space.

7

—space deleted—

8

REPRODUCTION FOR USE OF BLIND OR PHYSICALLY HANDICAPPED INDIVIDUALS A signature on this form at space 10 and a check in one of the boxes here in space 8 constitutes a non-exclusive grant of permission to the Library of Congress to reproduce and distribute solely for the blind and physically handicapped and under the conditions and limitations prescribed by the regulations of the Copyright Office: (1) copies of the work identified in space 1 of this application in Braille (or similar tactile symbols); or (2) phonorecords embodying a fixation of a reading of that work; or (3) both.

a☒ Copies and Phonorecords   b☐ Copies Only   c☐ Phonorecords Only

See instructions.

9

DEPOSIT ACCOUNT If the registration fee is to be charged to a Deposit Account established in the Copyright Office, give name and number of Account.
Name ▼   **Account Number** ▼

CORRESPONDENCE Give name and address to which correspondence about this application should be sent.   Name/Address/Apt/City/State/ZIP ▼

Micro Weird, Inc.
666 Dreary Lane
Marred Vista, CA
90000   Area Code and Telephone Number ▶ 818-555-1212

Be sure to give your daytime phone ◀ number

10

CERTIFICATION* I, the undersigned, hereby certify that I am the
Check only one ▶ {
☐ author
☐ other copyright claimant
☐ owner of exclusive right(s)
☒ authorized agent of ____ Micro Weird, Inc.
}
of the work identified in this application and that the statements made by me in this application are correct to the best of my knowledge.
Name of author or other copyright claimant, or owner of exclusive right(s) ▲

Typed or printed name and date ▼ If this application gives a date of publication in space 3, do not sign and submit it before that date.
Leslie Howard   Date ▶ 4/1/XX

☞   Handwritten signature (X) ▼

11

MAIL CERTIFICATE TO

Name ▼
Micro Weird, Inc.
Number/Street/Apt ▼
666 Dreary Lane
City/State/ZIP ▼
Marred Vista, CA 90000

Certificate will be mailed in window envelope

YOU MUST:
• Complete all necessary spaces
• Sign your application in space 10
SEND ALL 3 ELEMENTS IN THE SAME PACKAGE:
1. Application form
2. Nonrefundable $20 filing fee in check or money order payable to *Register of Copyrights*
3. Deposit material
MAIL TO:
Register of Copyrights
Library of Congress
Washington, D.C. 20559-6000

*17 U.S.C. § 506(e): Any person who knowingly makes a false representation of a material fact in the application for copyright registration provided for by section 409, or in any written statement filed in connection with the application, shall be fined not more than $2,500.
May 1995—300,000   ☆U.S. COPYRIGHT OFFICE WWW FORM: 1995

3 Published computer game created by joint authors; all rights transferred to publisher; screen displays listed in Nature of Authorship statement

FORM TX
For a Literary Work
UNITED STATES COPYRIGHT OFFICE

REGISTRATION NUMBER

| | |
| TX | TXU |

EFFECTIVE DATE OF REGISTRATION

| Month | Day | Year |

DO NOT WRITE ABOVE THIS LINE. IF YOU NEED MORE SPACE, USE A SEPARATE CONTINUATION SHEET.

1 **TITLE OF THIS WORK ▼**

You Are What You Eat

PREVIOUS OR ALTERNATIVE TITLES ▼

PUBLICATION AS A CONTRIBUTION If this work was published as a contribution to a periodical, serial, or collection, give information about the collective work in which the contribution appeared.   **Title of Collective Work ▼**

If published in a periodical or serial give: Volume ▼   Number ▼   Issue Date ▼   On Pages ▼

2

a **NAME OF AUTHOR ▼**
Ron Claiborne

DATES OF BIRTH AND DEATH
Year Born ▼   Year Died ▼
1950

Was this contribution to the work a "work made for hire"?
☐ Yes
☒ No

AUTHOR'S NATIONALITY OR DOMICILE
Name of Country
OR { Citizen of ▶ USA
      Domiciled in ▶

WAS THIS AUTHOR'S CONTRIBUTION TO THE WORK
Anonymous?   ☐ Yes ☒ No
Pseudonymous?   ☐ Yes ☒ No
If the answer to either of these questions is "Yes," see detailed instructions.

NATURE OF AUTHORSHIP Briefly describe nature of material created by this author in which copyright is claimed. ▼
Entire text of computer program and screen display with user documentation

NOTE
Under the law, the "author" of a "work made for hire" is generally the employer, not the employee (see instructions). For any part of this work that was "made for hire" check "Yes" in the space provided, give the employer (or other person for whom the work was prepared) as "Author" of that part, and leave the space for dates of birth and death blank.

b **NAME OF AUTHOR ▼**
Sue Sweet

DATES OF BIRTH AND DEATH
Year Born ▼   Year Died ▼
1960

Was this contribution to the work a "work made for hire"?
☐ Yes
☒ No

AUTHOR'S NATIONALITY OR DOMICILE
Name of Country
OR { Citizen of ▶ USA
      Domiciled in ▶

WAS THIS AUTHOR'S CONTRIBUTION TO THE WORK
Anonymous?   ☐ Yes ☒ No
Pseudonymous?   ☐ Yes ☒ No
If the answer to either of these questions is "Yes," see detailed instructions.

NATURE OF AUTHORSHIP Briefly describe nature of material created by this author in which copyright is claimed. ▼
Entire text of computer program and screen display with user documentation

c **NAME OF AUTHOR ▼**
Jesse Quicksilver

DATES OF BIRTH AND DEATH
Year Born ▼   Year Died ▼
1970

Was this contribution to the work a "work made for hire"?
☐ Yes
☒ No

AUTHOR'S NATIONALITY OR DOMICILE
Name of Country
OR { Citizen of ▶ USA
      Domiciled in ▶

WAS THIS AUTHOR'S CONTRIBUTION TO THE WORK
Anonymous?   ☐ Yes ☒ No
Pseudonymous?   ☐ Yes ☒ No
If the answer to either of these questions is "Yes," see detailed instructions.

NATURE OF AUTHORSHIP Briefly describe nature of material created by this author in which copyright is claimed. ▼
Entire text of computer program and screen display with user documentation

3
a **YEAR IN WHICH CREATION OF THIS WORK WAS COMPLETED** This information must be given   Year in all cases.
20XX

b **DATE AND NATION OF FIRST PUBLICATION OF THIS PARTICULAR WORK**
Complete this information ONLY if this work has been published.
Month ▶ 6   Day ▶ 1   Year ▶ XX
USA   ◀ Nation

4
See instructions before completing this space.

COPYRIGHT CLAIMANT(S) Name and address must be given even if the claimant is the same as the author given in space 2. ▼
Micro Games, Inc.
100 Commerce Way
Cambridge WA 01234

TRANSFER If the claimant(s) named here in space 4 is (are) different from the author(s) named in space 2, give a brief statement of how the claimant(s) obtained ownership of the copyright. ▼

By written contract

APPLICATION RECEIVED

ONE DEPOSIT RECEIVED

TWO DEPOSITS RECEIVED

FUNDS RECEIVED

DO NOT WRITE HERE — OFFICE USE ONLY

MORE ON BACK ▶   • Complete all applicable spaces (numbers 5-11) on the reverse side of this page.
• See detailed instructions.   • Sign the form at line 10.

DO NOT WRITE HERE
Page 1 of _____ pages

3   Published computer game created by joint authors; all rights transferred to publisher; screen displays listed in Nature of Authorship statement (back)

EXAMINED BY _____	FORM TX
CHECKED BY _____	
☐ CORRESPONDENCE Yes	FOR COPYRIGHT OFFICE USE ONLY

DO NOT WRITE ABOVE THIS LINE. IF YOU NEED MORE SPACE, USE A SEPARATE CONTINUATION SHEET.

5 **PREVIOUS REGISTRATION** Has registration for this work, or for an earlier version of this work, already been made in the Copyright Office?

☐ Yes   ☒ No   If your answer is "Yes," why is another registration being sought? (Check appropriate box) ▼

a. ☐ This is the first published edition of a work previously registered in unpublished form.

b. ☐ This is the first application submitted by this author as copyright claimant.

c. ☐ This is a changed version of the work, as shown by space 6 on this application.

If your answer is "Yes," give: **Previous Registration Number** ▼   **Year of Registration** ▼

6 **DERIVATIVE WORK OR COMPILATION** Complete both space 6a and 6b for a derivative work; complete only 6b for a compilation.

a. Preexisting Material Identify any preexisting work or works that this work is based on or incorporates. ▼

b. Material Added to This Work Give a brief, general statement of the material that has been added to this work and in which copyright is claimed. ▼

See instructions before completing this space.

7 —space deleted—

8 **REPRODUCTION FOR USE OF BLIND OR PHYSICALLY HANDICAPPED INDIVIDUALS** A signature on this form at space 10 and a check in one of the boxes here in space 8 constitutes a non-exclusive grant of permission to the Library of Congress to reproduce and distribute solely for the blind and physically handicapped and under the conditions and limitations prescribed by the regulations of the Copyright Office: (1) copies of the work identified in space 1 of this application in Braille (or similar tactile symbols); or (2) phonorecords embodying a fixation of a reading of that work; or (3) both.

a ☒ Copies and Phonorecords   **b** ☐ Copies Only   **c** ☐ Phonorecords Only

See instructions.

9 **DEPOSIT ACCOUNT** If the registration fee is to be charged to a Deposit Account established in the Copyright Office, give name and number of Account.

Name ▼   **Account Number** ▼

Micro Games, Inc.

CORRESPONDENCE Give name and address to which correspondence about this application should be sent.   Name/Address/Apt/City/State/ZIP ▼

Micro Games, Inc.
100 Commerce Way
Cambridge, MA 01234

Area Code and Telephone Number ▶   012-555-5555

Be sure to give your daytime phone ◄ number

10 **CERTIFICATION*** I, the undersigned, hereby certify that I am the

Check only one ▶

     ☒ author
     ☐ other copyright claimant
     ☐ owner of exclusive right(s)
     ☐ authorized agent of _____

of the work identified in this application and that the statements made by me in this application are correct to the best of my knowledge.

Name of author or other copyright claimant, or owner of exclusive right(s) ▲

Typed or printed name and date ▼ If this application gives a date of publication in space 3, do not sign and submit it before that date.

Art Atlas   Date ▶ 5/15/XX

☞ **Handwritten signature (X)** ▼

11 **MAIL CERTIFI-CATE TO**   **Certificate will be mailed in window envelope**

Name ▼
Micro Games, Inc.

Number/Street/Apt ▼
100 Commerce Way

City/State/ZIP ▼
Cambridge, MA 01234

YOU MUST:
• Complete all necessary spaces
• Sign your application in space 10

SEND ALL 3 ELEMENTS IN THE SAME PACKAGE:
1. Application form
2. Nonrefundable $20 filing fee in check or money order payable to *Register of Copyrights*
3. Deposit material

MAIL TO:
Register of Copyrights
Library of Congress
Washington, D.C. 20559-6000

*17 U.S.C. § 506(e): Any person who knowingly makes a false representation of a material fact in the application for copyright registration provided for by section 409, or in any written statement filed in connection with the application, shall be fined not more than $2,500.

May 1995—300,000   ☆U.S. COPYRIGHT OFFICE WWW FORM: 1995

4 Published derivative work made for hire; a new version of previously published program

FORM TX

For a Literary Work
UNITED STATES COPYRIGHT OFFICE

REGISTRATION NUMBER

_____
TX   TXU
EFFECTIVE DATE OF REGISTRATION

_____
Month   Day   Year

DO NOT WRITE ABOVE THIS LINE. IF YOU NEED MORE SPACE, USE A SEPARATE CONTINUATION SHEET.

1 TITLE OF THIS WORK ▼

Account Handler 2.0

PREVIOUS OR ALTERNATIVE TITLES ▼

PUBLICATION AS A CONTRIBUTION If this work was published as a contribution to a periodical, serial, or collection, give information about the collective work in which the contribution appeared.   **Title of Collective Work** ▼

If published in a periodical or serial give: **Volume** ▼   **Number** ▼   **Issue Date** ▼   **On Pages** ▼

2

a NAME OF AUTHOR ▼
CPA Software, Inc.

DATES OF BIRTH AND DEATH
Year Born ▼   Year Died ▼

Was this contribution to the work a "work made for hire"?
☒ Yes
☐ No

AUTHOR'S NATIONALITY OR DOMICILE
Name of Country
OR { Citizen of ▶ USA
Domiciled in ▶

WAS THIS AUTHOR'S CONTRIBUTION TO THE WORK
Anonymous?   ☐ Yes ☒ No
Pseudonymous? ☐ Yes ☒ No

If the answer to either of these questions is "Yes," see detailed instructions.

NATURE OF AUTHORSHIP Briefly describe nature of material created by this author in which copyright is claimed. ▼
Entire text of computer program

NOTE

Under the law, the "author" of a "work made for hire" is generally the employer, not the employee (see instructions). For any part of this work that was "made for hire" check "Yes" in the space provided, give the employer (or other person for whom the work was prepared) as "Author" of that part, and leave the space for dates of birth and death blank.

b NAME OF AUTHOR ▼

DATES OF BIRTH AND DEATH
Year Born ▼   Year Died ▼

Was this contribution to the work a "work made for hire"?
☐ Yes
☐ No

AUTHOR'S NATIONALITY OR DOMICILE
Name of Country
OR { Citizen of ▶
Domiciled in ▶

WAS THIS AUTHOR'S CONTRIBUTION TO THE WORK
Anonymous?   ☐ Yes ☐ No
Pseudonymous? ☐ Yes ☐ No

If the answer to either of these questions is "Yes," see detailed instructions.

NATURE OF AUTHORSHIP Briefly describe nature of material created by this author in which copyright is claimed. ▼

c NAME OF AUTHOR ▼

DATES OF BIRTH AND DEATH
Year Born ▼   Year Died ▼

Was this contribution to the work a "work made for hire"?
☐ Yes
☐ No

AUTHOR'S NATIONALITY OR DOMICILE
Name of Country
OR { Citizen of ▶
Domiciled in ▶

WAS THIS AUTHOR'S CONTRIBUTION TO THE WORK
Anonymous?   ☐ Yes ☐ No
Pseudonymous? ☐ Yes ☐ No

If the answer to either of these questions is "Yes," see detailed instructions.

NATURE OF AUTHORSHIP Briefly describe nature of material created by this author in which copyright is claimed. ▼

3

a YEAR IN WHICH CREATION OF THIS WORK WAS COMPLETED This information must be given in all cases.
20XX ◀ Year

b DATE AND NATION OF FIRST PUBLICATION OF THIS PARTICULAR WORK
Complete this information ONLY if this work has been published.
Month ▶ 11 Day ▶ 1 Year ▶ XX
USA ◀ Nation

4

See instructions before completing this space.

COPYRIGHT CLAIMANT(S) Name and address must be given even if the claimant is the same as the author given in space 2. ▼
CPA Software, Inc.
240 5th Ave.
New York, NY 12345

TRANSFER If the claimant(s) named here in space 4 is (are) different from the author(s) named in space 2, give a brief statement of how the claimant(s) obtained ownership of the copyright. ▼

APPLICATION RECEIVED

ONE DEPOSIT RECEIVED

TWO DEPOSITS RECEIVED

FUNDS RECEIVED

DO NOT WRITE HERE
OFFICE USE ONLY

MORE ON BACK ▶ • Complete all applicable spaces (numbers 5-11) on the reverse side of this page.
• See detailed instructions.   • Sign the form at line 10.

DO NOT WRITE HERE

Page 1 of _____ pages

4   Published derivative work made for hire; a new version of previously published program (back)

EXAMINED BY	**FORM TX**
CHECKED BY	
☐ CORRESPONDENCE ☐ Yes	FOR COPYRIGHT OFFICE USE ONLY

DO NOT WRITE ABOVE THIS LINE. IF YOU NEED MORE SPACE, USE A SEPARATE CONTINUATION SHEET.

PREVIOUS REGISTRATION Has registration for this work, or for an earlier version of this work, already been made in the Copyright Office?

☒ **Yes** ☐ **No** If your answer is "Yes," why is another registration being sought? (Check appropriate box) ▼

a. ☐ This is the first published edition of a work previously registered in unpublished form.

b. ☐ This is the first application submitted by this author as copyright claimant.

c. ☒ This is a changed version of the work, as shown by space 6 on this application.

If your answer is "Yes," give: **Previous Registration Number** ▼   **Year of Registration** ▼

TX123456   1999

5

DERIVATIVE WORK OR COMPILATION Complete both space 6a and 6b for a derivative work; complete only 6b for a compilation.

a. Preexisting Material Identify any preexisting work or works that this work is based on or incorporates. ▼

previous version

b. Material Added to This Work Give a brief, general statement of the material that has been added to this work and in which copyright is claimed. ▼

revised computer program

6

See instructions before completing this space.

—space deleted—

7

REPRODUCTION FOR USE OF BLIND OR PHYSICALLY HANDICAPPED INDIVIDUALS A signature on this form at space 10 and a check in one of the boxes here in space 8 constitutes a non-exclusive grant of permission to the Library of Congress to reproduce and distribute solely for the blind and physically handicapped and under the conditions and limitations prescribed by the regulations of the Copyright Office: (1) copies of the work identified in space 1 of this application in Braille (or similar tactile symbols); or (2) phonorecords embodying a fixation of a reading of that work; or (3) both.

a ☒ Copies and Phonorecords   **b** ☐ Copies Only   **c** ☐ Phonorecords Only

8

See instructions.

DEPOSIT ACCOUNT If the registration fee is to be charged to a Deposit Account established in the Copyright Office, give name and number of Account.

Name ▼   **Account Number** ▼

9

CORRESPONDENCE Give name and address to which correspondence about this application should be sent.   Name/Address/Apt/City/State/ZIP ▼

CPA Software, Inc.
240 5th Avenue
New York, NY 12345

Area Code and Telephone Number ▶ 212-555-6789

Be sure to give your daytime phone ◀ number

CERTIFICATION* I, the undersigned, hereby certify that I am the

Check only one ▶

☐ author
☐ other copyright claimant
☐ owner of exclusive right(s)
☒ authorized agent of   CPA Software, Inc.

of the work identified in this application and that the statements made by me in this application are correct to the best of my knowledge.

Name of author or other copyright claimant, or owner of exclusive right(s) ▲

Typed or printed name and date ▼ If this application gives a date of publication in space 3, do not sign and submit it before that date.

Sid Shuster

Date ▶ 1/2/XX

☞   Handwritten signature (X) ▼

10

MAIL CERTIFI-CATE TO

Name ▼
CPA Software, Inc.
Number/Street/Apt ▼
240 5th Ave.
City/State/ZIP ▼
New York, NY 12345

Certificate will be mailed in window envelope

YOU MUST:
• Complete all necessary spaces
• Sign your application in space 10

SEND ALL 3 ELEMENTS IN THE SAME PACKAGE:
1. Application form
2. Nonrefundable $20 filing fee in check or money order payable to *Register of Copyrights*
3. Deposit material

MAIL TO:
Register of Copyrights
Library of Congress
Washington, D.C. 20559-6000

11

*17 U.S.C. § 506(e): Any person who knowingly makes a false representation of a material fact in the application for copyright registration provided for by section 409, or in any written statement filed in connection with the application, shall be fined not more than $2,500.

May 1995—300,000   ☆U.S. COPYRIGHT OFFICE WWW FORM: 1995

5 Documentation registered separately from computer program

FORM TX
For a Literary Work
UNITED STATES COPYRIGHT OFFICE

REGISTRATION NUMBER

TX   TXU

EFFECTIVE DATE OF REGISTRATION

Month   Day   Year

DO NOT WRITE ABOVE THIS LINE. IF YOU NEED MORE SPACE, USE A SEPARATE CONTINUATION SHEET.

1 TITLE OF THIS WORK ▼

Acme Word Users' Manual

PREVIOUS OR ALTERNATIVE TITLES ▼

PUBLICATION AS A CONTRIBUTION If this work was published as a contribution to a periodical, serial, or collection, give information about the collective work in which the contribution appeared.   **Title of Collective Work ▼**

If published in a periodical or serial give: **Volume ▼**   **Number ▼**   **Issue Date ▼**   **On Pages ▼**

2   **a** NAME OF AUTHOR ▼

Acme Soft

DATES OF BIRTH AND DEATH
Year Born ▼   Year Died ▼

Was this contribution to the work a "work made for hire"?
☒ Yes
☐ No

AUTHOR'S NATIONALITY OR DOMICILE
Name of Country
OR { Citizen of ▶ USA
Domiciled in ▶

WAS THIS AUTHOR'S CONTRIBUTION TO THE WORK
Anonymous? ☐ Yes ☒ No
Pseudonymous? ☐ Yes ☒ No
If the answer to either of these questions is "Yes," see detailed instructions.

NATURE OF AUTHORSHIP Briefly describe nature of material created by this author in which copyright is claimed. ▼

NOTE
Under the law, the "author" of a "work made for hire" is generally the employer, not the employee (see instructions). For any part of this work that was "made for hire" check "Yes" in the space provided, give the employer (or other person for whom the work was prepared) as "Author" of that part, and leave the space for dates of birth and death blank.

b NAME OF AUTHOR ▼

DATES OF BIRTH AND DEATH
Year Born ▼   Year Died ▼

Was this contribution to the work a "work made for hire"?
☐ Yes
☐ No

AUTHOR'S NATIONALITY OR DOMICILE
Name of Country
OR { Citizen of ▶
Domiciled in ▶

WAS THIS AUTHOR'S CONTRIBUTION TO THE WORK
Anonymous? ☐ Yes ☐ No
Pseudonymous? ☐ Yes ☐ No
If the answer to either of these questions is "Yes," see detailed instructions.

NATURE OF AUTHORSHIP Briefly describe nature of material created by this author in which copyright is claimed. ▼

c NAME OF AUTHOR ▼

DATES OF BIRTH AND DEATH
Year Born ▼   Year Died ▼

Was this contribution to the work a "work made for hire"?
☐ Yes
☐ No

AUTHOR'S NATIONALITY OR DOMICILE
Name of Country
OR { Citizen of ▶
Domiciled in ▶

WAS THIS AUTHOR'S CONTRIBUTION TO THE WORK
Anonymous? ☐ Yes ☐ No
Pseudonymous? ☐ Yes ☐ No
If the answer to either of these questions is "Yes," see detailed instructions.

NATURE OF AUTHORSHIP Briefly describe nature of material created by this author in which copyright is claimed. ▼

3   **a** YEAR IN WHICH CREATION OF THIS WORK WAS COMPLETED   This information must be given in all cases.
20XX ◀ Year

b DATE AND NATION OF FIRST PUBLICATION OF THIS PARTICULAR WORK
Complete this information ONLY if this work has been published.
Month ▶ 12   Day ▶ 1   Year ▶ 20XX
USA ◀ Nation

4 COPYRIGHT CLAIMANT(S) Name and address must be given even if the claimant is the same as the author given in space 2. ▼

Acme Soft, Inc.
123 Computer Rd.
Silicon Valley, OR 80500

See instructions before completing this space.

TRANSFER If the claimant(s) named here in space 4 is (are) different from the author(s) named in space 2, give a brief statement of how the claimant(s) obtained ownership of the copyright. ▼

DO NOT WRITE HERE
OFFICE USE ONLY

APPLICATION RECEIVED

ONE DEPOSIT RECEIVED

TWO DEPOSITS RECEIVED

FUNDS RECEIVED

MORE ON BACK ▶ • Complete all applicable spaces (numbers 5-11) on the reverse side of this page.
• See detailed instructions.   • Sign the form at line 10.

DO NOT WRITE HERE
Page 1 of _____ pages

5 Documentation registered separately from computer program (back)

EXAMINED BY	FORM TX
CHECKED BY	
☐ CORRESPONDENCE Yes	FOR COPYRIGHT OFFICE USE ONLY

DO NOT WRITE ABOVE THIS LINE. IF YOU NEED MORE SPACE, USE A SEPARATE CONTINUATION SHEET.

PREVIOUS REGISTRATION Has registration for this work, or for an earlier version of this work, already been made in the Copyright Office?

☐ Yes ☒ No If your answer is "Yes," why is another registration being sought? (Check appropriate box) ▼

a.☐ This is the first published edition of a work previously registered in unpublished form.

b.☐ This is the first application submitted by this author as copyright claimant.

c.☐ This is a changed version of the work, as shown by space 6 on this application.

If your answer is "Yes," give: **Previous Registration Number ▼**   **Year of Registration ▼**

5

DERIVATIVE WORK OR COMPILATION Complete both space 6a and 6b for a derivative work; complete only 6b for a compilation.
a. **Preexisting Material** Identify any preexisting work or works that this work is based on or incorporates. ▼

b. **Material Added to This Work** Give a brief, general statement of the material that has been added to this work and in which copyright is claimed. ▼

6

See instructions before completing this space.

—space deleted—

7

REPRODUCTION FOR USE OF BLIND OR PHYSICALLY HANDICAPPED INDIVIDUALS A signature on this form at space 10 and a check in one of the boxes here in space 8 constitutes a non-exclusive grant of permission to the Library of Congress to reproduce and distribute solely for the blind and physically handicapped and under the conditions and limitations prescribed by the regulations of the Copyright Office: (1) copies of the work identified in space 1 of this application in Braille (or similar tactile symbols); or (2) phonorecords embodying a fixation of a reading of that work; or (3) both.

a ☒ Copies and Phonorecords   b ☐ Copies Only   c ☐ Phonorecords Only

8

See instructions.

DEPOSIT ACCOUNT If the registration fee is to be charged to a Deposit Account established in the Copyright Office, give name and number of Account.
Name ▼   **Account Number ▼**

9

CORRESPONDENCE Give name and address to which correspondence about this application should be sent.   Name/Address/Apt/City/State/ZIP ▼

Acme Soft, Inc., Attn. George Apley
123 Computer Rd.
Silicon Valley, OR 80500

Area Code and Telephone Number ▶ 555-555-5555

Be sure to give your daytime phone number ◀

CERTIFICATION* I, the undersigned, hereby certify that I am the

Check only one ▶ {
☐ author
☐ other copyright claimant
☐ owner of exclusive right(s)
☒ authorized agent of Acme Soft, Inc.
}

of the work identified in this application and that the statements made
by me in this application are correct to the best of my knowledge.

Name of author or other copyright claimant, or owner of exclusive right(s) ▲

Typed or printed name and date ▼ If this application gives a date of publication in space 3, do not sign and submit it before that date.

George Apley

Date ▶ 12/15/XX

☞   Handwritten signature (X) ▼

10

MAIL CERTIFI-CATE TO

Name ▼
Acme Soft, Inc.

Certificate will be mailed in window envelope

Number/Street/Apt ▼
123 Computer Rd.

City/State/ZIP ▼
Silicon Valley, OR 80500

YOU MUST:
• Complete all necessary spaces
• Sign your application in space 10
SEND ALL 3 ELEMENTS IN THE SAME PACKAGE:
1. Application form
2. Nonrefundable $20 filing fee in check or money order payable to *Register of Copyrights*
3. Deposit material
MAIL TO:
Register of Copyrights
Library of Congress
Washington, D.C. 20559-6000

11

*17 U.S.C. § 506(e): Any person who knowingly makes a false representation of a material fact in the application for copyright registration provided for by section 409, or in any written statement filed in connection with the application, shall be fined not more than $2,500.

May 1995—300,000

☆U.S. COPYRIGHT OFFICE WWW FORM: 1995

6   Computer game

FORM TX
For a Literary Work
UNITED STATES COPYRIGHT OFFICE

REGISTRATION NUMBER

_____

TX   TXU

EFFECTIVE DATE OF REGISTRATION

_____

Month   Day   Year

DO NOT WRITE ABOVE THIS LINE. IF YOU NEED MORE SPACE, USE A SEPARATE CONTINUATION SHEET.

1

TITLE OF THIS WORK ▼

Kill or Die

PREVIOUS OR ALTERNATIVE TITLES ▼

PUBLICATION AS A CONTRIBUTION If this work was published as a contribution to a periodical, serial, or collection, give information about the collective work in which the contribution appeared.   **Title of Collective Work ▼**

If published in a periodical or serial give: **Volume ▼**   **Number ▼**   **Issue Date ▼**   **On Pages ▼**

2

a **NAME OF AUTHOR ▼**

Game Soft, Inc.

DATES OF BIRTH AND DEATH
Year Born ▼   Year Died ▼

Was this contribution to the work a "work made for hire"?
☒ Yes
☐ No

AUTHOR'S NATIONALITY OR DOMICILE
Name of Country
OR { Citizen of ▶ USA
      Domiciled in ▶

WAS THIS AUTHOR'S CONTRIBUTION TO THE WORK
Anonymous?   ☐ Yes ☒ No
Pseudonymous?   ☐ Yes ☒ No
If the answer to either of these questions is "Yes," see detailed instructions.

NATURE OF AUTHORSHIP Briefly describe nature of material created by this author in which copyright is claimed. ▼
Text of program, game screens and sounds

NOTE

Under the law, the "author" of a "work made for hire" is generally the employer, not the employee (see instructions). For any part of this work that was "made for hire" check "Yes" in the space provided, give the employer (or other person for whom the work was prepared) as "Author" of that part, and leave the space for dates of birth and death blank.

b **NAME OF AUTHOR ▼**

DATES OF BIRTH AND DEATH
Year Born ▼   Year Died ▼

Was this contribution to the work a "work made for hire"?
☐ Yes
☐ No

AUTHOR'S NATIONALITY OR DOMICILE
Name of Country
OR { Citizen of ▶
      Domiciled in ▶

WAS THIS AUTHOR'S CONTRIBUTION TO THE WORK
Anonymous?   ☐ Yes ☐ No
Pseudonymous?   ☐ Yes ☐ No
If the answer to either of these questions is "Yes," see detailed instructions.

NATURE OF AUTHORSHIP Briefly describe nature of material created by this author in which copyright is claimed. ▼

c **NAME OF AUTHOR ▼**

DATES OF BIRTH AND DEATH
Year Born ▼   Year Died ▼

Was this contribution to the work a "work made for hire"?
☐ Yes
☐ No

AUTHOR'S NATIONALITY OR DOMICILE
Name of Country
OR { Citizen of ▶
      Domiciled in ▶

WAS THIS AUTHOR'S CONTRIBUTION TO THE WORK
Anonymous?   ☐ Yes ☐ No
Pseudonymous?   ☐ Yes ☐ No
If the answer to either of these questions is "Yes," see detailed instructions.

NATURE OF AUTHORSHIP Briefly describe nature of material created by this author in which copyright is claimed. ▼

3

a **YEAR IN WHICH CREATION OF THIS WORK WAS COMPLETED**   This information must be given   20XX   ◀ Year in all cases.

b **DATE AND NATION OF FIRST PUBLICATION OF THIS PARTICULAR WORK**
Complete this information ONLY if this work has been published.   Month ▶ 4   Day ▶ 1   Year ▶ 20XX
USA   ◀ Nation

4

See instructions before completing this space.

COPYRIGHT CLAIMANT(S) Name and address must be given even if the claimant is the same as the author given in space 2. ▼
Game Soft, Inc.
1000 3rd St.
Miami, FL 40600

TRANSFER If the claimant(s) named here in space 4 is (are) different from the author(s) named in space 2, give a brief statement of how the claimant(s) obtained ownership of the copyright. ▼

DO NOT WRITE HERE
OFFICE USE ONLY

APPLICATION RECEIVED

ONE DEPOSIT RECEIVED

TWO DEPOSITS RECEIVED

FUNDS RECEIVED

MORE ON BACK ▶   • Complete all applicable spaces (numbers 5-11) on the reverse side of this page.
• See detailed instructions.   • Sign the form at line 10.

DO NOT WRITE HERE
Page 1 of _____ pages

6   Computer game (back)

EXAMINED BY	FORM TX
CHECKED BY	
☐ CORRESPONDENCE Yes	FOR COPYRIGHT OFFICE USE ONLY

DO NOT WRITE ABOVE THIS LINE. IF YOU NEED MORE SPACE, USE A SEPARATE CONTINUATION SHEET.

5

PREVIOUS REGISTRATION Has registration for this work, or for an earlier version of this work, already been made in the Copyright Office?

☐ Yes ☒ No If your answer is "Yes," why is another registration being sought? (Check appropriate box) ▼

a. ☐ This is the first published edition of a work previously registered in unpublished form.

b. ☐ This is the first application submitted by this author as copyright claimant.

c. ☐ This is a changed version of the work, as shown by space 6 on this application.

If your answer is "Yes," give: **Previous Registration Number ▼**   **Year of Registration ▼**

6

DERIVATIVE WORK OR COMPILATION Complete both space 6a and 6b for a derivative work; complete only 6b for a compilation.

a. Preexisting Material Identify any preexisting work or works that this work is based on or incorporates. ▼

b. Material Added to This Work Give a brief, general statement of the material that has been added to this work and in which copyright is claimed. ▼

See instructions before completing this space.

7

—space deleted—

8

REPRODUCTION FOR USE OF BLIND OR PHYSICALLY HANDICAPPED INDIVIDUALS A signature on this form at space 10 and a check in one of the boxes here in space 8 constitutes a non-exclusive grant of permission to the Library of Congress to reproduce and distribute solely for the blind and physically handicapped and under the conditions and limitations prescribed by the regulations of the Copyright Office: (1) copies of the work identified in space 1 of this application in Braille (or similar tactile symbols); or (2) phonorecords embodying a fixation of a reading of that work; or (3) both.

a ☒ Copies and Phonorecords   **b** ☐ Copies Only   **c** ☐ Phonorecords Only

See instructions.

9

DEPOSIT ACCOUNT If the registration fee is to be charged to a Deposit Account established in the Copyright Office, give name and number of Account.

Name ▼   **Account Number ▼**

CORRESPONDENCE Give name and address to which correspondence about this application should be sent.   Name/Address/Apt/City/State/ZIP ▼

Game Soft, Inc.
1000 3rd St.
Miami, FL 40600

Area Code and Telephone Number ▶ 123-456-7890

Be sure to give your daytime phone ◀ number

10

CERTIFICATION* I, the undersigned, hereby certify that I am the

Check only one ▶

☐ author
☐ other copyright claimant
☐ owner of exclusive right(s)
☒ authorized agent of _Game Soft, Inc._

of the work identified in this application and that the statements made by me in this application are correct to the best of my knowledge.

Name of author or other copyright claimant, or owner of exclusive right(s) ▲

Typed or printed name and date ▼ If this application gives a date of publication in space 3, do not sign and submit it before that date.

Andrea Andrews   Date ▶ 4/15/XX

☞ **Handwritten signature (X) ▼**

11

MAIL CERTIFI-CATE TO

Certificate will be mailed in window envelope

Name ▼
Game Soft, Inc.
Number/Street/Apt ▼
1000 3rd St.
City/State/ZIP ▼
Miami, FL 40600

YOU MUST:
• Complete all necessary spaces
• Sign your application in space 10
SEND ALL 3 ELEMENTS IN THE SAME PACKAGE:
1. Application form
2. Nonrefundable $20 filing fee in check or money order payable to *Register of Copyrights*
3. Deposit material
MAIL TO:
Register of Copyrights
Library of Congress
Washington, D.C. 20559-6000

*17 U.S.C. § 506(e): Any person who knowingly makes a false representation of a material fact in the application for copyright registration provided for by section 409, or in any written statement filed in connection with the application, shall be fined not more than $2,500.

May 1995—300,000   ☆U.S. COPYRIGHT OFFICE WWW FORM: 1995

7 Published multimedia program; work made for hire

FORM PA
For a Work of the Performing Arts
UNITED STATES COPYRIGHT OFFICE

REGISTRATION NUMBER

_____

PA   PAU

EFFECTIVE DATE OF REGISTRATION

_____

Month   Day   Year

DO NOT WRITE ABOVE THIS LINE. IF YOU NEED MORE SPACE, USE A SEPARATE CONTINUATION SHEET.

1

TITLE OF THIS WORK ▼

History of Art

PREVIOUS OR ALTERNATIVE TITLES ▼

NATURE OF THIS WORK ▼ See instructions

2

a NAME OF AUTHOR ▼

Acme Soft, Inc.

DATES OF BIRTH AND DEATH
Year Born ▼   Year Died ▼

Was this contribution to the work a "work made for hire"?
☒ Yes
☐ No

AUTHOR'S NATIONALITY OR DOMICILE
Name of Country
OR { Citizen of ▶ USA
Domiciled in ▶

WAS THIS AUTHOR'S CONTRIBUTION TO THE WORK
Anonymous?   ☐ Yes ☒ No
Pseudonymous? ☐ Yes ☒ No
If the answer to either of these questions is "Yes," see detailed instructions.

NATURE OF AUTHORSHIP Briefly describe nature of material created by this author in which copyright is claimed. ▼

NOTE

Under the law, the "author" of a "work made for hire" is generally the employer, not the employee (see instructions). For any part of this work that was "made for hire" check "Yes" in the space provided, give the employer (or other person for whom the work was prepared) as "Author" of that part, and leave the space for dates of birth and death blank.

b NAME OF AUTHOR ▼

DATES OF BIRTH AND DEATH
Year Born ▼   Year Died ▼

Was this contribution to the work a "work made for hire"?
☐ Yes
☐ No

AUTHOR'S NATIONALITY OR DOMICILE
Name of Country
OR { Citizen of ▶
Domiciled in ▶

WAS THIS AUTHOR'S CONTRIBUTION TO THE WORK
Anonymous?   ☐ Yes ☐ No
Pseudonymous? ☐ Yes ☐ No
If the answer to either of these questions is "Yes," see detailed instructions.

NATURE OF AUTHORSHIP Briefly describe nature of material created by this author in which copyright is claimed. ▼

c NAME OF AUTHOR ▼

DATES OF BIRTH AND DEATH
Year Born ▼   Year Died ▼

Was this contribution to the work a "work made for hire"?
☐ Yes
☐ No

AUTHOR'S NATIONALITY OR DOMICILE
Name of Country
OR { Citizen of ▶
Domiciled in ▶

WAS THIS AUTHOR'S CONTRIBUTION TO THE WORK
Anonymous?   ☐ Yes ☐ No
Pseudonymous? ☐ Yes ☐ No
If the answer to either of these questions is "Yes," see detailed instructions.

NATURE OF AUTHORSHIP Briefly describe nature of material created by this author in which copyright is claimed. ▼

3

a YEAR IN WHICH CREATION OF THIS WORK WAS COMPLETED This information must be given in all cases.
20XX ◀ Year

b DATE AND NATION OF FIRST PUBLICATION OF THIS PARTICULAR WORK Complete this information ONLY if this work has been published.
Month ▶ 11   Day ▶ 1   Year ▶ 20XX
USA ◀ Nation

4

See instructions before completing this space.

a COPYRIGHT CLAIMANT(S) Name and address must be given even if the claimant is the same as the author given in space 2. ▼

Acme Soft, Inc.
100 Broadway
Chicago, IL 12345

b TRANSFER If the claimant(s) named here in space 4 is (are) different from the author(s) named in space 2, give a brief statement of how the claimant(s) obtained ownership of the copyright. ▼

DO NOT WRITE HERE
OFFICE USE ONLY

APPLICATION RECEIVED

ONE DEPOSIT RECEIVED

TWO DEPOSITS RECEIVED

FUNDS RECEIVED

MORE ON BACK ▶ • Complete all applicable spaces (numbers 5-9) on the reverse side of this page.
• See detailed instructions.   • Sign the form at line 8.

DO NOT WRITE HERE
Page 1 of _____ pages

7   Published multimedia program; work made for hire (back)

EXAMINED BY	FORM PA
CHECKED BY	

☐ CORRESPONDENCE
Yes

FOR
COPYRIGHT
OFFICE
USE
ONLY

DO NOT WRITE ABOVE THIS LINE. IF YOU NEED MORE SPACE, USE A SEPARATE CONTINUATION SHEET.

PREVIOUS REGISTRATION Has registration for this work, or for an earlier version of this work, already been made in the Copyright Office?

☐ Yes ☒ No If your answer is "Yes," why is another registration being sought? (Check appropriate box) ▼

a. ☐ This is the first published edition of a work previously registered in unpublished form.

b. ☐ This is the first application submitted by this author as copyright claimant.

c. ☐ This is a changed version of the work, as shown by space 6 on this application.

If your answer is "Yes," give: **Previous Registration Number** ▼   **Year of Registration** ▼

5

DERIVATIVE WORK OR COMPILATION Complete both space 6a and 6b for a derivative work; complete only 6b for a compilation.

a. Preexisting Material Identify any preexisting work or works that this work is based on or incorporates. ▼

Previously published text, photos, artwork, video footage and music.

b. Material Added to This Work Give a brief, general statement of the material that has been added to this work and in which copyright is claimed. ▼

Compilaton and editing of preexisting text, photos, video clips and music plus new original text

6

See instructions
before completing
this space.

DEPOSIT ACCOUNT If the registration fee is to be charged to a Deposit Account established in the Copyright Office, give name and number of Account.

Name ▼   **Account Number** ▼

a

7

CORRESPONDENCE Give name and address to which correspondence about this application should be sent.   Name/Address/Apt/City/State/ZIP ▼

Acme Soft, Inc.
100 Broadway
Chicago, IL 12345

b

Area Code and Daytime Telephone Number ▶ 123-456-7890   Fax Number ▶

CERTIFICATION* I, the undersigned, hereby certify that I am the

Check only one ▼

☐ author

☐ other copyright claimant

☐ owner of exclusive right(s)

☒ authorized agent of Acme Soft, Inc.
Name of author or other copyright claimant, or owner of exclusive right(s) ▲

8

of the work identified in this application and that the statements made
by me in this application are correct to the best of my knowledge.

Typed or printed name and date ▼ If this application gives a date of publication in space 3, do not sign and submit it before that date.

Sue Smitters   Date ▶ 12/10/XX

👉 Handwritten signature (X) ▼

| Mail certificate to: | Name ▼ |
| Acme Soft, Inc. |
| **Certificate will be mailed in window envelope** | Number/Street/Apt ▼ |
| 100 Broadway |
| City/State/ZIP ▼ |
| Chicago, IL 12345 |

YOU MUST:
• Complete all necessary spaces
• Sign your application in space 8

SEND ALL 3 ELEMENTS IN THE SAME PACKAGE:
1. Application form
2. Nonrefundable $20 filing fee in check or money order payable to *Register of Copyrights*
3. Deposit material

MAIL TO:
Register of Copyrights
Library of Congress
Washington, D.C. 20559-6000

9

8   Computer database; group registration for patent database updated weekly

FORM TX

For a Literary Work
UNITED STATES COPYRIGHT OFFICE

REGISTRATION NUMBER

TX _____ TXU

EFFECTIVE DATE OF REGISTRATION

Month _____ Day _____ Year _____

DO NOT WRITE ABOVE THIS LINE. IF YOU NEED MORE SPACE, USE A SEPARATE CONTINUATION SHEET.

1

TITLE OF THIS WORK ▼

Group registration for automated database titled U.S. Patent
Database; published updates from 2/1/95 thru 5/1/95

PREVIOUS OR ALTERNATIVE TITLES ▼

PUBLICATION AS A CONTRIBUTION If this work was published as a contribution to a periodical, serial, or collection, give information about the collective work in which the contribution appeared.   **Title of Collective Work ▼**

2/1/95 updated weekly

If published in a periodical or serial give: **Volume ▼**   **Number ▼**   **Issue Date ▼**   **On Pages ▼**

2

a
NAME OF AUTHOR ▼

Patent Soft, Inc.

DATES OF BIRTH AND DEATH
Year Born ▼   Year Died ▼

Was this contribution to the work a "work made for hire"?
☒ Yes
☐ No

AUTHOR'S NATIONALITY OR DOMICILE
Name of Country
OR { Citizen of ▶ USA
Domiciled in ▶ USA

WAS THIS AUTHOR'S CONTRIBUTION TO THE WORK
Anonymous?   ☐ Yes ☒ No
Pseudonymous?   ☐ Yes ☒ No

If the answer to either of these questions is "Yes," see detailed instructions.

NATURE OF AUTHORSHIP Briefly describe nature of material created by this author in which copyright is claimed. ▼

NOTE

Under the law, the "author" of a "work made for hire" is generally the employer, not the employee (see instructions). For any part of this work that was "made for hire" check "Yes" in the space provided, give the employer (or other person for whom the work was prepared) as "Author" of that part, and leave the space for dates of birth and death blank.

b
NAME OF AUTHOR ▼

DATES OF BIRTH AND DEATH
Year Born ▼   Year Died ▼

Was this contribution to the work a "work made for hire"?
☐ Yes
☐ No

AUTHOR'S NATIONALITY OR DOMICILE
Name of Country
OR { Citizen of ▶
Domiciled in ▶

WAS THIS AUTHOR'S CONTRIBUTION TO THE WORK
Anonymous?   ☐ Yes ☐ No
Pseudonymous?   ☐ Yes ☐ No

If the answer to either of these questions is "Yes," see detailed instructions.

NATURE OF AUTHORSHIP Briefly describe nature of material created by this author in which copyright is claimed. ▼

c
NAME OF AUTHOR ▼

DATES OF BIRTH AND DEATH
Year Born ▼   Year Died ▼

Was this contribution to the work a "work made for hire"?
☐ Yes
☐ No

AUTHOR'S NATIONALITY OR DOMICILE
Name of Country
OR { Citizen of ▶
Domiciled in ▶

WAS THIS AUTHOR'S CONTRIBUTION TO THE WORK
Anonymous?   ☐ Yes ☐ No
Pseudonymous?   ☐ Yes ☐ No

If the answer to either of these questions is "Yes," see detailed instructions.

NATURE OF AUTHORSHIP Briefly describe nature of material created by this author in which copyright is claimed. ▼

3

a
YEAR IN WHICH CREATION OF THIS WORK WAS COMPLETED This information must be given ◀ Year in all cases.
20XX

b
DATE AND NATION OF FIRST PUBLICATION OF THIS PARTICULAR WORK Complete this information ONLY if this work has been published.
Month ▶ 5   Day ▶ 1   Year ▶ 20XX
USA   ◀ Nation

4

COPYRIGHT CLAIMANT(S) Name and address must be given even if the claimant is the same as the author given in space 2. ▼

Patent Soft, Inc.
950 2nd St.
Washington, D.C. 10100

See instructions before completing this space.

TRANSFER If the claimant(s) named here in space 4 is (are) different from the author(s) named in space 2, give a brief statement of how the claimant(s) obtained ownership of the copyright. ▼

APPLICATION RECEIVED

ONE DEPOSIT RECEIVED

TWO DEPOSITS RECEIVED

FUNDS RECEIVED

DO NOT WRITE HERE
OFFICE USE ONLY

MORE ON BACK ▶   • Complete all applicable spaces (numbers 5-11) on the reverse side of this page.
• See detailed instructions.   • Sign the form at line 10.

DO NOT WRITE HERE
Page 1 of _____ pages

8 Computer database; group registration for patent database updated weekly (back)

DO NOT WRITE ABOVE THIS LINE. IF YOU NEED MORE SPACE, USE A SEPARATE CONTINUATION SHEET.

PREVIOUS REGISTRATION Has registration for this work, or for an earlier version of this work, already been made in the Copyright Office?
☒ Yes ☐ No If your answer is "Yes," why is another registration being sought? (Check appropriate box) ▼
a.☐ This is the first published edition of a work previously registered in unpublished form.
b.☐ This is the first application submitted by this author as copyright claimant.
c.☒ This is a changed version of the work, as shown by space 6 on this application.
If your answer is "Yes," give: **Previous Registration Number** ▼   **Year of Registration** ▼
   TX18742   20XX

5

DERIVATIVE WORK OR COMPILATION Complete both space 6a and 6b for a derivative work; complete only 6b for a compilation.
a. **Preexisting Material** Identify any preexisting work or works that this work is based on or incorporates. ▼
   public domain data

b. **Material Added to This Work** Give a brief, general statement of the material that has been added to this work and in which copyright is claimed. ▼
   weekly updates

6

See instructions
before completing
this space.

—space deleted—

7

REPRODUCTION FOR USE OF BLIND OR PHYSICALLY HANDICAPPED INDIVIDUALS A signature on this form at space 10 and a check in one of the boxes here in space 8 constitutes a non-exclusive grant of permission to the Library of Congress to reproduce and distribute solely for the blind and physically handicapped and under the conditions and limitations prescribed by the regulations of the Copyright Office: (1) copies of the work identified in space 1 of this application in Braille (or similar tactile symbols); or (2) phonorecords embodying a fixation of a reading of that work; or (3) both.

a☒ Copies and Phonorecords   b☐ Copies Only   c☐ Phonorecords Only

8

See instructions.

DEPOSIT ACCOUNT If the registration fee is to be charged to a Deposit Account established in the Copyright Office, give name and number of Account.
Name ▼   **Account Number** ▼

9

CORRESPONDENCE Give name and address to which correspondence about this application should be sent.   Name/Address/Apt/City/State/ZIP ▼

Patent Soft, Inc.
950 2nd St.
Washington, D.C. 10100
                              Area Code and Telephone Number ▶ 212-555-1115

Be sure to
give your
daytime phone
◀ number

CERTIFICATION* I, the undersigned, hereby certify that I am the
                                          ☐ author
                Check only one ▶ {   ☐ other copyright claimant
                                          ☐ owner of exclusive right(s)
of the work identified in this application and that the statements made   ☒ authorized agent of Patent Soft, Inc.
by me in this application are correct to the best of my knowledge.   Name of author or other copyright claimant, or owner of exclusive right(s) ▲

10

Typed or printed name and date ▼ If this application gives a date of publication in space 3, do not sign and submit it before that date.
David Edison   Date ▶ 5/1/XX

☞   Handwritten signature (X) ▼

**MAIL
CERTIFI-
CATE TO**

Name ▼
   Patent Soft, Inc.
Number/Street/Apt ▼
   950 2nd St.
City/State/ZIP ▼
   Washington, D.C. 10100

**Certificate
will be
mailed in
window
envelope**

11

*17 U.S.C. § 506(e): Any person who knowingly makes a false representation of a material fact in the application for copyright registration provided for by section 409, or in any written statement filed in connection with the application, shall be fined not more than $2,500.

May 1995—300,000   ☆U.S. COPYRIGHT OFFICE WWW FORM: 1995

Blank Forms

- Form TX (3 copies)

- Form PA (2 copies)

- Form VA

- Request for Special Handling

- Form _____ /CON (Continuation Sheet for Application Forms)

- Form CA

- Search Request Form

- Document Cover Sheet

FORM TX
For a Literary Work
UNITED STATES COPYRIGHT OFFICE

REGISTRATION NUMBER

TX	TXU

EFFECTIVE DATE OF REGISTRATION

Month	Day	Year

DO NOT WRITE ABOVE THIS LINE. IF YOU NEED MORE SPACE, USE A SEPARATE CONTINUATION SHEET.

1

TITLE OF THIS WORK ▼

PREVIOUS OR ALTERNATIVE TITLES ▼

PUBLICATION AS A CONTRIBUTION If this work was published as a contribution to a periodical, serial, or collection, give information about the collective work in which the contribution appeared.   **Title of Collective Work ▼**

If published in a periodical or serial give: **Volume ▼**   **Number ▼**   **Issue Date ▼**   **On Pages ▼**

2

a

NAME OF AUTHOR ▼

DATES OF BIRTH AND DEATH
Year Born ▼   Year Died ▼

Was this contribution to the work a "work made for hire"?
☐ Yes
☐ No

AUTHOR'S NATIONALITY OR DOMICILE
Name of Country
OR { Citizen of ▶ _____
Domiciled in ▶ _____

WAS THIS AUTHOR'S CONTRIBUTION TO THE WORK
Anonymous?   ☐ Yes ☐ No
Pseudonymous?   ☐ Yes ☐ No
If the answer to either of these questions is "Yes," see detailed instructions.

NATURE OF AUTHORSHIP Briefly describe nature of material created by this author in which copyright is claimed. ▼

NOTE

Under the law, the "author" of a "work made for hire" is generally the employer, not the employee (see instructions). For any part of this work that was "made for hire" check "Yes" in the space provided, give the employer (or other person for whom the work was prepared) as "Author" of that part, and leave the space for dates of birth and death blank.

b

NAME OF AUTHOR ▼

DATES OF BIRTH AND DEATH
Year Born ▼   Year Died ▼

Was this contribution to the work a "work made for hire"?
☐ Yes
☐ No

AUTHOR'S NATIONALITY OR DOMICILE
Name of Country
OR { Citizen of ▶ _____
Domiciled in ▶ _____

WAS THIS AUTHOR'S CONTRIBUTION TO THE WORK
Anonymous?   ☐ Yes ☐ No
Pseudonymous?   ☐ Yes ☐ No
If the answer to either of these questions is "Yes," see detailed instructions.

NATURE OF AUTHORSHIP Briefly describe nature of material created by this author in which copyright is claimed. ▼

c

NAME OF AUTHOR ▼

DATES OF BIRTH AND DEATH
Year Born ▼   Year Died ▼

Was this contribution to the work a "work made for hire"?
☐ Yes
☐ No

AUTHOR'S NATIONALITY OR DOMICILE
Name of Country
OR { Citizen of ▶ _____
Domiciled in ▶ _____

WAS THIS AUTHOR'S CONTRIBUTION TO THE WORK
Anonymous?   ☐ Yes ☐ No
Pseudonymous?   ☐ Yes ☐ No
If the answer to either of these questions is "Yes," see detailed instructions.

NATURE OF AUTHORSHIP Briefly describe nature of material created by this author in which copyright is claimed. ▼

3

a
YEAR IN WHICH CREATION OF THIS WORK WAS COMPLETED   This information must be given ◀ Year in all cases.

b
DATE AND NATION OF FIRST PUBLICATION OF THIS PARTICULAR WORK   Complete this information ONLY if this work has been published.   Month ▶ _____ Day ▶ _____ Year ▶ _____ ◀ Nation

4

See instructions before completing this space.

COPYRIGHT CLAIMANT(S) Name and address must be given even if the claimant is the same as the author given in space 2. ▼

TRANSFER If the claimant(s) named here in space 4 is (are) different from the author(s) named in space 2, give a brief statement of how the claimant(s) obtained ownership of the copyright. ▼

DO NOT WRITE HERE — OFFICE USE ONLY

APPLICATION RECEIVED

ONE DEPOSIT RECEIVED

TWO DEPOSITS RECEIVED

FUNDS RECEIVED

MORE ON BACK ▶   • Complete all applicable spaces (numbers 5-11) on the reverse side of this page.
• See detailed instructions.   • Sign the form at line 10.

DO NOT WRITE HERE

Page 1 of _____ pages

DO NOT WRITE ABOVE THIS LINE. IF YOU NEED MORE SPACE, USE A SEPARATE CONTINUATION SHEET.

PREVIOUS REGISTRATION Has registration for this work, or for an earlier version of this work, already been made in the Copyright Office?

☐ **Yes**   ☐ **No**   If your answer is "Yes," why is another registration being sought? (Check appropriate box) ▼

a. ☐ This is the first published edition of a work previously registered in unpublished form.

b. ☐ This is the first application submitted by this author as copyright claimant.

c. ☐ This is a changed version of the work, as shown by space 6 on this application.

If your answer is "Yes," give: **Previous Registration Number** ▼   **Year of Registration** ▼

5

DERIVATIVE WORK OR COMPILATION   Complete both space 6a and 6b for a derivative work; complete only 6b for a compilation.

a. Preexisting Material   Identify any preexisting work or works that this work is based on or incorporates. ▼

b. Material Added to This Work   Give a brief, general statement of the material that has been added to this work and in which copyright is claimed. ▼

6

See instructions
before completing
this space.

7

—space deleted—

REPRODUCTION FOR USE OF BLIND OR PHYSICALLY HANDICAPPED INDIVIDUALS   A signature on this form at space 10 and a check in one of the boxes here in space 8 constitutes a non-exclusive grant of permission to the Library of Congress to reproduce and distribute solely for the blind and physically handicapped and under the conditions and limitations prescribed by the regulations of the Copyright Office: (1) copies of the work identified in space 1 of this application in Braille (or similar tactile symbols); or (2) phonorecords embodying a fixation of a reading of that work; or (3) both.

a ☐ Copies and Phonorecords   **b** ☐ Copies Only   **c** ☐ Phonorecords Only

8

See instructions.

DEPOSIT ACCOUNT   If the registration fee is to be charged to a Deposit Account established in the Copyright Office, give name and number of Account.

Name ▼   **Account Number** ▼

9

CORRESPONDENCE   Give name and address to which correspondence about this application should be sent.   Name/Address/Apt/City/State/ZIP ▼

Area Code and Telephone Number ▶

Be sure to
give your
daytime phone
◀ number

CERTIFICATION*   I, the undersigned, hereby certify that I am the

Check only one ▶ {
☐ author
☐ other copyright claimant
☐ owner of exclusive right(s)
☐ authorized agent of _____

of the work identified in this application and that the statements made
by me in this application are correct to the best of my knowledge.

Name of author or other copyright claimant, or owner of exclusive right(s) ▲

10

Typed or printed name and date ▼ If this application gives a date of publication in space 3, do not sign and submit it before that date.

_____   Date ▶ _____

Handwritten signature (X) ▼

MAIL CERTIFI-CATE TO

Name ▼

Number/Street/Apt ▼

Certificate will be mailed in window envelope

City/State/ZIP ▼

11

*17 U.S.C. § 506(e): Any person who knowingly makes a false representation of a material fact in the application for copyright registration provided for by section 409, or in any written statement filed in connection with the application, shall be fined not more than $2,500.

May 1995—300,000

☆U.S. COPYRIGHT OFFICE WWW FORM: 1995

FORM TX
For a Literary Work
UNITED STATES COPYRIGHT OFFICE

REGISTRATION NUMBER

_____

TX   TXU
EFFECTIVE DATE OF REGISTRATION

_____

Month _____ Day _____ Year _____

DO NOT WRITE ABOVE THIS LINE. IF YOU NEED MORE SPACE, USE A SEPARATE CONTINUATION SHEET.

1

TITLE OF THIS WORK ▼

PREVIOUS OR ALTERNATIVE TITLES ▼

PUBLICATION AS A CONTRIBUTION If this work was published as a contribution to a periodical, serial, or collection, give information about the collective work in which the contribution appeared.   **Title of Collective Work ▼**

If published in a periodical or serial give: **Volume ▼**   **Number ▼**   **Issue Date ▼**   **On Pages ▼**

2

a

NAME OF AUTHOR ▼

DATES OF BIRTH AND DEATH
Year Born ▼   Year Died ▼

Was this contribution to the work a "work made for hire"?
☐ Yes
☐ No

AUTHOR'S NATIONALITY OR DOMICILE
Name of Country
OR { Citizen of ▶ _____
     Domiciled in ▶ _____

WAS THIS AUTHOR'S CONTRIBUTION TO THE WORK
Anonymous?   ☐ Yes ☐ No
Pseudonymous? ☐ Yes ☐ No
If the answer to either of these questions is "Yes," see detailed instructions.

NATURE OF AUTHORSHIP Briefly describe nature of material created by this author in which copyright is claimed. ▼

NOTE

Under the law, the "author" of a "work made for hire" is generally the employer, not the employee (see instructions). For any part of this work that was "made for hire" check "Yes" in the space provided, give the employer (or other person for whom the work was prepared) as "Author" of that part, and leave the space for dates of birth and death blank.

b

NAME OF AUTHOR ▼

DATES OF BIRTH AND DEATH
Year Born ▼   Year Died ▼

Was this contribution to the work a "work made for hire"?
☐ Yes
☐ No

AUTHOR'S NATIONALITY OR DOMICILE
Name of Country
OR { Citizen of ▶ _____
     Domiciled in ▶ _____

WAS THIS AUTHOR'S CONTRIBUTION TO THE WORK
Anonymous?   ☐ Yes ☐ No
Pseudonymous? ☐ Yes ☐ No
If the answer to either of these questions is "Yes," see detailed instructions.

NATURE OF AUTHORSHIP Briefly describe nature of material created by this author in which copyright is claimed. ▼

c

NAME OF AUTHOR ▼

DATES OF BIRTH AND DEATH
Year Born ▼   Year Died ▼

Was this contribution to the work a "work made for hire"?
☐ Yes
☐ No

AUTHOR'S NATIONALITY OR DOMICILE
Name of Country
OR { Citizen of ▶ _____
     Domiciled in ▶ _____

WAS THIS AUTHOR'S CONTRIBUTION TO THE WORK
Anonymous?   ☐ Yes ☐ No
Pseudonymous? ☐ Yes ☐ No
If the answer to either of these questions is "Yes," see detailed instructions.

NATURE OF AUTHORSHIP Briefly describe nature of material created by this author in which copyright is claimed. ▼

3

a
YEAR IN WHICH CREATION OF THIS WORK WAS COMPLETED   This information must be given ◄Year in all cases.

b
DATE AND NATION OF FIRST PUBLICATION OF THIS PARTICULAR WORK
Complete this information ONLY if this work has been published.
Month ▶ _____ Day ▶ _____ Year ▶ _____
_____ ◄ Nation

4

See instructions before completing this space.

COPYRIGHT CLAIMANT(S) Name and address must be given even if the claimant is the same as the author given in space 2. ▼

TRANSFER If the claimant(s) named here in space 4 is (are) different from the author(s) named in space 2, give a brief statement of how the claimant(s) obtained ownership of the copyright. ▼

**DO NOT WRITE HERE
OFFICE USE ONLY**

APPLICATION RECEIVED

ONE DEPOSIT RECEIVED

TWO DEPOSITS RECEIVED

FUNDS RECEIVED

MORE ON BACK ▶ • Complete all applicable spaces (numbers 5-11) on the reverse side of this page.
• See detailed instructions.   • Sign the form at line 10.

DO NOT WRITE HERE
Page 1 of _____ pages

EXAMINED BY

CHECKED BY

☐ CORRESPONDENCE
  Yes

FORM TX

FOR
COPYRIGHT
OFFICE
USE
ONLY

DO NOT WRITE ABOVE THIS LINE. IF YOU NEED MORE SPACE, USE A SEPARATE CONTINUATION SHEET.

PREVIOUS REGISTRATION Has registration for this work, or for an earlier version of this work, already been made in the Copyright Office?

☐ Yes ☐ No If your answer is "Yes," why is another registration being sought? (Check appropriate box) ▼

a. ☐ This is the first published edition of a work previously registered in unpublished form.

b. ☐ This is the first application submitted by this author as copyright claimant.

c. ☐ This is a changed version of the work, as shown by space 6 on this application.

If your answer is "Yes," give: **Previous Registration Number** ▼   **Year of Registration** ▼

5

DERIVATIVE WORK OR COMPILATION Complete both space 6a and 6b for a derivative work; complete only 6b for a compilation.

a. Preexisting Material Identify any preexisting work or works that this work is based on or incorporates. ▼

b. Material Added to This Work Give a brief, general statement of the material that has been added to this work and in which copyright is claimed. ▼

6

See instructions
before completing
this space.

—space deleted—

7

REPRODUCTION FOR USE OF BLIND OR PHYSICALLY HANDICAPPED INDIVIDUALS A signature on this form at space 10 and a check in one of the boxes here in space 8 constitutes a non-exclusive grant of permission to the Library of Congress to reproduce and distribute solely for the blind and physically handicapped and under the conditions and limitations prescribed by the regulations of the Copyright Office: (1) copies of the work identified in space 1 of this application in Braille (or similar tactile symbols); or (2) phonorecords embodying a fixation of a reading of that work; or (3) both.

a ☐ Copies and Phonorecords   **b** ☐ Copies Only   **c** ☐ Phonorecords Only

8

See instructions.

DEPOSIT ACCOUNT If the registration fee is to be charged to a Deposit Account established in the Copyright Office, give name and number of Account.

Name ▼   **Account Number** ▼

9

CORRESPONDENCE Give name and address to which correspondence about this application should be sent.   Name/Address/Apt/City/State/ZIP ▼

Area Code and Telephone Number ▶

Be sure to
give your
daytime phone
◀ number

CERTIFICATION* I, the undersigned, hereby certify that I am the

Check only one ▶

☐ author
☐ other copyright claimant
☐ owner of exclusive right(s)
☐ authorized agent of _____

of the work identified in this application and that the statements made by me in this application are correct to the best of my knowledge.

Name of author or other copyright claimant, or owner of exclusive right(s) ▲

10

Typed or printed name and date ▼ If this application gives a date of publication in space 3, do not sign and submit it before that date.

_____ Date ▶ _____

☞ Handwritten signature (X) ▼

MAIL CERTIFI-CATE TO

Name ▼

Number/Street/Apt ▼

City/State/ZIP ▼

Certificate will be mailed in window envelope

YOU MUST:
• Complete all necessary spaces
• Sign your application in space 10

SEND ALL 3 ELEMENTS IN THE SAME PACKAGE:
1. Application form
2. Nonrefundable $20 filing fee in check or money order payable to *Register of Copyrights*
3. Deposit material

MAIL TO:
Register of Copyrights
Library of Congress
Washington, D.C. 20559-6000

11

*17 U.S.C. § 506(e): Any person who knowingly makes a false representation of a material fact in the application for copyright registration provided for by section 409, or in any written statement filed in connection with the application, shall be fined not more than $2,500.

May 1995—300,000

☆U.S. COPYRIGHT OFFICE WWW FORM: 1995

FORM TX

For a Literary Work
UNITED STATES COPYRIGHT OFFICE

REGISTRATION NUMBER

_____

TX _____ TXU _____

EFFECTIVE DATE OF REGISTRATION

_____

Month _____ Day _____ Year _____

DO NOT WRITE ABOVE THIS LINE. IF YOU NEED MORE SPACE, USE A SEPARATE CONTINUATION SHEET.

1

TITLE OF THIS WORK ▼

PREVIOUS OR ALTERNATIVE TITLES ▼

PUBLICATION AS A CONTRIBUTION If this work was published as a contribution to a periodical, serial, or collection, give information about the collective work in which the contribution appeared. **Title of Collective Work ▼**

If published in a periodical or serial give: **Volume ▼**   **Number ▼**   **Issue Date ▼**   **On Pages ▼**

2

a

NAME OF AUTHOR ▼

DATES OF BIRTH AND DEATH
Year Born ▼   Year Died ▼

Was this contribution to the work a "work made for hire"?
☐ Yes
☐ No

AUTHOR'S NATIONALITY OR DOMICILE
Name of Country
OR { Citizen of ▶ _____
      Domiciled in ▶ _____

WAS THIS AUTHOR'S CONTRIBUTION TO THE WORK
Anonymous? ☐ Yes ☐ No
Pseudonymous? ☐ Yes ☐ No

If the answer to either of these questions is "Yes," see detailed instructions.

NATURE OF AUTHORSHIP Briefly describe nature of material created by this author in which copyright is claimed. ▼

b

NAME OF AUTHOR ▼

DATES OF BIRTH AND DEATH
Year Born ▼   Year Died ▼

Was this contribution to the work a "work made for hire"?
☐ Yes
☐ No

AUTHOR'S NATIONALITY OR DOMICILE
Name of Country
OR { Citizen of ▶ _____
      Domiciled in ▶ _____

WAS THIS AUTHOR'S CONTRIBUTION TO THE WORK
Anonymous? ☐ Yes ☐ No
Pseudonymous? ☐ Yes ☐ No

If the answer to either of these questions is "Yes," see detailed instructions.

NATURE OF AUTHORSHIP Briefly describe nature of material created by this author in which copyright is claimed. ▼

c

NAME OF AUTHOR ▼

DATES OF BIRTH AND DEATH
Year Born ▼   Year Died ▼

Was this contribution to the work a "work made for hire"?
☐ Yes
☐ No

AUTHOR'S NATIONALITY OR DOMICILE
Name of Country
OR { Citizen of ▶ _____
      Domiciled in ▶ _____

WAS THIS AUTHOR'S CONTRIBUTION TO THE WORK
Anonymous? ☐ Yes ☐ No
Pseudonymous? ☐ Yes ☐ No

If the answer to either of these questions is "Yes," see detailed instructions.

NATURE OF AUTHORSHIP Briefly describe nature of material created by this author in which copyright is claimed. ▼

NOTE

Under the law, the "author" of a "work made for hire" is generally the employer, not the employee (see instructions). For any part of this work that was "made for hire" check "Yes" in the space provided, give the employer (or other person for whom the work was prepared) as "Author" of that part, and leave the space for dates of birth and death blank.

3

a
YEAR IN WHICH CREATION OF THIS WORK WAS COMPLETED This information must be given ◀ Year in all cases.

b
DATE AND NATION OF FIRST PUBLICATION OF THIS PARTICULAR WORK
Complete this information ONLY if this work has been published.
Month ▶ _____ Day ▶ _____ Year ▶ _____
◀ Nation

4

See instructions before completing this space.

COPYRIGHT CLAIMANT(S) Name and address must be given even if the claimant is the same as the author given in space 2. ▼

TRANSFER If the claimant(s) named here in space 4 is (are) different from the author(s) named in space 2, give a brief statement of how the claimant(s) obtained ownership of the copyright. ▼

DO NOT WRITE HERE — OFFICE USE ONLY

APPLICATION RECEIVED

ONE DEPOSIT RECEIVED

TWO DEPOSITS RECEIVED

FUNDS RECEIVED

MORE ON BACK ▶ • Complete all applicable spaces (numbers 5-11) on the reverse side of this page.
• See detailed instructions.   • Sign the form at line 10.

DO NOT WRITE HERE
Page 1 of _____ pages

DO NOT WRITE ABOVE THIS LINE. IF YOU NEED MORE SPACE, USE A SEPARATE CONTINUATION SHEET.

PREVIOUS REGISTRATION Has registration for this work, or for an earlier version of this work, already been made in the Copyright Office?

☐ Yes ☐ No   If your answer is "Yes," why is another registration being sought? (Check appropriate box) ▼

a. ☐ This is the first published edition of a work previously registered in unpublished form.

b. ☐ This is the first application submitted by this author as copyright claimant.

c. ☐ This is a changed version of the work, as shown by space 6 on this application.

If your answer is "Yes," give: **Previous Registration Number** ▼ _____   **Year of Registration** ▼ _____

5

DERIVATIVE WORK OR COMPILATION   Complete both space 6a and 6b for a derivative work; complete only 6b for a compilation.

a. Preexisting Material   Identify any preexisting work or works that this work is based on or incorporates. ▼

b. Material Added to This Work   Give a brief, general statement of the material that has been added to this work and in which copyright is claimed. ▼

6

See instructions before completing this space.

—space deleted—

7

REPRODUCTION FOR USE OF BLIND OR PHYSICALLY HANDICAPPED INDIVIDUALS   A signature on this form at space 10 and a check in one of the boxes here in space 8 constitutes a non-exclusive grant of permission to the Library of Congress to reproduce and distribute solely for the blind and physically handicapped and under the conditions and limitations prescribed by the regulations of the Copyright Office: (1) copies of the work identified in space 1 of this application in Braille (or similar tactile symbols); or (2) phonorecords embodying a fixation of a reading of that work; or (3) both.

a ☐ Copies and Phonorecords   b ☐ Copies Only   c ☐ Phonorecords Only

8

See instructions.

DEPOSIT ACCOUNT   If the registration fee is to be charged to a Deposit Account established in the Copyright Office, give name and number of Account.

Name ▼   **Account Number** ▼

9

CORRESPONDENCE   Give name and address to which correspondence about this application should be sent.   Name/Address/Apt/City/State/ZIP ▼

Area Code and Telephone Number ▶

Be sure to give your daytime phone number ◀

CERTIFICATION*   I, the undersigned, hereby certify that I am the

Check only one ▶ {
☐ author
☐ other copyright claimant
☐ owner of exclusive right(s)
☐ authorized agent of _____
}

of the work identified in this application and that the statements made by me in this application are correct to the best of my knowledge.

Name of author or other copyright claimant, or owner of exclusive right(s) ▲

Typed or printed name and date ▼ If this application gives a date of publication in space 3, do not sign and submit it before that date.

_____   Date ▶ _____

☞ Handwritten signature (X) ▼

10

MAIL CERTIFI-CATE TO

Name ▼

Number/Street/Apt ▼

Certificate will be mailed in window envelope

City/State/ZIP ▼

YOU MUST:
• Complete all necessary spaces
• Sign your application in space 10

SEND ALL 3 ELEMENTS IN THE SAME PACKAGE:
1. Application form
2. Nonrefundable $20 filing fee in check or money order payable to *Register of Copyrights*
3. Deposit material

MAIL TO:
Register of Copyrights
Library of Congress
Washington, D.C. 20559-6000

11

FORM PA

For a Work of the Performing Arts
UNITED STATES COPYRIGHT OFFICE

REGISTRATION NUMBER

PA   PAU

EFFECTIVE DATE OF REGISTRATION

_____ Month   Day   Year

DO NOT WRITE ABOVE THIS LINE. IF YOU NEED MORE SPACE, USE A SEPARATE CONTINUATION SHEET.

1

TITLE OF THIS WORK ▼

PREVIOUS OR ALTERNATIVE TITLES ▼

NATURE OF THIS WORK ▼ See instructions

2

a

NAME OF AUTHOR ▼

DATES OF BIRTH AND DEATH
Year Born ▼   Year Died ▼

Was this contribution to the work a "work made for hire"?
☐ Yes
☐ No

AUTHOR'S NATIONALITY OR DOMICILE
Name of Country
OR { Citizen of ▶ _____
Domiciled in ▶ _____

WAS THIS AUTHOR'S CONTRIBUTION TO THE WORK
Anonymous? ☐ Yes ☐ No
Pseudonymous? ☐ Yes ☐ No
If the answer to either of these questions is "Yes," see detailed instructions.

NATURE OF AUTHORSHIP Briefly describe nature of material created by this author in which copyright is claimed. ▼

NOTE

Under the law, the "author" of a "work made for hire" is generally the employer, not the employee (see instructions). For any part of this work that was "made for hire" check "Yes" in the space provided, give the employer (or other person for whom the work was prepared) as "Author" of that part, and leave the space for dates of birth and death blank.

b

NAME OF AUTHOR ▼

DATES OF BIRTH AND DEATH
Year Born ▼   Year Died ▼

Was this contribution to the work a "work made for hire"?
☐ Yes
☐ No

AUTHOR'S NATIONALITY OR DOMICILE
Name of Country
OR { Citizen of ▶ _____
Domiciled in ▶ _____

WAS THIS AUTHOR'S CONTRIBUTION TO THE WORK
Anonymous? ☐ Yes ☐ No
Pseudonymous? ☐ Yes ☐ No
If the answer to either of these questions is "Yes," see detailed instructions.

NATURE OF AUTHORSHIP Briefly describe nature of material created by this author in which copyright is claimed. ▼

c

NAME OF AUTHOR ▼

DATES OF BIRTH AND DEATH
Year Born ▼   Year Died ▼

Was this contribution to the work a "work made for hire"?
☐ Yes
☐ No

AUTHOR'S NATIONALITY OR DOMICILE
Name of Country
OR { Citizen of ▶ _____
Domiciled in ▶ _____

WAS THIS AUTHOR'S CONTRIBUTION TO THE WORK
Anonymous? ☐ Yes ☐ No
Pseudonymous? ☐ Yes ☐ No
If the answer to either of these questions is "Yes," see detailed instructions.

NATURE OF AUTHORSHIP Briefly describe nature of material created by this author in which copyright is claimed. ▼

3

a **YEAR IN WHICH CREATION OF THIS WORK WAS COMPLETED** This information must be given in all cases.
_____ ◀ Year

b **DATE AND NATION OF FIRST PUBLICATION OF THIS PARTICULAR WORK** Complete this information ONLY if this work has been published.
Month ▶ _____ Day ▶ _____ Year ▶ _____ ◀ Nation

4

a **COPYRIGHT CLAIMANT(S)** Name and address must be given even if the claimant is the same as the author given in space 2. ▼

See instructions before completing this space.

b **TRANSFER** If the claimant(s) named here in space 4 is (are) different from the author(s) named in space 2, give a brief statement of how the claimant(s) obtained ownership of the copyright. ▼

DO NOT WRITE HERE OFFICE USE ONLY

APPLICATION RECEIVED

ONE DEPOSIT RECEIVED

TWO DEPOSITS RECEIVED

FUNDS RECEIVED

MORE ON BACK ▶ • Complete all applicable spaces (numbers 5-9) on the reverse side of this page.
• See detailed instructions.   • Sign the form at line 8.

DO NOT WRITE HERE
Page 1 of _____ pages

DO NOT WRITE ABOVE THIS LINE. IF YOU NEED MORE SPACE, USE A SEPARATE CONTINUATION SHEET.

PREVIOUS REGISTRATION Has registration for this work, or for an earlier version of this work, already been made in the Copyright Office?

☐ Yes ☐ No If your answer is "Yes," why is another registration being sought? (Check appropriate box) ▼

a. ☐ This is the first published edition of a work previously registered in unpublished form.

b. ☐ This is the first application submitted by this author as copyright claimant.

c. ☐ This is a changed version of the work, as shown by space 6 on this application.

If your answer is "Yes," give: **Previous Registration Number** ▼   **Year of Registration** ▼

5

DERIVATIVE WORK OR COMPILATION Complete both space 6a and 6b for a derivative work; complete only 6b for a compilation.
a. Preexisting Material Identify any preexisting work or works that this work is based on or incorporates. ▼

b. Material Added to This Work Give a brief, general statement of the material that has been added to this work and in which copyright is claimed. ▼

6

See instructions
before completing
this space.

DEPOSIT ACCOUNT If the registration fee is to be charged to a Deposit Account established in the Copyright Office, give name and number of Account.
Name ▼   **Account Number ▼**

a

7

CORRESPONDENCE Give name and address to which correspondence about this application should be sent.   Name/Address/Apt/City/State/ZIP ▼

b

Area Code and Daytime Telephone Number ▶   Fax Number ▶

CERTIFICATION* I, the undersigned, hereby certify that I am the

Check only one ▼

☐ author

☐ other copyright claimant

☐ owner of exclusive right(s)

☐ authorized agent of ―――――――――――――――――――――――――
                      Name of author or other copyright claimant, or owner of exclusive right(s) ▲

of the work identified in this application and that the statements made
by me in this application are correct to the best of my knowledge.

Typed or printed name and date ▼ If this application gives a date of publication in space 3, do not sign and submit it before that date.

                                                              Date ▶

☞   Handwritten signature (X) ▼

8

Mail
certificate
to:

Certificate
will be
mailed in
window
envelope

Name ▼

Number/Street/Apt ▼

City/State/ZIP ▼

9

*17 U.S.C. § 506(e): Any person who knowingly makes a false representation of a material fact in the application for copyright registration provided for by section 409, or in any written statement filed in connection with the application, shall be fined not more than $2,500.

September 1995—400,000   ♻ PRINTED ON RECYCLED PAPER   ☆U.S. GOVERNMENT PRINTING OFFICE: 1995-387-237/20,024

FORM PA

For a Work of the Performing Arts
UNITED STATES COPYRIGHT OFFICE

REGISTRATION NUMBER

_____
PA   PAU

EFFECTIVE DATE OF REGISTRATION

_____
Month   Day   Year

DO NOT WRITE ABOVE THIS LINE. IF YOU NEED MORE SPACE, USE A SEPARATE CONTINUATION SHEET.

1

TITLE OF THIS WORK ▼

_____

PREVIOUS OR ALTERNATIVE TITLES ▼

_____

NATURE OF THIS WORK ▼ See instructions

_____

2

a

NAME OF AUTHOR ▼
_____

DATES OF BIRTH AND DEATH
Year Born ▼   Year Died ▼

Was this contribution to the work a "work made for hire"?
☐ Yes
☐ No

AUTHOR'S NATIONALITY OR DOMICILE
Name of Country
OR { Citizen of ▶ _____
Domiciled in ▶ _____

WAS THIS AUTHOR'S CONTRIBUTION TO THE WORK
Anonymous?   ☐ Yes ☐ No
Pseudonymous? ☐ Yes ☐ No
If the answer to either of these questions is "Yes," see detailed instructions.

NATURE OF AUTHORSHIP Briefly describe nature of material created by this author in which copyright is claimed. ▼

NOTE

Under the law, the "author" of a "work made for hire" is generally the employer, not the employee (see instructions). For any part of this work that was "made for hire" check "Yes" in the space provided, give the employer (or other person for whom the work was prepared) as "Author" of that part, and leave the space for dates of birth and death blank.

b

NAME OF AUTHOR ▼
_____

DATES OF BIRTH AND DEATH
Year Born ▼   Year Died ▼

Was this contribution to the work a "work made for hire"?
☐ Yes
☐ No

AUTHOR'S NATIONALITY OR DOMICILE
Name of Country
OR { Citizen of ▶ _____
Domiciled in ▶ _____

WAS THIS AUTHOR'S CONTRIBUTION TO THE WORK
Anonymous?   ☐ Yes ☐ No
Pseudonymous? ☐ Yes ☐ No
If the answer to either of these questions is "Yes," see detailed instructions.

NATURE OF AUTHORSHIP Briefly describe nature of material created by this author in which copyright is claimed. ▼

c

NAME OF AUTHOR ▼
_____

DATES OF BIRTH AND DEATH
Year Born ▼   Year Died ▼

Was this contribution to the work a "work made for hire"?
☐ Yes
☐ No

AUTHOR'S NATIONALITY OR DOMICILE
Name of Country
OR { Citizen of ▶ _____
Domiciled in ▶ _____

WAS THIS AUTHOR'S CONTRIBUTION TO THE WORK
Anonymous?   ☐ Yes ☐ No
Pseudonymous? ☐ Yes ☐ No
If the answer to either of these questions is "Yes," see detailed instructions.

NATURE OF AUTHORSHIP Briefly describe nature of material created by this author in which copyright is claimed. ▼

3

a
YEAR IN WHICH CREATION OF THIS WORK WAS COMPLETED This information must be given in all cases.
_____ ◀ Year

b
DATE AND NATION OF FIRST PUBLICATION OF THIS PARTICULAR WORK
Complete this information ONLY if this work has been published.
Month ▶ _____ Day ▶ _____ Year ▶ _____
_____ ◀ Nation

4

a
COPYRIGHT CLAIMANT(S) Name and address must be given even if the claimant is the same as the author given in space 2. ▼

See instructions before completing this space.

b
TRANSFER If the claimant(s) named here in space 4 is (are) different from the author(s) named in space 2, give a brief statement of how the claimant(s) obtained ownership of the copyright. ▼

DO NOT WRITE HERE OFFICE USE ONLY

APPLICATION RECEIVED

ONE DEPOSIT RECEIVED

TWO DEPOSITS RECEIVED

FUNDS RECEIVED

MORE ON BACK ▶ • Complete all applicable spaces (numbers 5-9) on the reverse side of this page.
• See detailed instructions.   • Sign the form at line 8.

DO NOT WRITE HERE
Page 1 of _____ pages

DO NOT WRITE ABOVE THIS LINE. IF YOU NEED MORE SPACE, USE A SEPARATE CONTINUATION SHEET.

PREVIOUS REGISTRATION Has registration for this work, or for an earlier version of this work, already been made in the Copyright Office?

☐ Yes ☐ No If your answer is "Yes," why is another registration being sought? (Check appropriate box) ▼

a. ☐ This is the first published edition of a work previously registered in unpublished form.

b. ☐ This is the first application submitted by this author as copyright claimant.

c. ☐ This is a changed version of the work, as shown by space 6 on this application.

If your answer is "Yes," give: **Previous Registration Number** ▼ _____ **Year of Registration** ▼ _____

5

DERIVATIVE WORK OR COMPILATION Complete both space 6a and 6b for a derivative work; complete only 6b for a compilation.
a. Preexisting Material Identify any preexisting work or works that this work is based on or incorporates. ▼

_____
_____

b. Material Added to This Work Give a brief, general statement of the material that has been added to this work and in which copyright is claimed. ▼

_____
_____
_____

6

See instructions
before completing
this space.

DEPOSIT ACCOUNT If the registration fee is to be charged to a Deposit Account established in the Copyright Office, give name and number of Account.
Name ▼   **Account Number** ▼

a

_____

CORRESPONDENCE Give name and address to which correspondence about this application should be sent.   Name/Address/Apt/City/State/ZIP ▼

b

_____
_____
_____

Area Code and Daytime Telephone Number ▶ _____   Fax Number ▶ _____

7

CERTIFICATION* I, the undersigned, hereby certify that I am the

Check only one ▼

☐ author

☐ other copyright claimant

☐ owner of exclusive right(s)

☐ authorized agent of _____
                          Name of author or other copyright claimant, or owner of exclusive right(s) ▲

of the work identified in this application and that the statements made
by me in this application are correct to the best of my knowledge.

Typed or printed name and date ▼ If this application gives a date of publication in space 3, do not sign and submit it before that date.

_____   Date ▶ _____

👉 **Handwritten signature** (X) ▼

_____

8

**Mail
certificate
to:**

**Certificate
will be
mailed in
window
envelope**

Name ▼ _____

Number/Street/Apt ▼ _____

City/State/ZIP ▼ _____

YOU MUST:
• Complete all necessary spaces
• Sign your application in space 8
**SEND ALL 3 ELEMENTS
IN THE SAME PACKAGE:**
1. Application form
2. Nonrefundable $20 filing fee
   in check or money order
   payable to *Register of Copyrights*
3. Deposit material
MAIL TO:
Register of Copyrights
Library of Congress
Washington, D.C. 20559-6000

9

FORM VA
For a Work of the Visual Arts
UNITED STATES COPYRIGHT OFFICE

REGISTRATION NUMBER

VA	VAU

EFFECTIVE DATE OF REGISTRATION

Month	Day	Year

DO NOT WRITE ABOVE THIS LINE. IF YOU NEED MORE SPACE, USE A SEPARATE CONTINUATION SHEET.

1

TITLE OF THIS WORK ▼

NATURE OF THIS WORK ▼ See instructions

PREVIOUS OR ALTERNATIVE TITLES ▼

PUBLICATION AS A CONTRIBUTION If this work was published as a contribution to a periodical, serial, or collection, give information about the collective work in which the contribution appeared.   **Title of Collective Work ▼**

If published in a periodical or serial give: **Volume ▼**   **Number ▼**   **Issue Date ▼**   **On Pages ▼**

2   a

NAME OF AUTHOR ▼

DATES OF BIRTH AND DEATH
Year Born ▼   Year Died ▼

Was this contribution to the work a "work made for hire"?
☐ Yes
☐ No

AUTHOR'S NATIONALITY OR DOMICILE
Name of Country
OR { Citizen of ▶
Domiciled in▶

WAS THIS AUTHOR'S CONTRIBUTION TO THE WORK
Anonymous? ☐ Yes ☐ No
Pseudonymous? ☐ Yes ☐ No
If the answer to either of these questions is "Yes," see detailed instructions.

NATURE OF AUTHORSHIP Check appropriate box(es). **See instructions**
☐ 3-Dimensional sculpture   ☐ Map   ☐ Technical drawing
☐ 2-Dimensional artwork   ☐ Photograph   ☐ Text
☐ Reproduction of work of art ☐ Jewelry design ☐ Architectural work
☐ Design on sheetlike material

NOTE

Under the law, the "author" of a "work made for hire" is generally the employer, not the employee (see instructions). For any part of this work that was "made for hire" check "Yes" in the space provided, give the employer (or other person for whom the work was prepared) as "Author" of that part, and leave the space for dates of birth and death blank.

b

NAME OF AUTHOR ▼

DATES OF BIRTH AND DEATH
Year Born ▼   Year Died ▼

Was this contribution to the work a "work made for hire"?
☐ Yes
☐ No

AUTHOR'S NATIONALITY OR DOMICILE
Name of Country
OR { Citizen of ▶
Domiciled in▶

WAS THIS AUTHOR'S CONTRIBUTION TO THE WORK
Anonymous? ☐ Yes ☐ No
Pseudonymous? ☐ Yes ☐ No
If the answer to either of these questions is "Yes," see detailed instructions.

NATURE OF AUTHORSHIP Check appropriate box(es). **See instructions**
☐ 3-Dimensional sculpture   ☐ Map   ☐ Technical drawing
☐ 2-Dimensional artwork   ☐ Photograph   ☐ Text
☐ Reproduction of work of art ☐ Jewelry design ☐ Architectural work
☐ Design on sheetlike material

3   a   b

YEAR IN WHICH CREATION OF THIS WORK WAS COMPLETED This information must be given ◀ Year in all cases.

DATE AND NATION OF FIRST PUBLICATION OF THIS PARTICULAR WORK
Complete this information ONLY if this work has been published.
Month ▶ _____ Day ▶ _____ Year ▶ _____ ◀ Nation

4

See instructions before completing this space.

COPYRIGHT CLAIMANT(S) Name and address must be given even if the claimant is the same as the author given in space 2. ▼

TRANSFER If the claimant(s) named here in space 4 is (are) different from the author(s) named in space 2, give a brief statement of how the claimant(s) obtained ownership of the copyright. ▼

DO NOT WRITE HERE
OFFICE USE ONLY

APPLICATION RECEIVED

ONE DEPOSIT RECEIVED

TWO DEPOSITS RECEIVED

FUNDS RECEIVED

MORE ON BACK ▶ • Complete all applicable spaces (numbers 5-9) on the reverse side of this page.
• See detailed instructions.   • Sign the form at line 8.

DO NOT WRITE HERE
Page 1 of _____ pages

DO NOT WRITE ABOVE THIS LINE. IF YOU NEED MORE SPACE, USE A SEPARATE CONTINUATION SHEET.

PREVIOUS REGISTRATION Has registration for this work, or for an earlier version of this work, already been made in the Copyright Office?

☐ **Yes** ☐ **No** If your answer is "Yes," why is another registration being sought? (Check appropriate box) ▼

a. ☐ This is the first published edition of a work previously registered in unpublished form.

b. ☐ This is the first application submitted by this author as copyright claimant.

c. ☐ This is a changed version of the work, as shown by space 6 on this application.

If your answer is "Yes," give: **Previous Registration Number** ▼　　　　**Year of Registration** ▼

5

DERIVATIVE WORK OR COMPILATION Complete both space 6a and 6b for a derivative work; complete only 6b for a compilation.

a. Preexisting Material Identify any preexisting work or works that this work is based on or incorporates. ▼

b. Material Added to This Work Give a brief, general statement of the material that has been added to this work and in which copyright is claimed. ▼

6

See instructions
before completing
this space.

DEPOSIT ACCOUNT If the registration fee is to be charged to a Deposit Account established in the Copyright Office, give name and number of Account.

Name ▼　　　　　　　　　　　　　　　**Account Number** ▼

7

CORRESPONDENCE Give name and address to which correspondence about this application should be sent.　Name/Address/Apt/City/State/ZIP ▼

Area Code and Telephone Number ▶

Be sure to
give your
daytime phone
◀ number

CERTIFICATION* I, the undersigned, hereby certify that I am the

check only one ▼

☐ author

☐ other copyright claimant

☐ owner of exclusive right(s)

☐ authorized agent of _____
　　　　Name of author or other copyright claimant, or owner of exclusive right(s) ▲

of the work identified in this application and that the statements made
by me in this application are correct to the best of my knowledge.

8

Typed or printed name and date ▼ If this application gives a date of publication in space 3, do not sign and submit it before that date.

_____　Date▶ _____

☞　**Handwritten signature (X)** ▼

request for
special handling

1

SPECIAL HANDLING IS NOT FOR CONVENIENCE ONLY !

NOTE: The special handling of a registration application or other fee service severely disrupts the entire registration process and workflow of the Copyright Office. It is granted only in the most urgent of cases. A request for special handling is subject to the approval of the Chief of the Receiving and Processing Division, who takes into account the workload situation of the office at the time the request is made. A minimum period of five working days is required to process a registration application under special handling procedures.

Why is there an urgent need for special handling?

☐ Litigation   ☐ Contractual/Publishing Deadlines

☐ Customs Matter   ☐ Other, Specify

2

If you must have the requested action to go forward with the litigation, please answer the following questions.

a. Is the litigation actual or prospective?

Unless <u>all</u> blanks are completed your request <u>cannot</u> be processed.

b. Are you (or your client) the plaintiff or defendant in the action? Please specify.

c. What are the names of the parties and what is the name of the court where the action is pending or expected?

I certify that the statements made above are correct to the best of my knowledge.

(Signature)

(Address)

(Phone)   (Date)

FOR COPYRIGHT
OFFICE USE ONLY

Information Specialist handling matter

remarks

C-2 August 1987 - 1,000

CONTINUATION SHEET
FOR APPLICATION FORMS

- This Continuation Sheet is used in conjunction with Forms CA, PA, SE, SR, TX, and VA **only**. Indicate which basic form you are continuing in the space in the upper right-hand corner.

- If at all possible, try to fit the information called for into the spaces provided on the basic form.

- If you do not have space enough for all the information you need to give on the basic form, use this Continuation Sheet and submit it with the basic form.

- If you submit this Continuation Sheet, clip (do not tape or staple) it to the basic form and fold the two together before submitting them.

- **Part A of this sheet is intended to identify the basic application.**
  Part B is a continuation of Space 2 on the basic application.
  Part C (on the reverse side of this sheet) is for the continuation of Spaces 1, 4, or 6 on the basic application.

DO NOT WRITE ABOVE THIS LINE. FOR COPYRIGHT OFFICE USE ONLY

⊘ FORM _____ /CON

UNITED STATES COPYRIGHT OFFICE

REGISTRATION NUMBER

PA PAU SE SEG SEU SR SRU TX TXU VA VAU

EFFECTIVE DATE OF REGISTRATION

_____
(Month)   (Day)   (Year)

CONTINUATION SHEET RECEIVED

Page _____ of _____ pages

A
Identification of Application

IDENTIFICATION OF CONTINUATION SHEET: This sheet is a continuation of the application for copyright registration on the basic form submitted for the following work:
- TITLE: (Give the title as given under the heading "Title of this Work" in Space 1 of the basic form.)

- NAME(S) AND ADDRESS(ES) OF COPYRIGHT CLAIMANT(S) : (Give the name and address of at least one copyright claimant as given in Space 4 of the basic form.)

B
Continuation of Space 2

d

NAME OF AUTHOR ▼

DATES OF BIRTH AND DEATH
Year Born▼   Year Died▼

Was this contribution to the work a "work made for hire"?
☐ Yes
☐ No

AUTHOR'S NATIONALITY OR DOMICILE
Name of Country
OR { Citizen of ▶ _____
Domiciled in ▶ _____

WAS THIS AUTHOR'S CONTRIBUTION TO THE WORK
Anonymous? ☐ Yes ☐ No
Pseudonymous? ☐ Yes ☐ No

If the answer to either of these questions is "Yes" see detailed instructions.

NATURE OF AUTHORSHIP Briefly describe nature of the material created by the author in which copyright is claimed. ▼

---

e

NAME OF AUTHOR ▼

DATES OF BIRTH AND DEATH
Year Born▼   Year Died▼

Was this contribution to the work a "work made for hire"?
☐ Yes
☐ No

AUTHOR'S NATIONALITY OR DOMICILE
Name of Country
OR { Citizen of ▶ _____
Domiciled in ▶ _____

WAS THIS AUTHOR'S CONTRIBUTION TO THE WORK
Anonymous? ☐ Yes ☐ No
Pseudonymous? ☐ Yes ☐ No

If the answer to either of these questions is "Yes" see detailed instructions.

NATURE OF AUTHORSHIP Briefly describe nature of the material created by the author in which copyright is claimed. ▼

---

f

NAME OF AUTHOR ▼

DATES OF BIRTH AND DEATH
Year Born▼   Year Died▼

Was this contribution to the work a "work made for hire"?
☐ Yes
☐ No

AUTHOR'S NATIONALITY OR DOMICILE
Name of Country
OR { Citizen of ▶ _____
Domiciled in ▶ _____

WAS THIS AUTHOR'S CONTRIBUTION TO THE WORK
Anonymous? ☐ Yes ☐ No
Pseudonymous? ☐ Yes ☐ No

If the answer to either of these questions is "Yes" see detailed instructions.

NATURE OF AUTHORSHIP Briefly describe nature of the material created by the author in which copyright is claimed. ▼

Use the reverse side of this sheet if you need more space for continuation of Spaces 1, 4, or 6 of the basic form.

CONTINUATION OF (Check which):   ☐ **Space 1**   ☐ **Space 4**   ☐ **Space 6**

C

**Continuation
of other
Spaces**

**MAIL
TO**

**Certificate
will be
mailed in
window
envelope**

Name ▼

Number/Street/Apt ▼

City/State/ZIP ▼

YOU MUST:
• Complete all necessary spaces
• Sign your application

**SEND ALL 3 ELEMENTS
IN THE SAME PACKAGE:**

1. Application form
2. Nonrefundable $20 filing fee
in check or money order
payable to *Register of Copyrights*

MAIL TO:
Register of Copyrights
Library of Congress
Washington, D.C. 20559-6000

D

**Address for
return of
certificate**

August 1995–150,000

☆U.S.COPYRIGHT OFFICE WWW FORM: 1995

REGISTRATION NUMBER

TX	TXU	PA	PAU	VA	VAU	SR	SRU	RE

EFFECTIVE DATE OF SUPPLEMENTARY REGISTRATION

_____
Month   Day   Year

DO NOT WRITE ABOVE THIS LINE. IF YOU NEED MORE SPACE, USE A SEPARATE CONTINUATION SHEET.

A

TITLE OF WORK ▼

REGISTRATION NUMBER OF THE BASIC REGISTRATION ▼   **YEAR OF BASIC REGISTRATION ▼**

NAME(S) OF AUTHOR(S) ▼   **NAME(S) OF COPYRIGHT CLAIMANT(S) ▼**

B

LOCATION AND NATURE OF INCORRECT INFORMATION IN BASIC REGISTRATION ▼

Line Number . . . . Line Heading or Description . . . .

INCORRECT INFORMATION AS IT APPEARS IN BASIC REGISTRATION ▼

CORRECTED INFORMATION ▼

EXPLANATION OF CORRECTION ▼

C

LOCATION AND NATURE OF INFORMATION IN BASIC REGISTRATION TO BE AMPLIFIED ▼

Line Number . . . . Line Heading or Description . . . .

AMPLIFIED INFORMATION ▼

EXPLANATION OF AMPLIFIED INFORMATION ▼

MORE ON BACK ▶   • Complete all applicable spaces (D -G) on the reverse side of this page.   **DO NOT WRITE HERE**
      • See detailed instructions.   • Sign the form at space F.

Page 1 of _____ pages

DO NOT WRITE ABOVE THIS LINE. IF YOU NEED MORE SPACE, USE A SEPARATE CONTINUATION SHEET.

CONTINUATION OF: (Check which) ☐ PART B OR ☐ PART C

D

DEPOSIT ACCOUNT: If the registration fee is to be charged to a Deposit Account established in the Copyright Office, give name and number of Account.

Name _____

_____

Account Number _____

CORRESPONDENCE: Give name and address to which correspondence about this application should be sent.

Name _____

Address _____
                                                                    (Apt)
_____
(City)   (State)   (ZIP)
Area Code and Telephone Number ▶ _____

Be sure to
give your
daytime phone
number ◀

E

CERTIFICATION* I, the undersigned, hereby certify that I am the: (Check one)
☐ author ☐ other copyright claimant ☐ owner of exclusive right(s) M duly authorized agent of_____
                                                                              (Name of author or other copyright claimant, or owner of exclusive right(s) ▲
of the work identified in this application and that the statements made by me in this application are correct to the best of my knowledge.

Typed or printed name ▼   Date ▼

☞   **Handwritten signature (X)** ▼

F

*17 U.S.C. § 506(e): Any person who knowingly makes a false representation of a material fact in the application for copyright registration provided for by section 409, or in any written statement filed in connection with the application, shall be fined not more than $2,500.

October 1994

☆U.S. COPYRIGHT OFFICE WWW FORM: 1996

Copyright Office • Library of Congress • Washington, D.C. 20559-6000

search request form

Copyright Office
Library of Congress

Reference & Bibliography
Section
(202) 707-6850
8:30 a.m. - 5 p.m. Monday-Friday

Type of work:

Book   Music   Motion Picture   Drama   Sound Recording

Photograph/Artwork   Map   Periodical   Contribution   Architectural Work

Search information you require:

Registration   Renewal   Assignment   Address

Specifics of work to be searched:

TITLE:

AUTHOR:

COPYRIGHT CLAIMANT (if known):

(name in © notice)

APPROXIMATE YEAR DATE OF PUBLICATION CREATION:

REGISTRATION NUMBER (if known):

OTHER IDENTIFYING INFORMATION:

If you need more space please attach additional pages

Estimates are based on the Copyright Office fee of $20 an hour or fraction of an hour consumed. The more information you furnish as a basis for the search the better service we can provide.

Names, titles and short phases are not copyrightable.

Please read Circular 22 for more information on copyright searches.

DOCUMENT COVER SHEET

For Recordation of Documents
UNITED STATES COPYRIGHT OFFICE

DATE OF RECORDATION
(Assigned by Copyright Office)

Month	Day	Year

Volume _____ Page _____

Volume _____ Page _____

REMITTANCE _____

FUNDS RECEIVED) _____

─────────Do not write above this line.─────────

Before you complete this form, please read the instructions on the reverse side. If additional space is needed, use white 8½ x 11 inch paper.

Attachments to Cover Sheet? Yes ❑ No ❑ If so, how many?_____

To the Register of Copyrights:
Please record the accompanying original document or copy thereof.

1 Name of the Party or Parties to the Document Spelled as They Appear in the Document.

Party 1: (assignor, grantor, etc.)_____

Party 2: (assignee, grantee, etc.)_____

_____

_____

_____

2 Description of the Document:
- ❑ Transfer of Copyright
- ❑ Security Interest
- ❑ Change of Name of Owner
- ❑ Termination of Transfer(s) [Section 304]
- ❑ Shareware
- ❑ Life, Identity, Death Statement [Section 302]
- ❑ Transfer of Mask Works
- ❑ Other _____

3 Title(s) of Work(s), Author(s), Registration Number(s), and Other Information to Identify Work.

Title	Author(s)	Registration Number	Registration Date/Year

4
- ❑ Document is complete by its own terms.
- ❑ Document is not complete. Record "as is."

5 Number of titles in Document: _____

6 Amount of fee enclosed or authorized to be charged to a Deposit Account _____ .

7 Deposit account number _____

Deposit account name _____

8 Date of execution and/or effective date of accompanying document _____ .

(Month)   (Day)   (Year)

9 **Affirmation:*** I hereby affirm to the Copyright Office that the information given on this form is a true and correct representation of the accompanying document. This affirmation will not suffice as a certification of a photocopy signature on the document.
(Affirmation *must* be signed.)

Signature _____

Date _____

Phone Number _____ Fax Number _____

10 **Certification:*** Complete this certification in addition to the Affirmation if a photocopy of the original signed document is submitted in lieu of a document bearing the actual signature.

I certify under penalty of perjury under the laws of the United States of America that the accompanying document is a true copy of the original document.

Signature _____

Duly Authorized Agent of: _____

Date _____

MAIL RECORDA-TION TO

Name▼ _____

Number/Street/Apt▼ _____

City/State/ZIP▼ _____

YOU MUST:
- Complete all necessary spaces
- Sign your cover sheet in Space 9

SEND ALL 3 ELEMENTS IN THE SAME PACKAGE:
1. Two copies of the Document Cover Sheet
2. Fee in check or money order payable to *Register of Copyrights*
3. Document

MAIL TO:
Documents Unit, Cataloging Division
Copyright Office, Library of Congress
Washington, D.C. 20559-6000

*Knowingly and willfully falsifying material facts on this form may result in criminal liability. 18 U.S.C.§1001.

September 1996

☆ U.S. COPYRIGHT OFFICE WWW FORM: 1997

Document Cover Sheet

*Read these instructions before completing this form. Make sure all applicable spaces
have been filled in before you return this form, or the form cannot be used.*

BASIC INFORMATION

When to Use This Form: Use the Document Cover Sheet when you are submitting a document for recordation in the U.S. Copyright Office.

Mailing Requirements: It is important that you send two copies of the Document Cover Sheet, any additional sheets, the document, and the fee together in the same envelope or package. The Copyright Office cannot process them unless they are received together. Send to: *Documents Unit, LM-462, Cataloging Division, Copyright Office, Library of Congress, Washington, D.C. 20559-6000.*

Two copies of this Document Cover Sheet and any additional sheets you include, which must measure 8 ½ x 11 inches, should accompany **each document**. Cover sheets should be typed or printed. The cover sheet, when completed, should contain all of the information necessary for the Copyright Office to process the document and ensure that the correct data is recorded promptly. The Copyright Office will process the document on the basis of information contained in the cover sheet without verifying its correctness from the document itself. However, to be recordable, a document must satisfy the recordation requirements of the Copyright Act and Copyright Office regulations.

The person(s) submitting a document with a cover sheet is (are) solely responsible for verifying the correctness of the cover sheet and the sufficiency of the document. Recording a document submitted with or without a cover sheet does not constitute a determination by the Copyright Office of the document's validity or the effect of that document. Only a court of law may make such determinations.

This cover sheet and any additional sheets will be recorded with the document as part of the official recordation.

SPACE-BY-SPACE INSTRUCTIONS

1 SPACE 1: Name of Party or Parties to the Document

Name all of the parties to this document. If additional space is needed, use a white 8½ x 11 inch sheet of paper to list the parties. The document will be indexed under the names of these parties. For transfers, notices of termination, and other two-party documents, indicate which is assignor, grantor, or party 1 and which is assignee, grantee, or party 2.

2 SPACE 2: Description of Document

Describe the document. This description will be entered in the catalog record of the recordation.

3 SPACE 3: Title(s) of Work(s)

List the titles of all works which are included in the document. Include registration number, names of authors, and other information to identify the work(s) and link them to the original registration. Additional sheets the same size as the cover sheet may be attached, if needed. Indicate that the titles on any additional sheets are additions to Space 3.

4 SPACE 4: Completeness of Document

All section 205 documents must be complete by their own terms in order to be recordable. Examples of section 205 documents include transfers of copyright ownerships and other documents pertaining to a copyright such as exclusive and non-exclusive licenses, contracts, mortgages, powers of attorney, certificates of change of corporate name or title, wills, and decrees of distribution.

5 SPACE 5: Number of Titles in Document

The number of titles determines the recordation fee. The fee for a document of any length containing one title is $20. Additional titles are $10 for each group of 10 or fewer. The Copyright Office will verify title counts.

6 SPACE 6: Fee

Calculate the fee from the information given in Space 5.

7 SPACE 7: Deposit Account

If a Deposit Account is to be charged, give the Deposit Account number and name.

8 SPACE 8: Date of Execution

Give the date the accompanying document (not this Cover Sheet) was executed and/or became effective.

9 SPACE 9: Affirmation

This space must be completed by all applicants. The party to the document submitting it for recordation or his/her authorized agent should sign the affirmation and authorization contained in this space. This affirmation and authorization is not a substitute for the certification required for documents containing a photocopy signature. (See Certification, Space 10.)

10 SPACE 10: Certification

Complete this section only if submitting photocopied documents in lieu of a document bearing the actual signature.

Certification: Any transfer of copyright ownership or other document pertaining to a copyright (section 205) may be recorded in the Copyright Office if the document bears the actual signature of the person or persons who executed (signed) the documents. If a photocopy of the original signed document is submitted, it must be accompanied by a sworn or official certification. A sworn certification signed by at least one of the parties to the document or their authorized representative (who is identified as such) at Space 10 will satisfy that requirement.

Copies of documents on file in a Federal, state, or local government office must be accompanied by an official certification.

Index

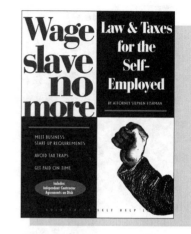

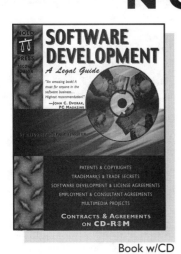
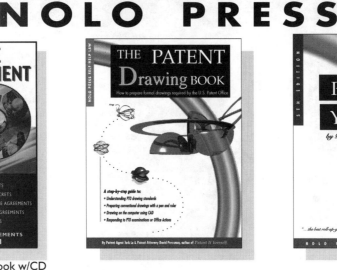

With our quarterly magazine, the **NOLO** *News*, you'll

- **Learn** about important legal changes that affect you
- **Find out first** about new Nolo products
- **Keep current** with practical articles on everyday law
- **Get answers** to your legal questions in *Ask Auntie Nolo's* advice column
- **Save money** with special Subscriber Only discounts
- **Tickle your funny bone** with our famous *Lawyer Joke* column.

It only takes a minute to reserve your free 1-year subscription or to extend your **NOLO** *News* subscription.

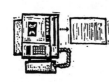

C A L L
1-800-992-6656

F A X
1-800-645-0895

E - M A I L
NOLOSUB@NOLOPRESS.com

OR MAIL US THIS REGISTRATION CARD

🌐 *U.S. ADDRESSES ONLY. ONE YEAR INTERNATIONAL SUBSCRIPTIONS: CANADA & MEXICO $10.00; ALL OTHER FOREIGN ADDRESSES $20.00.

fold here

- -

NOLO PRESS

REGISTRATION CARD

NAME _____ DATE _____

ADDRESS _____

_____

CITY _____ STATE _____ ZIP _____

PHONE _____ E-MAIL _____

WHERE DID YOU HEAR ABOUT THIS PRODUCT? _____

WHERE DID YOU PURCHASE THIS PRODUCT? _____

DID YOU CONSULT A LAWYER? (PLEASE CIRCLE ONE)   YES   NO   NOT APPLICABLE

DID YOU FIND THIS BOOK HELPFUL?   (VERY)   5   4   3   2   1   (NOT AT ALL)

COMMENTS _____

_____

_____

_____

WAS IT EASY TO USE?   (VERY EASY)   5   4   3   2   1   (VERY DIFFICULT)

DO YOU OWN A COMPUTER? IF SO, WHICH FORMAT? (PLEASE CIRCLE ONE)   WINDOWS   DOS   MAC

❑ If you do not wish to receive mailings from these companies, please check this box.

❑ You can quote me in future Nolo Press promotional materials. Daytime phone number _____.

CYS 2.0

NOLO IN THE NEWS

fold here

- -

Place
stamp here

NOLO PRESS
950 Parker Street
Berkeley, CA 94710-9867

Attn: CYS 2.0